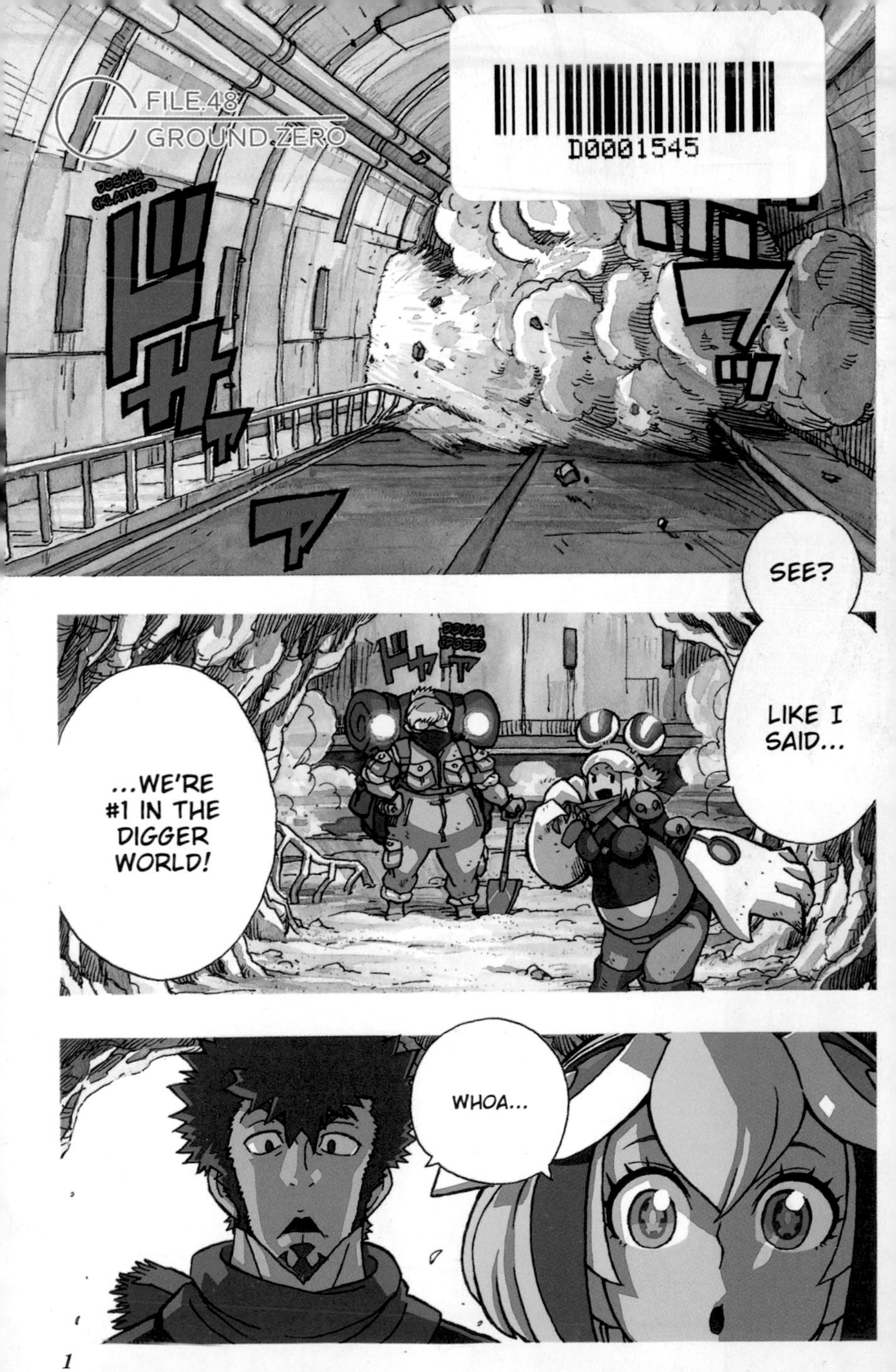
FILE.48
GROUND.ZERO
DOGAAA (KLATTER)
SEE?
LIKE I SAID...
...WE'RE #1 IN THE DIGGER WORLD!
DOVAA (POSE)
WHOA...

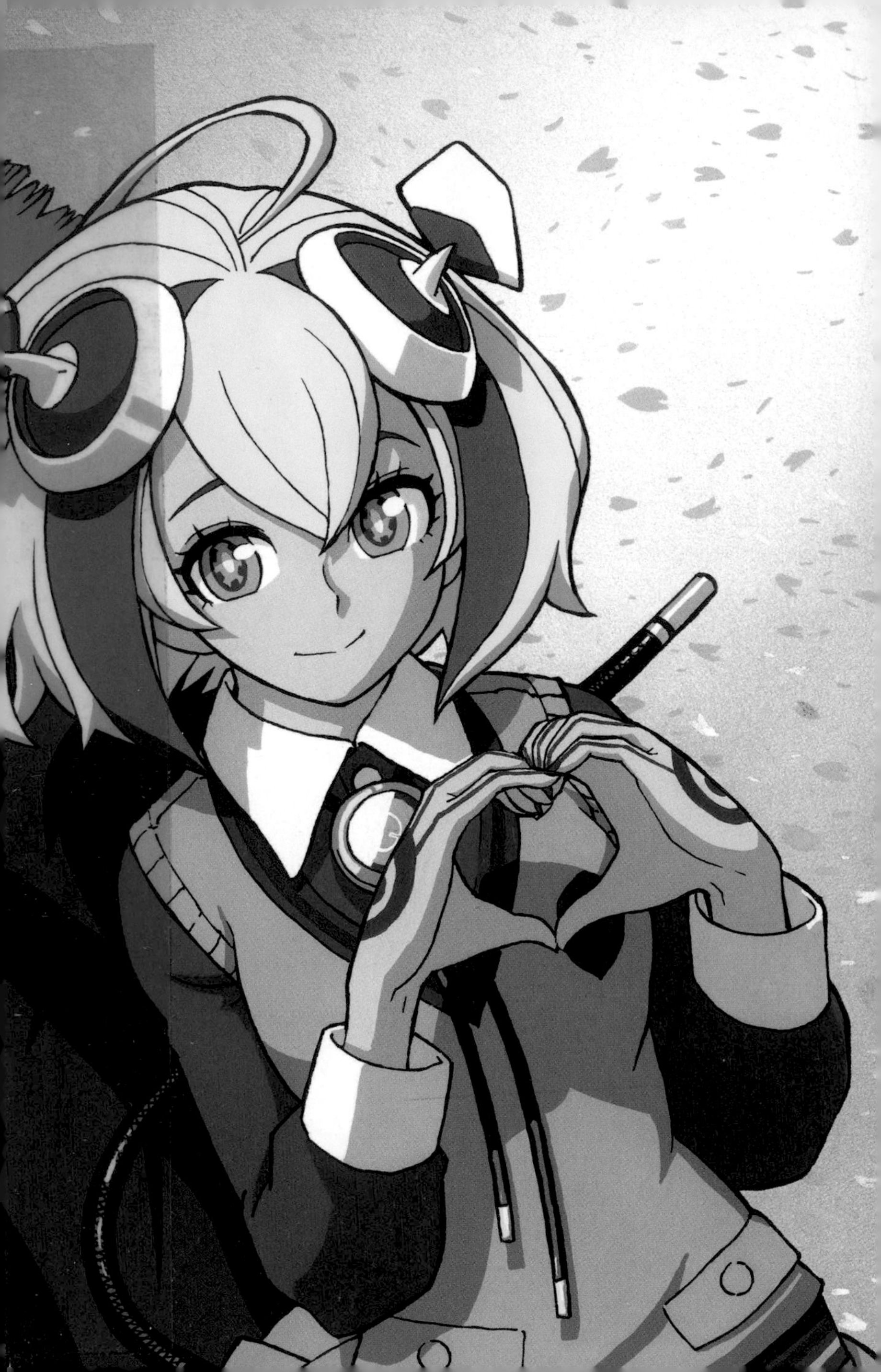

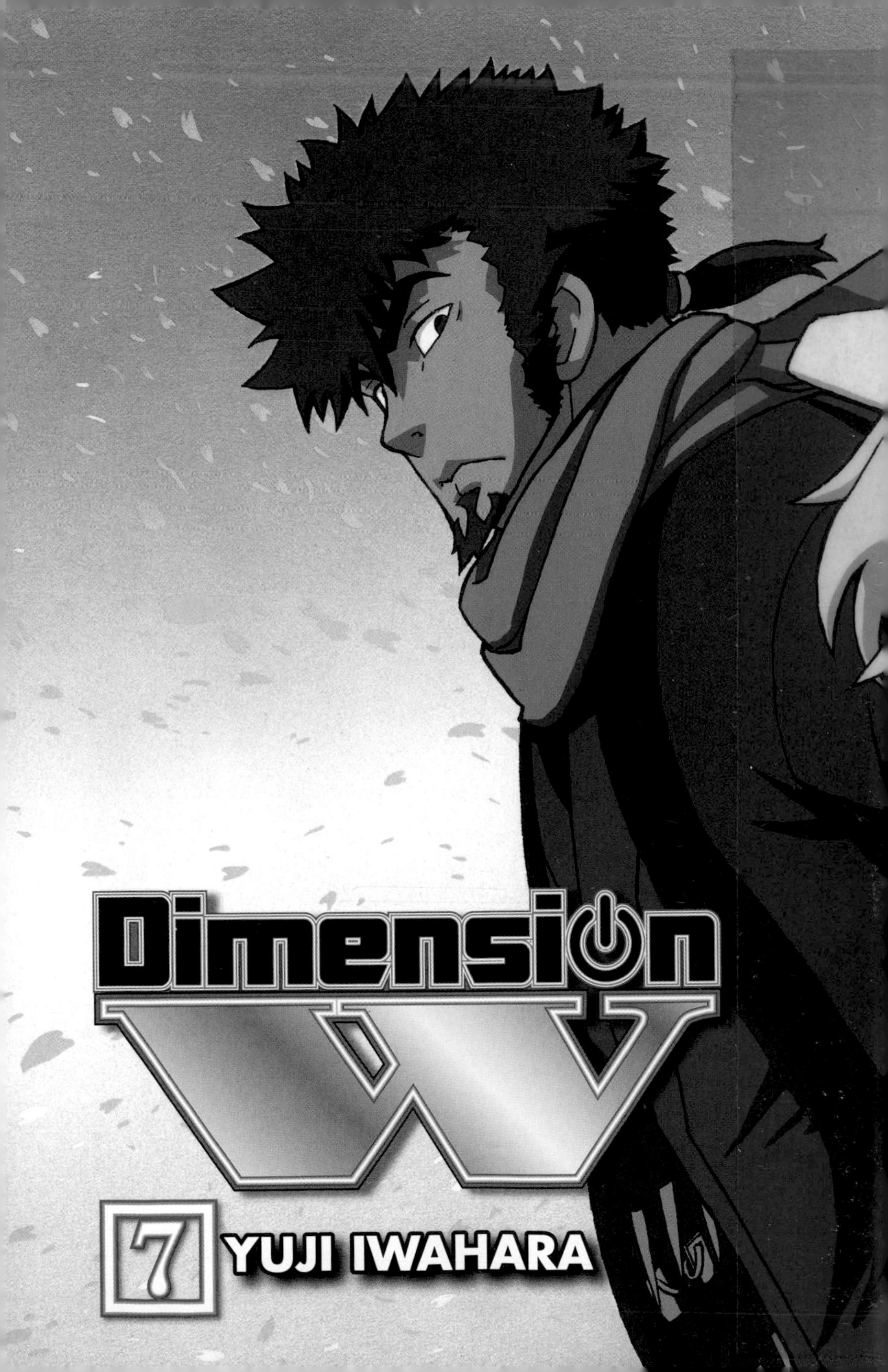
Dimension W
7
YUJI IWAHARA

CONTENTS

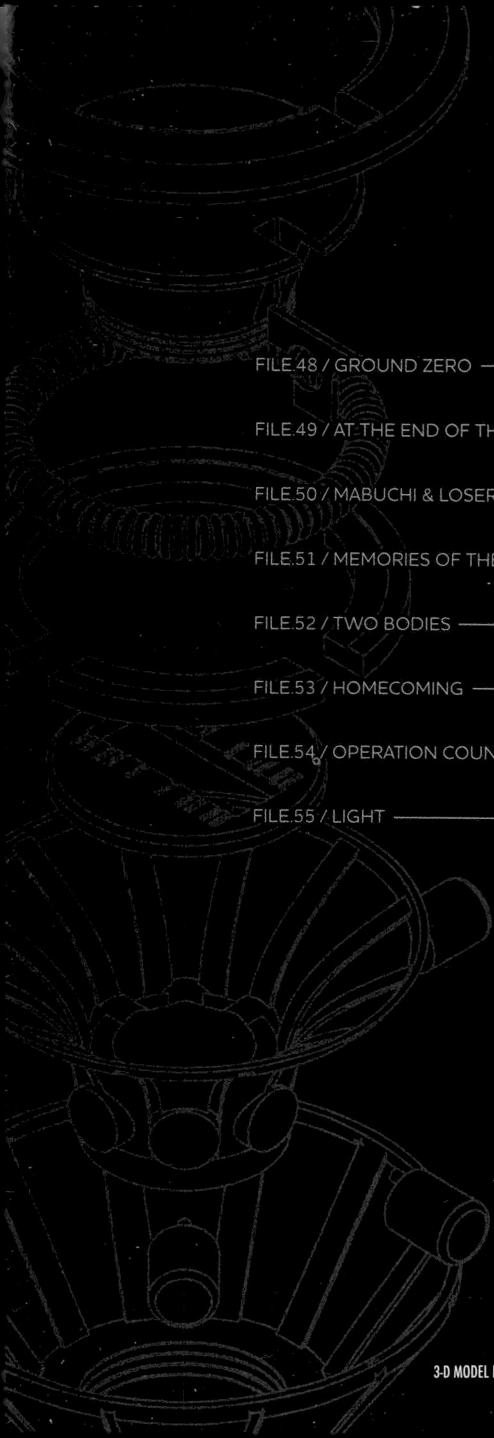

3-D MODEL DESIGN: TOSHIKAZU SENBA

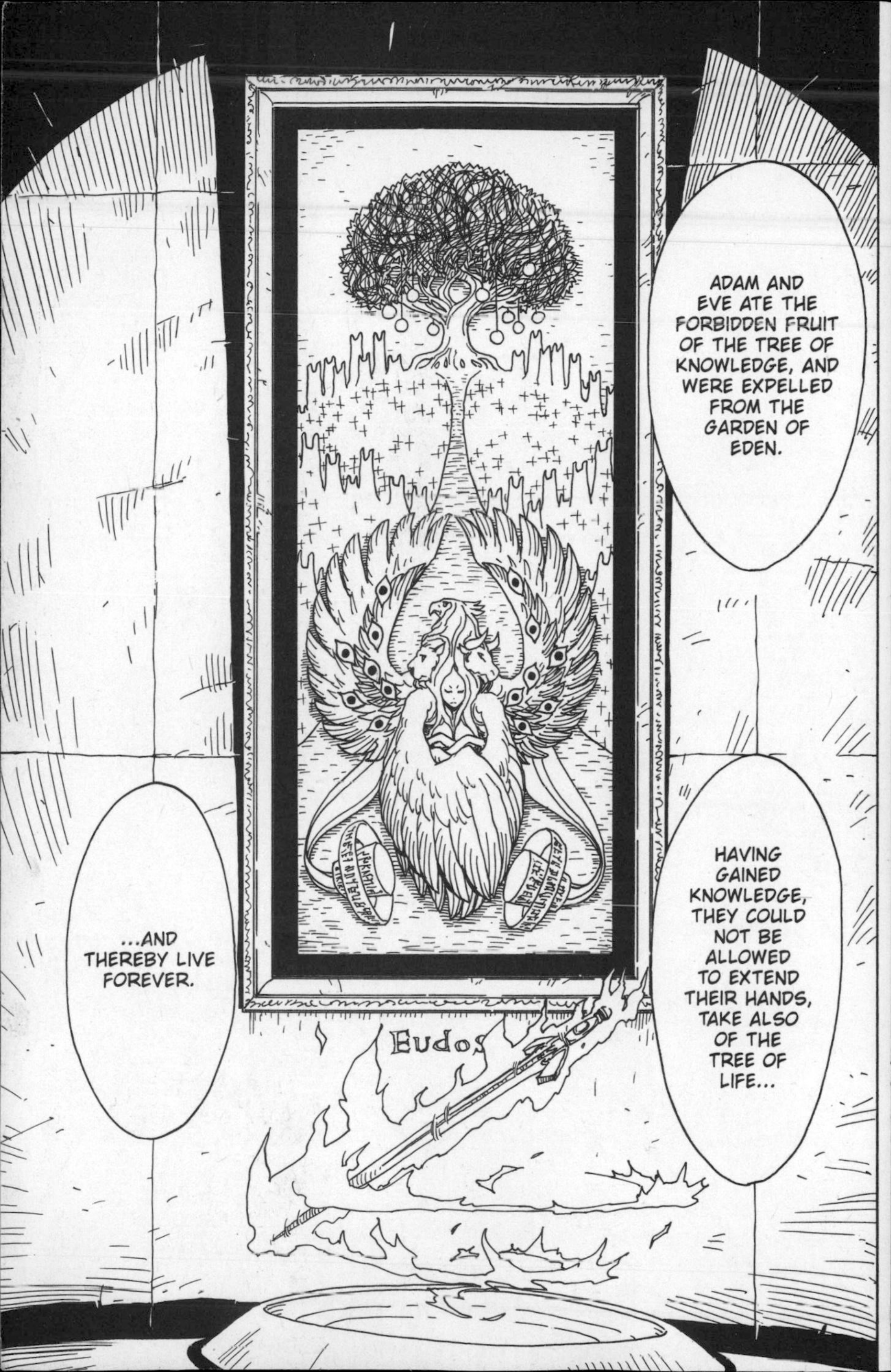
ADAM AND EVE ATE THE FORBIDDEN FRUIT OF THE TREE OF KNOWLEDGE, AND WERE EXPELLED FROM THE GARDEN OF EDEN.
Eudos
HAVING GAINED KNOWLEDGE, THEY COULD NOT BE ALLOWED TO EXTEND THEIR HANDS, TAKE ALSO OF THE TREE OF LIFE...
...AND THEREBY LIVE FOREVER.

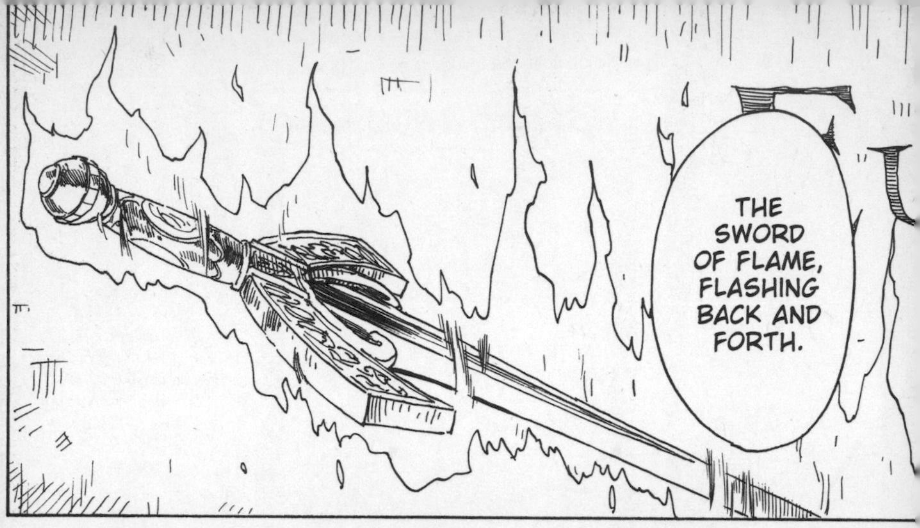
THE SWORD OF FLAME, FLASHING BACK AND FORTH.

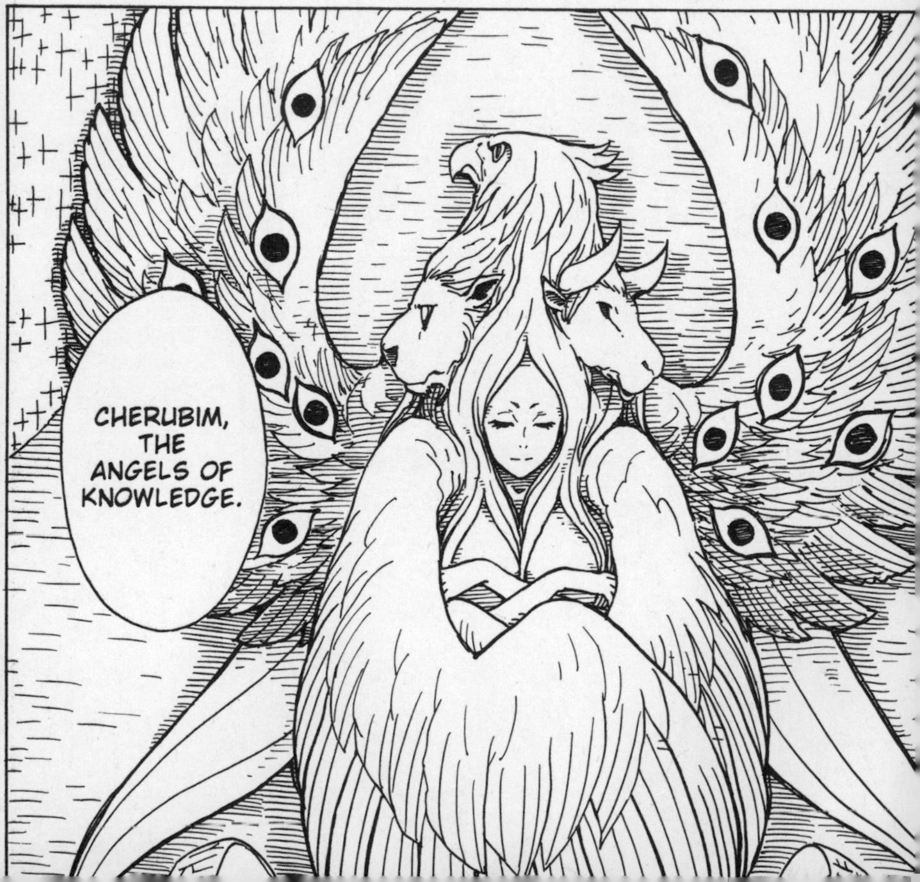
CHERUBIM, THE ANGELS OF KNOWLEDGE.

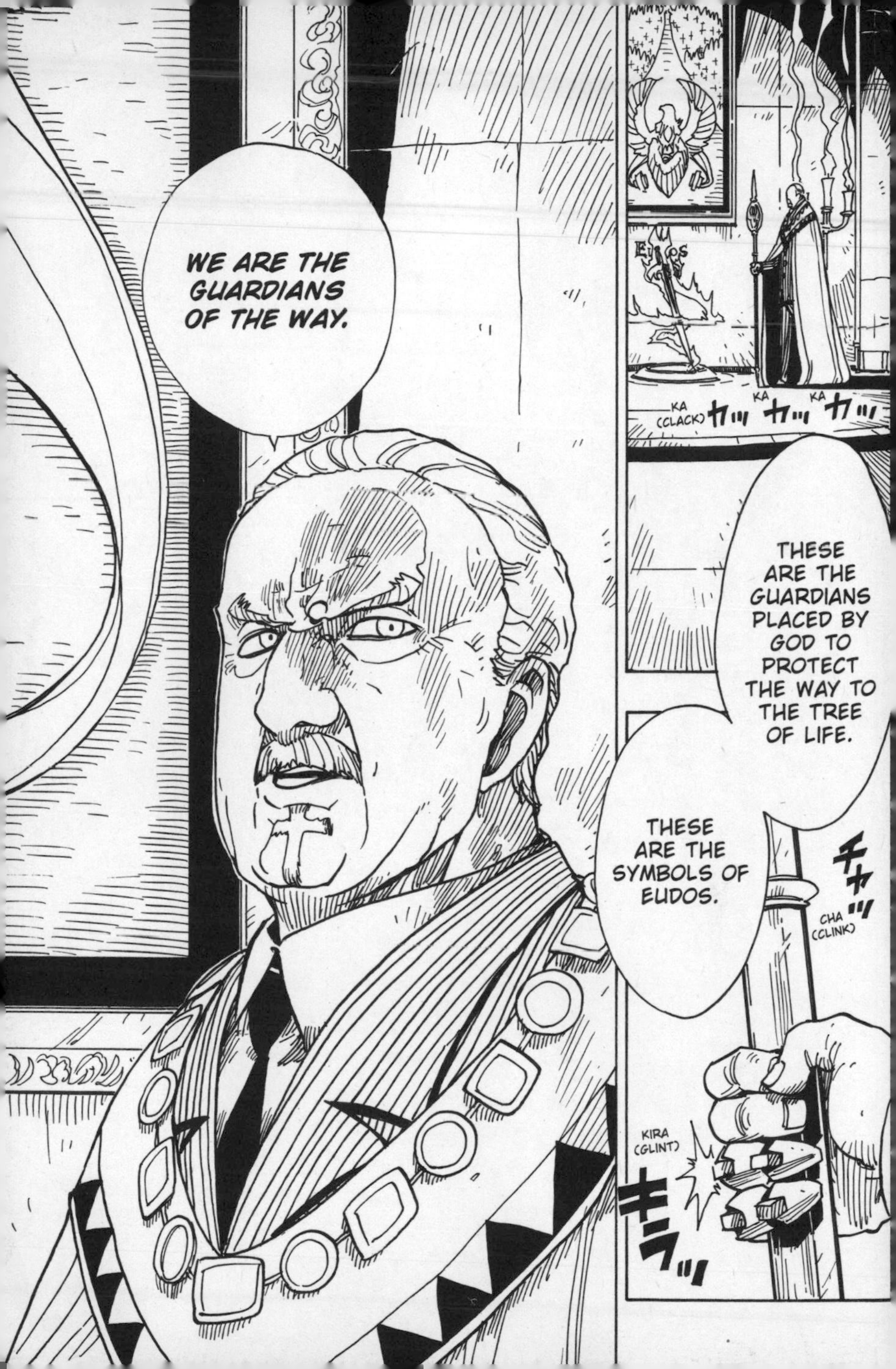
KA (CLACK) カッ
KA カッ
KA カッ
THESE ARE THE GUARDIANS PLACED BY GOD TO PROTECT THE WAY TO THE TREE OF LIFE.
THESE ARE THE SYMBOLS OF EUDOS.
チャッ
CHA (CLINK)
KIRA (GLINT)
キラッ
WE ARE THE GUARDIANS OF THE WAY.

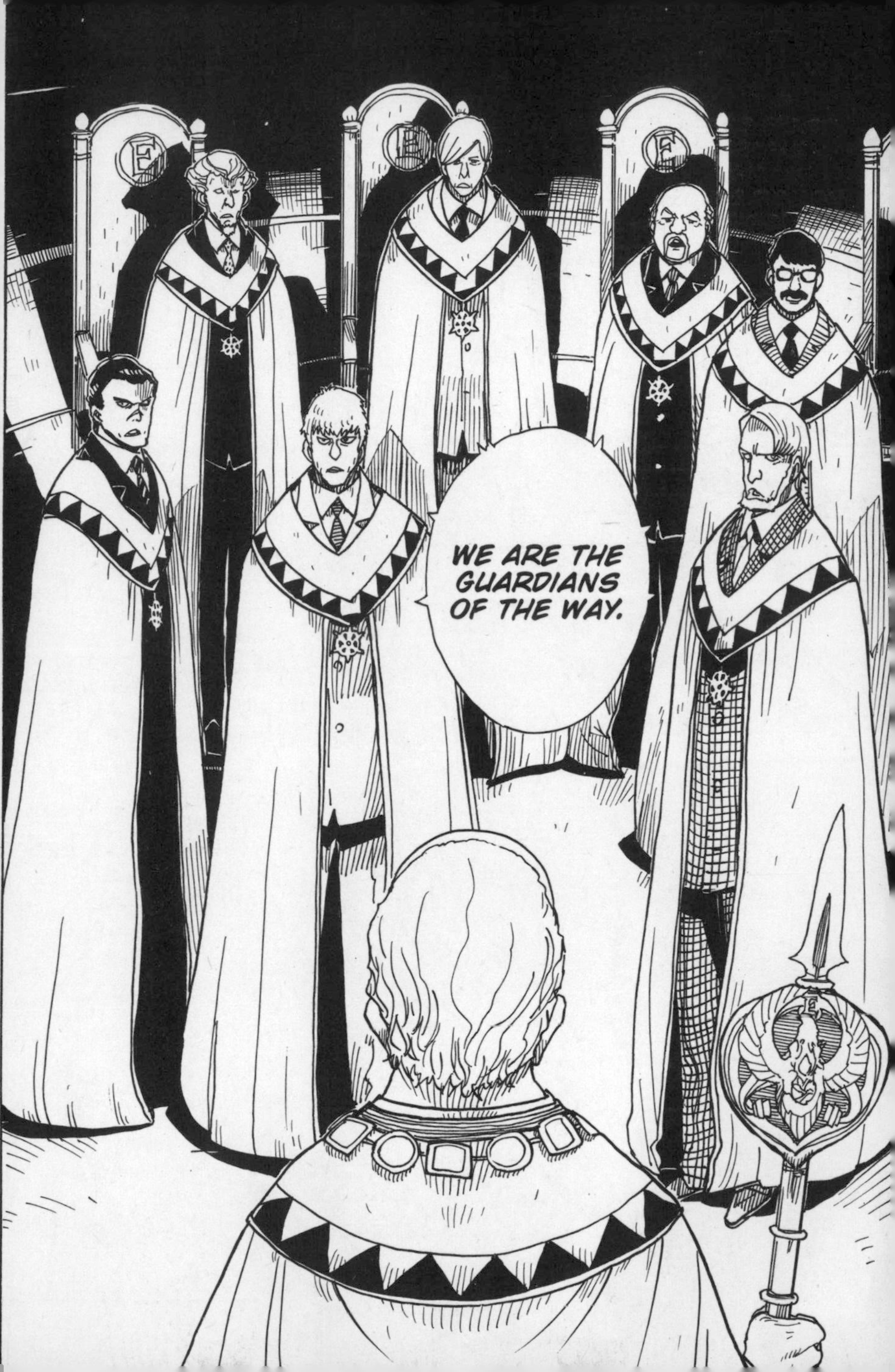
WE ARE THE GUARDIANS OF THE WAY.

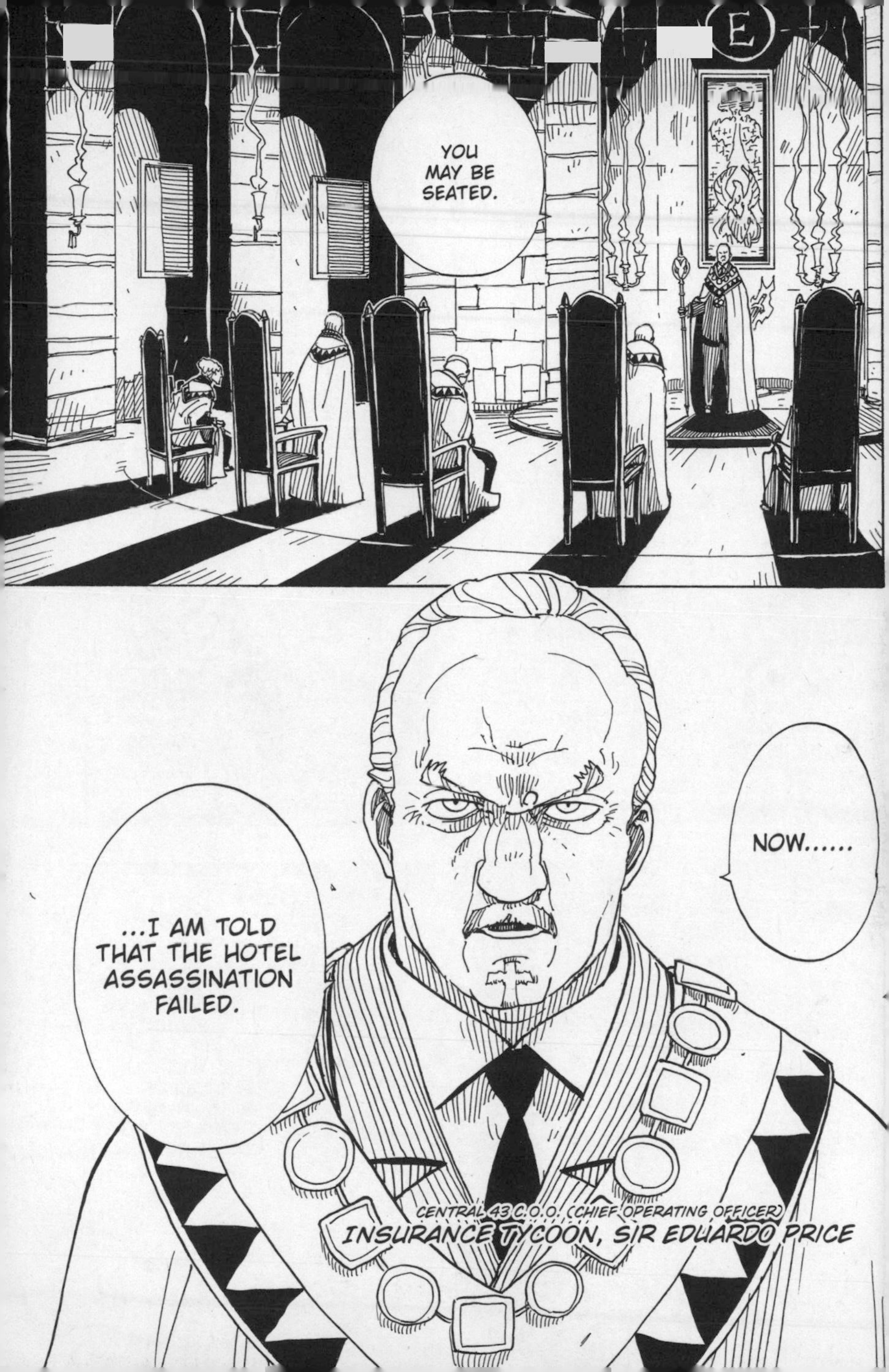
YOU MAY BE SEATED.
NOW......
...I AM TOLD THAT THE HOTEL ASSASSINATION FAILED.
CENTRAL 43 C.O.O. (CHIEF OPERATING OFFICER)
INSURANCE TYCOON, SIR EDUARDO PRICE

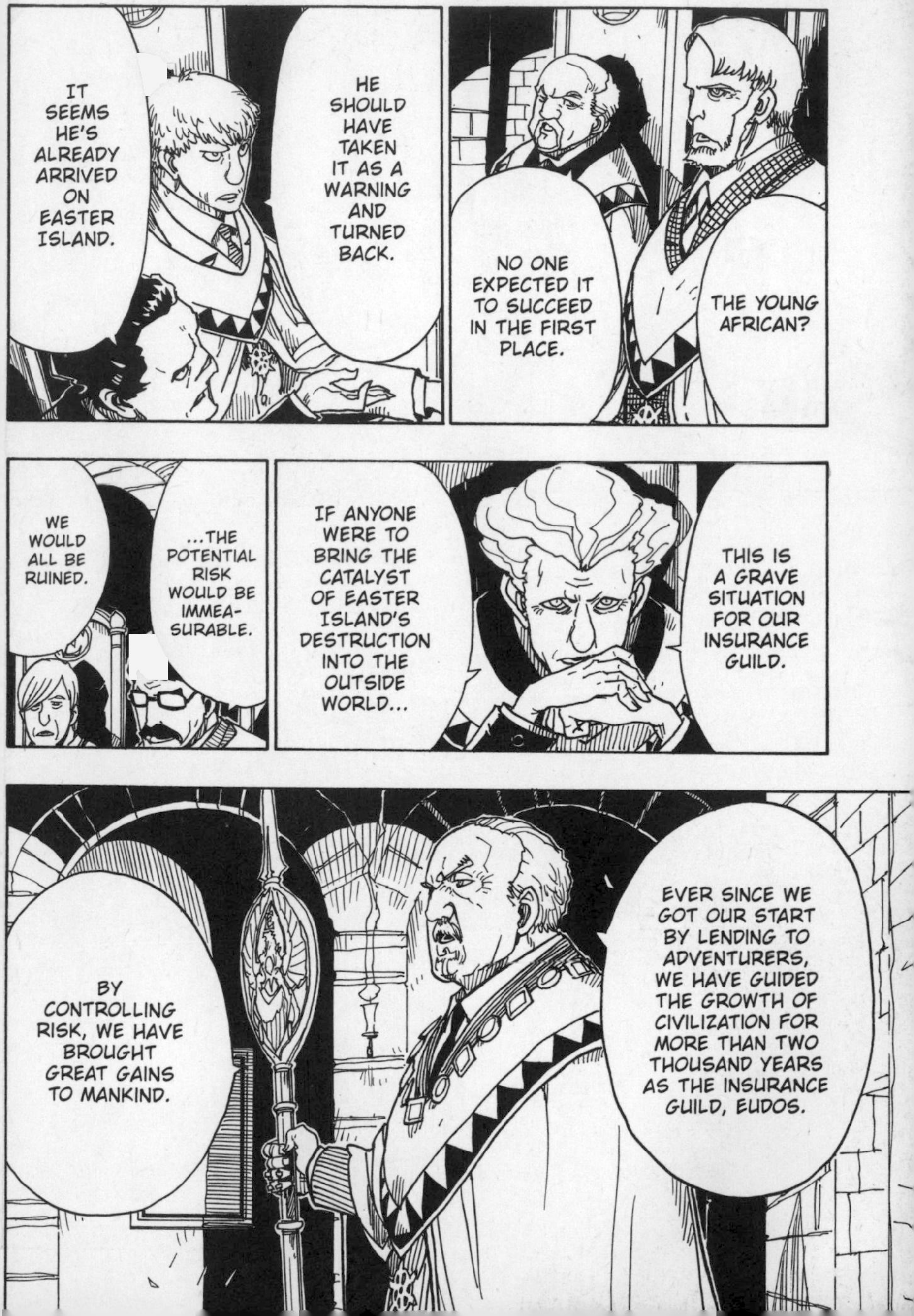
THE YOUNG AFRICAN?
NO ONE EXPECTED IT TO SUCCEED IN THE FIRST PLACE.
HE SHOULD HAVE TAKEN IT AS A WARNING AND TURNED BACK.
IT SEEMS HE'S ALREADY ARRIVED ON EASTER ISLAND.
THIS IS A GRAVE SITUATION FOR OUR INSURANCE GUILD.
IF ANYONE WERE TO BRING THE CATALYST OF EASTER ISLAND'S DESTRUCTION INTO THE OUTSIDE WORLD...
...THE POTENTIAL RISK WOULD BE IMMEASURABLE.
WE WOULD ALL BE RUINED.
EVER SINCE WE GOT OUR START BY LENDING TO ADVENTURERS, WE HAVE GUIDED THE GROWTH OF CIVILIZATION FOR MORE THAN TWO THOUSAND YEARS AS THE INSURANCE GUILD, EUDOS.
BY CONTROLLING RISK, WE HAVE BROUGHT GREAT GAINS TO MANKIND.

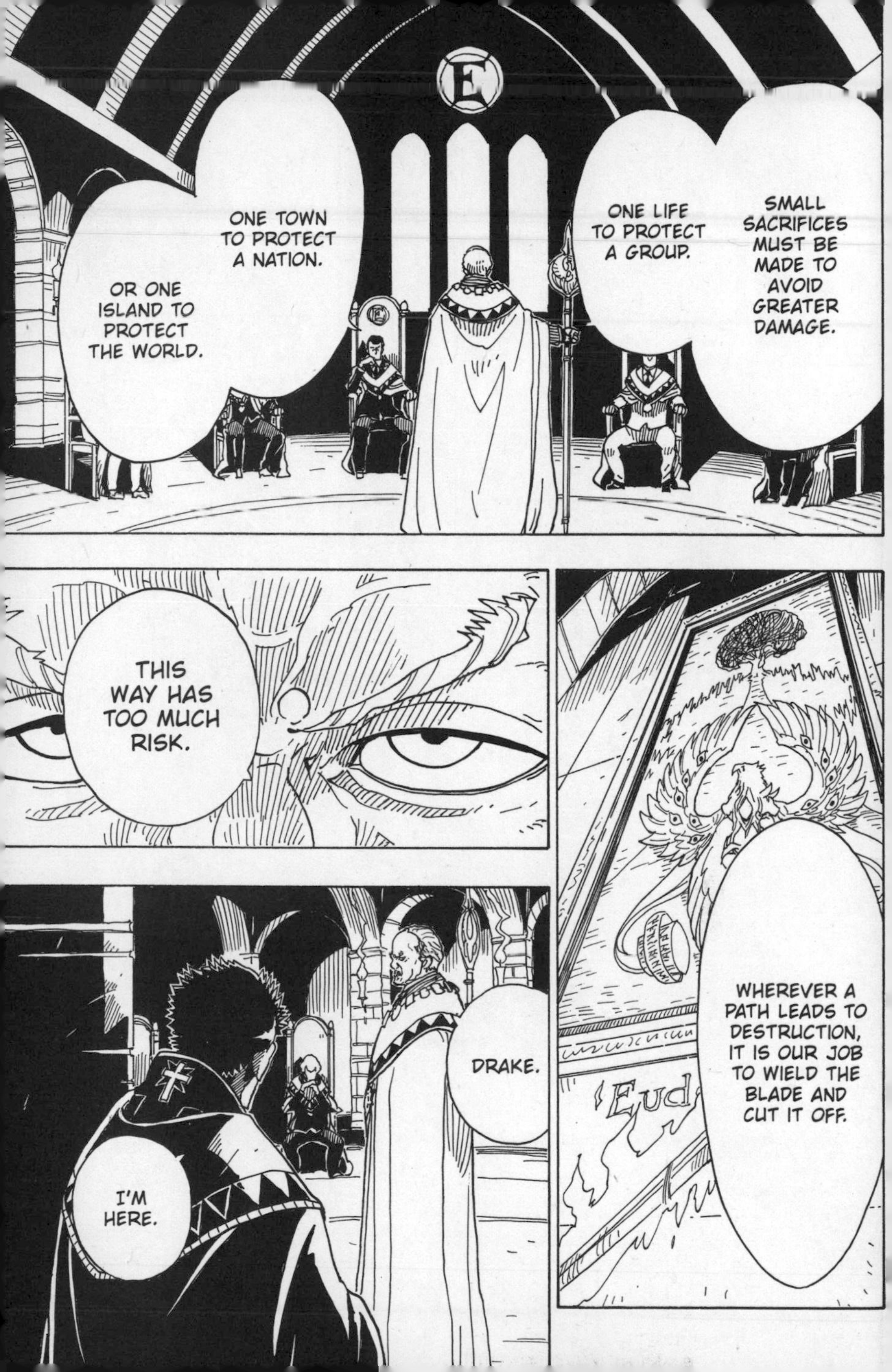
SMALL SACRIFICES MUST BE MADE TO AVOID GREATER DAMAGE.
ONE LIFE TO PROTECT A GROUP.
ONE TOWN TO PROTECT A NATION.
OR ONE ISLAND TO PROTECT THE WORLD.
WHEREVER A PATH LEADS TO DESTRUCTION, IT IS OUR JOB TO WIELD THE BLADE AND CUT IT OFF.
THIS WAY HAS TOO MUCH RISK.
DRAKE.
I'M HERE.

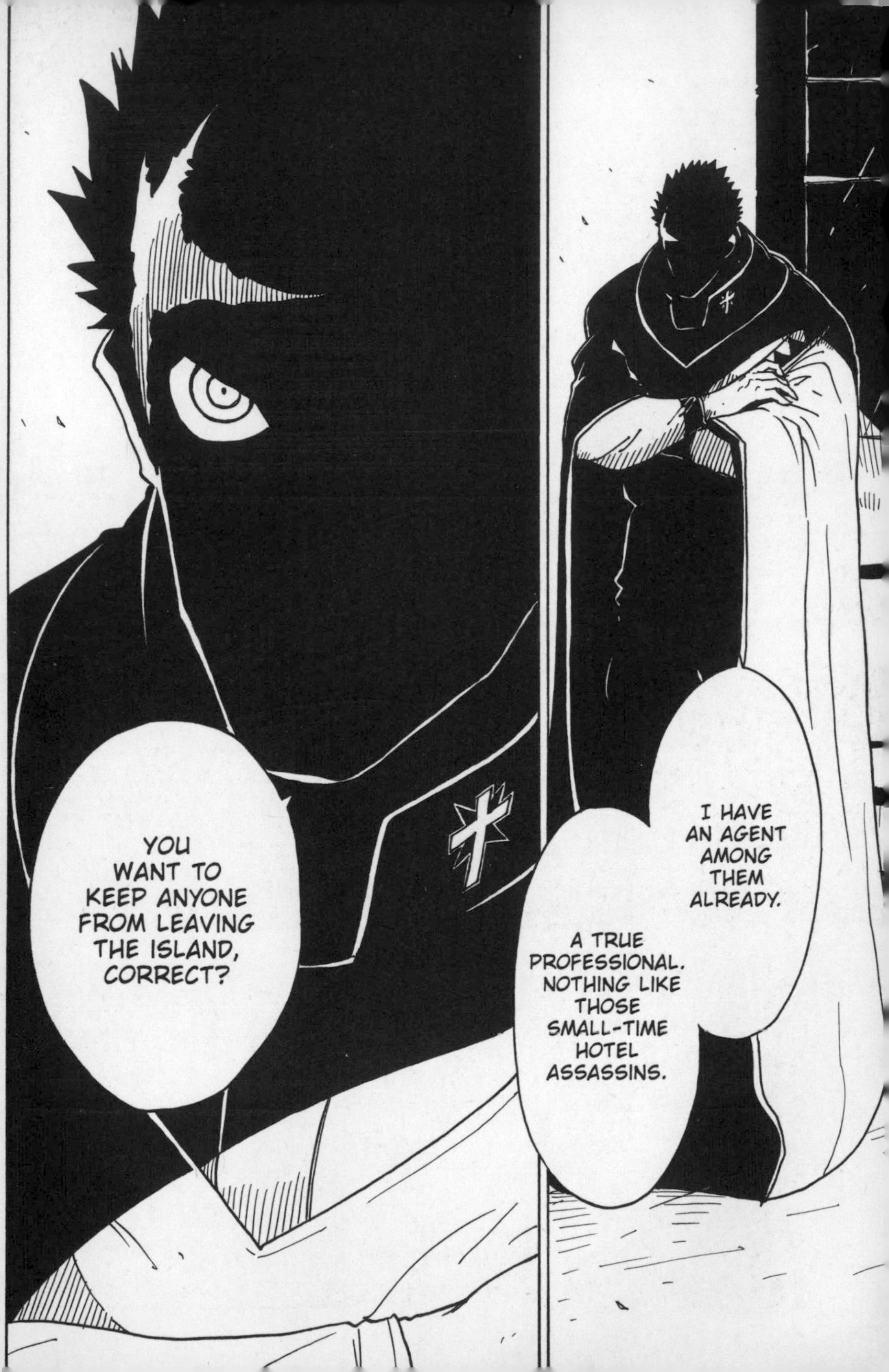
I HAVE AN AGENT AMONG THEM ALREADY.
A TRUE PROFESSIONAL. NOTHING LIKE THOSE SMALL-TIME HOTEL ASSASSINS.
YOU WANT TO KEEP ANYONE FROM LEAVING THE ISLAND, CORRECT?

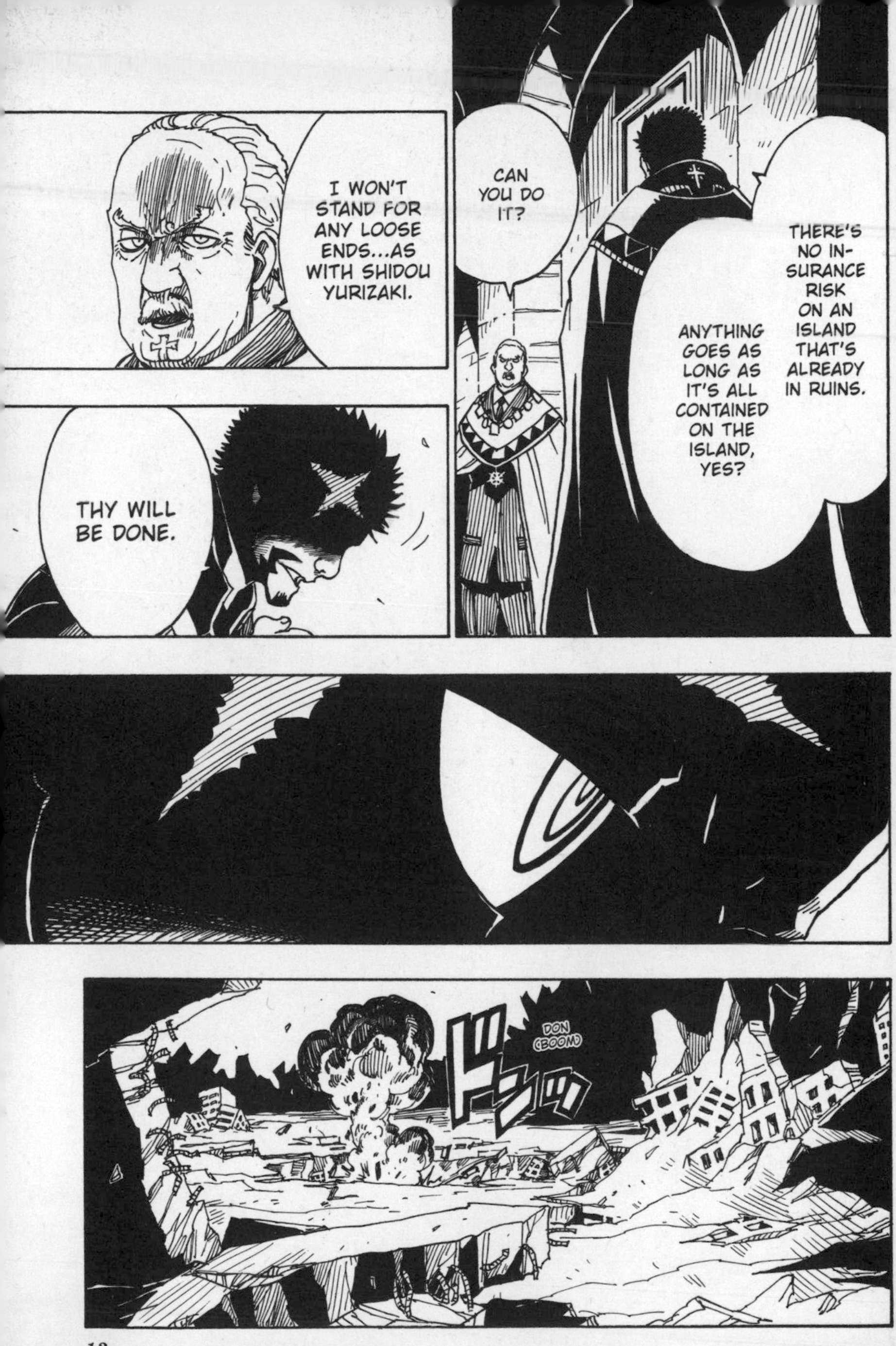
THERE'S NO INSURANCE RISK ON AN ISLAND THAT'S ALREADY IN RUINS.
ANYTHING GOES AS LONG AS IT'S ALL CONTAINED ON THE ISLAND, YES?
CAN YOU DO IT?
I WON'T STAND FOR ANY LOOSE ENDS...AS WITH SHIDOU YURIZAKI.
THY WILL BE DONE.
DON (BOOM)

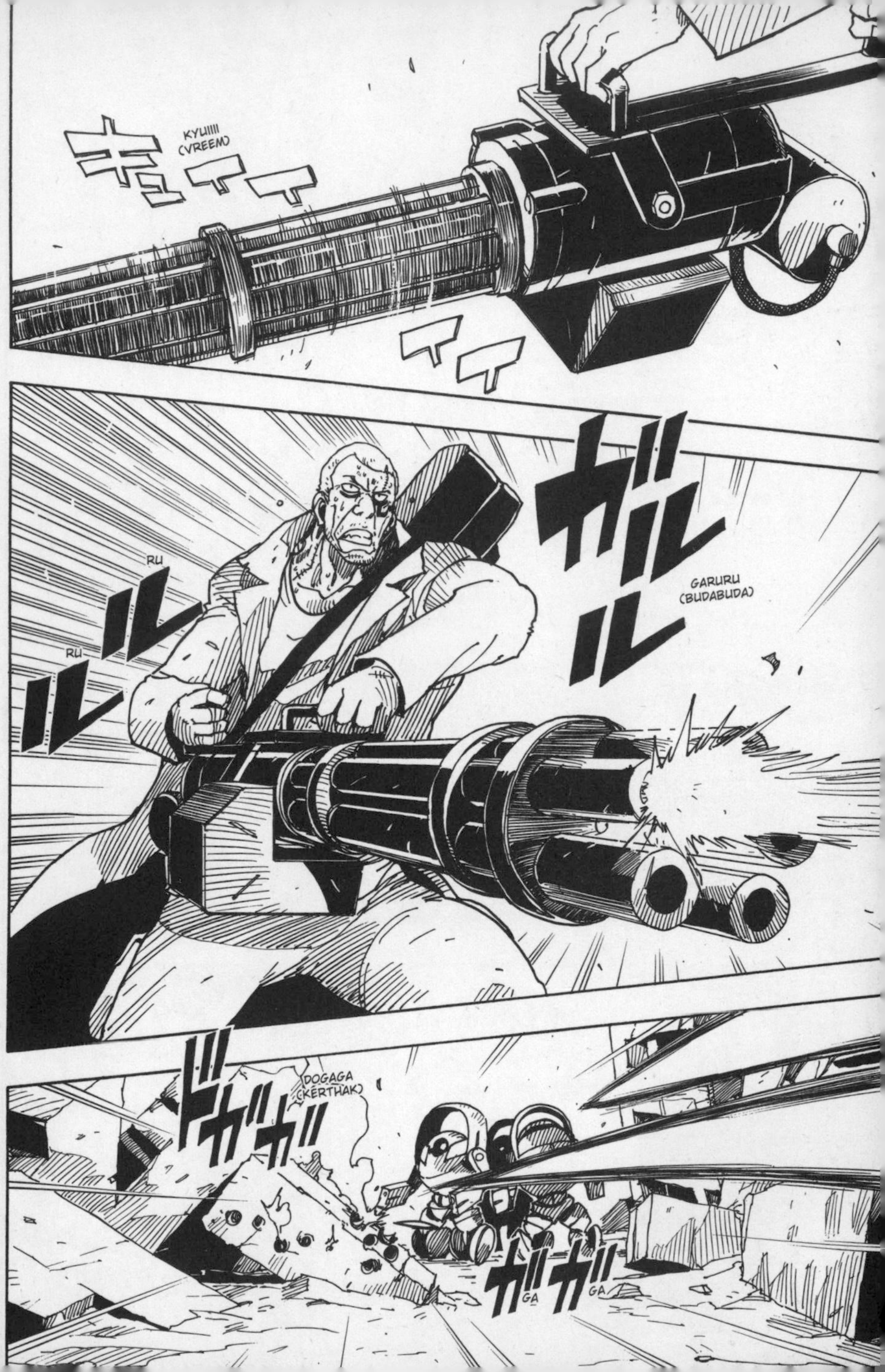
KYUIIII
(VREEM)
GARURU
(BUDABUDA)
RU
RU
DOGAGA
(KERTHAK)
GA
GA

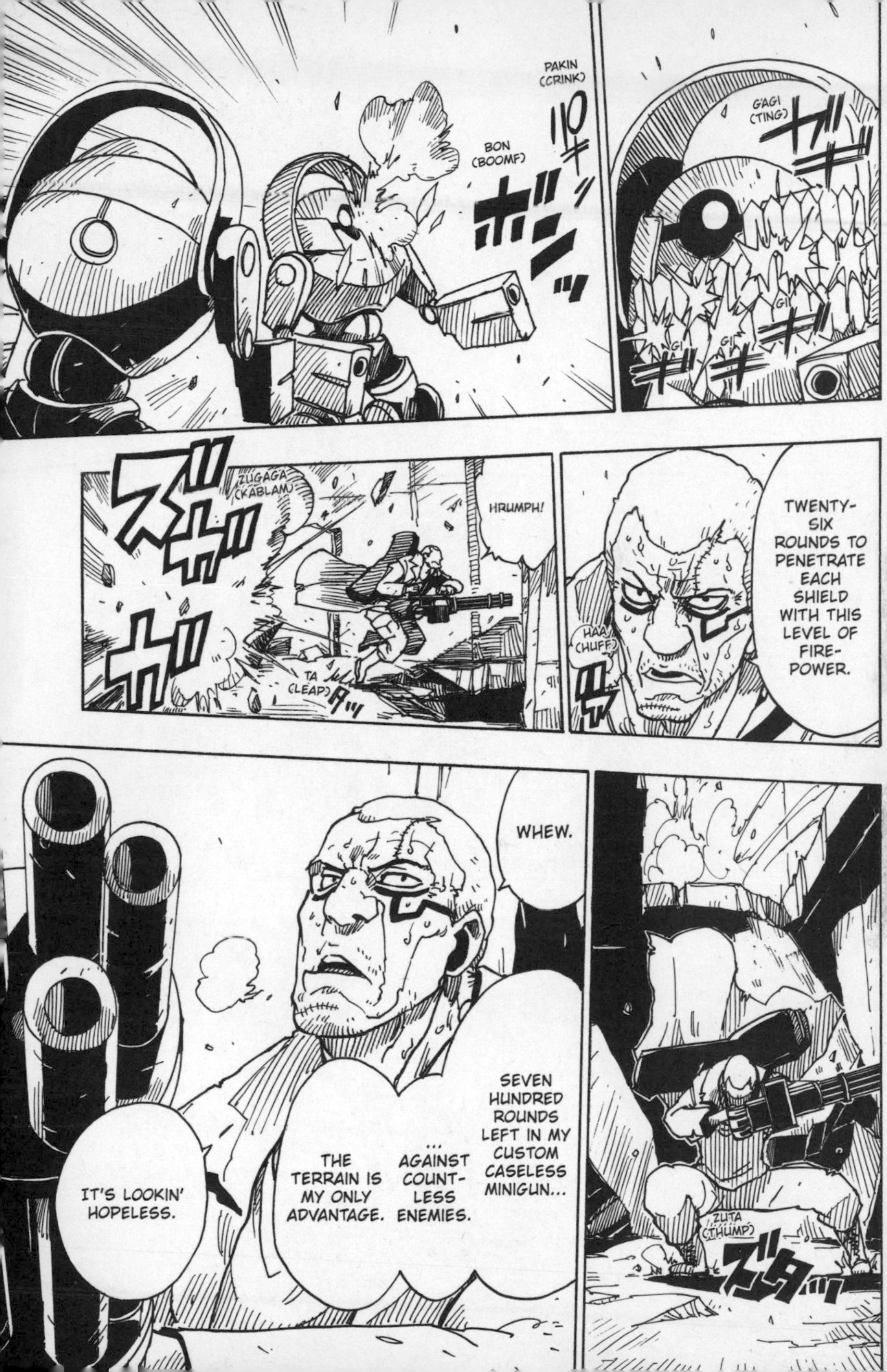
GAGI (TING)
GI
GI
GI
PAKIN (CRINK)
BON (BOOMF)
TWENTY-SIX ROUNDS TO PENETRATE EACH SHIELD WITH THIS LEVEL OF FIRE-POWER.
HAA (CHUFF)
HRUMPH!
ZUGAGA (KABLAM)
TA (LEAP)
ZUTA (THUMP)
WHEW.
SEVEN HUNDRED ROUNDS LEFT IN MY CUSTOM CASELESS MINIGUN...
...AGAINST COUNT-LESS ENEMIES.
THE TERRAIN IS MY ONLY ADVANTAGE.
IT'S LOOKIN' HOPELESS.

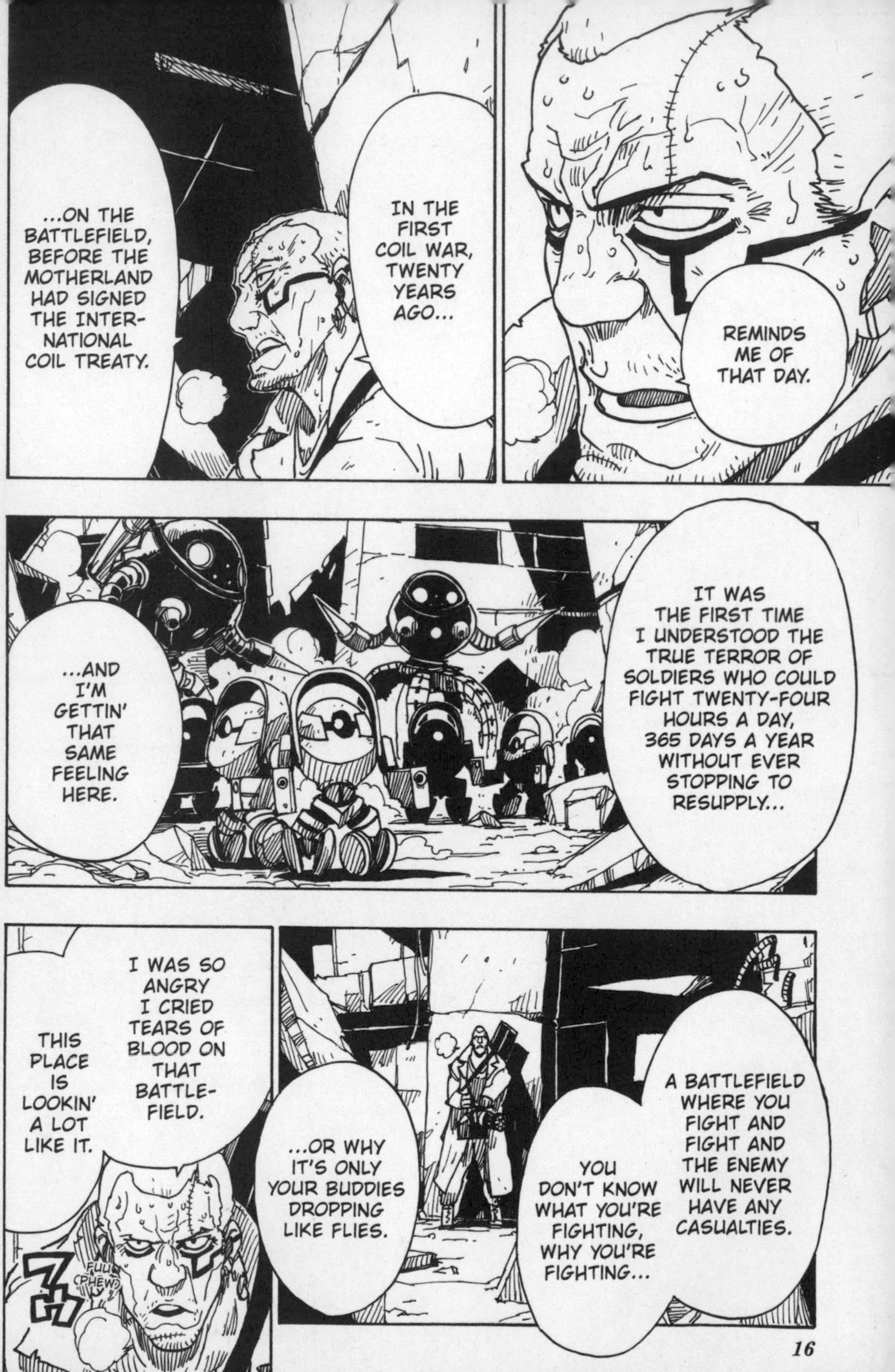
REMINDS ME OF THAT DAY.
IN THE FIRST COIL WAR, TWENTY YEARS AGO...
...ON THE BATTLEFIELD, BEFORE THE MOTHERLAND HAD SIGNED THE INTER-NATIONAL COIL TREATY.
IT WAS THE FIRST TIME I UNDERSTOOD THE TRUE TERROR OF SOLDIERS WHO COULD FIGHT TWENTY-FOUR HOURS A DAY, 365 DAYS A YEAR WITHOUT EVER STOPPING TO RESUPPLY...
...AND I'M GETTIN' THAT SAME FEELING HERE.
A BATTLEFIELD WHERE YOU FIGHT AND FIGHT AND THE ENEMY WILL NEVER HAVE ANY CASUALTIES.
YOU DON'T KNOW WHAT YOU'RE FIGHTING, WHY YOU'RE FIGHTING...
...OR WHY IT'S ONLY YOUR BUDDIES DROPPING LIKE FLIES.
I WAS SO ANGRY I CRIED TEARS OF BLOOD ON THAT BATTLE-FIELD.
THIS PLACE IS LOOKIN' A LOT LIKE IT.
FUU
(PHEW)

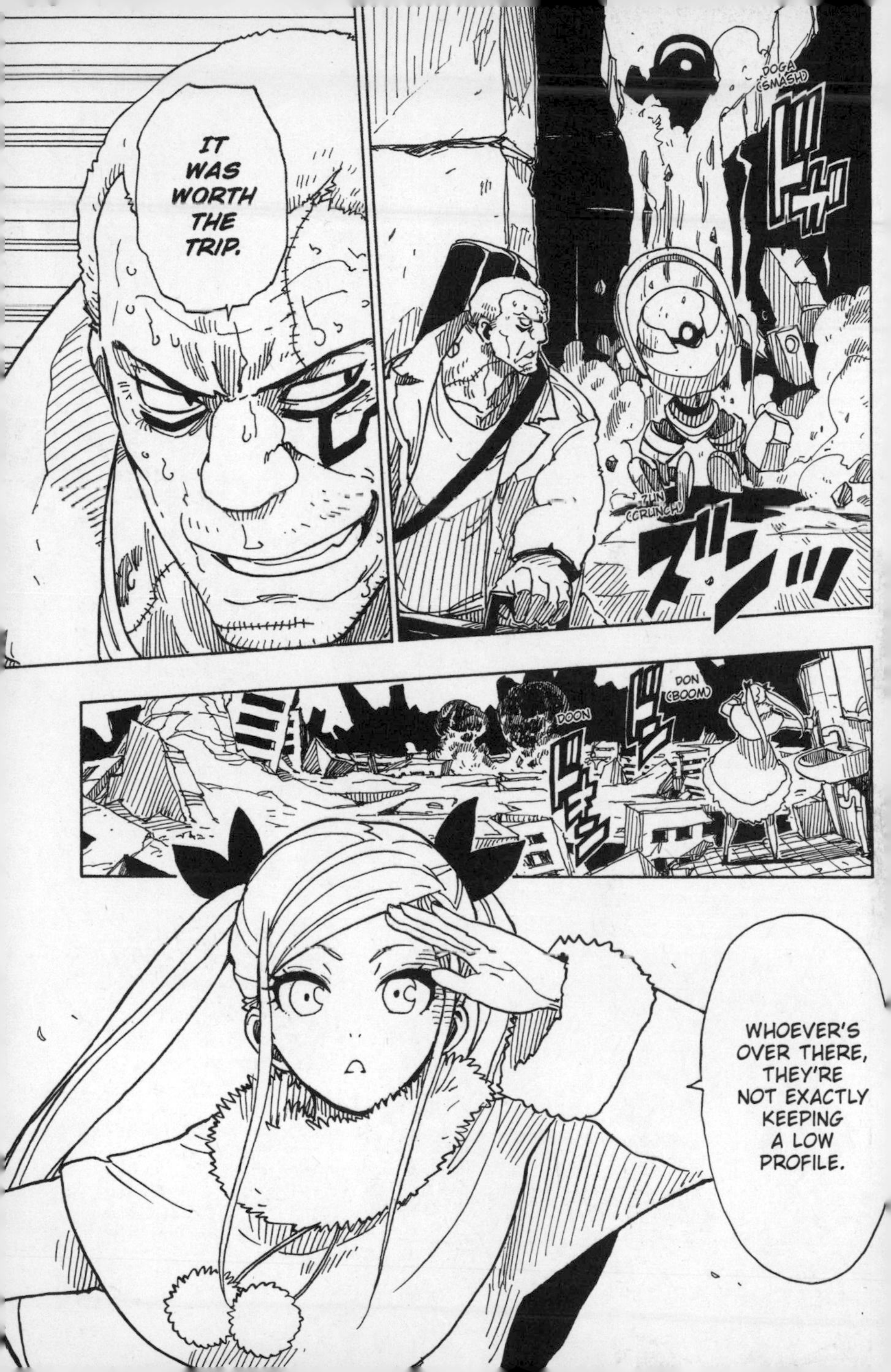
DOGA (SMASH)
ZUN (CRUNCH)
IT WAS WORTH THE TRIP.
DON (BOOM)
DOON
WHOEVER'S OVER THERE, THEY'RE NOT EXACTLY KEEPING A LOW PROFILE.

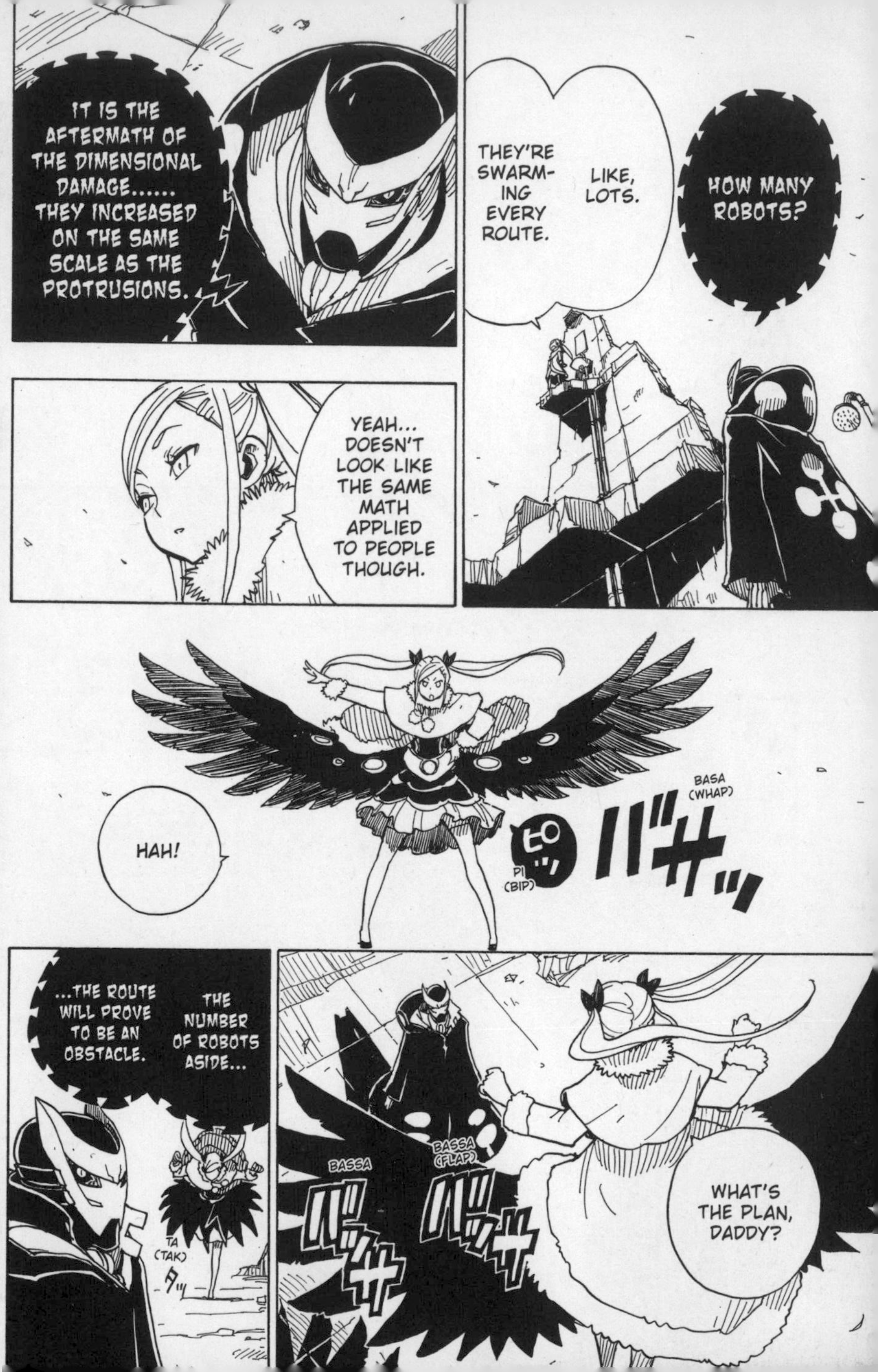
HOW MANY ROBOTS?
LIKE, LOTS.
THEY'RE SWARMING EVERY ROUTE.
IT IS THE AFTERMATH OF THE DIMENSIONAL DAMAGE...... THEY INCREASED ON THE SAME SCALE AS THE PROTRUSIONS.
YEAH... DOESN'T LOOK LIKE THE SAME MATH APPLIED TO PEOPLE THOUGH.
BASA (WHAP)
PI (BIP)
HAH!
WHAT'S THE PLAN, DADDY?
BASSA (FLAP)
BASSA
THE NUMBER OF ROBOTS ASIDE...
...THE ROUTE WILL PROVE TO BE AN OBSTACLE.
TA (TAK)

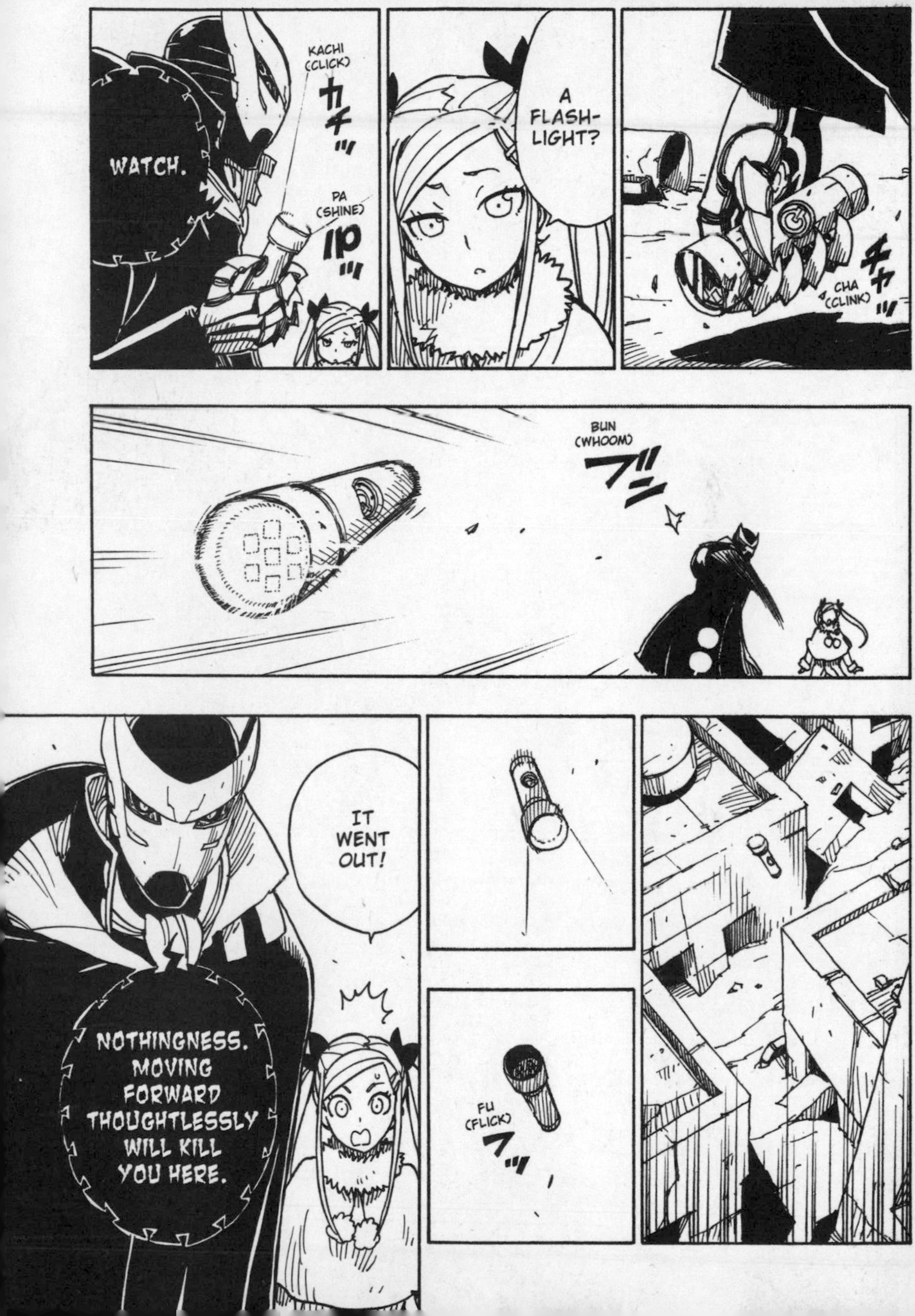
CHA (CLINK)
A FLASH-LIGHT?
KACHI (CLICK)
WATCH.
PA (SHINE)
BUN (WHOOM)
FU (FLICK)
IT WENT OUT!
NOTHINGNESS. MOVING FORWARD THOUGHTLESSLY WILL KILL YOU HERE.

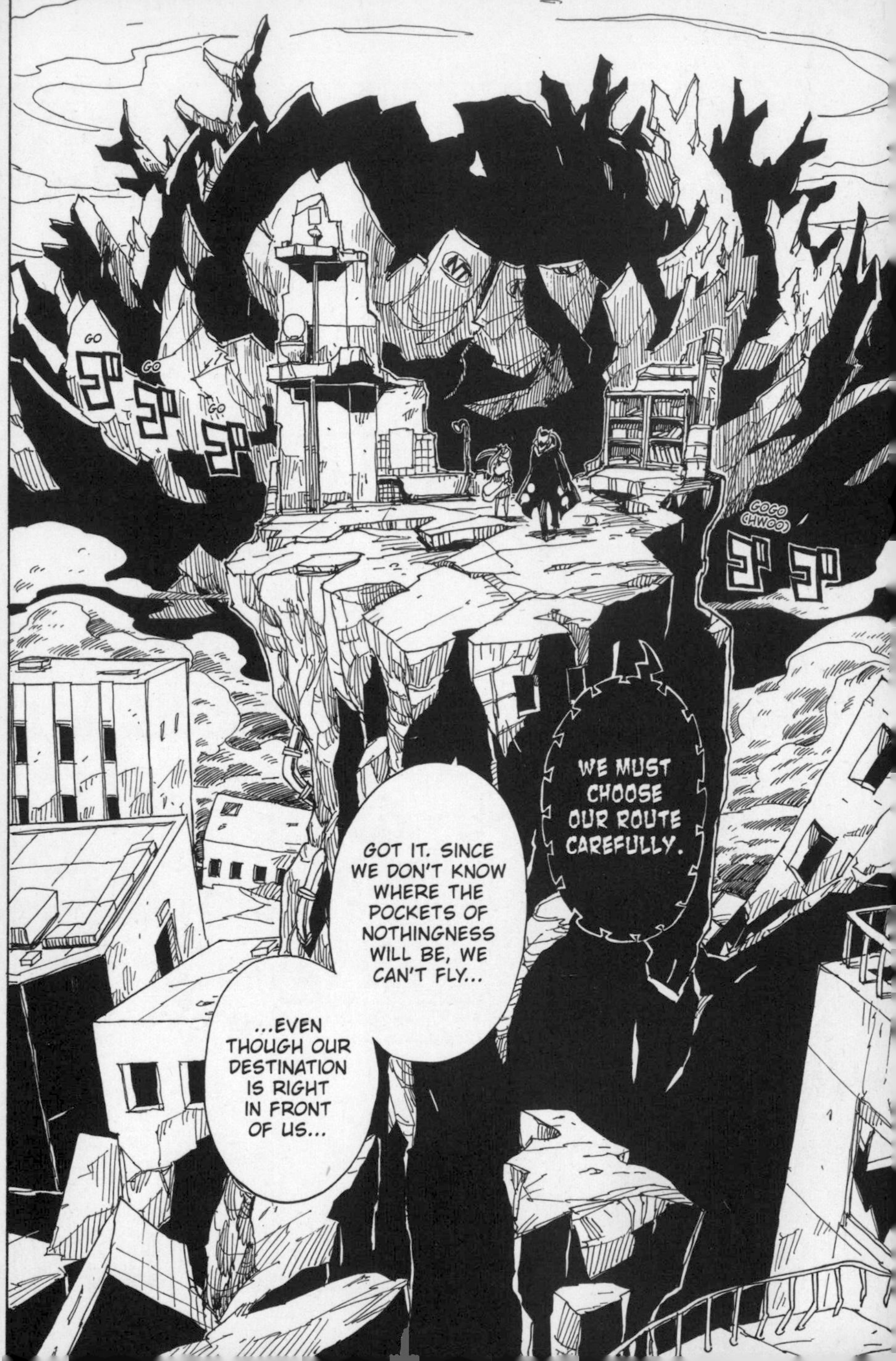
GO GO GO
GOGO (HWOO)
WE MUST CHOOSE OUR ROUTE CAREFULLY.
GOT IT. SINCE WE DON'T KNOW WHERE THE POCKETS OF NOTHINGNESS WILL BE, WE CAN'T FLY...
...EVEN THOUGH OUR DESTINATION IS RIGHT IN FRONT OF US...

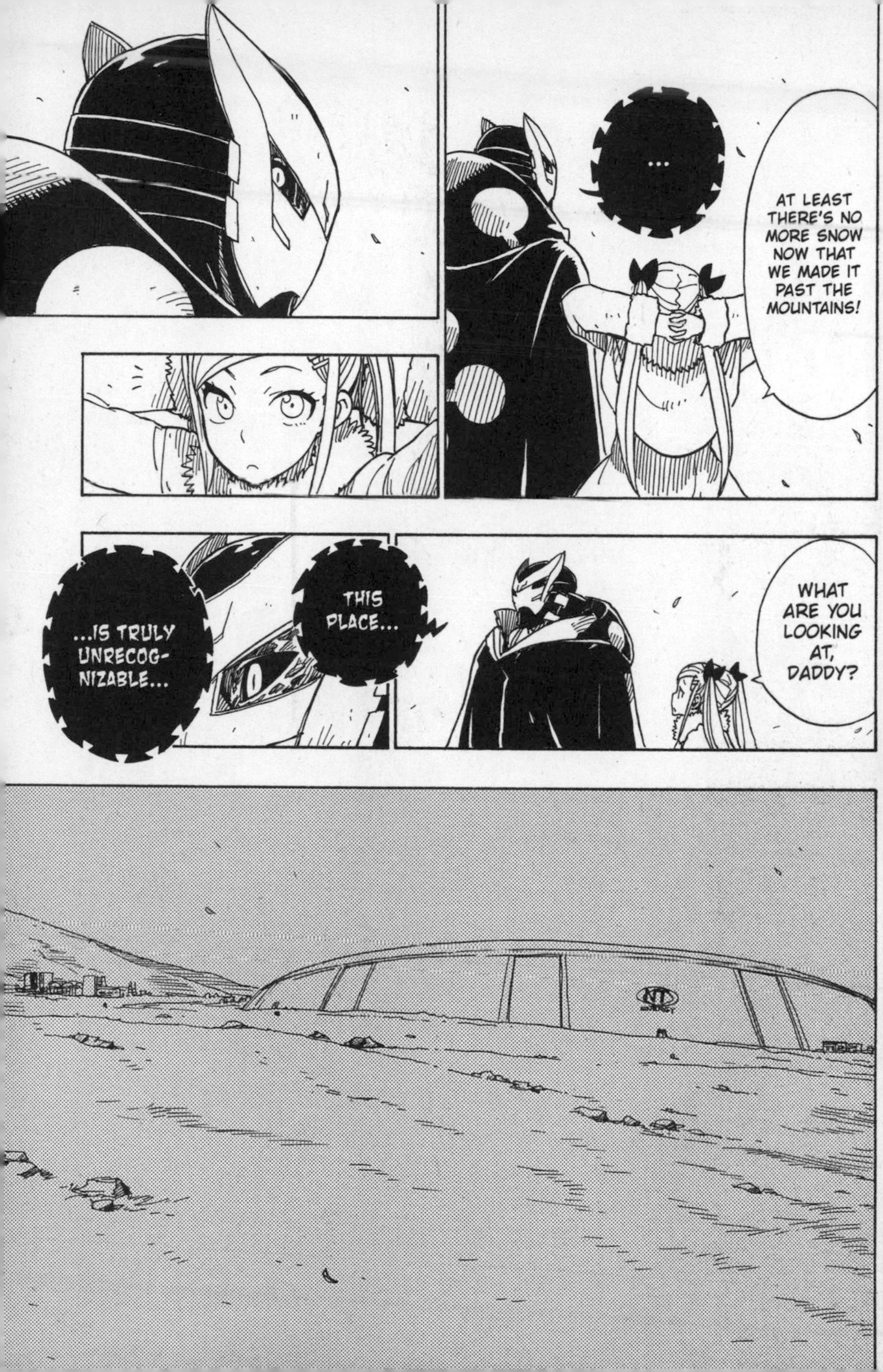
AT LEAST THERE'S NO MORE SNOW NOW THAT WE MADE IT PAST THE MOUNTAINS!
...
WHAT ARE YOU LOOKING AT, DADDY?
THIS PLACE...
...IS TRULY UNRECOG-NIZABLE...

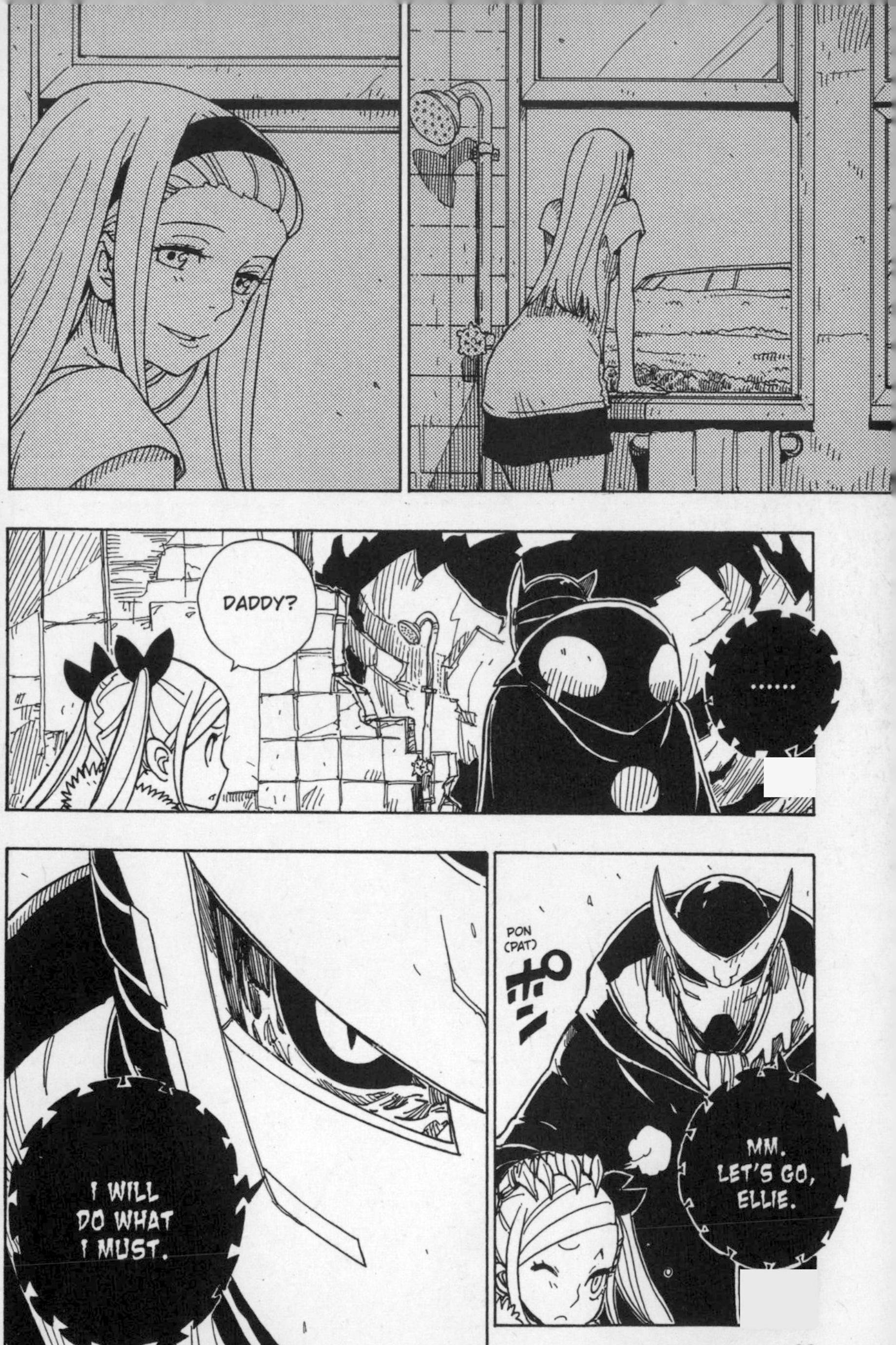
DADDY?
......
PON (PAT)
MM. LET'S GO, ELLIE.
I WILL DO WHAT I MUST.

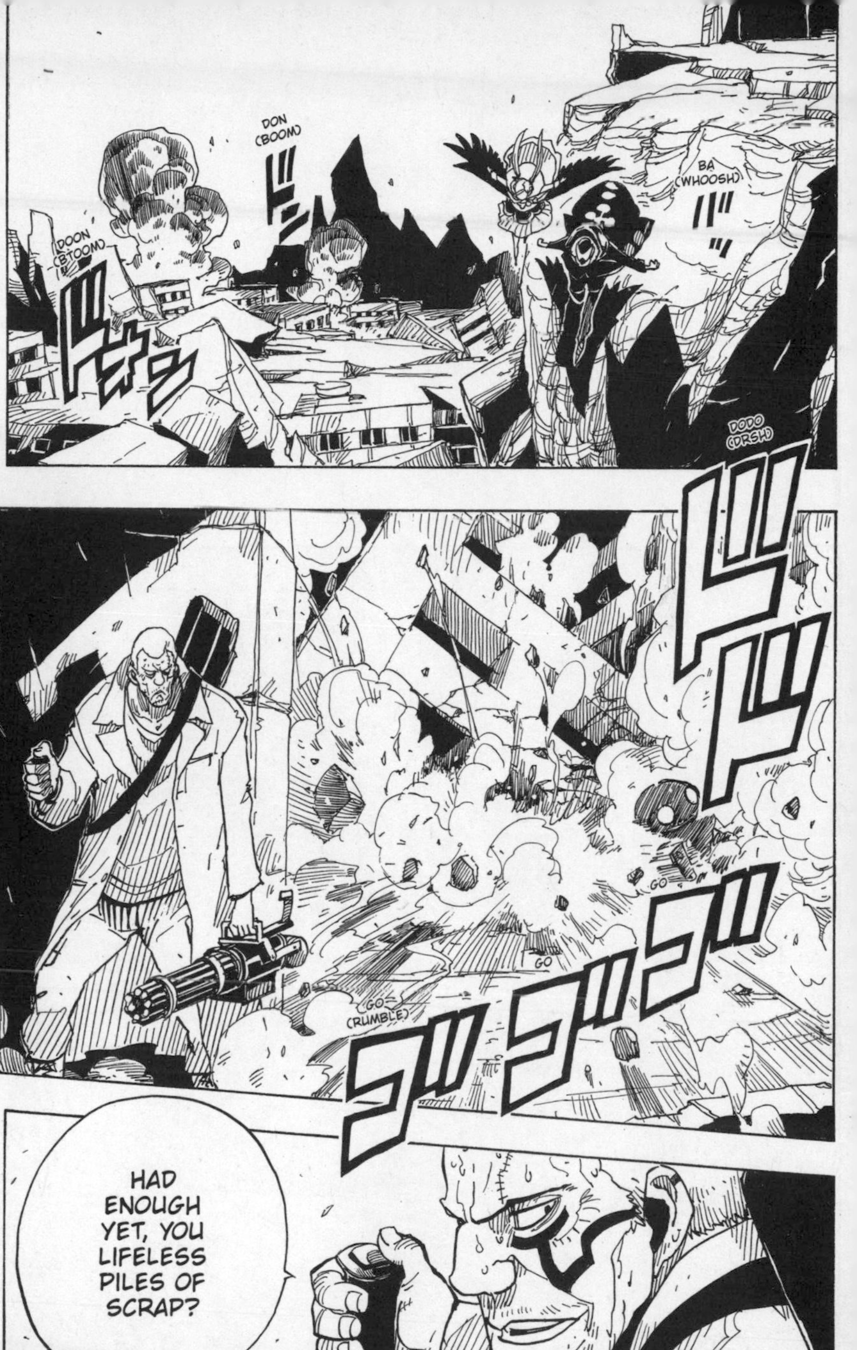
BA (WHOOSH)
DON (BOOM)
DOON (BTOOM)
DODO (DRSH)
GO
GO
GO (RUMBLE)
HAD ENOUGH YET, YOU LIFELESS PILES OF SCRAP?

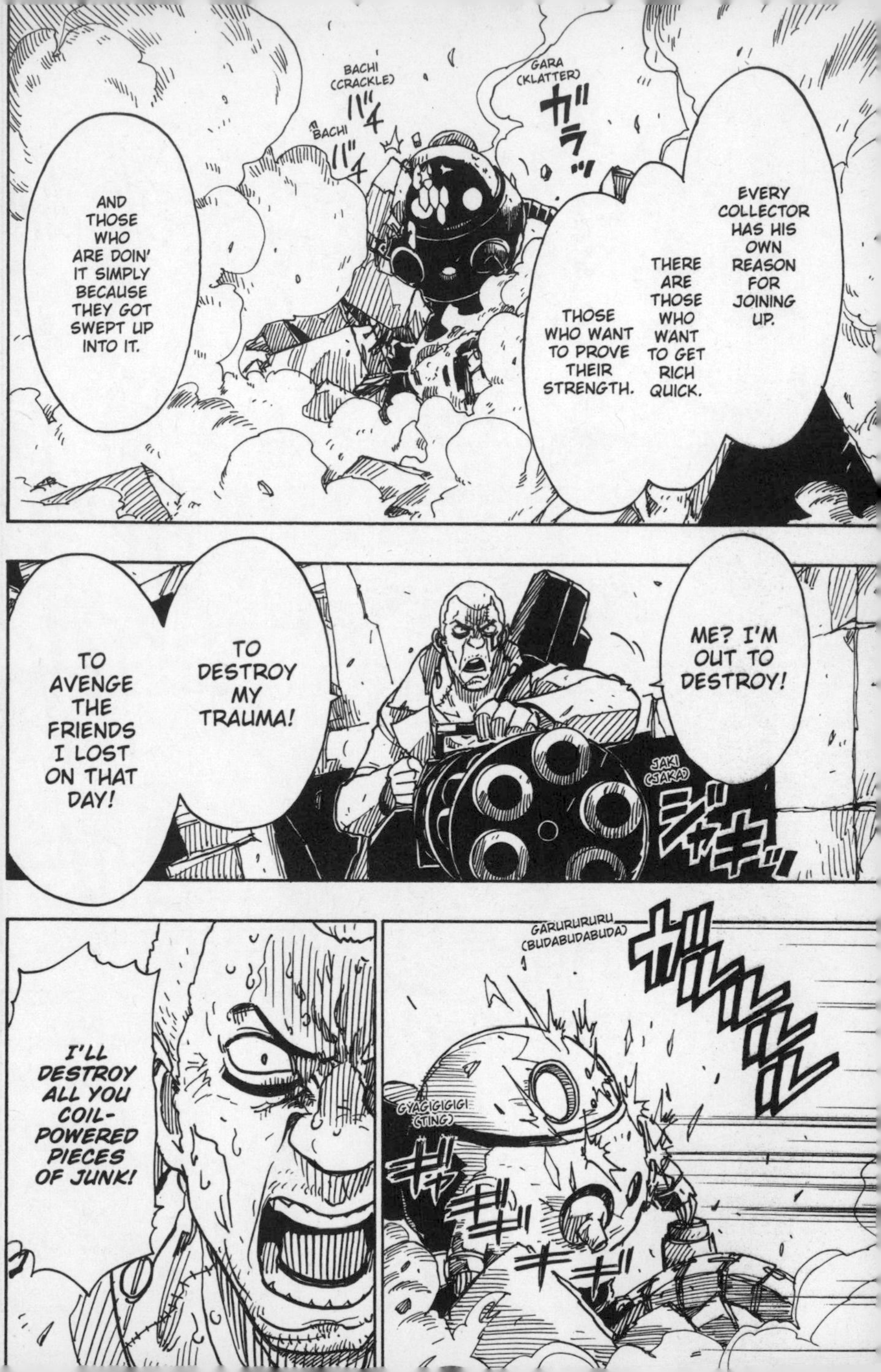
GARA (KLATTER)
EVERY COLLECTOR HAS HIS OWN REASON FOR JOINING UP.
THERE ARE THOSE WHO WANT TO GET RICH QUICK.
THOSE WHO WANT TO PROVE THEIR STRENGTH.
BACHI (CRACKLE)
BACHI
AND THOSE WHO ARE DOIN' IT SIMPLY BECAUSE THEY GOT SWEPT UP INTO IT.
ME? I'M OUT TO DESTROY!
JAKI (JAKA)
TO DESTROY MY TRAUMA!
TO AVENGE THE FRIENDS I LOST ON THAT DAY!
GARURURURU (BUDABUDABUDA)
GYAGIGIGIGI (TING)
I'LL DESTROY ALL YOU COIL-POWERED PIECES OF JUNK!

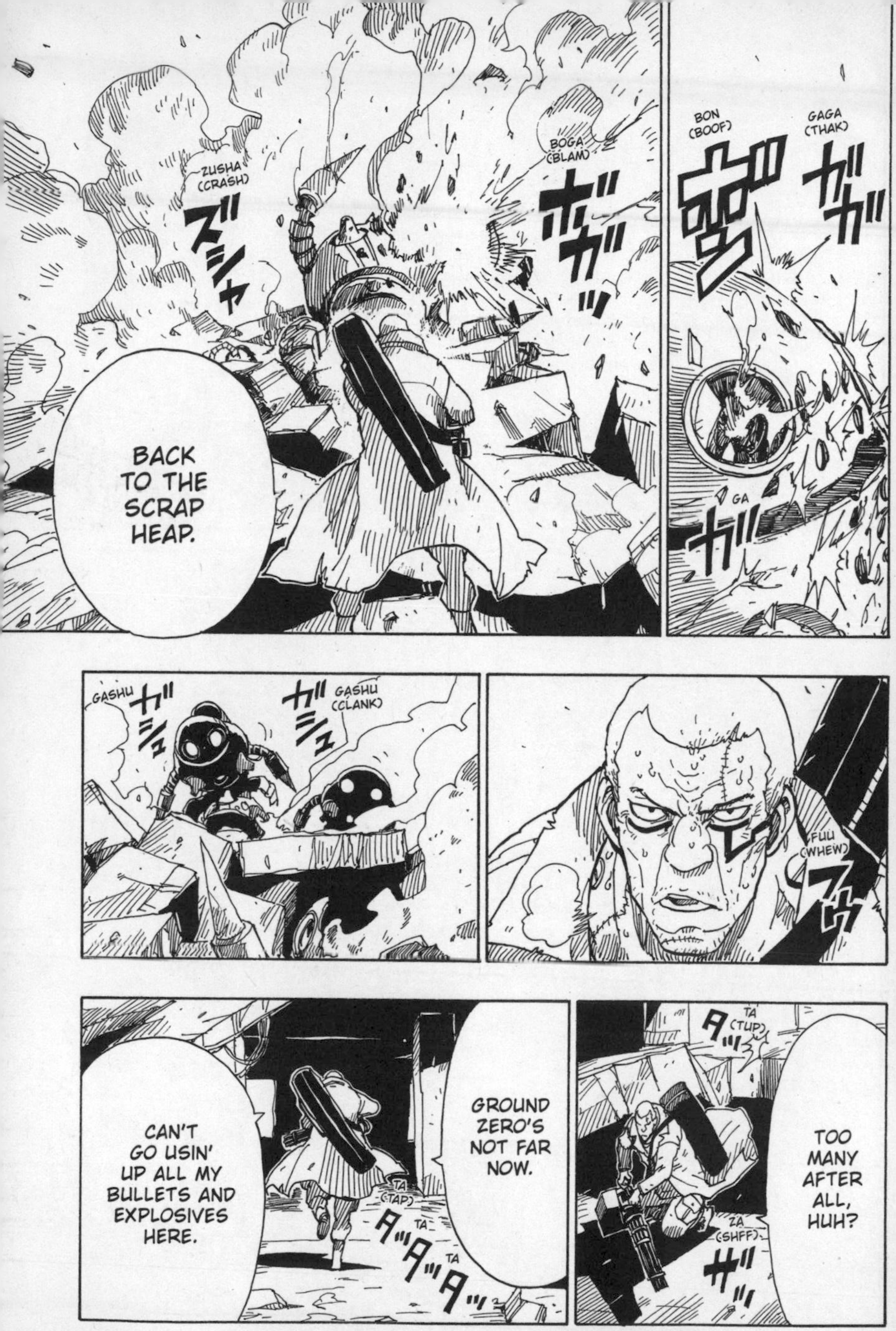
BON (BOOF)
GAGA (THAK)
GA
BOGA (BLAM)
ZUSHA (CRASH)
BACK TO THE SCRAP HEAP.
FUU (WHEW)
GASHU (CLANK)
GASHU
TA (TUP)
TOO MANY AFTER ALL, HUH?
ZA (SHFF)
GROUND ZERO'S NOT FAR NOW.
CAN'T GO USIN' UP ALL MY BULLETS AND EXPLOSIVES HERE.
TA (TAP)
TA
TA

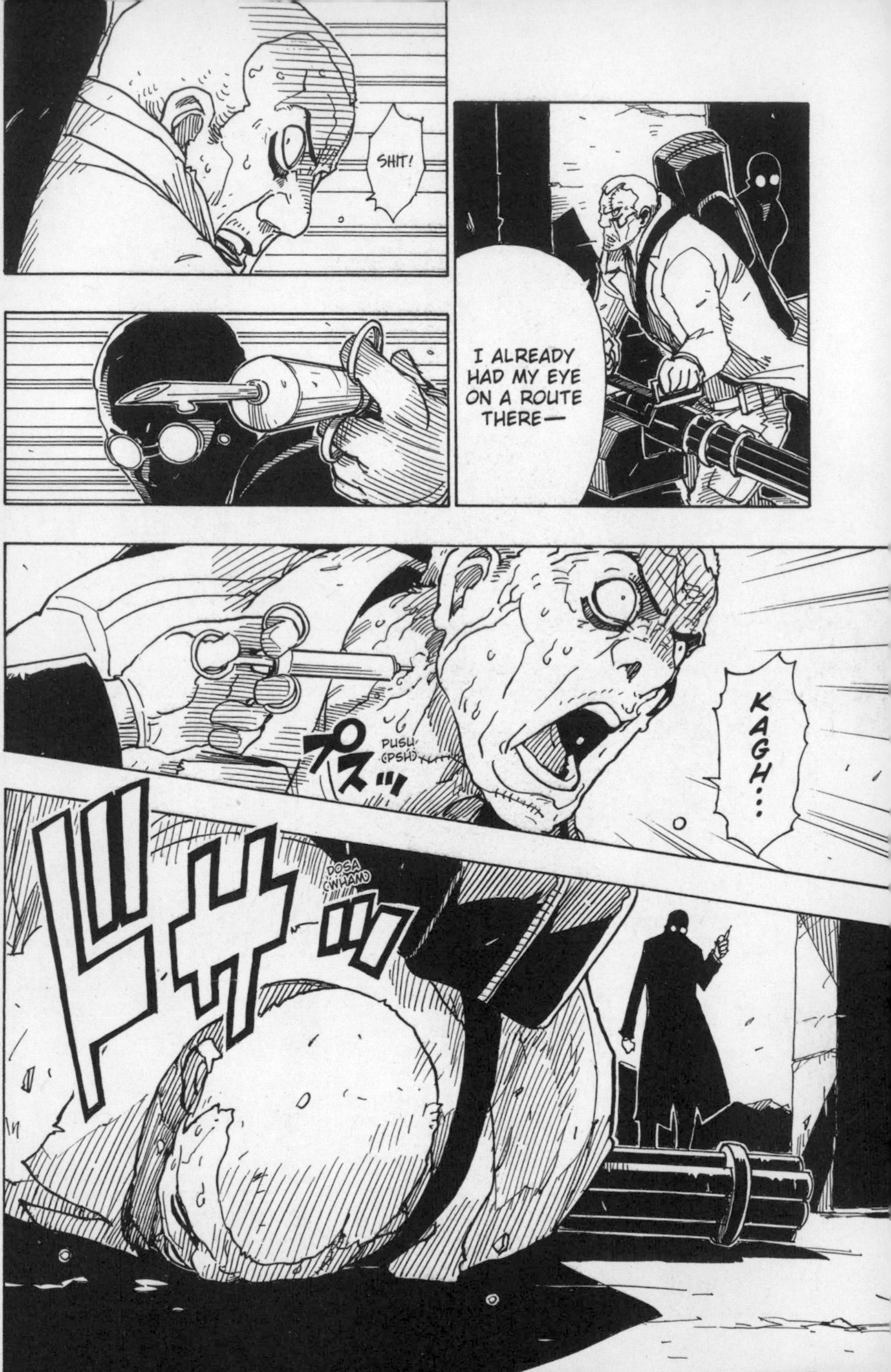
I ALREADY HAD MY EYE ON A ROUTE THERE—
SHIT!
KAGH...
PUSU (PSH)
プスッ
DOSA (WHAM)
ドサッ

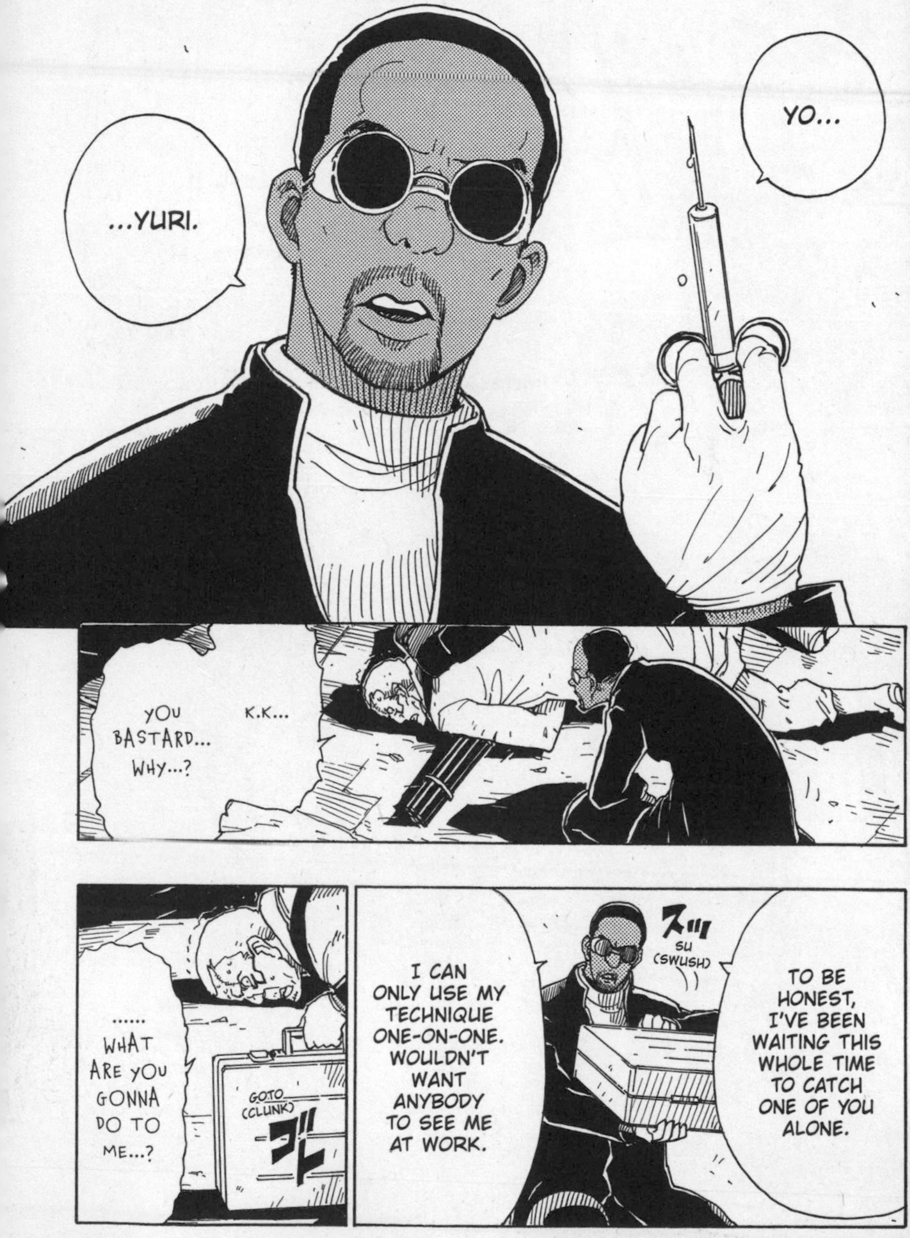
YO...
...YURI.
K.K...
YOU BASTARD... WHY...?
TO BE HONEST, I'VE BEEN WAITING THIS WHOLE TIME TO CATCH ONE OF YOU ALONE.
スッ
SU (SWUSH)
I CAN ONLY USE MY TECHNIQUE ONE-ON-ONE. WOULDN'T WANT ANYBODY TO SEE ME AT WORK.
ゴト
GOTO (CLUNK)
...... WHAT ARE YOU GONNA DO TO ME...?

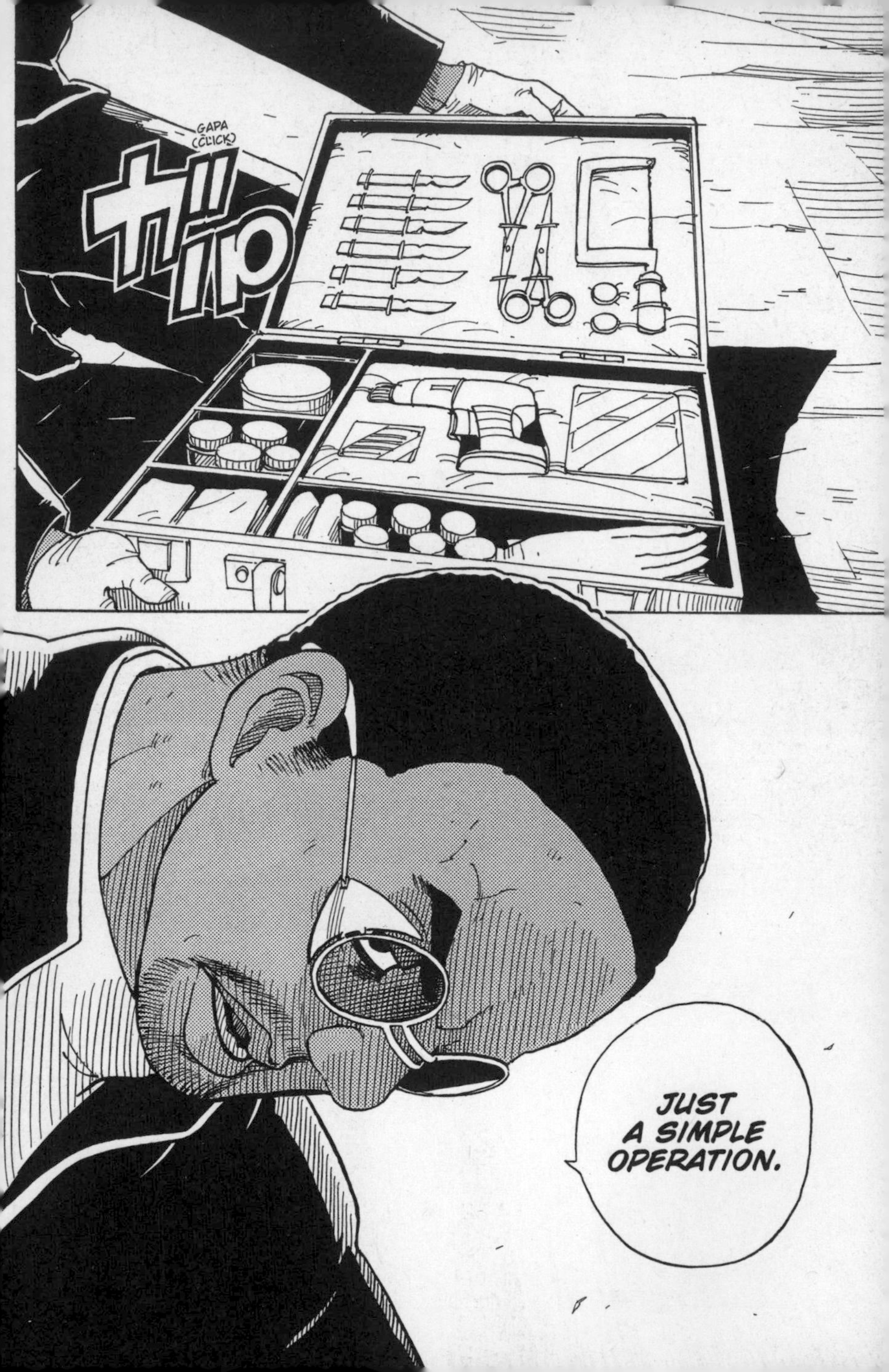
GAPA (CLICK)
JUST A SIMPLE OPERATION.

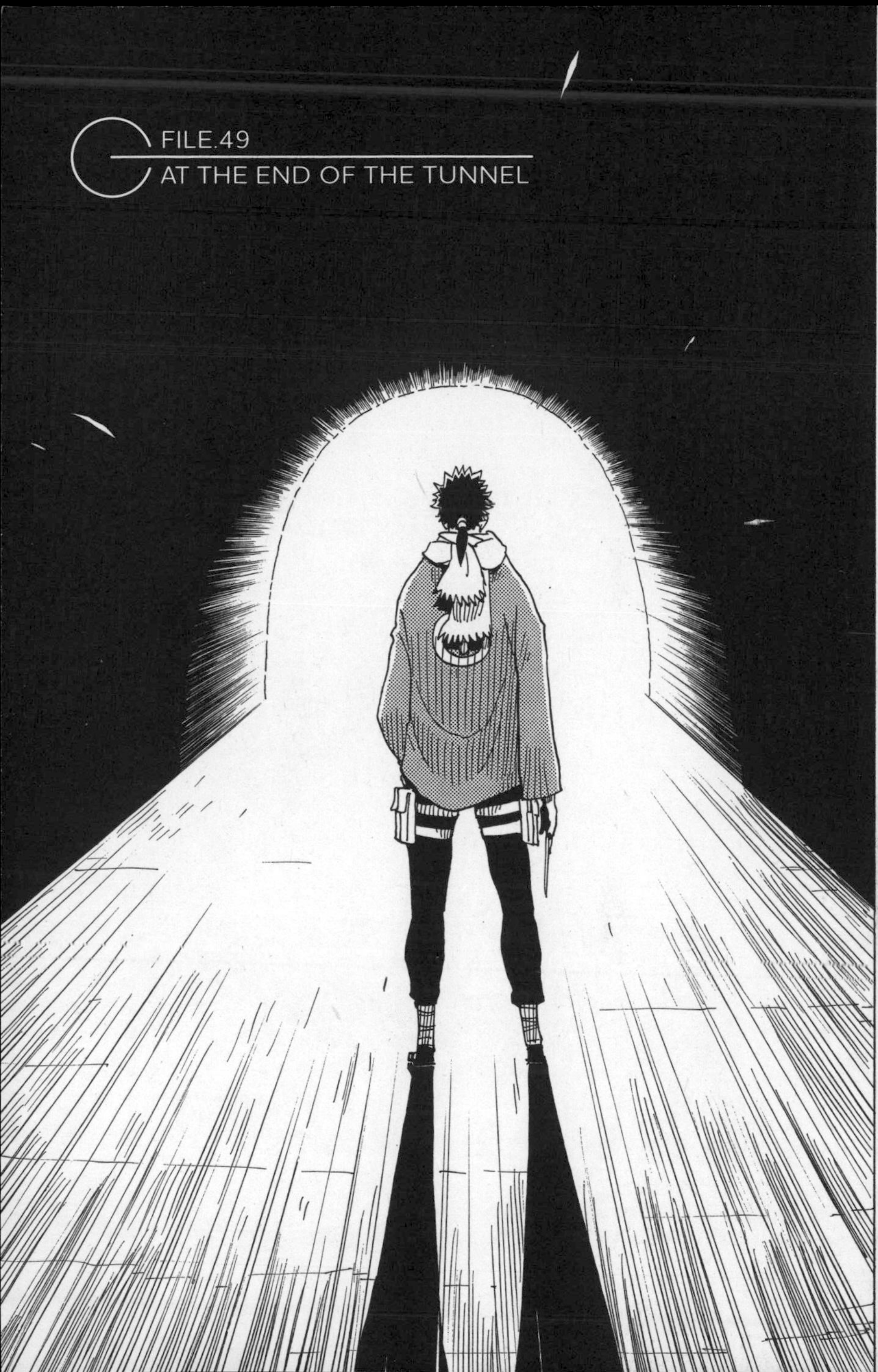
FILE.49
AT THE END OF THE TUNNEL

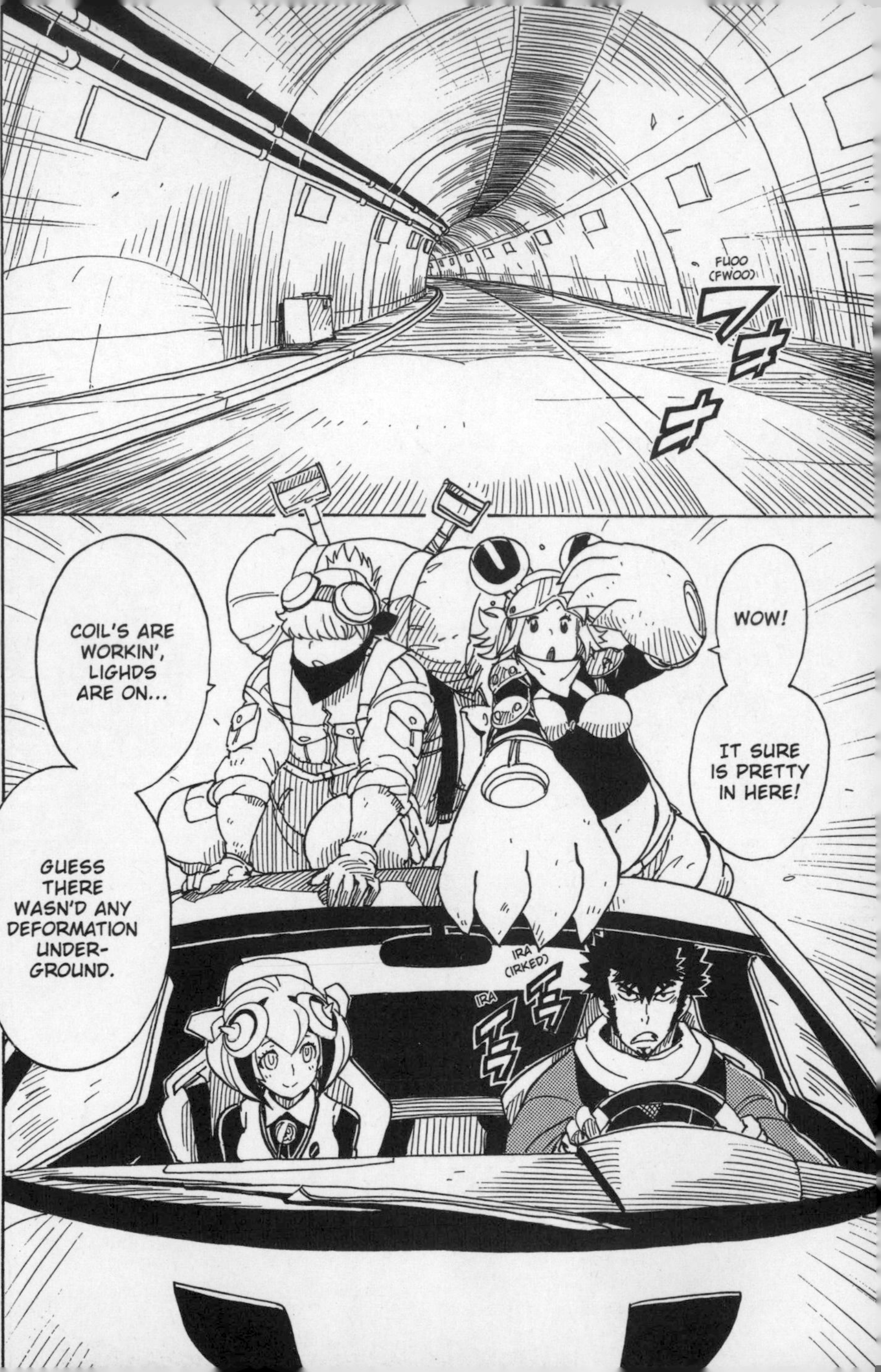
FUOO (FWOO)
WOW!
IT SURE IS PRETTY IN HERE!
COIL'S ARE WORKIN', LIGHDS ARE ON...
GUESS THERE WASN'D ANY DEFORMATION UNDER-GROUND.
IRA (IRKED)
IRA

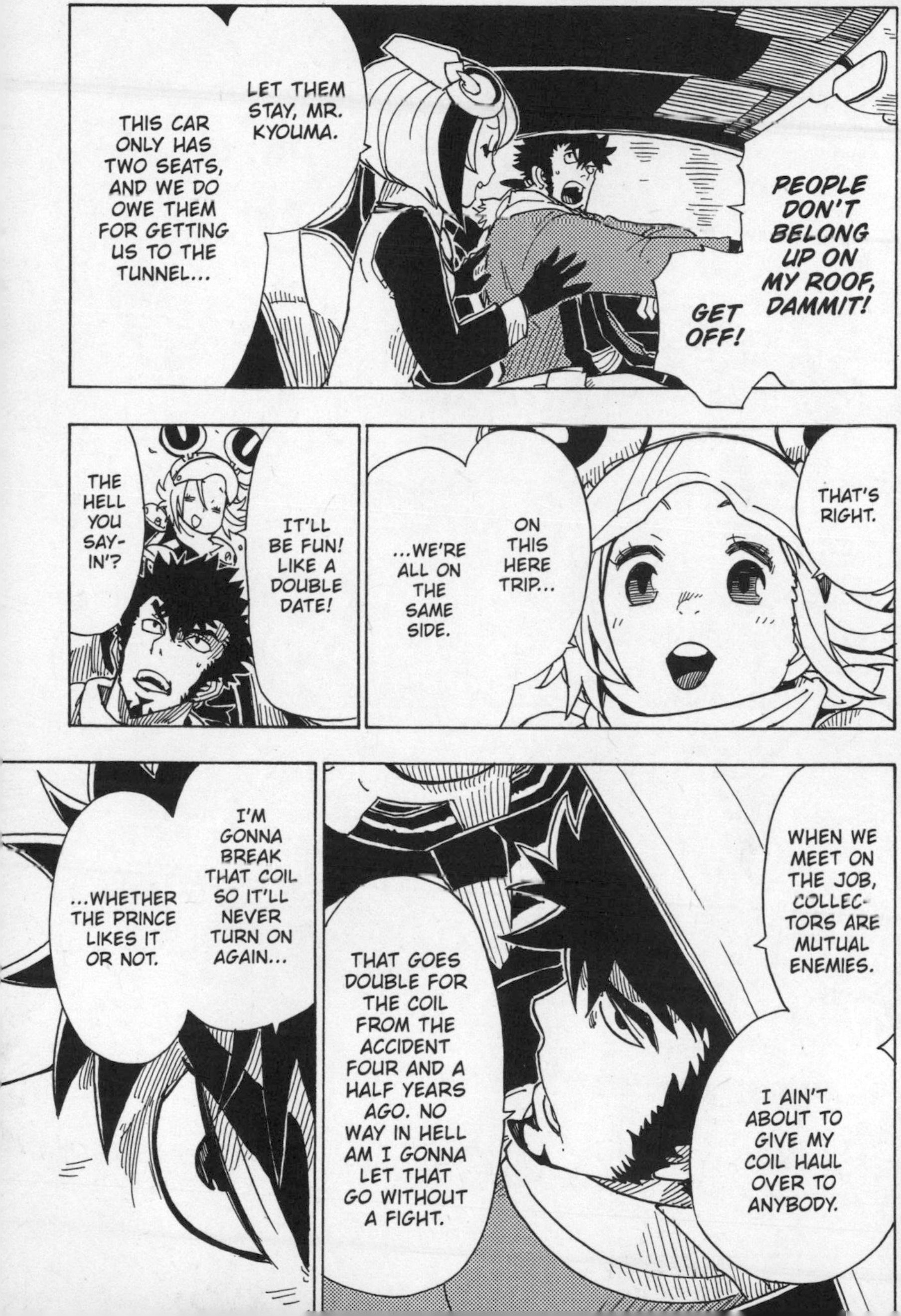
PEOPLE DON'T BELONG UP ON MY ROOF, DAMMIT!
GET OFF!
LET THEM STAY, MR. KYOUMA.
THIS CAR ONLY HAS TWO SEATS, AND WE DO OWE THEM FOR GETTING US TO THE TUNNEL...
THAT'S RIGHT.
ON THIS HERE TRIP...
...WE'RE ALL ON THE SAME SIDE.
IT'LL BE FUN! LIKE A DOUBLE DATE!
THE HELL YOU SAY-IN'?
WHEN WE MEET ON THE JOB, COLLEC-TORS ARE MUTUAL ENEMIES.
I AIN'T ABOUT TO GIVE MY COIL HAUL OVER TO ANYBODY.
THAT GOES DOUBLE FOR THE COIL FROM THE ACCIDENT FOUR AND A HALF YEARS AGO. NO WAY IN HELL AM I GONNA LET THAT GO WITHOUT A FIGHT.
I'M GONNA BREAK THAT COIL SO IT'LL NEVER TURN ON AGAIN...
...WHETHER THE PRINCE LIKES IT OR NOT.

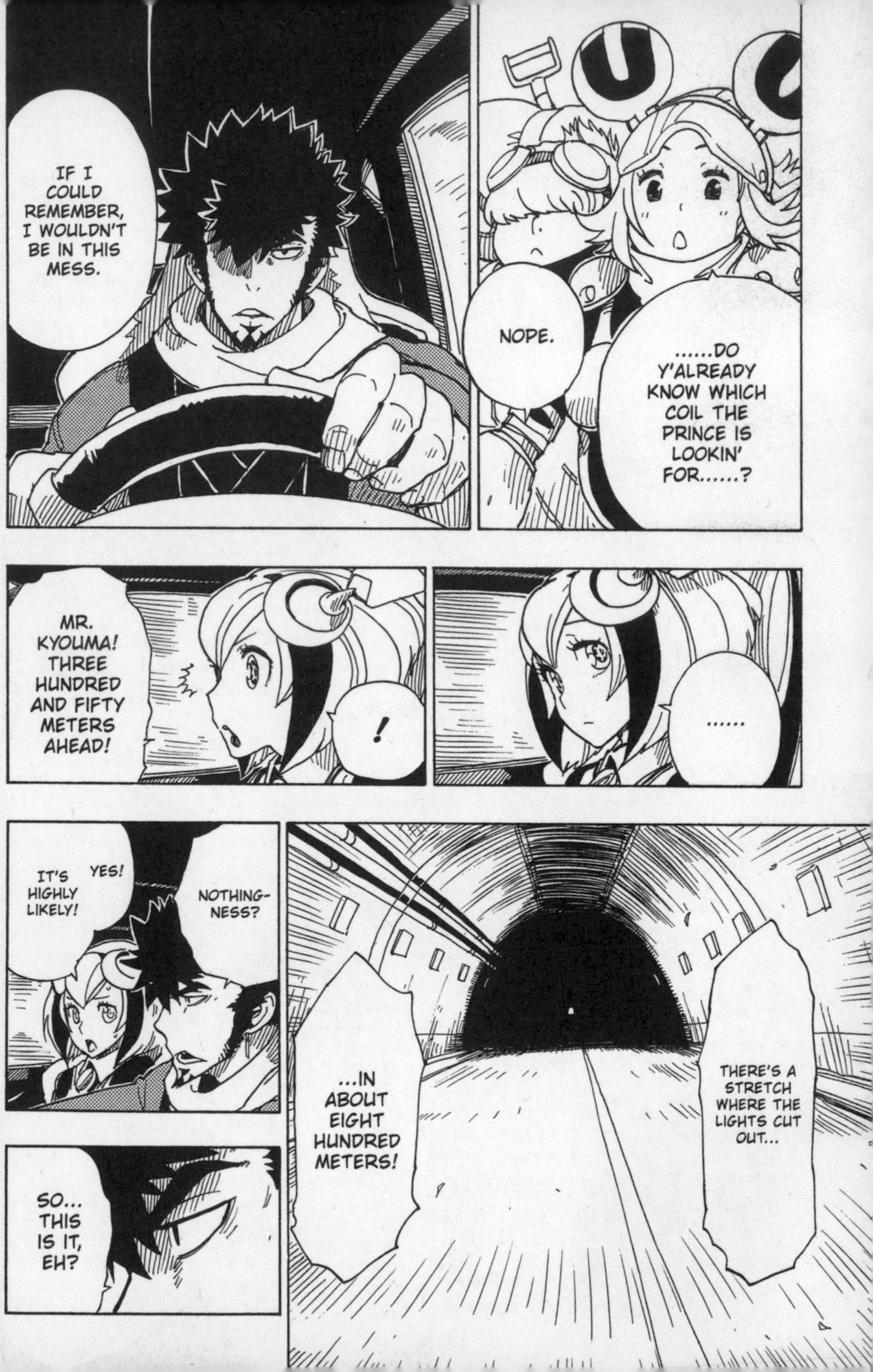

......DO Y'ALREADY KNOW WHICH COIL THE PRINCE IS LOOKIN' FOR......?
NOPE.
IF I COULD REMEMBER, I WOULDN'T BE IN THIS MESS.
......
!
MR. KYOUMA! THREE HUNDRED AND FIFTY METERS AHEAD!
THERE'S A STRETCH WHERE THE LIGHTS CUT OUT...
...IN ABOUT EIGHT HUNDRED METERS!
NOTHING-NESS?
YES!
IT'S HIGHLY LIKELY!
SO... THIS IS IT, EH?

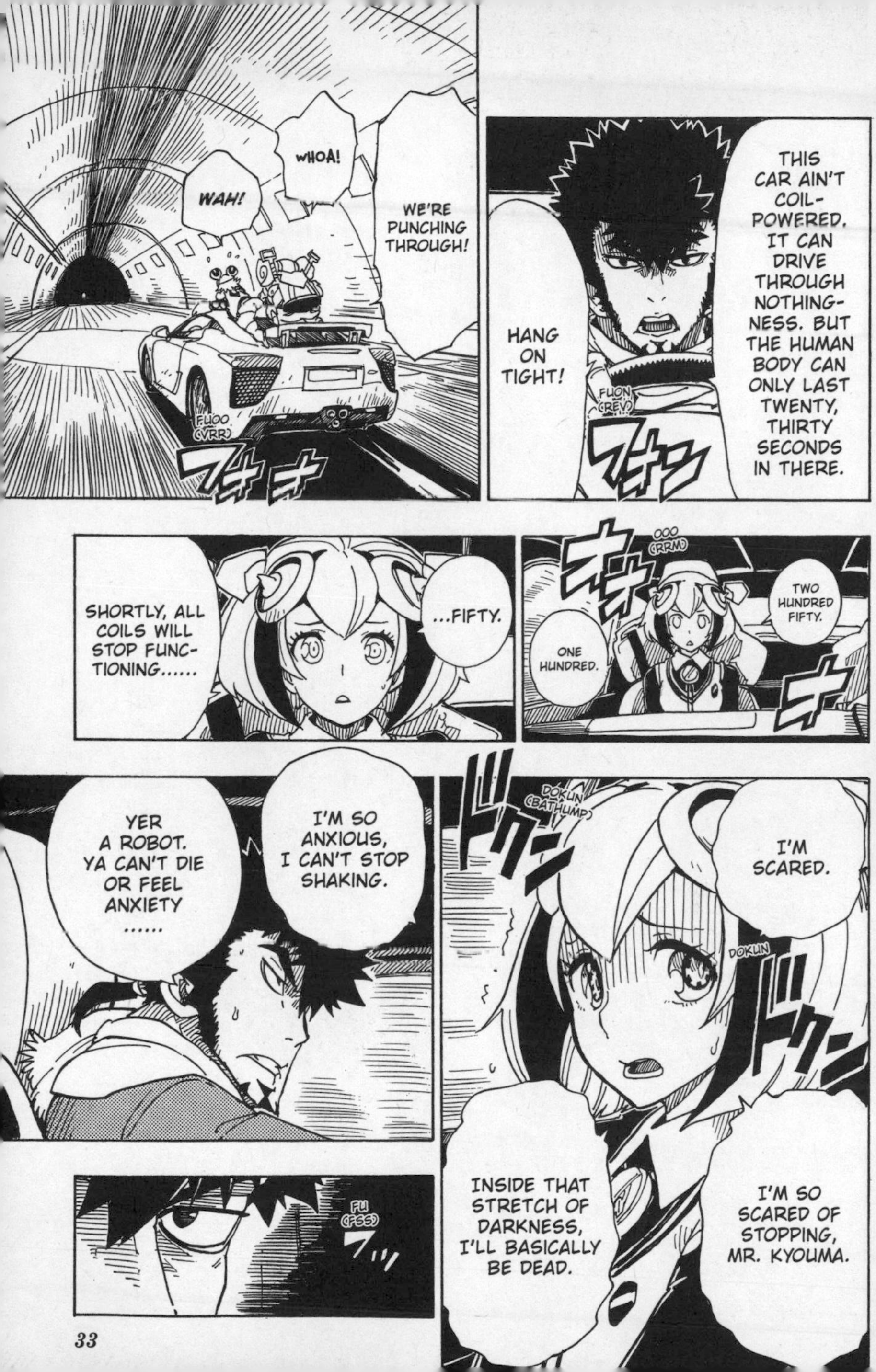
THIS CAR AIN'T COIL-POWERED. IT CAN DRIVE THROUGH NOTHINGNESS. BUT THE HUMAN BODY CAN ONLY LAST TWENTY, THIRTY SECONDS IN THERE.
HANG ON TIGHT!
FUON (REV)
WE'RE PUNCHING THROUGH!
WHOA!
WAH!
FUOO (VRR)
OOO (RRM)
TWO HUNDRED FIFTY.
ONE HUNDRED.
...FIFTY.
SHORTLY, ALL COILS WILL STOP FUNCTIONING......
DOKUN (BATHUMP)
I'M SCARED.
DOKUN
I'M SO SCARED OF STOPPING, MR. KYOUMA.
INSIDE THAT STRETCH OF DARKNESS, I'LL BASICALLY BE DEAD.
I'M SO ANXIOUS, I CAN'T STOP SHAKING.
YER A ROBOT. YA CAN'T DIE OR FEEL ANXIETY ......
FU (FSS)

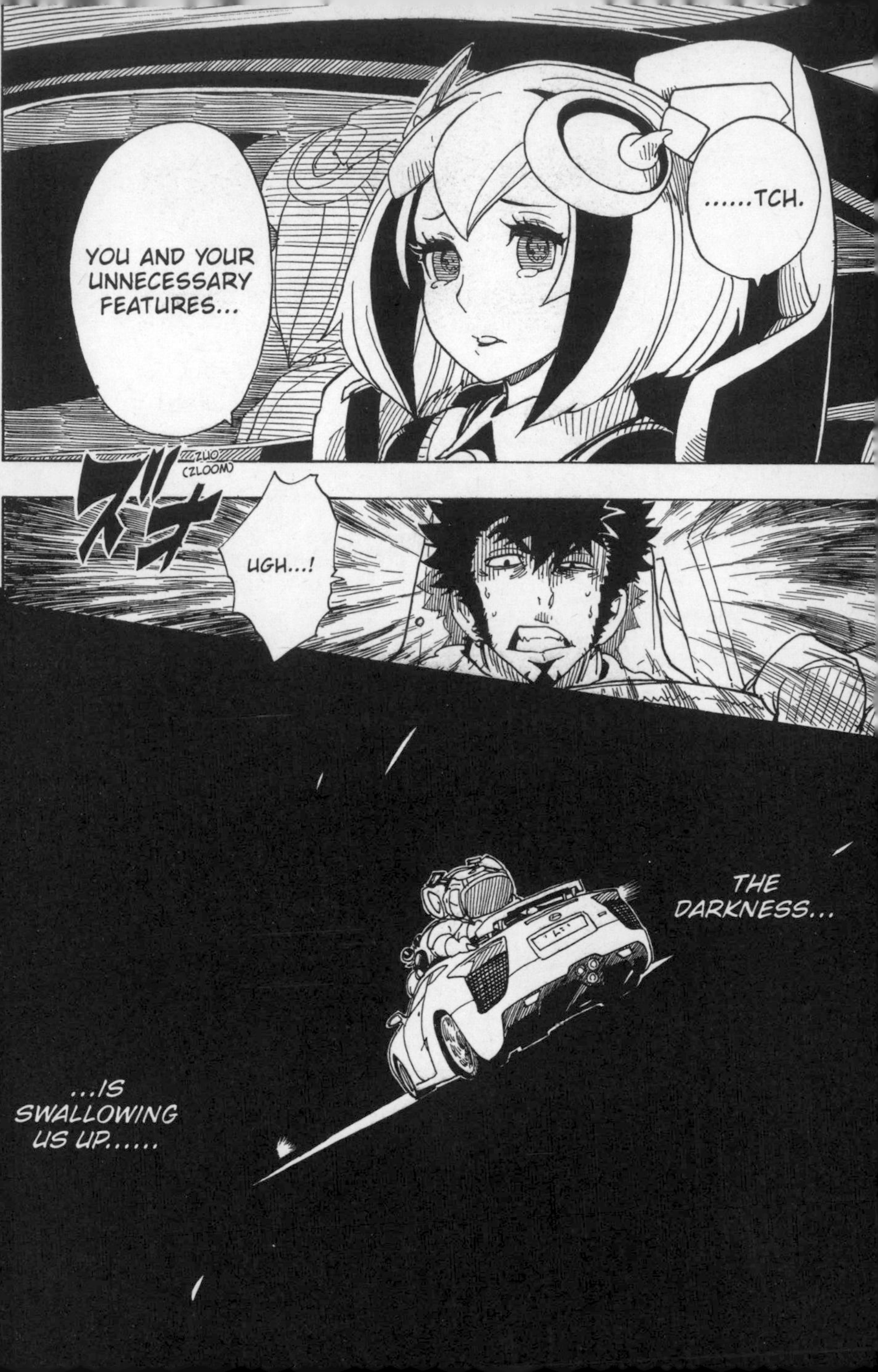
......TCH.
YOU AND YOUR UNNECESSARY FEATURES...
UGH...!
ZUO
(ZLOOM)
THE DARKNESS...
...IS SWALLOWING US UP......

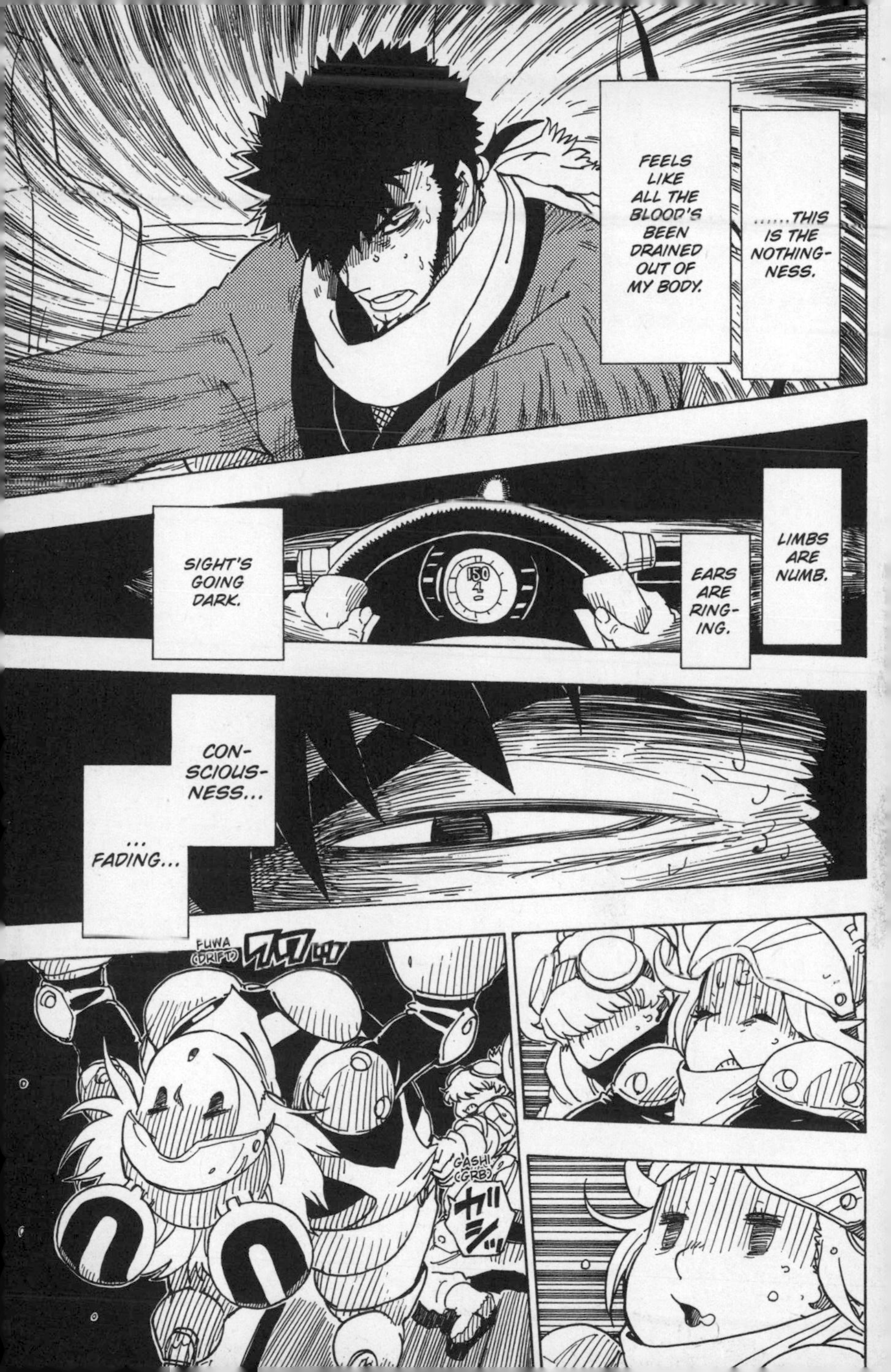
......THIS IS THE NOTHINGNESS.
FEELS LIKE ALL THE BLOOD'S BEEN DRAINED OUT OF MY BODY.
LIMBS ARE NUMB.
EARS ARE RINGING.
SIGHT'S GOING DARK.
CONSCIOUSNESS...
... FADING...
FUWA (DRIFT)
GASHI (GRB)

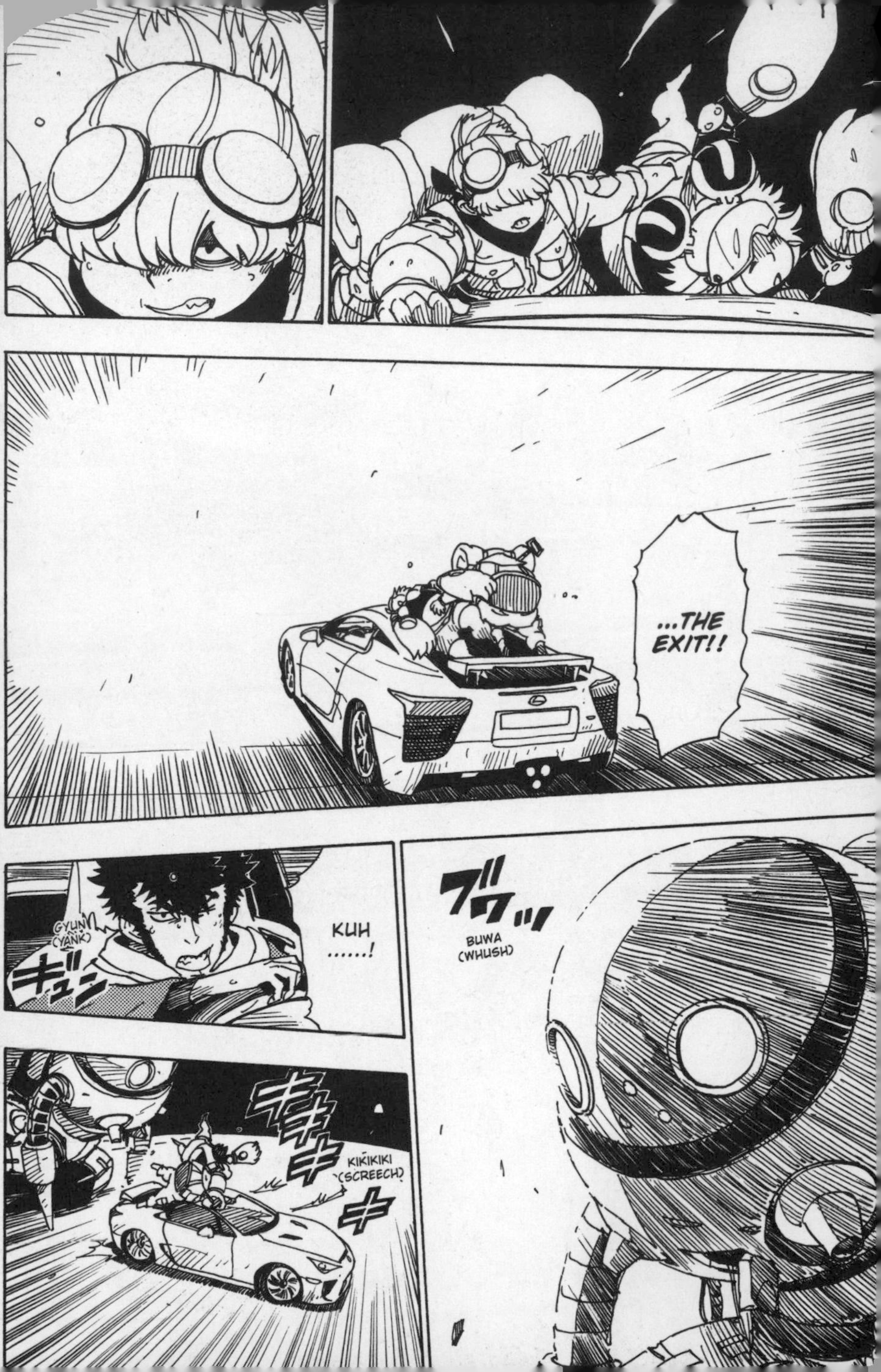
...THE EXIT!!
ブワッ
BUWA (WHUSH)
KUH ......!
GYUN (YANK)
ギュン
キキキキ
KIKIKIKI (SCREECH)

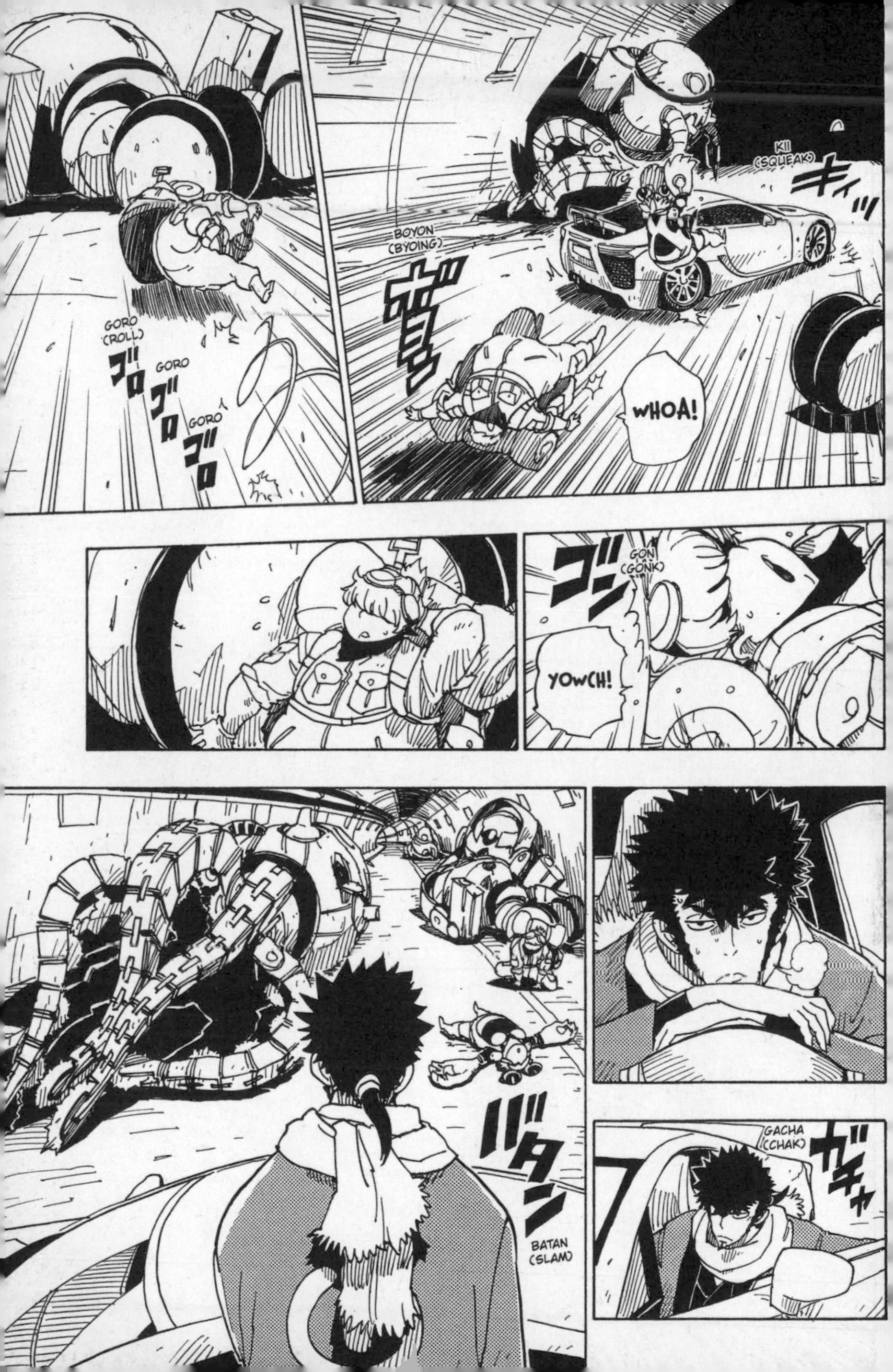
KII (SQUEAK)
キィッ
BOYON (BYOING)
WHOA!
GORO (ROLL)
ゴロ
GORO
ゴロ
GORO
ゴロ
GON (GONK)
ゴン
YOWCH!
GACHA (CHAK)
ガチャ
バタン
BATAN (SLAM)

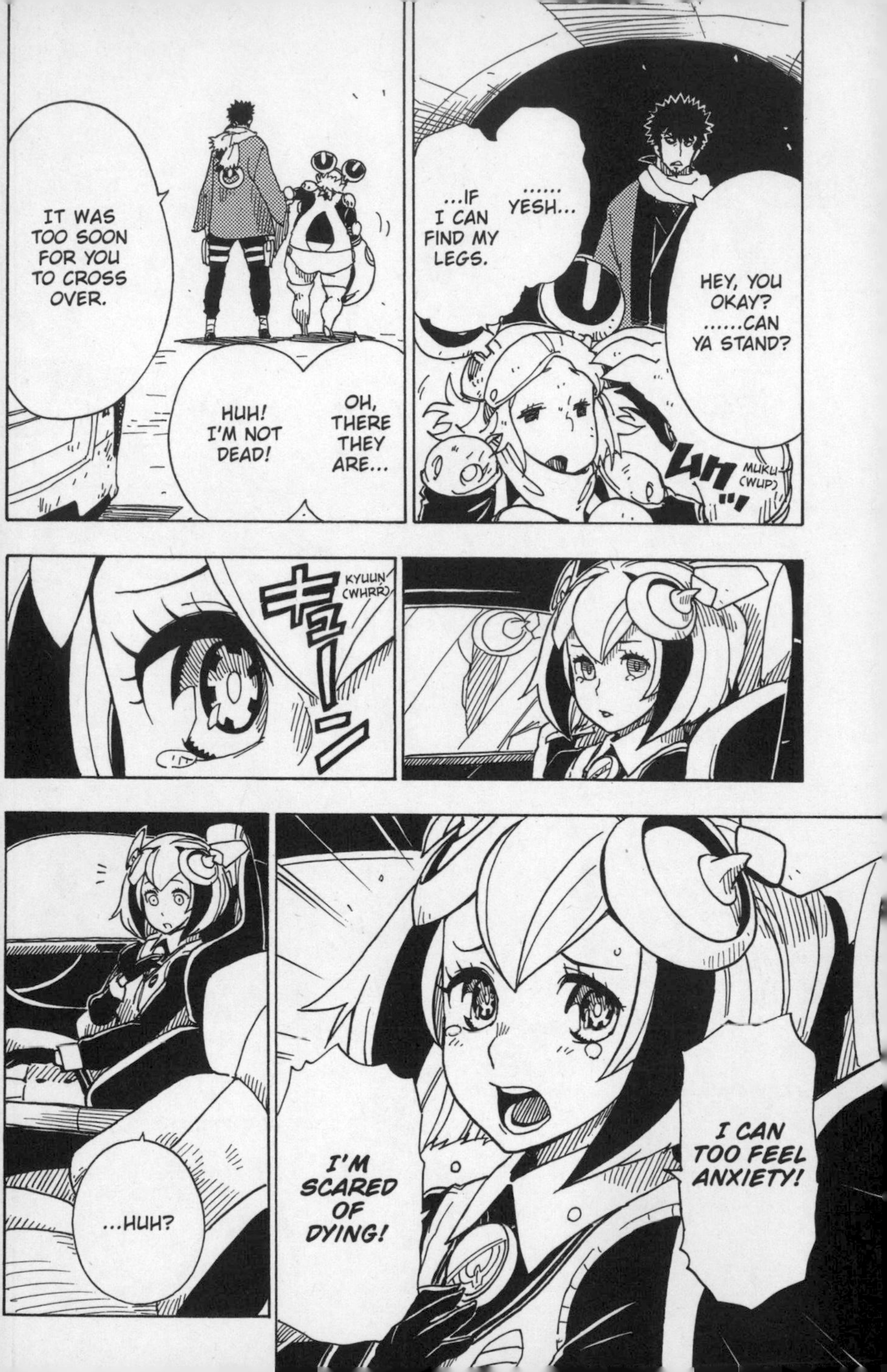
HEY, YOU OKAY? ......CAN YA STAND?
...... YESH...
...IF I CAN FIND MY LEGS.
MUKU (WUP)
OH, THERE THEY ARE...
HUH! I'M NOT DEAD!
IT WAS TOO SOON FOR YOU TO CROSS OVER.
KYUUN (WHRR)
I CAN TOO FEEL ANXIETY!
I'M SCARED OF DYING!
...HUH?

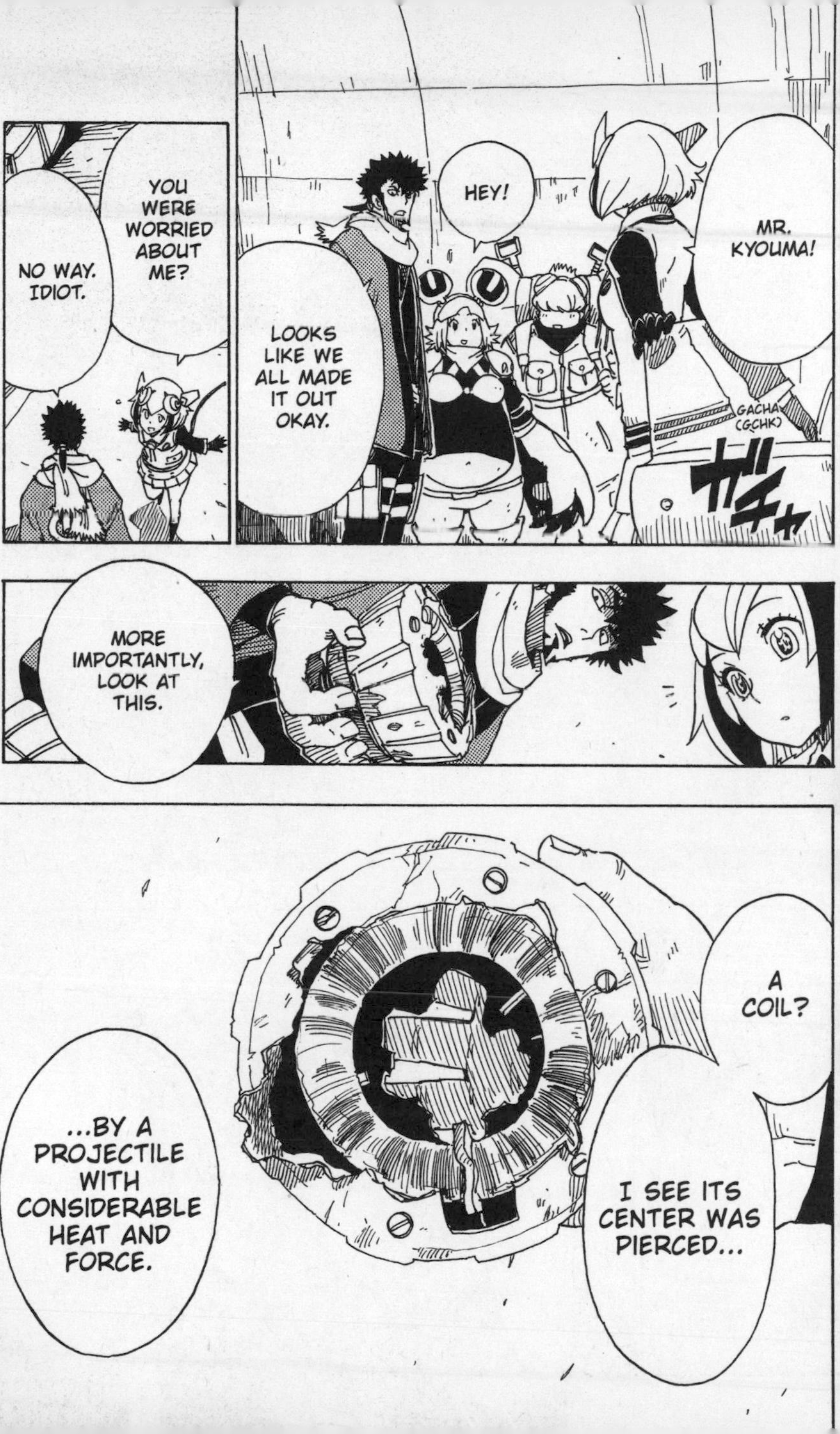
MR. KYOUMA!
GACHA (GCHK)
ガチャ
HEY!
LOOKS LIKE WE ALL MADE IT OUT OKAY.
YOU WERE WORRIED ABOUT ME?
NO WAY. IDIOT.
MORE IMPORTANTLY, LOOK AT THIS.
A COIL?
I SEE ITS CENTER WAS PIERCED...
...BY A PROJECTILE WITH CONSIDERABLE HEAT AND FORCE.

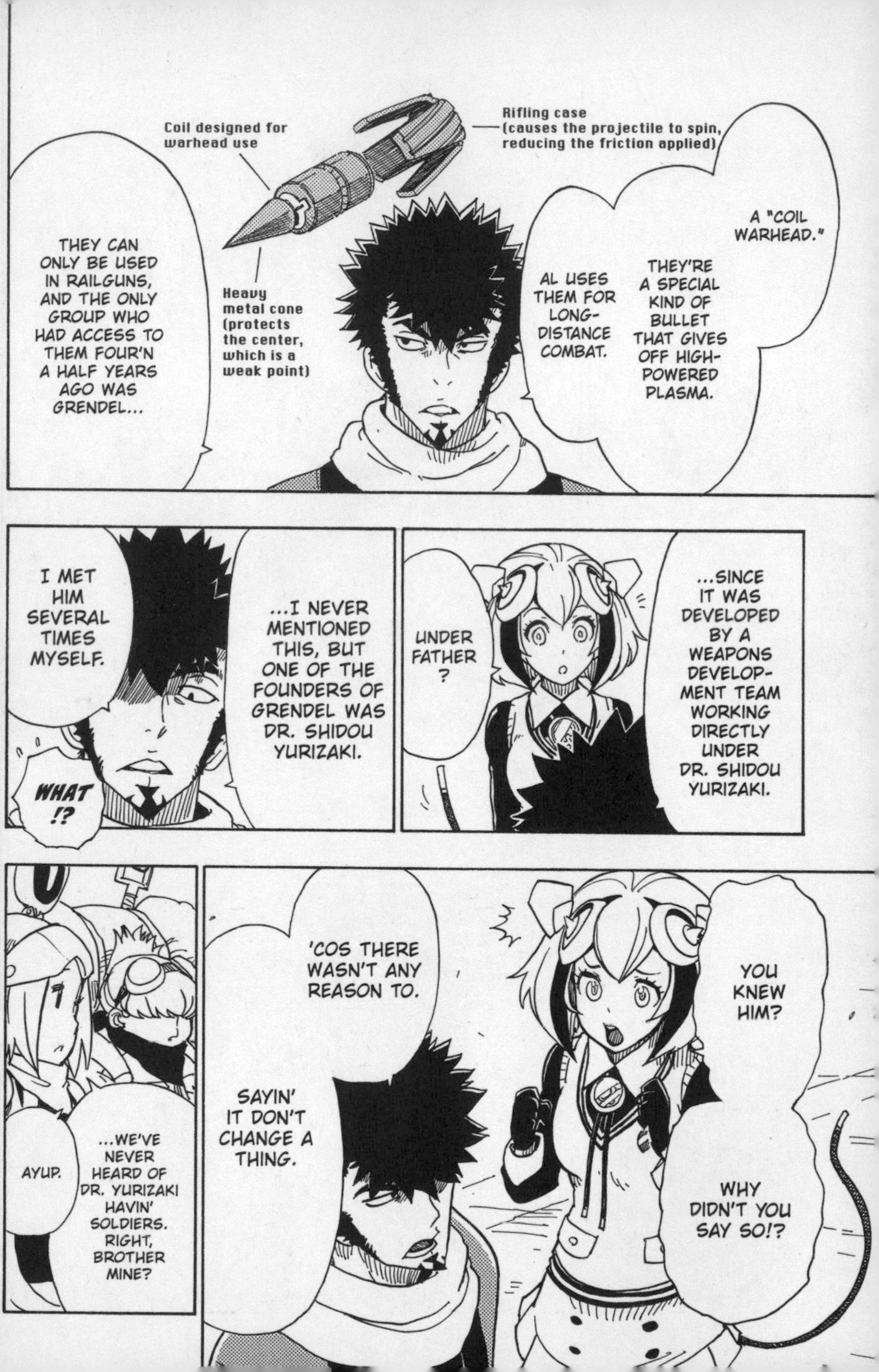
Rifling case (causes the projectile to spin, reducing the friction applied)
Coil designed for warhead use
A "COIL WARHEAD."
THEY'RE A SPECIAL KIND OF BULLET THAT GIVES OFF HIGH-POWERED PLASMA.
AL USES THEM FOR LONG-DISTANCE COMBAT.
Heavy metal cone (protects the center, which is a weak point)
THEY CAN ONLY BE USED IN RAILGUNS, AND THE ONLY GROUP WHO HAD ACCESS TO THEM FOUR'N A HALF YEARS AGO WAS GRENDEL...
...SINCE IT WAS DEVELOPED BY A WEAPONS DEVELOPMENT TEAM WORKING DIRECTLY UNDER DR. SHIDOU YURIZAKI.
UNDER FATHER?
...I NEVER MENTIONED THIS, BUT ONE OF THE FOUNDERS OF GRENDEL WAS DR. SHIDOU YURIZAKI.
I MET HIM SEVERAL TIMES MYSELF.
WHAT!?
YOU KNEW HIM?
'COS THERE WASN'T ANY REASON TO.
WHY DIDN'T YOU SAY SO!?
SAYIN' IT DON'T CHANGE A THING.
...WE'VE NEVER HEARD OF DR. YURIZAKI HAVIN' SOLDIERS. RIGHT, BROTHER MINE?
AYUP.

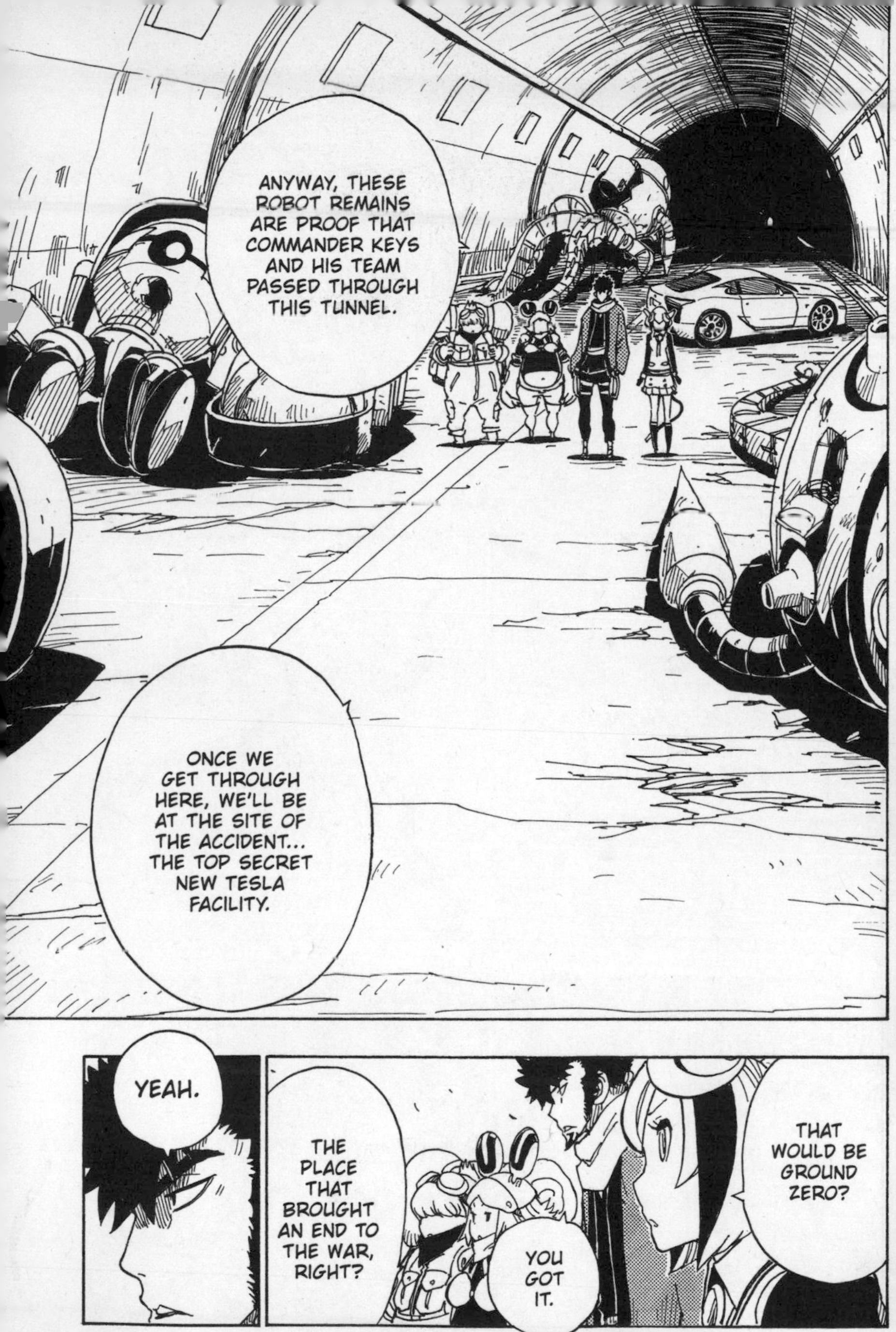
ANYWAY, THESE ROBOT REMAINS ARE PROOF THAT COMMANDER KEYS AND HIS TEAM PASSED THROUGH THIS TUNNEL.
ONCE WE GET THROUGH HERE, WE'LL BE AT THE SITE OF THE ACCIDENT... THE TOP SECRET NEW TESLA FACILITY.
THAT WOULD BE GROUND ZERO?
THE PLACE THAT BROUGHT AN END TO THE WAR, RIGHT?
YOU GOT IT.
YEAH.

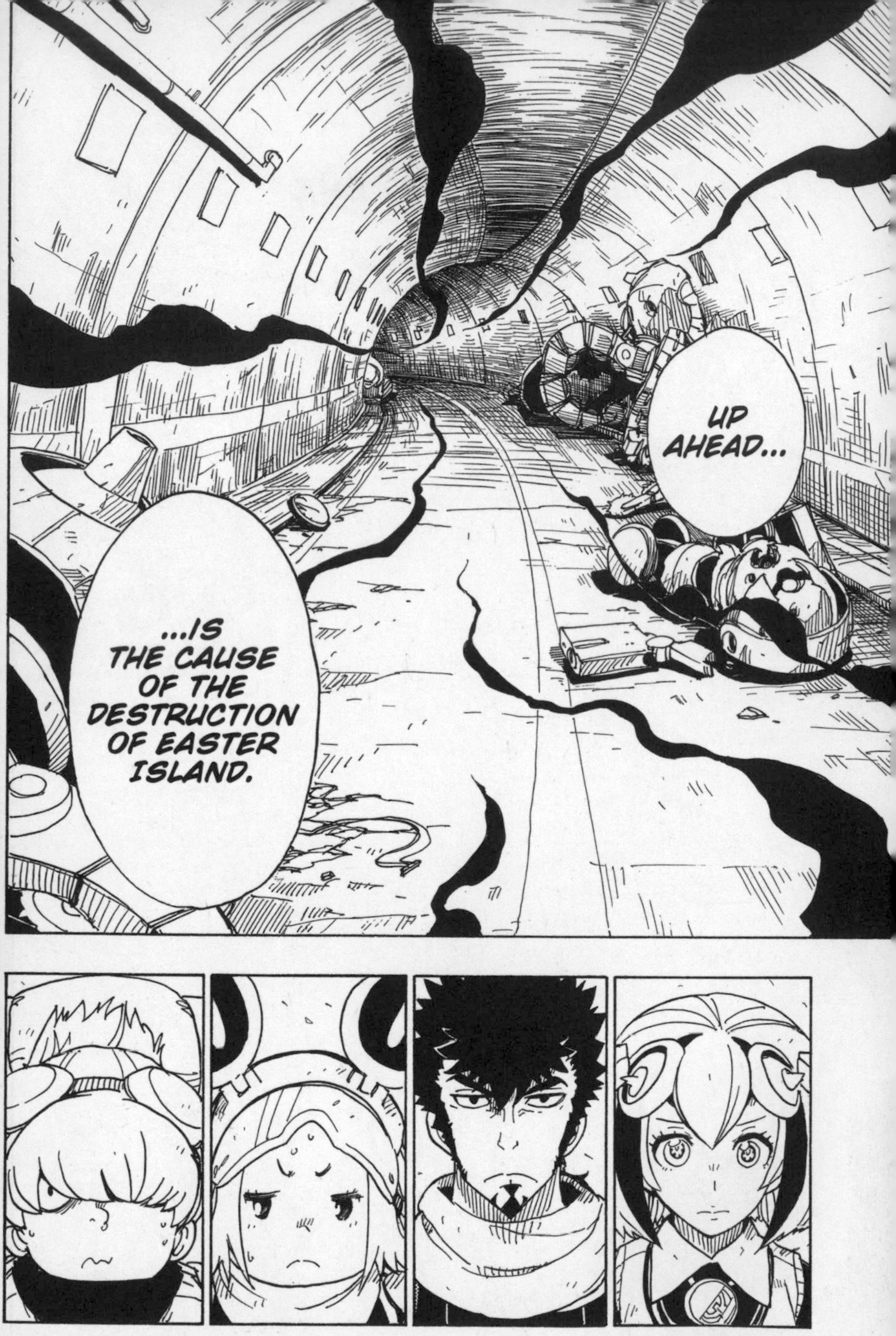
UP AHEAD...
...IS THE CAUSE OF THE DESTRUCTION OF EASTER ISLAND.

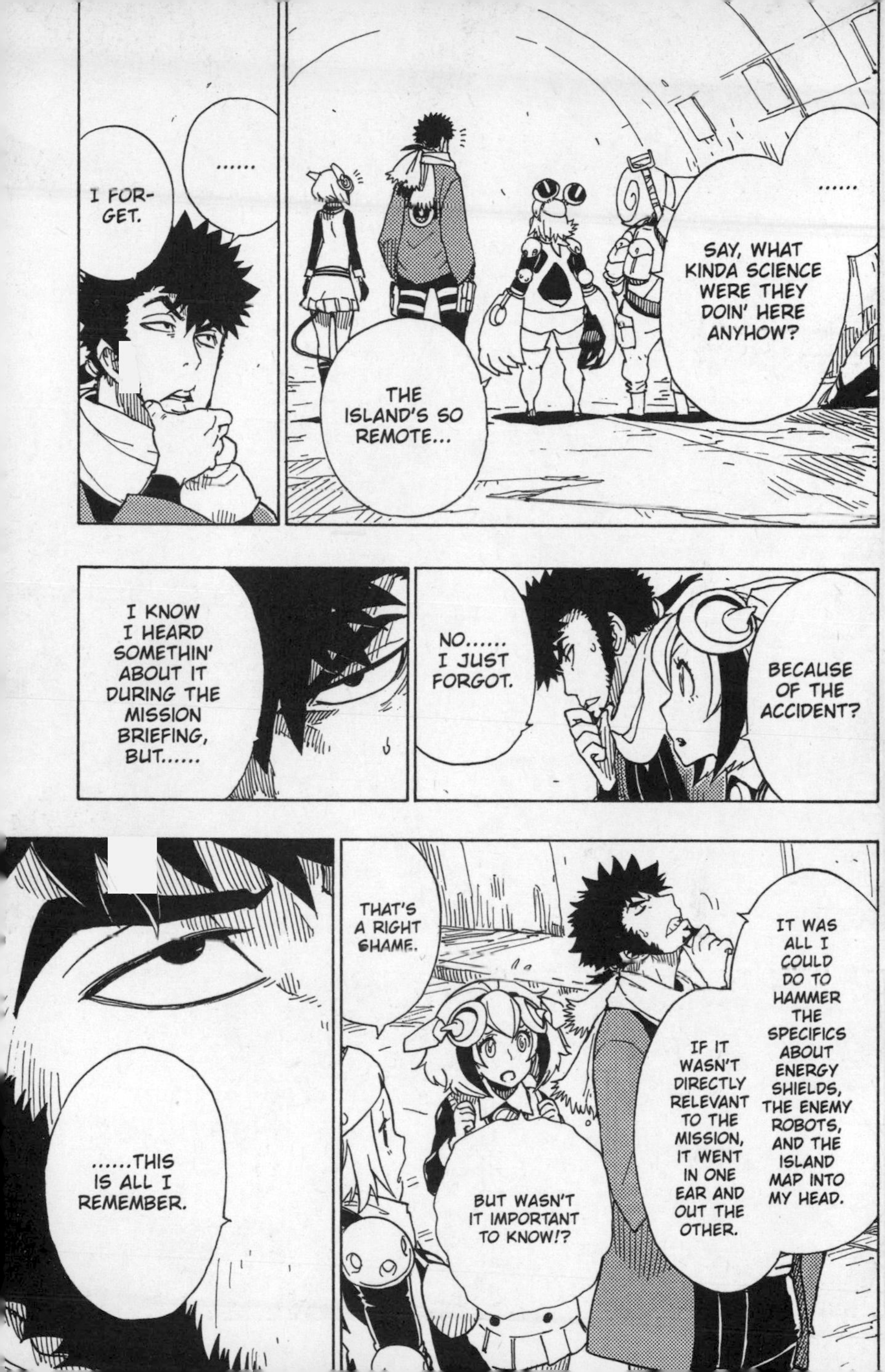
......
SAY, WHAT KINDA SCIENCE WERE THEY DOIN' HERE ANYHOW?
THE ISLAND'S SO REMOTE...
......
I FOR-GET.
BECAUSE OF THE ACCIDENT?
NO...... I JUST FORGOT.
I KNOW I HEARD SOMETHIN' ABOUT IT DURING THE MISSION BRIEFING, BUT......
IT WAS ALL I COULD DO TO HAMMER THE SPECIFICS ABOUT ENERGY SHIELDS, THE ENEMY ROBOTS, AND THE ISLAND MAP INTO MY HEAD.
IF IT WASN'T DIRECTLY RELEVANT TO THE MISSION, IT WENT IN ONE EAR AND OUT THE OTHER.
THAT'S A RIGHT SHAME.
BUT WASN'T IT IMPORTANT TO KNOW!?
......THIS IS ALL I REMEMBER.

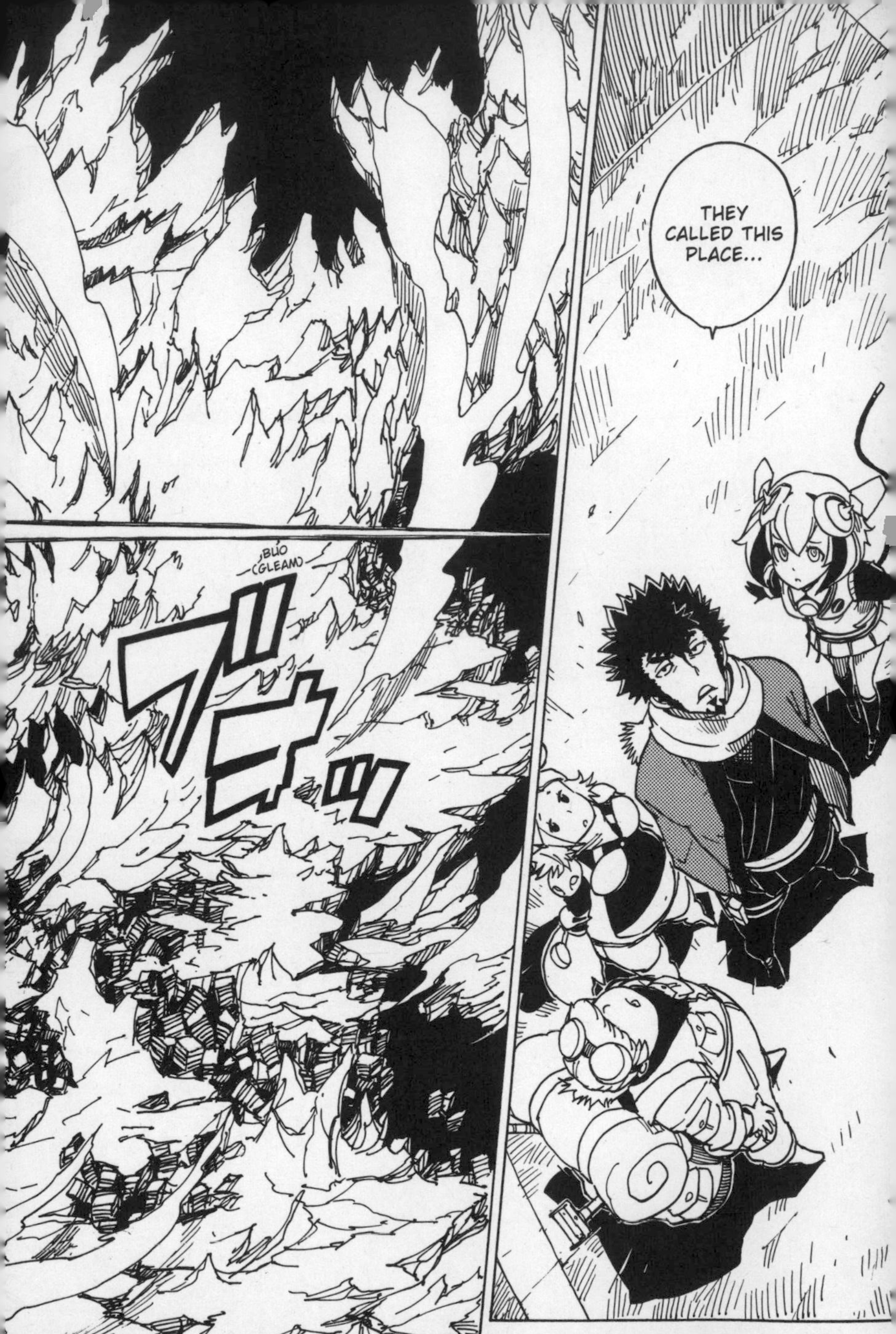
THEY CALLED THIS PLACE...
BUO (GLEAM)

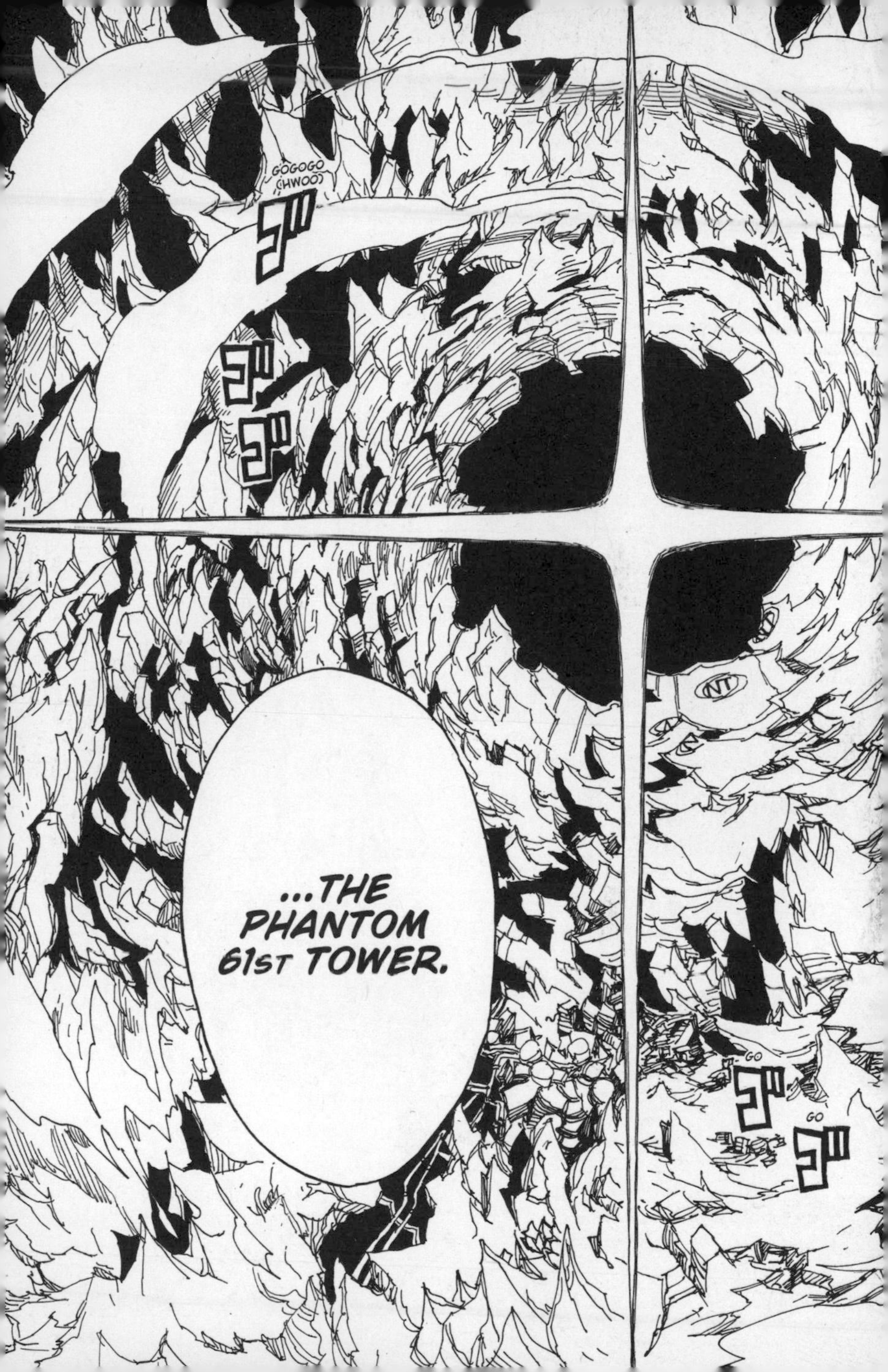
GOGOGO (HWOO)
...THE PHANTOM 61ST TOWER.
GO
GO

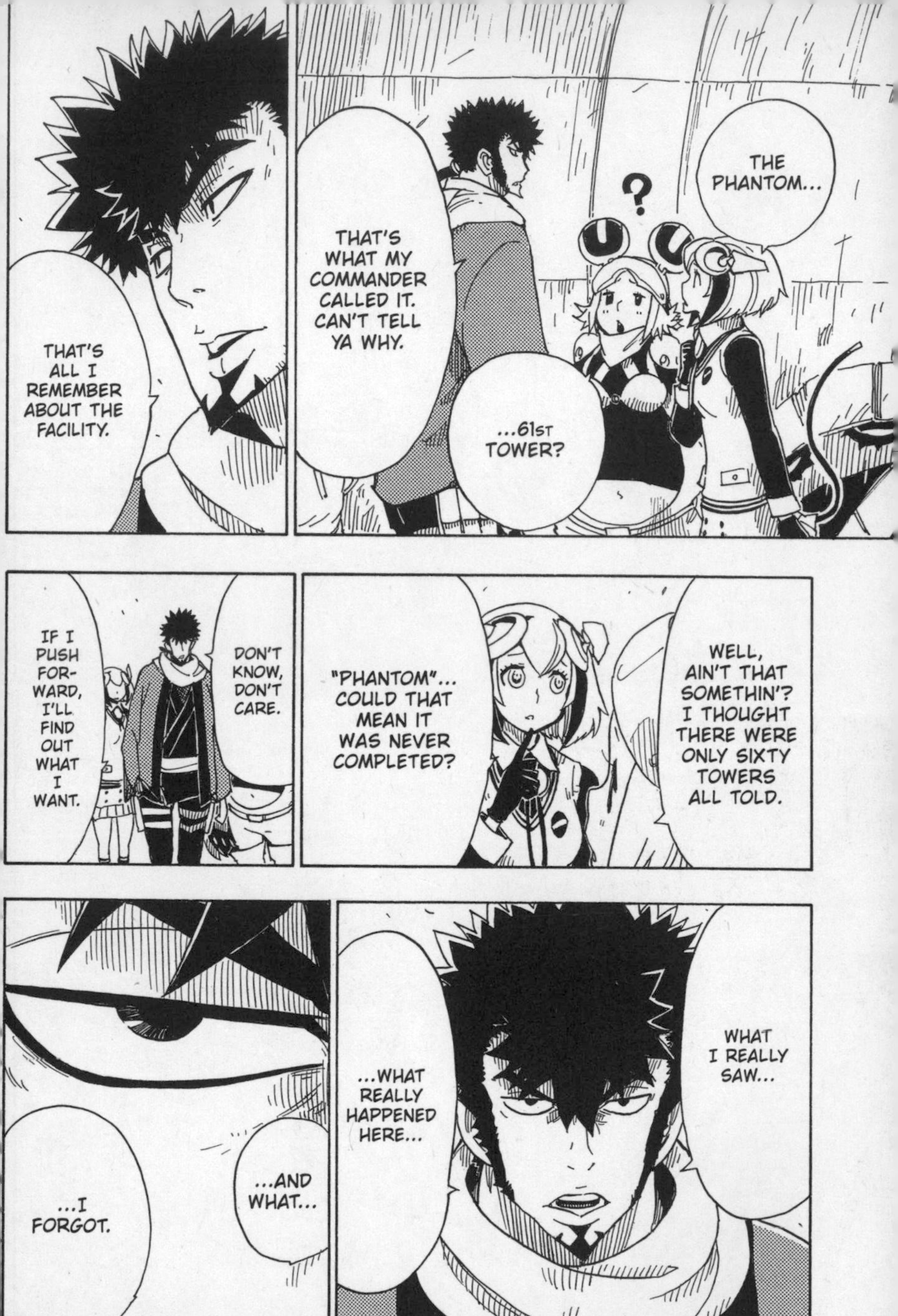
THE PHANTOM...
?
THAT'S WHAT MY COMMANDER CALLED IT. CAN'T TELL YA WHY.
...61ST TOWER?
THAT'S ALL I REMEMBER ABOUT THE FACILITY.
WELL, AIN'T THAT SOMETHIN'? I THOUGHT THERE WERE ONLY SIXTY TOWERS ALL TOLD.
"PHANTOM"... COULD THAT MEAN IT WAS NEVER COMPLETED?
DON'T KNOW, DON'T CARE.
IF I PUSH FOR-WARD, I'LL FIND OUT WHAT I WANT.
WHAT I REALLY SAW...
...WHAT REALLY HAPPENED HERE...
...AND WHAT...
...I FORGOT.

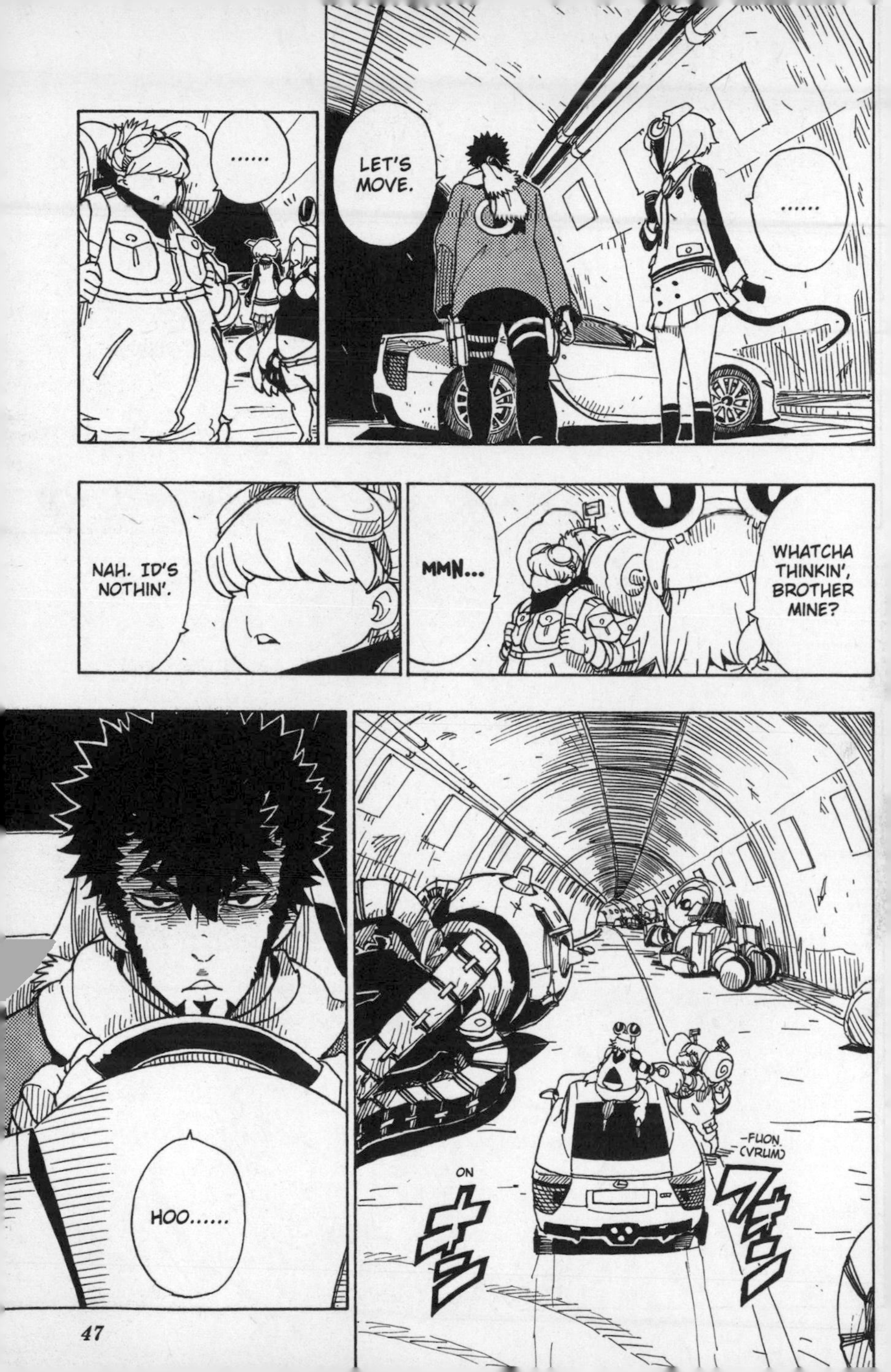
......
LET'S MOVE.
......
WHATCHA THINKIN', BROTHER MINE?
MMN...
NAH. ID'S NOTHIN'.
-FUON. (VRUM)
ON
HOO......

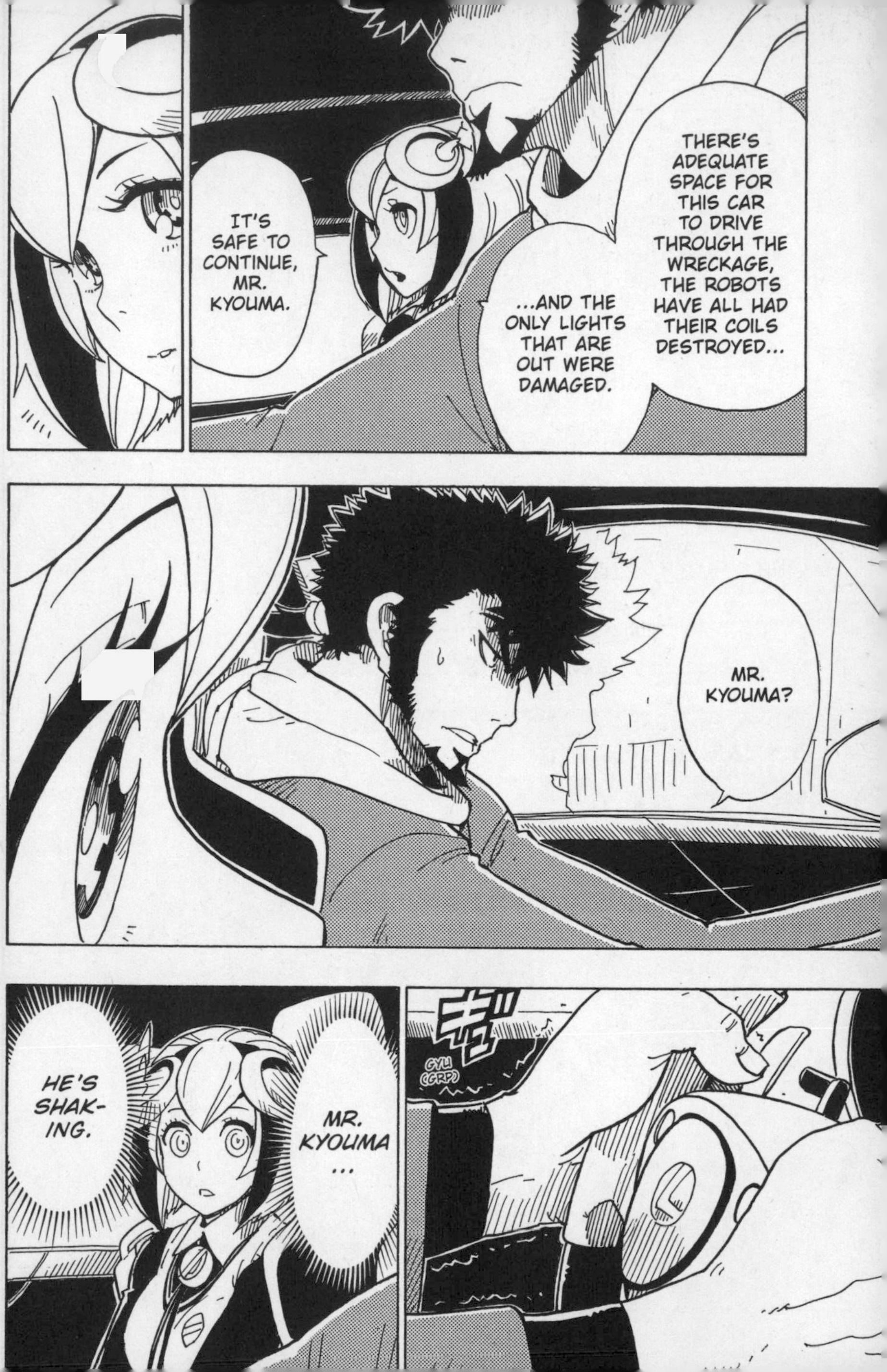
THERE'S ADEQUATE SPACE FOR THIS CAR TO DRIVE THROUGH THE WRECKAGE, THE ROBOTS HAVE ALL HAD THEIR COILS DESTROYED...
...AND THE ONLY LIGHTS THAT ARE OUT WERE DAMAGED.
IT'S SAFE TO CONTINUE, MR. KYOUMA.
MR. KYOUMA?
ギュ
GYU (GRP)
MR. KYOUMA...
HE'S SHAK-ING.

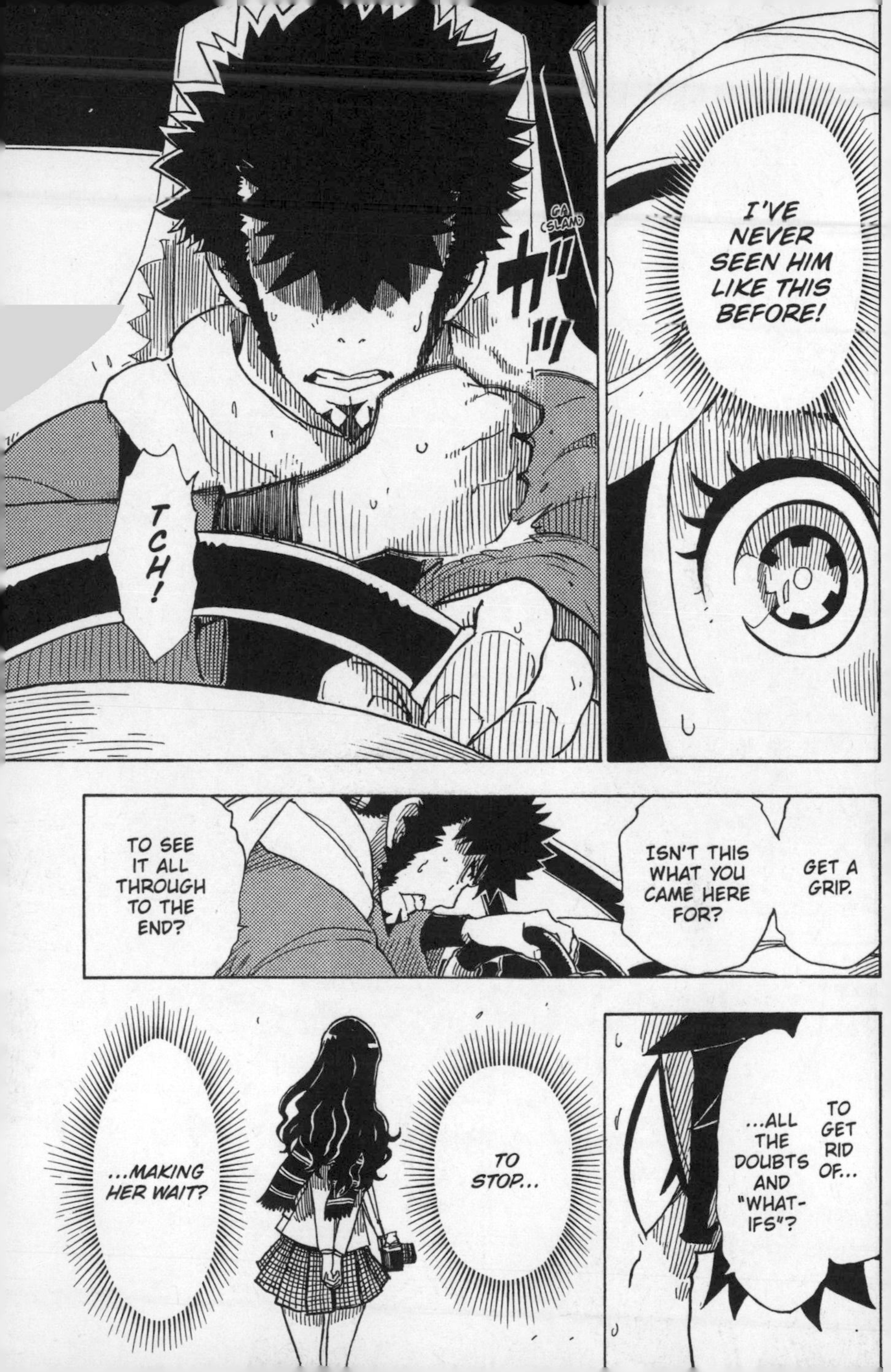
I'VE NEVER SEEN HIM LIKE THIS BEFORE!
GA SLAM
TCH!
GET A GRIP.
ISN'T THIS WHAT YOU CAME HERE FOR?
TO SEE IT ALL THROUGH TO THE END?
TO GET RID OF...
...ALL THE DOUBTS AND "WHAT-IFS"?
TO STOP...
...MAKING HER WAIT?

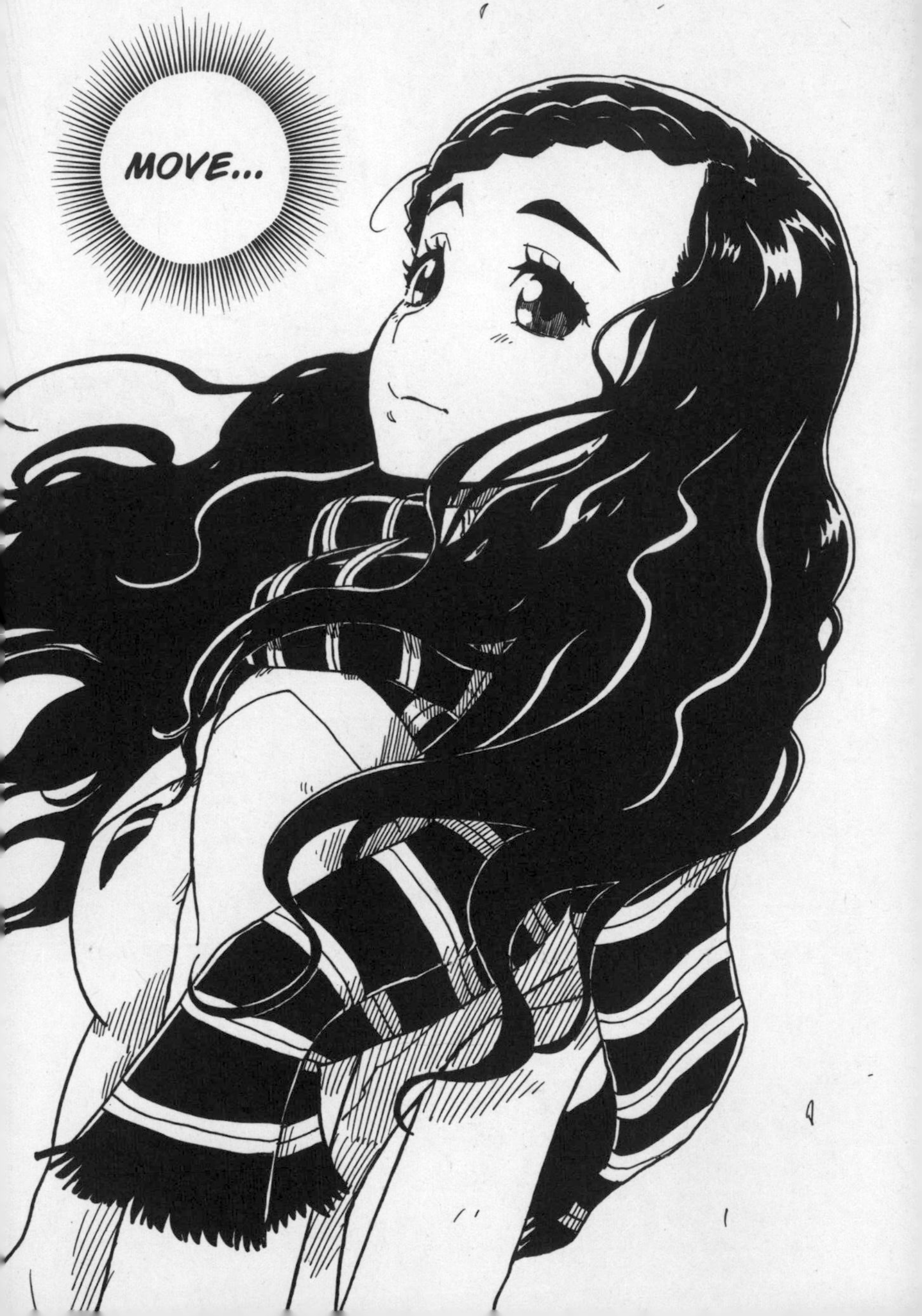
MOVE...

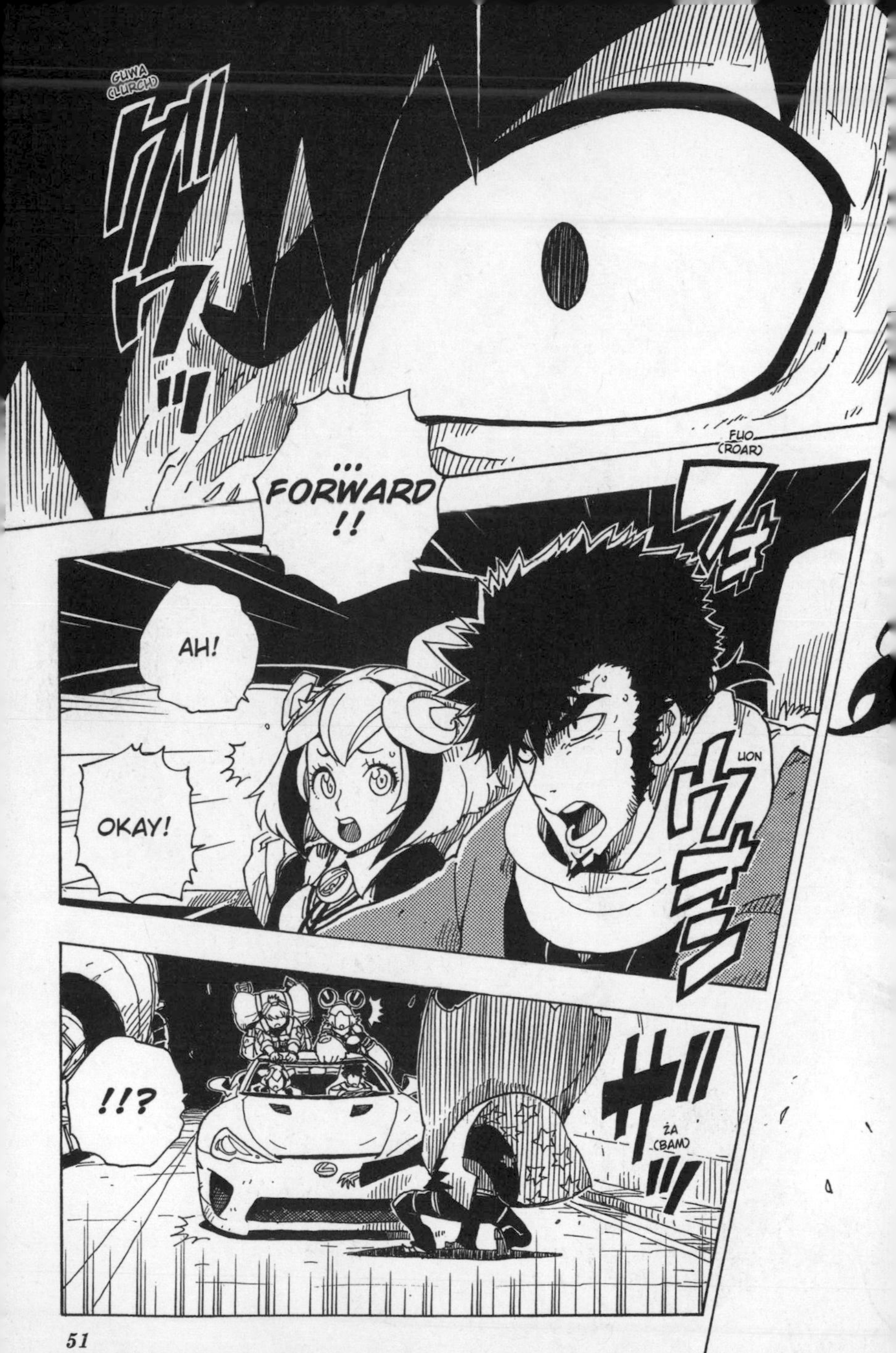
GUWA (LURCH)
...FORWARD!!
FUO (ROAR)
LIJON
AH!
OKAY!
ZA (BAM)
!!?

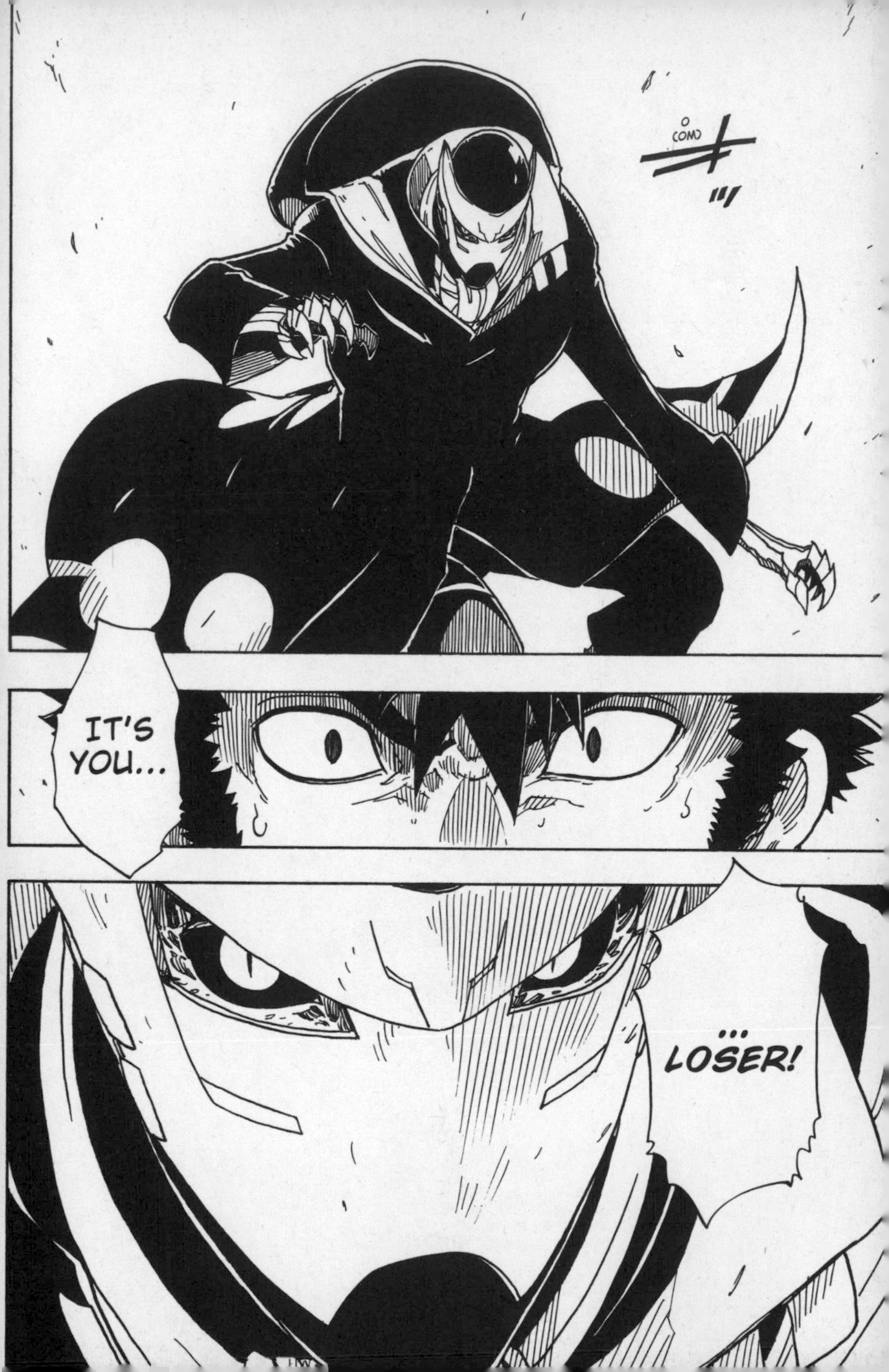
IT'S YOU...
...LOSER!

Dimension W

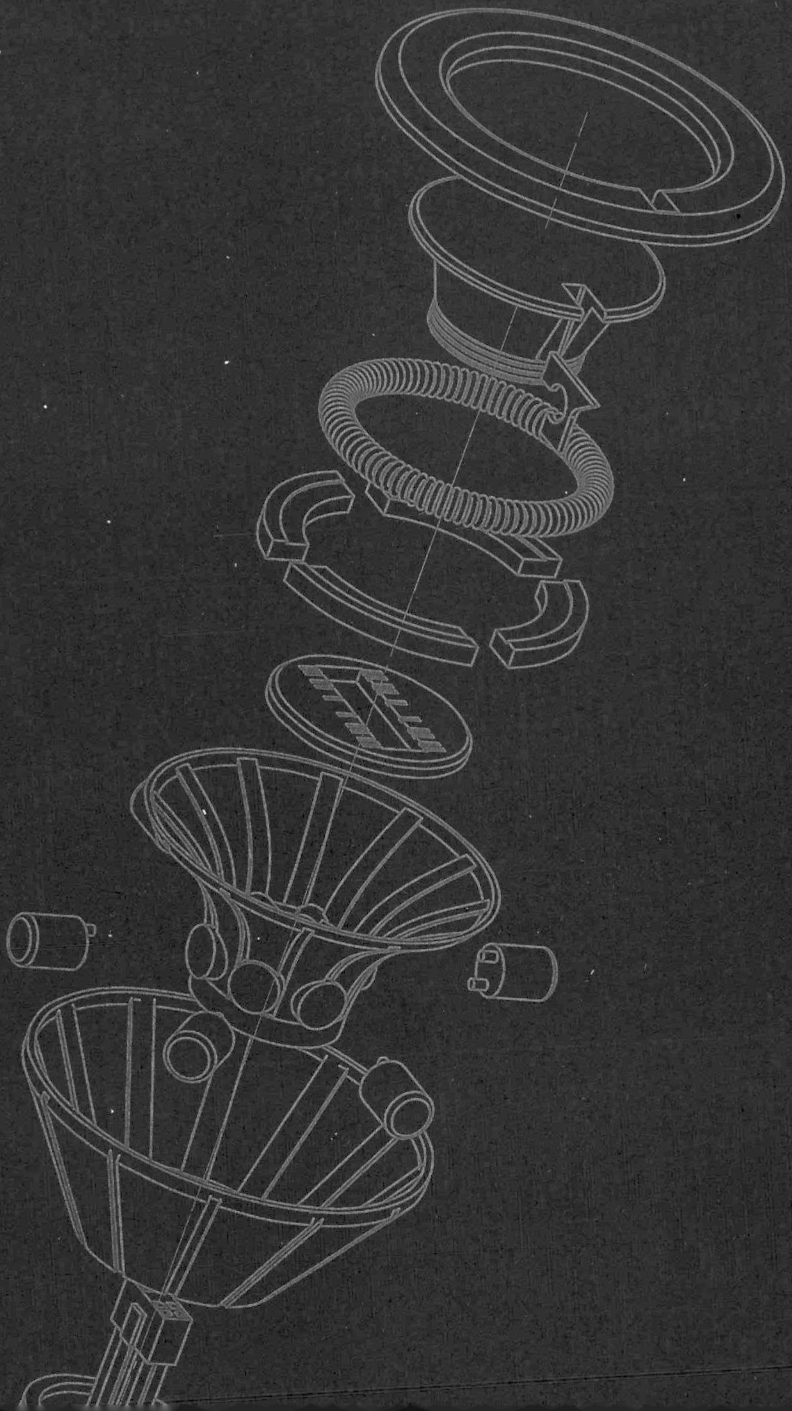

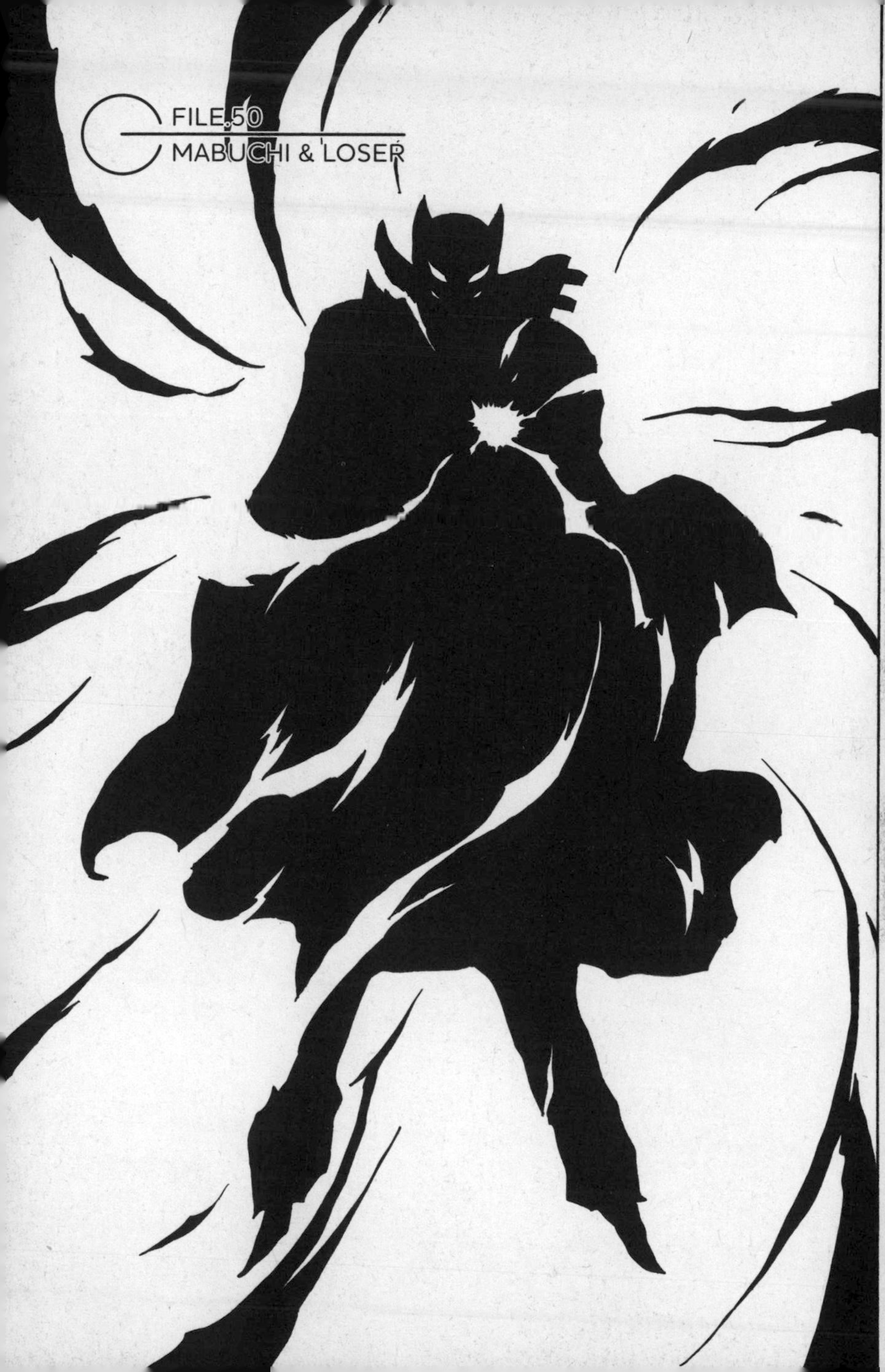
FILE.50
MABUCHI & LOSER

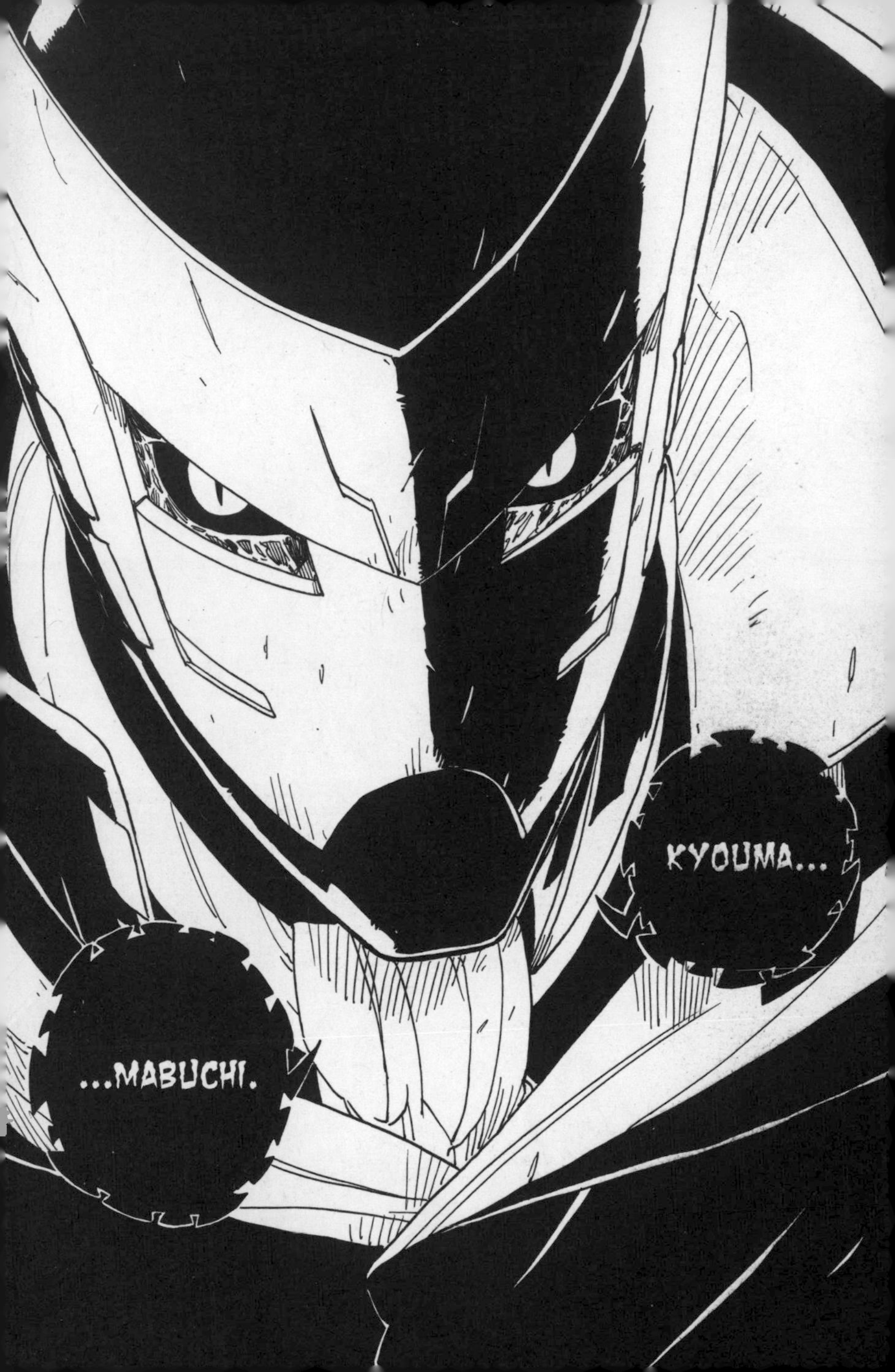
KYOUMA...
...MABUCHI.

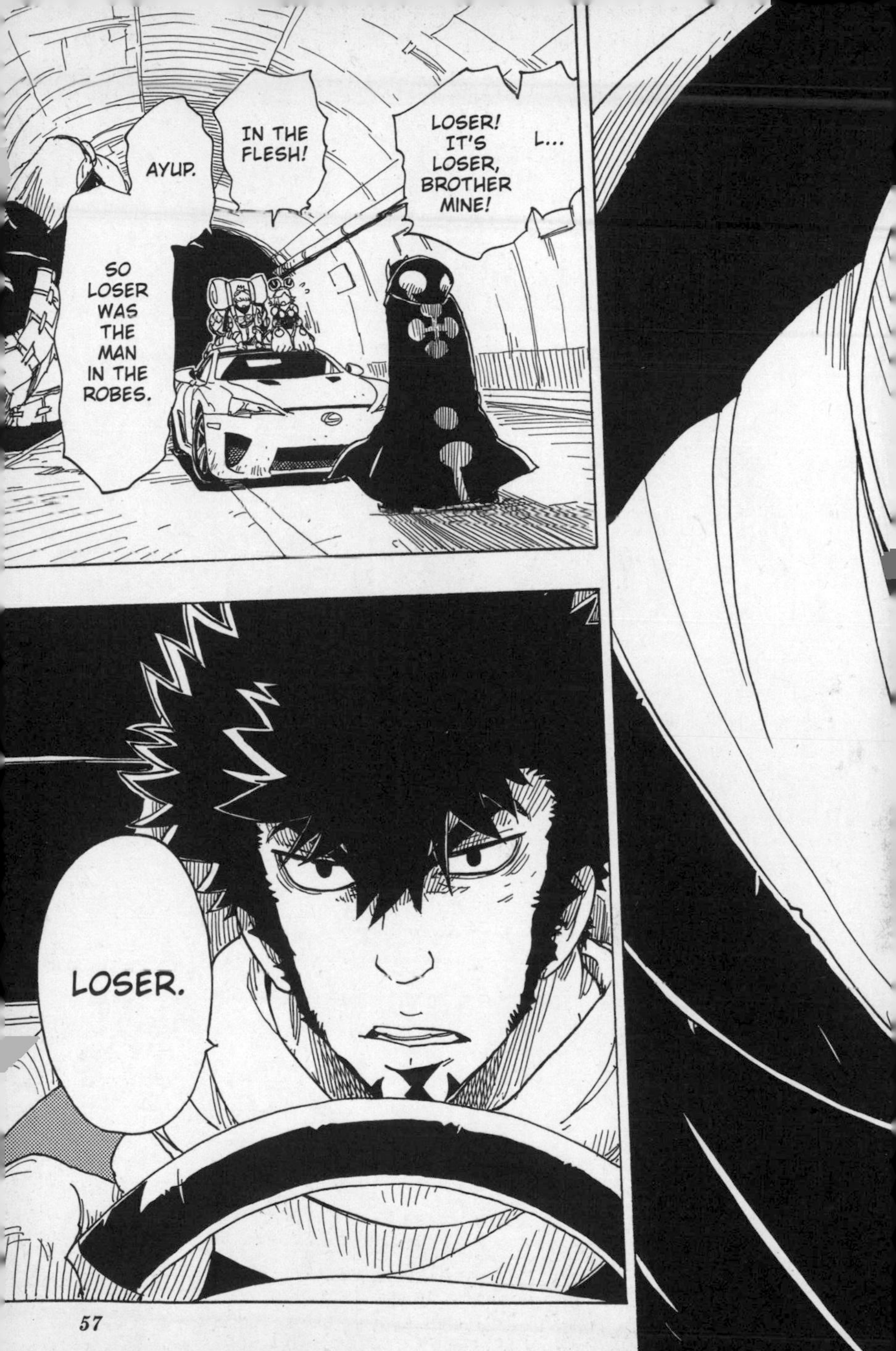
L...
LOSER! IT'S LOSER, BROTHER MINE!
IN THE FLESH!
AYUP.
SO LOSER WAS THE MAN IN THE ROBES.
LOSER.

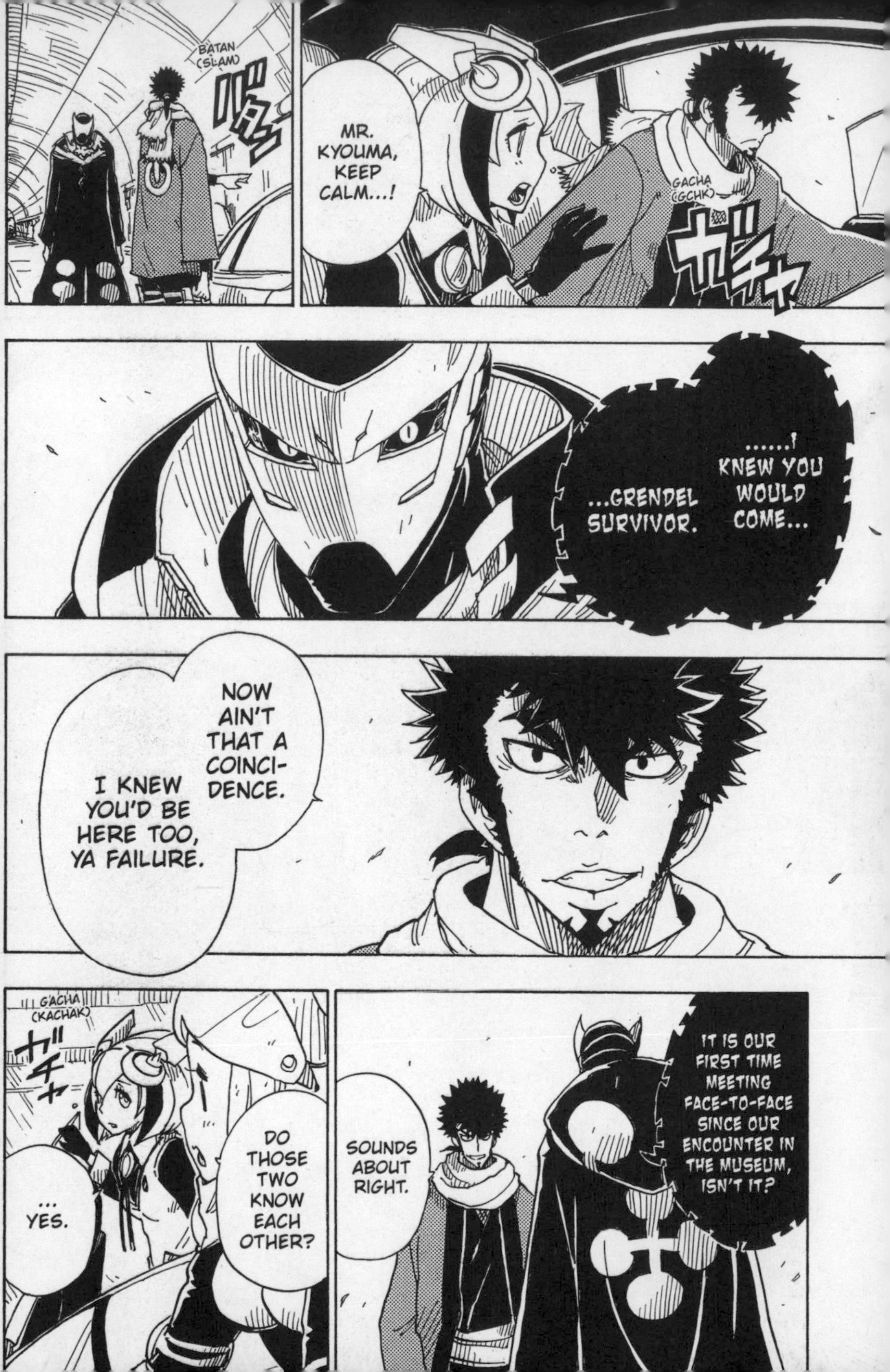
MR. KYOUMA, KEEP CALM...!
GACHA (GCHK)
ガチャ
BATAN (SLAM)
バタン
......I KNEW YOU WOULD COME...
...GRENDEL SURVIVOR.
NOW AIN'T THAT A COINCI-DENCE.
I KNEW YOU'D BE HERE TOO, YA FAILURE.
IT IS OUR FIRST TIME MEETING FACE-TO-FACE SINCE OUR ENCOUNTER IN THE MUSEUM, ISN'T IT?
SOUNDS ABOUT RIGHT.
DO THOSE TWO KNOW EACH OTHER?
GACHA (KACHAK)
ガチャ
... YES.

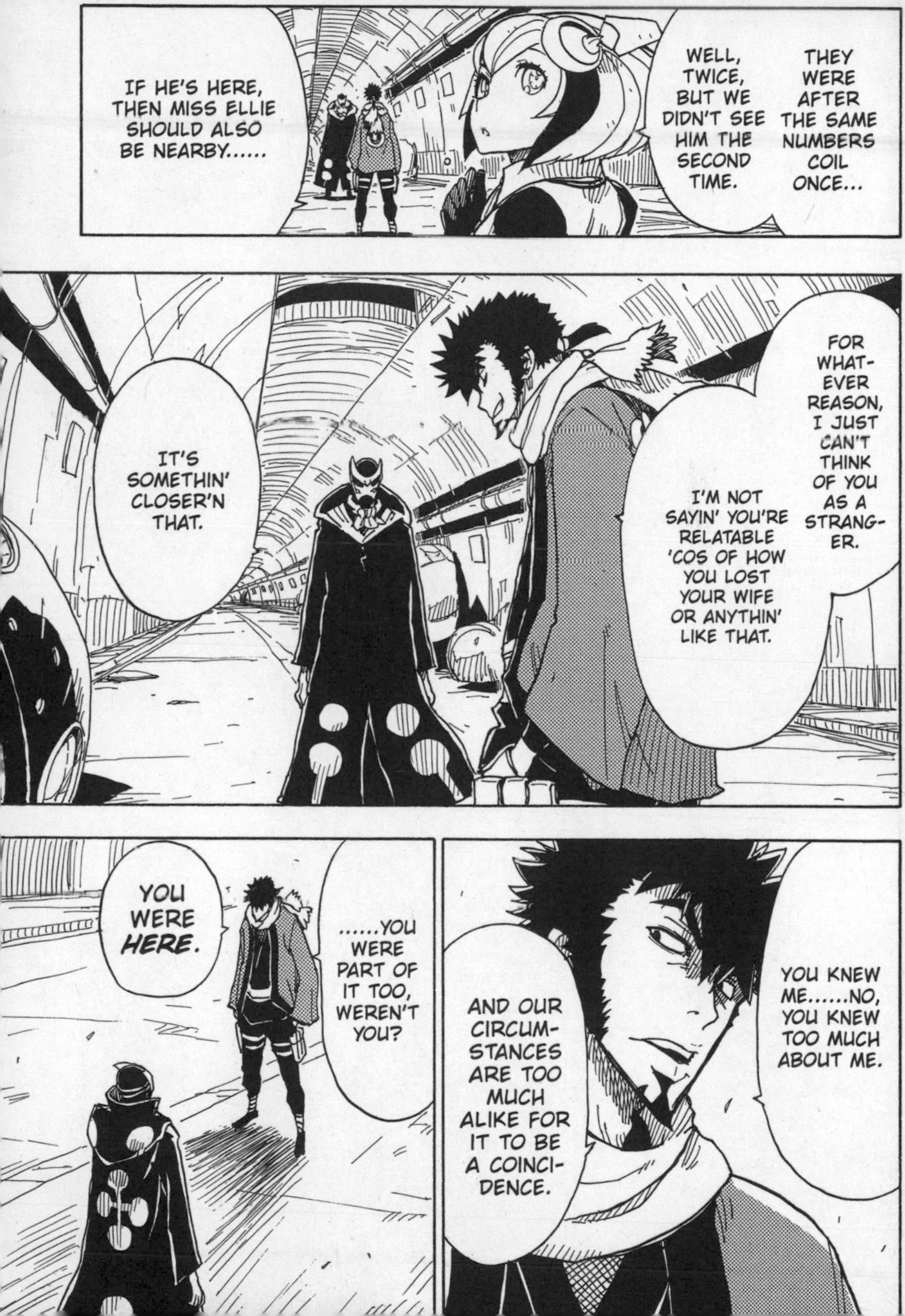
THEY WERE AFTER THE SAME NUMBERS COIL ONCE...
WELL, TWICE, BUT WE DIDN'T SEE HIM THE SECOND TIME.
IF HE'S HERE, THEN MISS ELLIE SHOULD ALSO BE NEARBY......
FOR WHATEVER REASON, I JUST CAN'T THINK OF YOU AS A STRANGER.
I'M NOT SAYIN' YOU'RE RELATABLE 'COS OF HOW YOU LOST YOUR WIFE OR ANYTHIN' LIKE THAT.
IT'S SOMETHIN' CLOSER'N THAT.
YOU KNEW ME......NO, YOU KNEW TOO MUCH ABOUT ME.
AND OUR CIRCUMSTANCES ARE TOO MUCH ALIKE FOR IT TO BE A COINCIDENCE.
......YOU WERE PART OF IT TOO, WEREN'T YOU?
YOU WERE *HERE*.

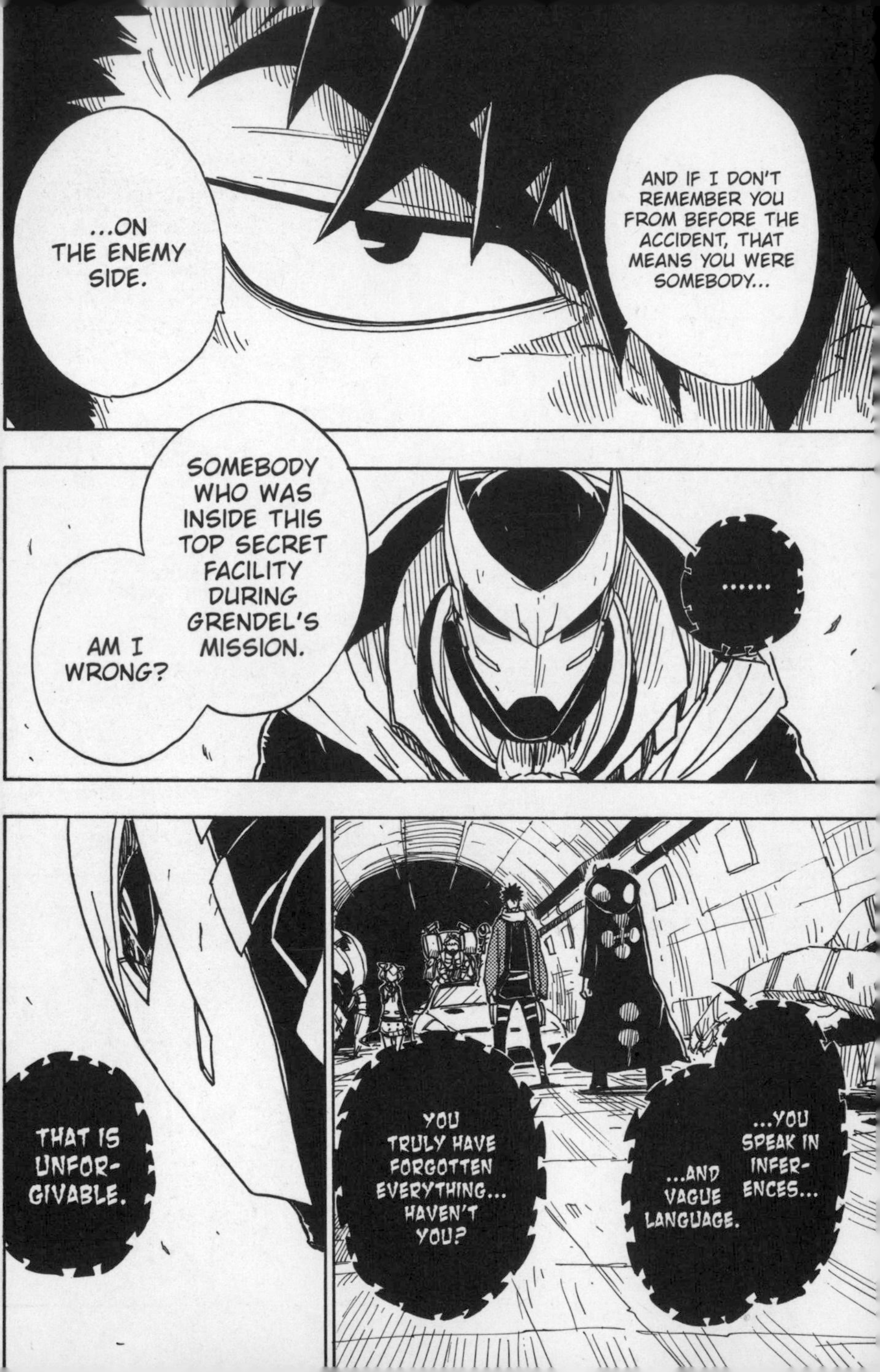
AND IF I DON'T REMEMBER YOU FROM BEFORE THE ACCIDENT, THAT MEANS YOU WERE SOMEBODY...
...ON THE ENEMY SIDE.
SOMEBODY WHO WAS INSIDE THIS TOP SECRET FACILITY DURING GRENDEL'S MISSION.
AM I WRONG?
......
...YOU SPEAK IN INFER-ENCES...
...AND VAGUE LANGUAGE.
YOU TRULY HAVE FORGOTTEN EVERYTHING... HAVEN'T YOU?
THAT IS UNFOR-GIVABLE.

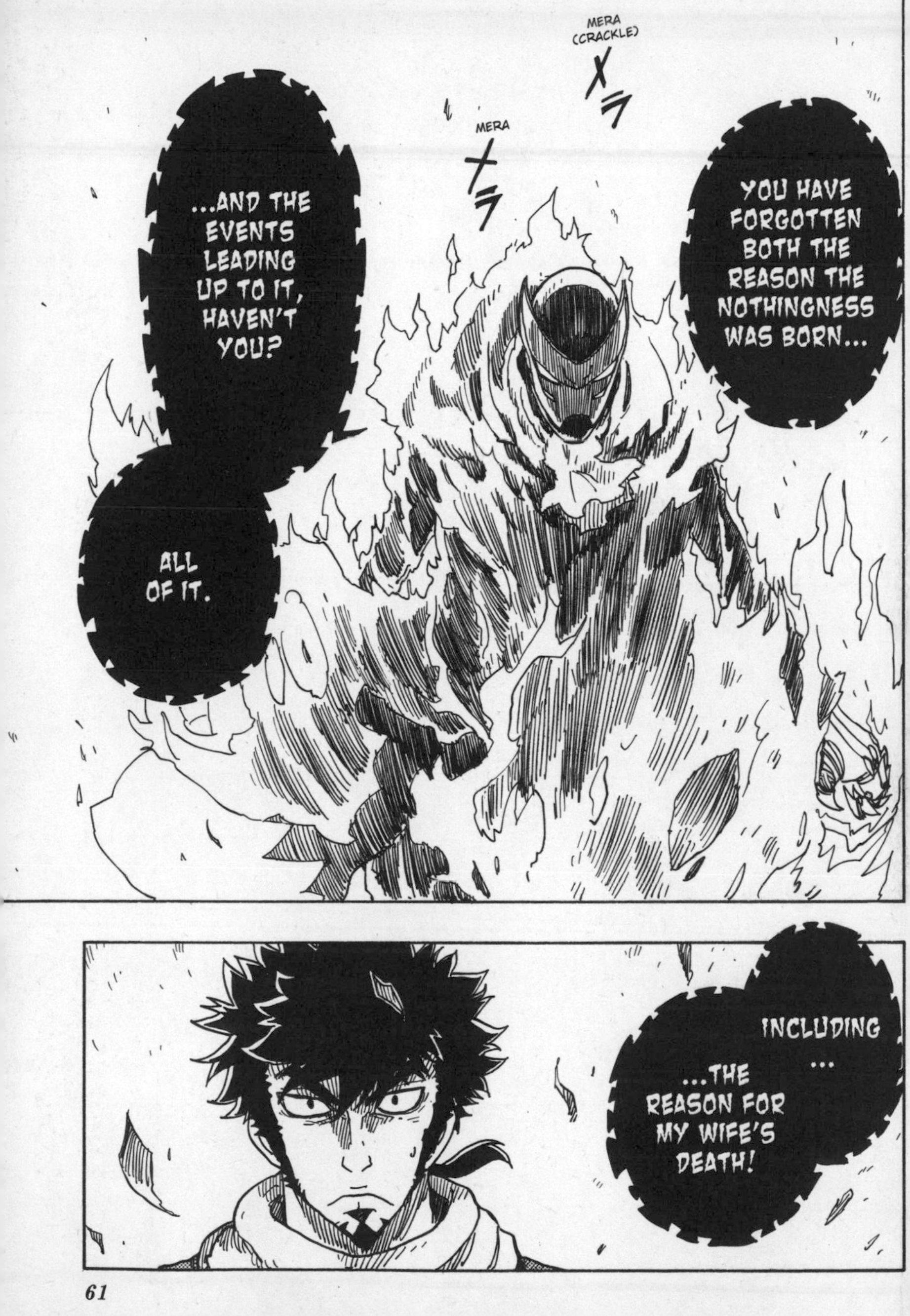
MERA (CRACKLE)
メラ
MERA
メラ
YOU HAVE FORGOTTEN BOTH THE REASON THE NOTHINGNESS WAS BORN...
...AND THE EVENTS LEADING UP TO IT, HAVEN'T YOU?
ALL OF IT.
INCLUDING ...
...THE REASON FOR MY WIFE'S DEATH!

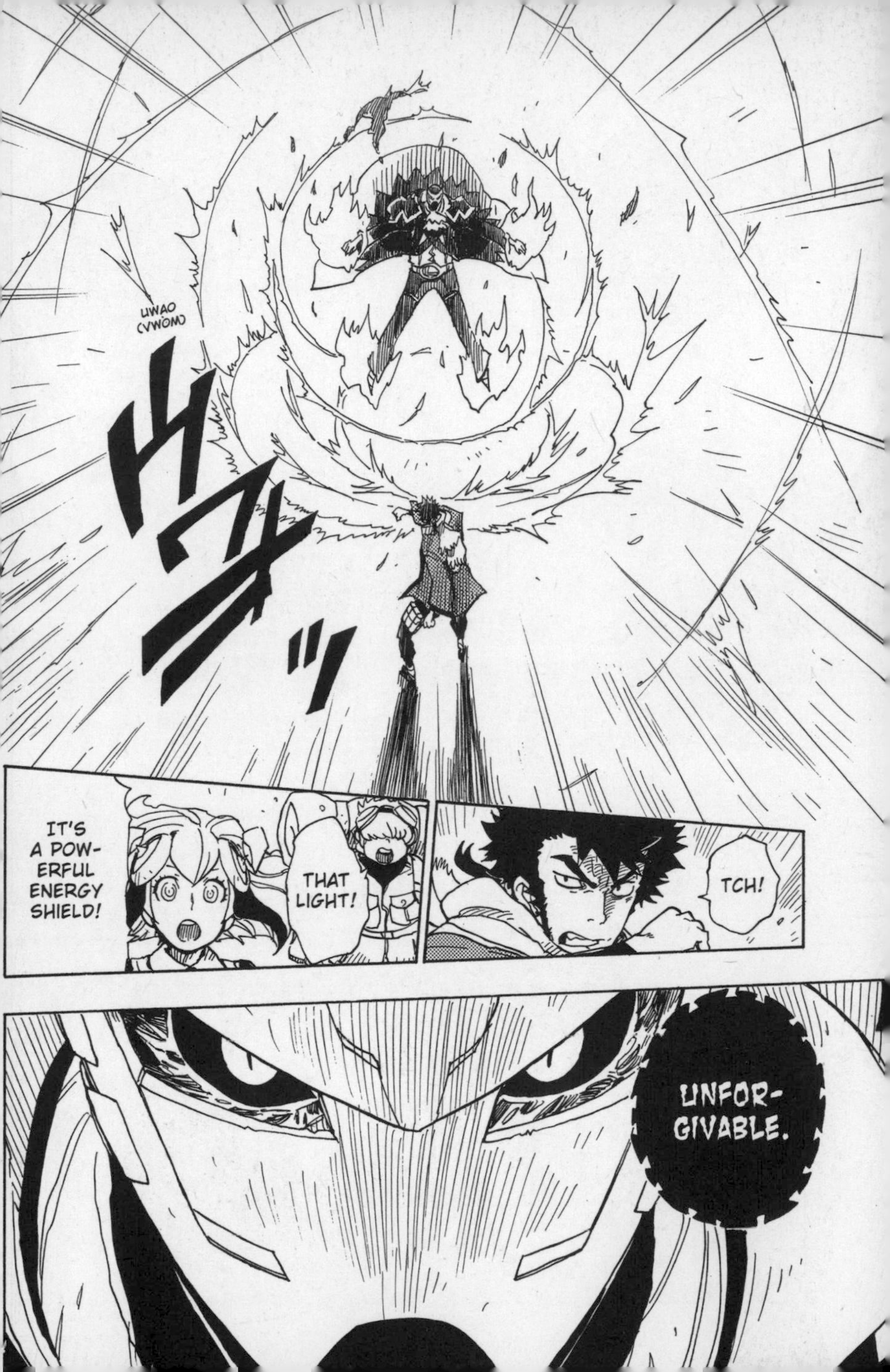
UWAO
(VWOM)
TCH!
THAT LIGHT!
IT'S A POW-ERFUL ENERGY SHIELD!
UNFOR-GIVABLE.

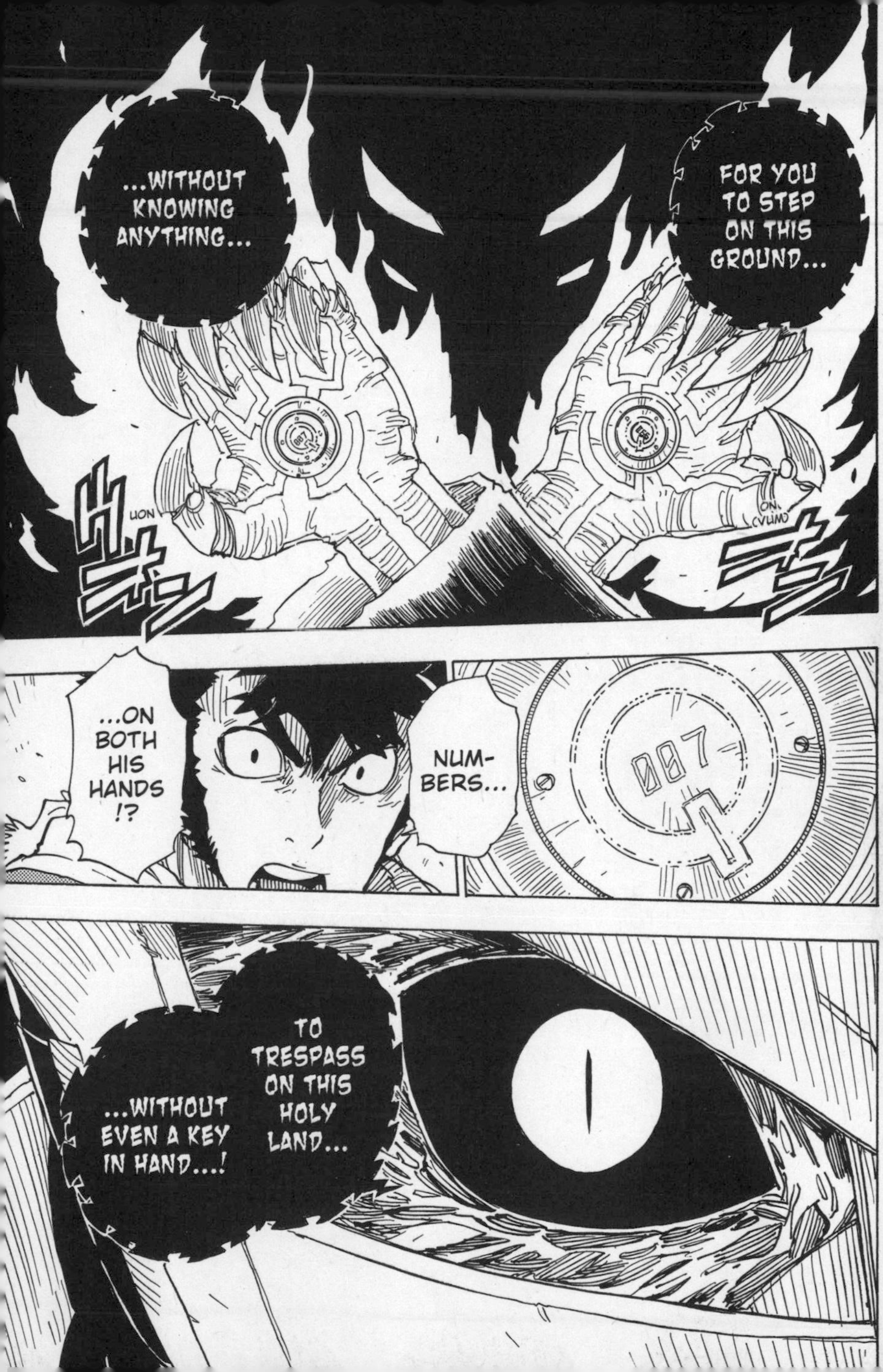
FOR YOU TO STEP ON THIS GROUND...
...WITHOUT KNOWING ANYTHING...
ON (VUM)
UON
NUM-BERS...
...ON BOTH HIS HANDS!?
007
TO TRESPASS ON THIS HOLY LAND...
...WITHOUT EVEN A KEY IN HAND...!

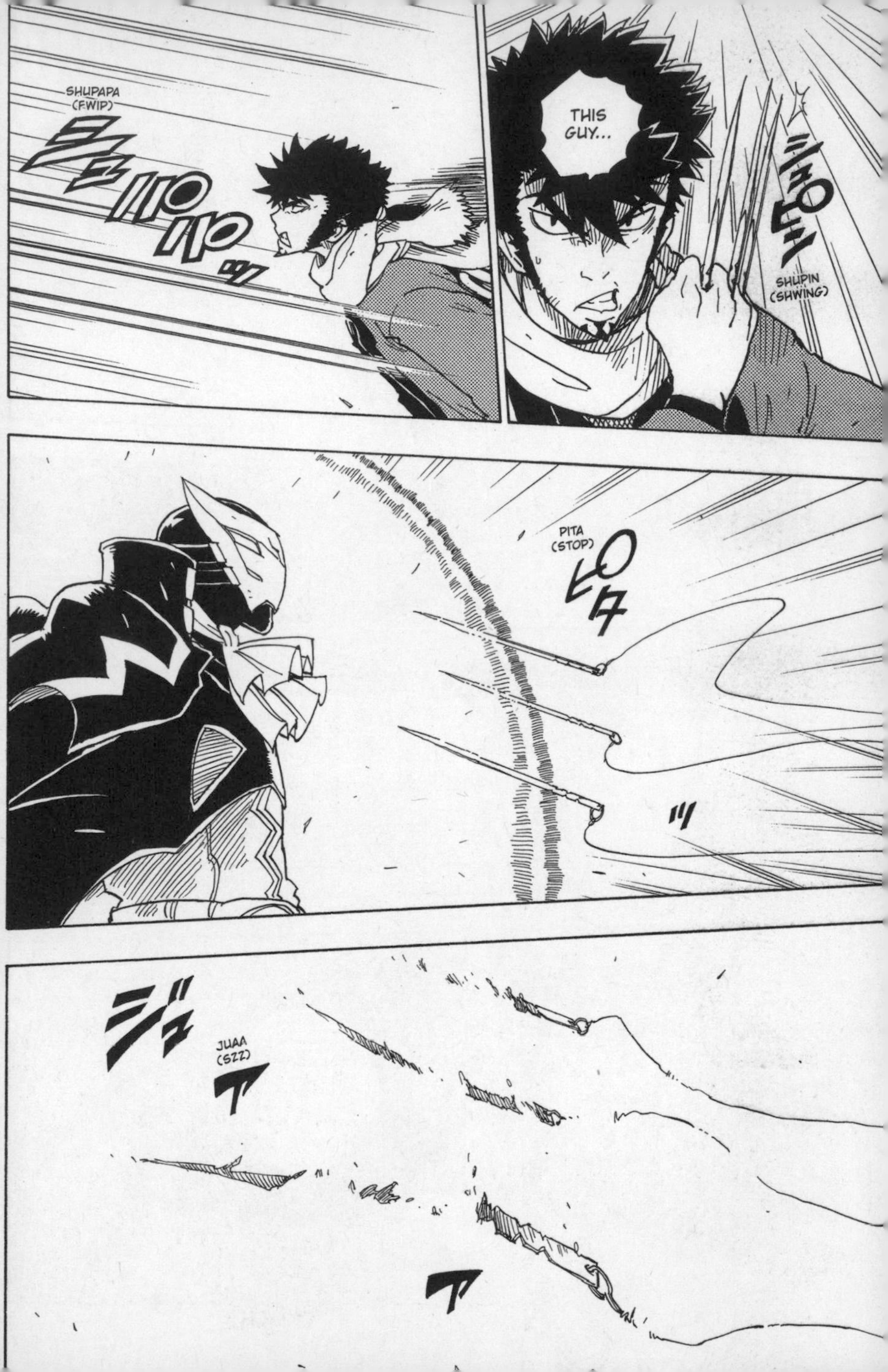
THIS GUY...
シュピン
SHUPIN (SHWING)
シュパパッ
SHUPAPA (FWIP)
ピタッ
PITA (STOP)
ジュアア
JUAA (SZZ)

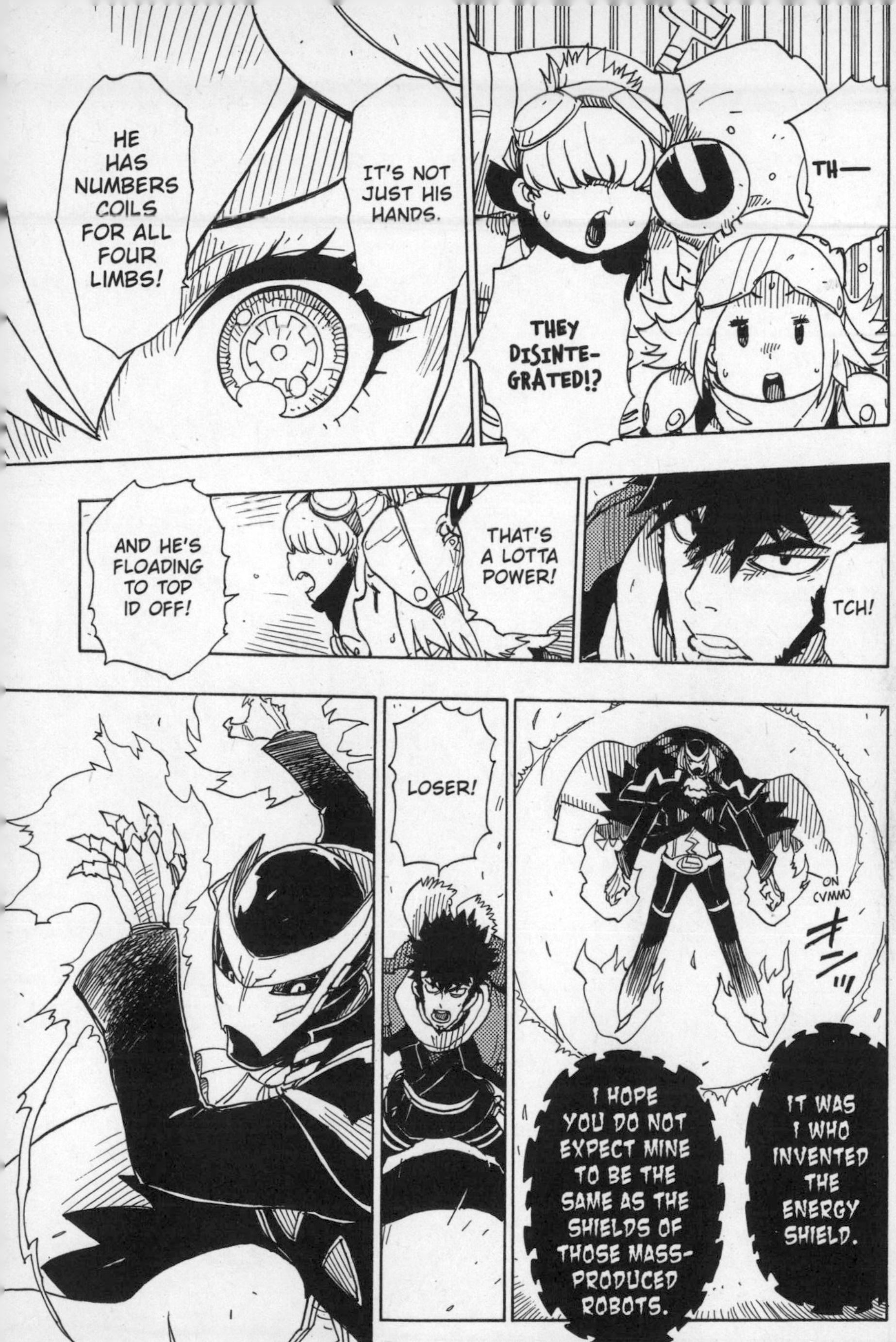
TH—
THEY DISINTE-GRATED!?
IT'S NOT JUST HIS HANDS.
HE HAS NUMBERS COILS FOR ALL FOUR LIMBS!
TCH!
THAT'S A LOTTA POWER!
AND HE'S FLOADING TO TOP ID OFF!
ON (VMM)
IT WAS I WHO INVENTED THE ENERGY SHIELD.
I HOPE YOU DO NOT EXPECT MINE TO BE THE SAME AS THE SHIELDS OF THOSE MASS-PRODUCED ROBOTS.
LOSER!

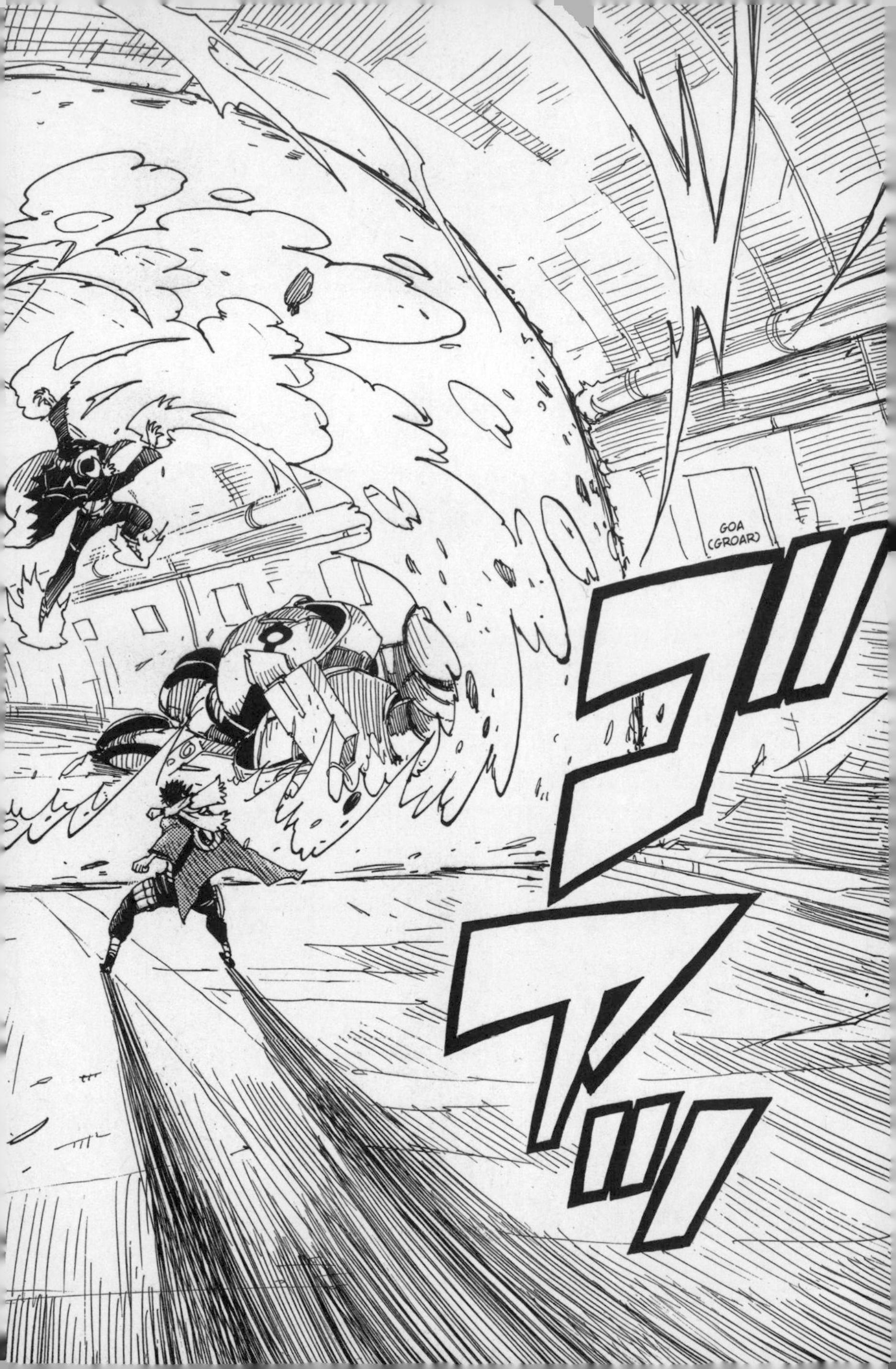
GOA
(GROAR)
ゴァッ

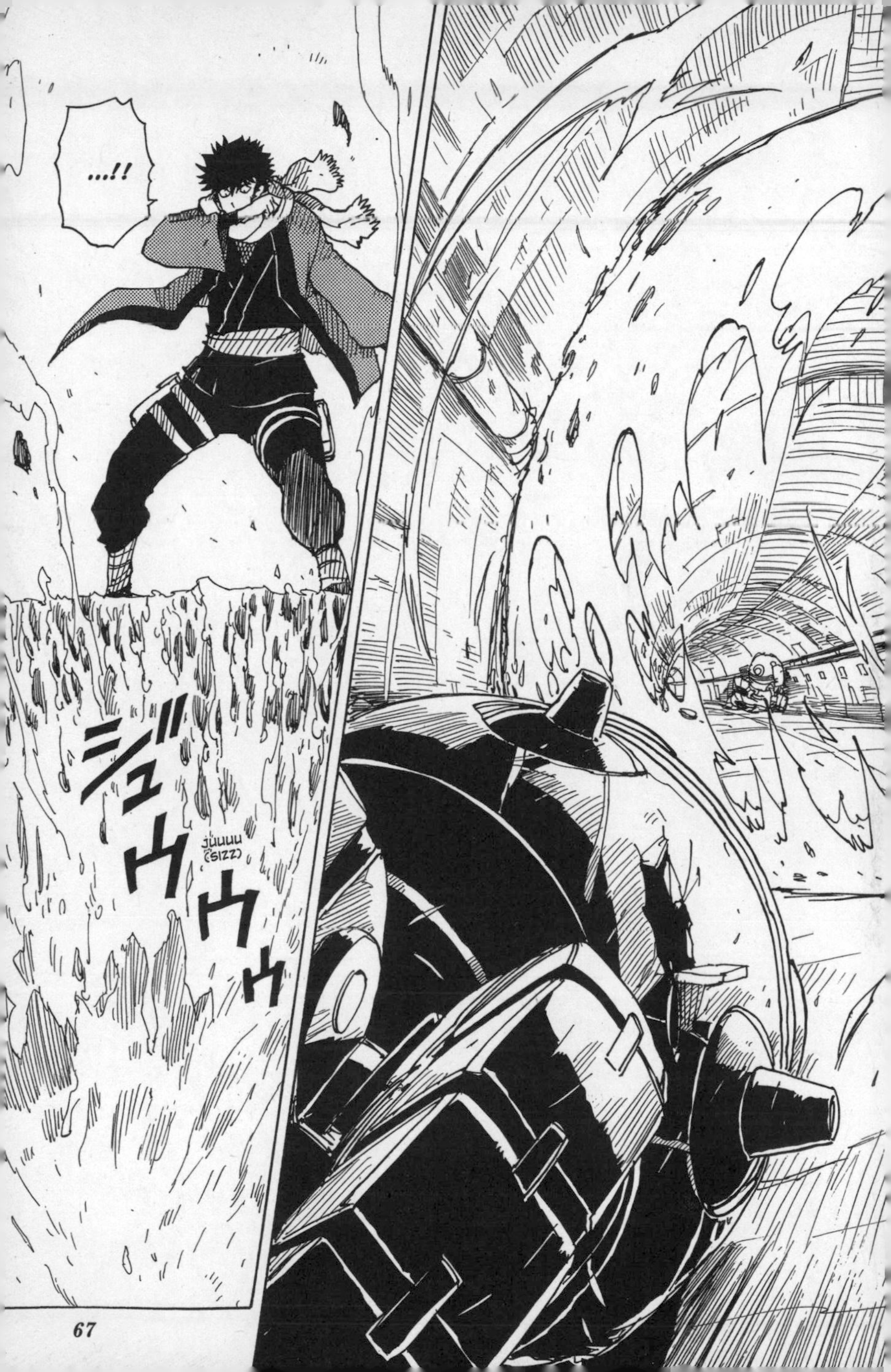
...!!
ジュウウウ
JUUUU (SIZZ)

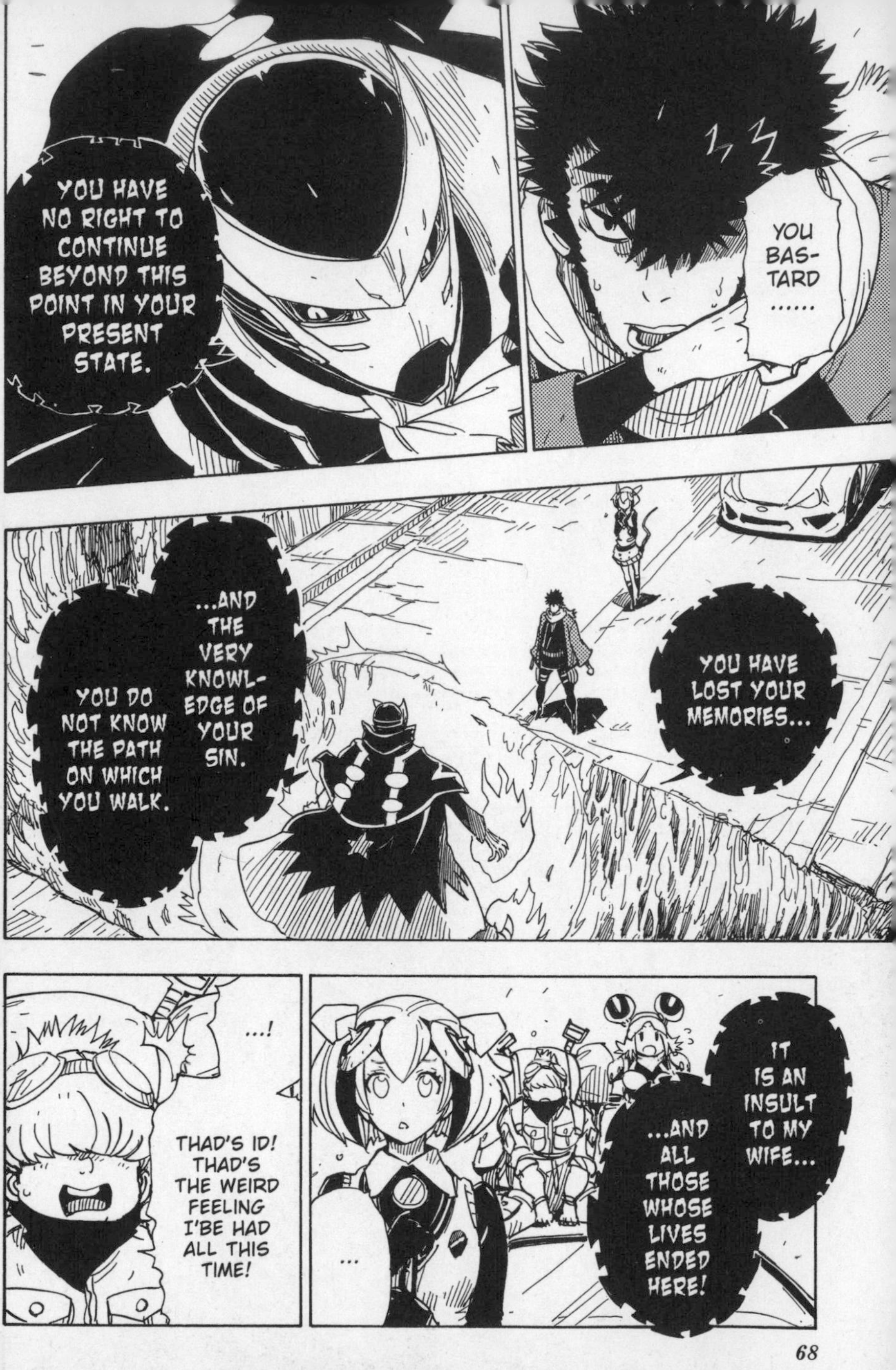
YOU BASTARD ......
YOU HAVE NO RIGHT TO CONTINUE BEYOND THIS POINT IN YOUR PRESENT STATE.
YOU HAVE LOST YOUR MEMORIES...
...AND THE VERY KNOWLEDGE OF YOUR SIN.
YOU DO NOT KNOW THE PATH ON WHICH YOU WALK.
IT IS AN INSULT TO MY WIFE...
...AND ALL THOSE WHOSE LIVES ENDED HERE!
...
...!
THAD'S ID! THAD'S THE WEIRD FEELING I'BE HAD ALL THIS TIME!

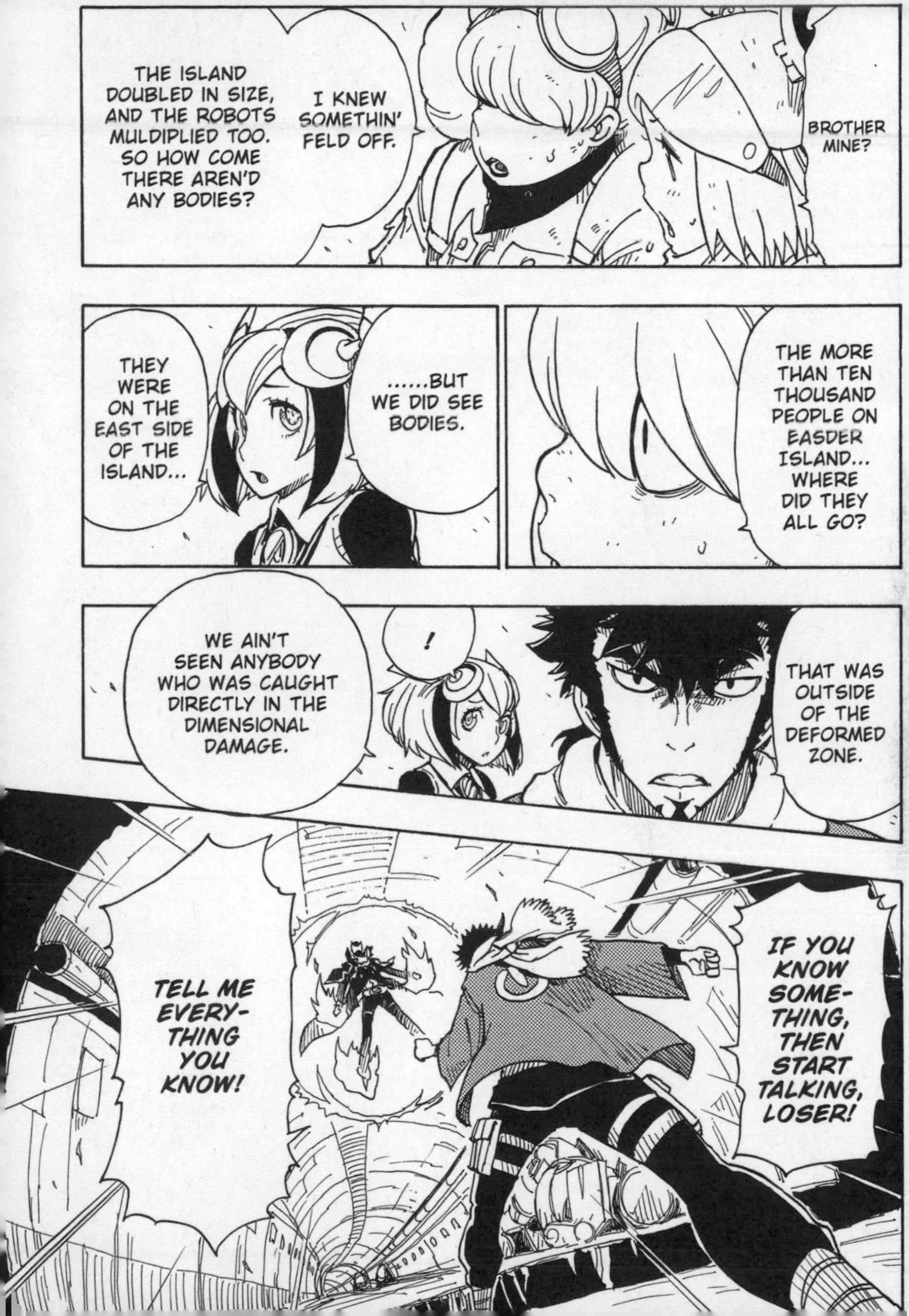
BROTHER MINE?
I KNEW SOMETHIN' FELD OFF.
THE ISLAND DOUBLED IN SIZE, AND THE ROBOTS MULDIPLIED TOO. SO HOW COME THERE AREN'D ANY BODIES?
THE MORE THAN TEN THOUSAND PEOPLE ON EASDER ISLAND... WHERE DID THEY ALL GO?
......BUT WE DID SEE BODIES.
THEY WERE ON THE EAST SIDE OF THE ISLAND...
THAT WAS OUTSIDE OF THE DEFORMED ZONE.
!
WE AIN'T SEEN ANYBODY WHO WAS CAUGHT DIRECTLY IN THE DIMENSIONAL DAMAGE.
IF YOU KNOW SOME-THING, THEN START TALKING, LOSER!
TELL ME EVERY-THING YOU KNOW!

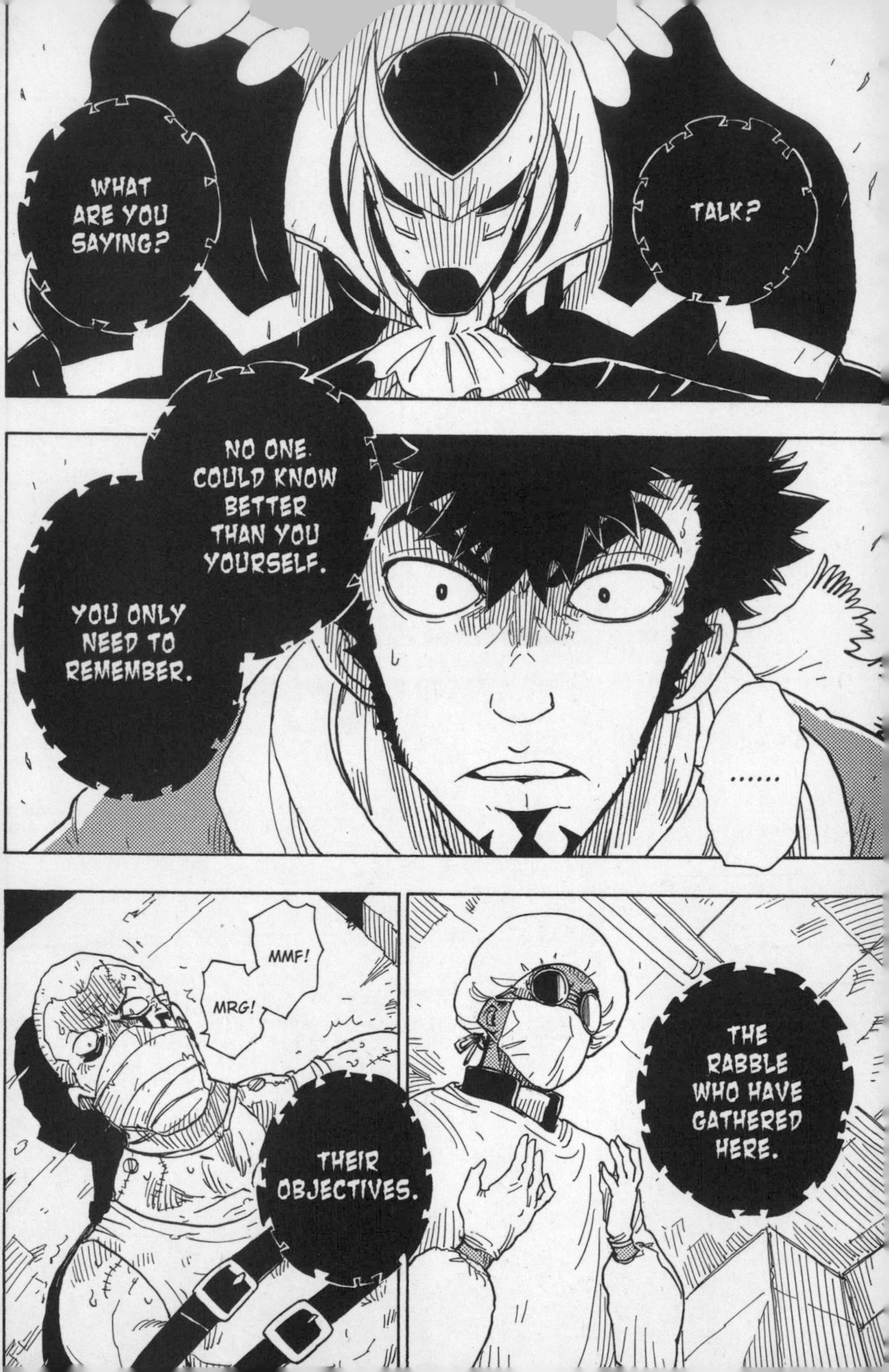

TALK?
WHAT ARE YOU SAYING?
NO ONE COULD KNOW BETTER THAN YOU YOURSELF.
YOU ONLY NEED TO REMEMBER.
......
THE RABBLE WHO HAVE GATHERED HERE.
MMF!
MRG!
THEIR OBJECTIVES.

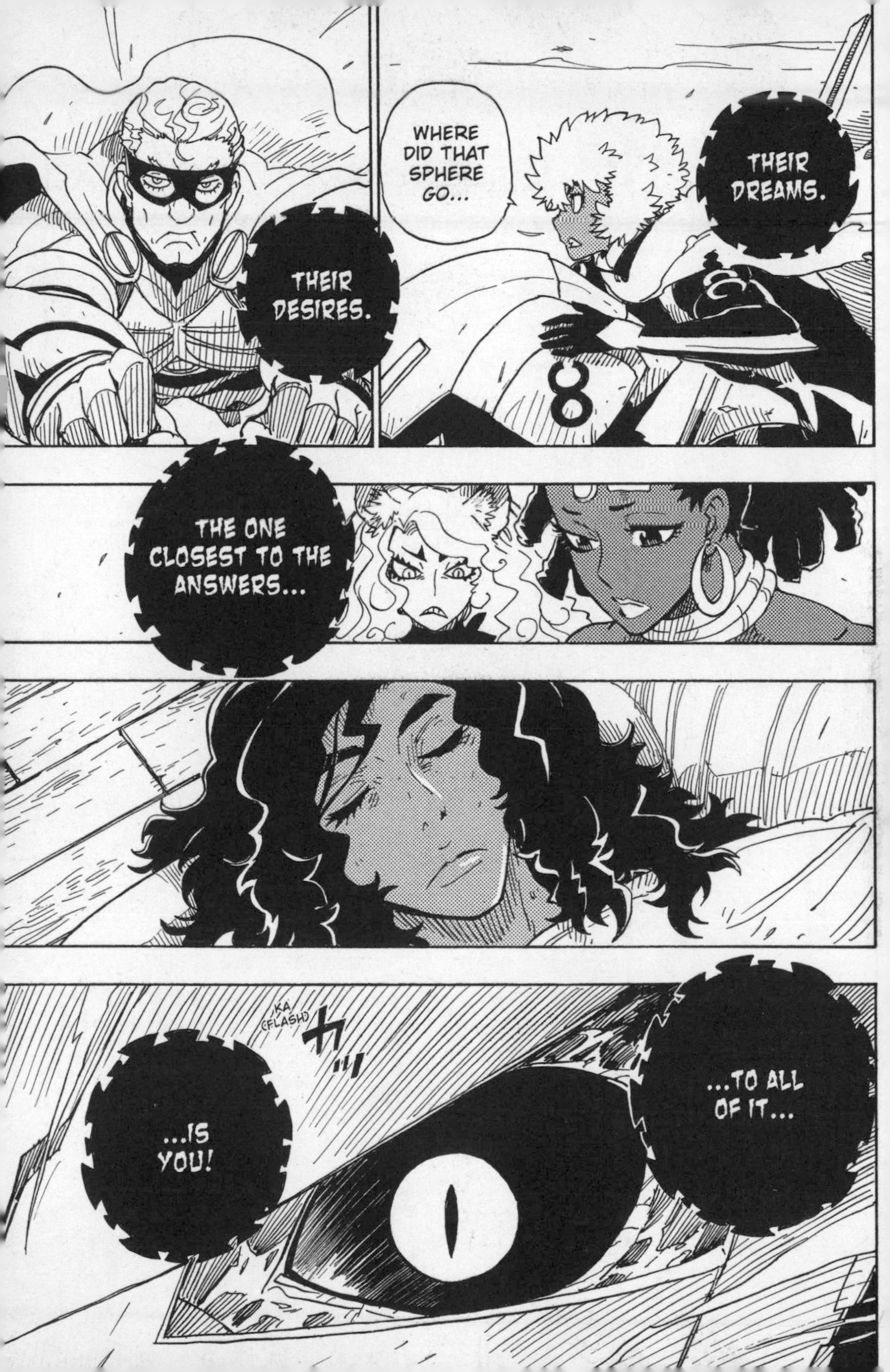
THEIR DREAMS.
WHERE DID THAT SPHERE GO...
THEIR DESIRES.
THE ONE CLOSEST TO THE ANSWERS...
...TO ALL OF IT...
KA (FLASH)
カッ
...IS YOU!

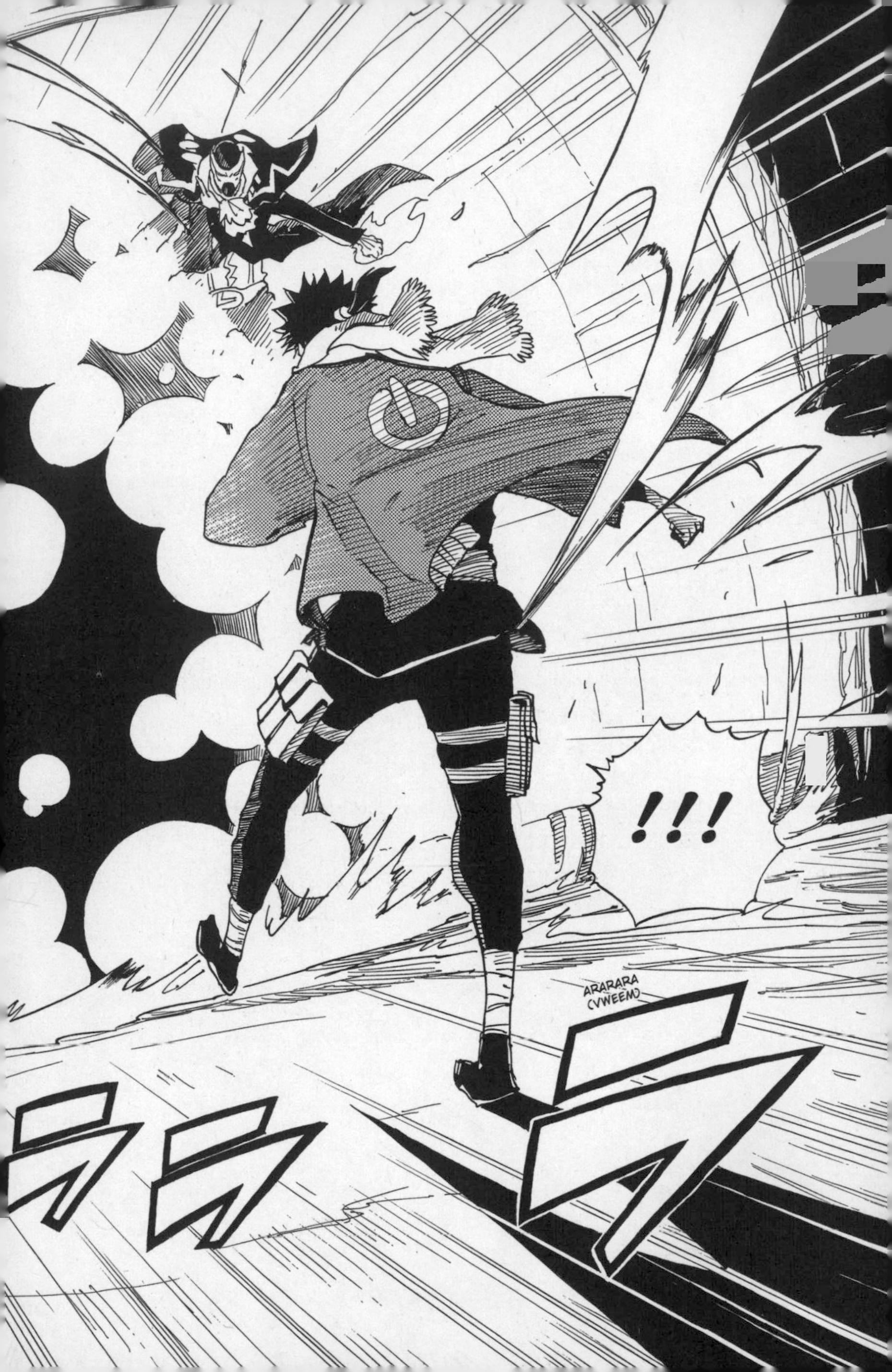

!!!
ARARARA
(VWEEM)

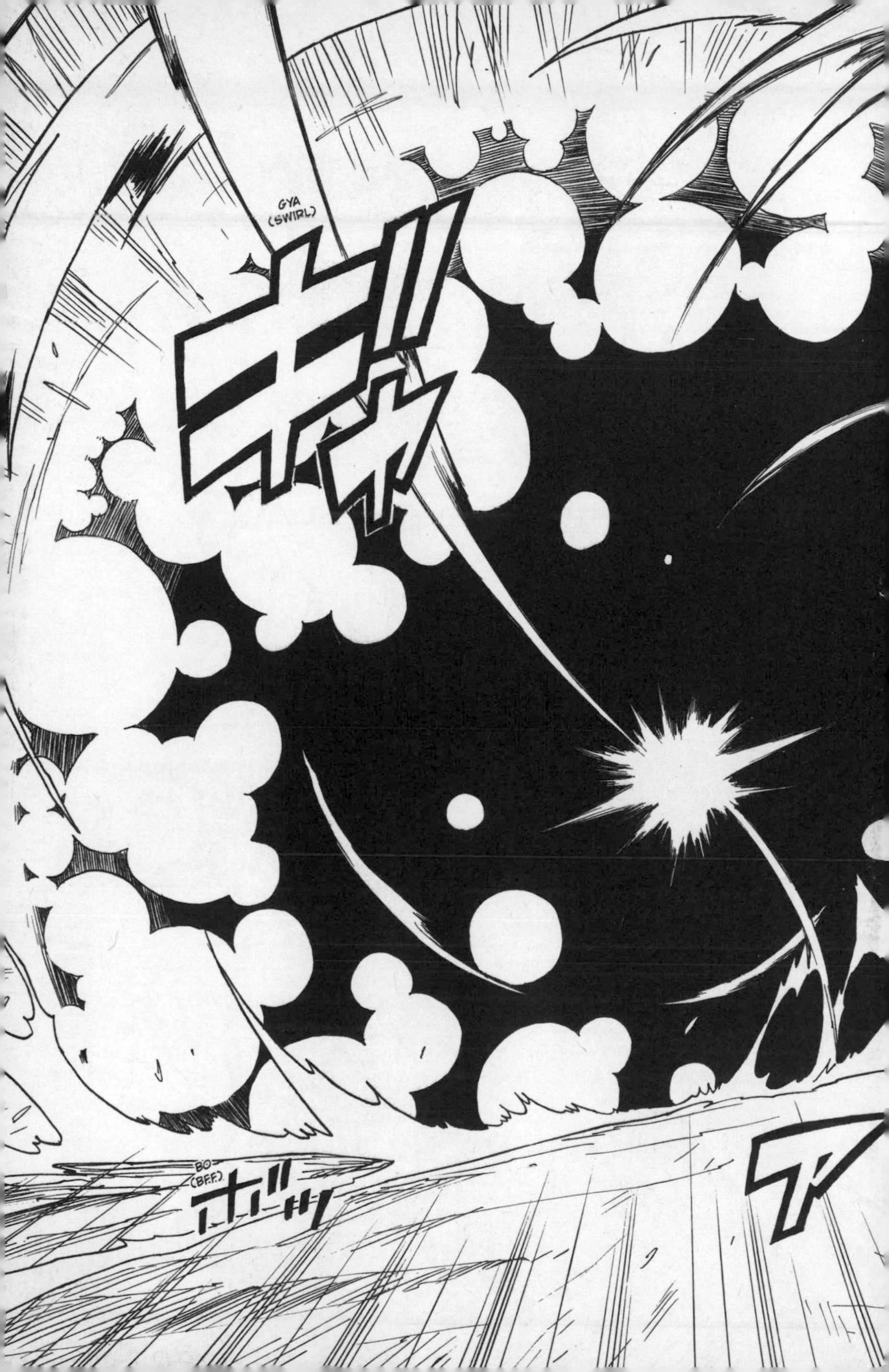
GYA
(SWIRL)
BO
(BF.F.)

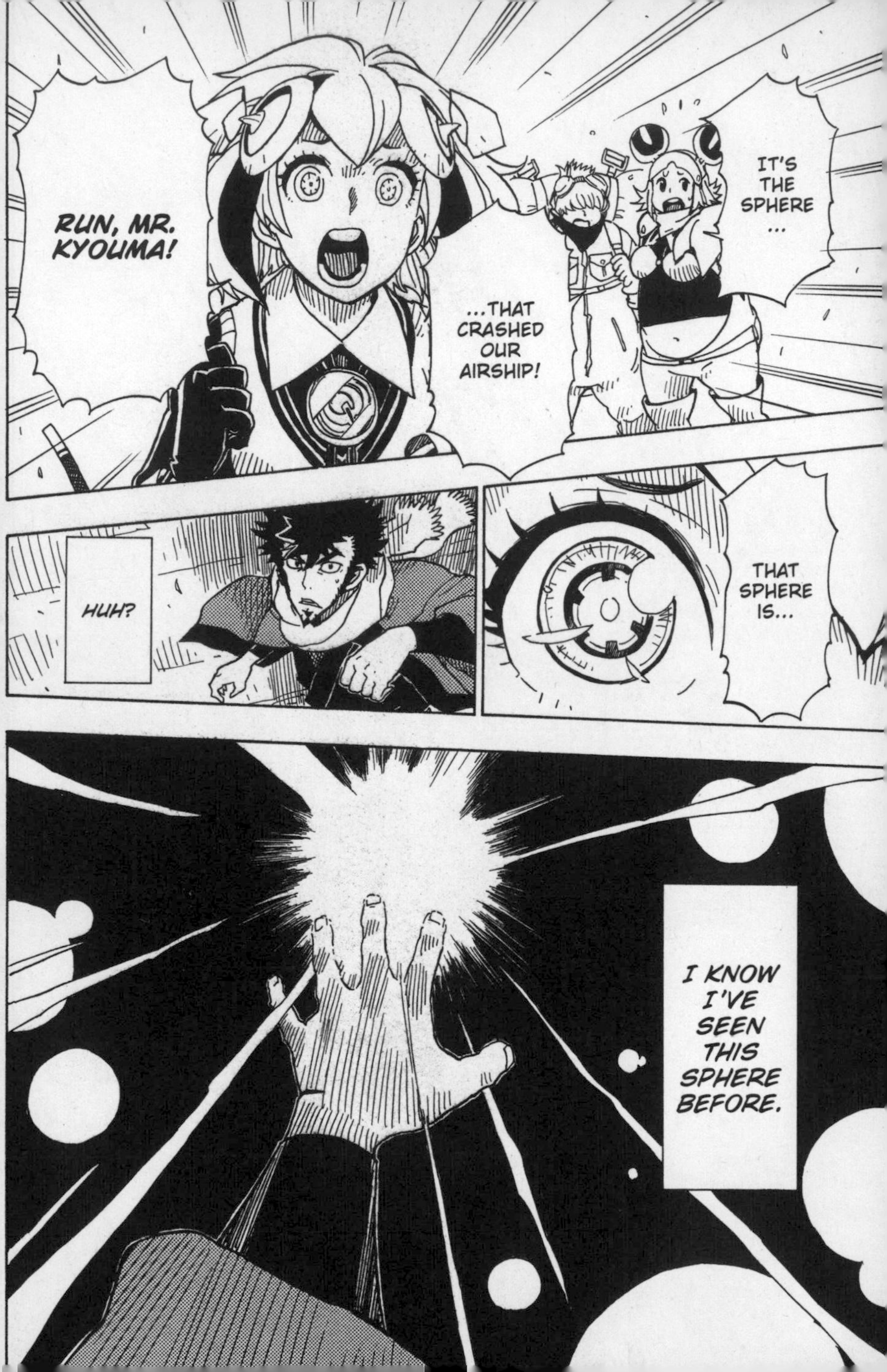
IT'S THE SPHERE ...
...THAT CRASHED OUR AIRSHIP!
RUN, MR. KYOUMA!
THAT SPHERE IS...
HUH?
I KNOW I'VE SEEN THIS SPHERE BEFORE.

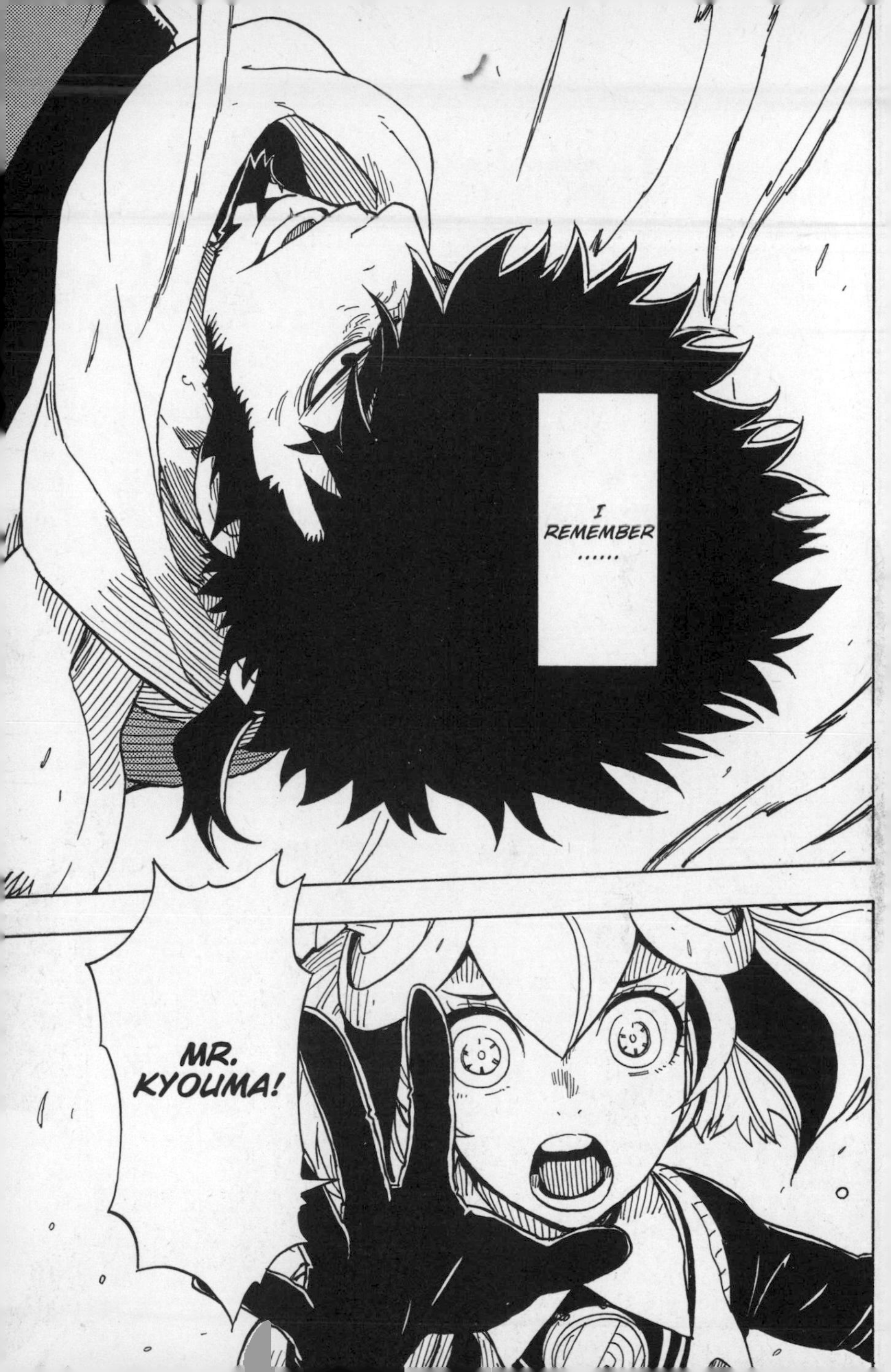
I REMEMBER ......
MR. KYOUMA!

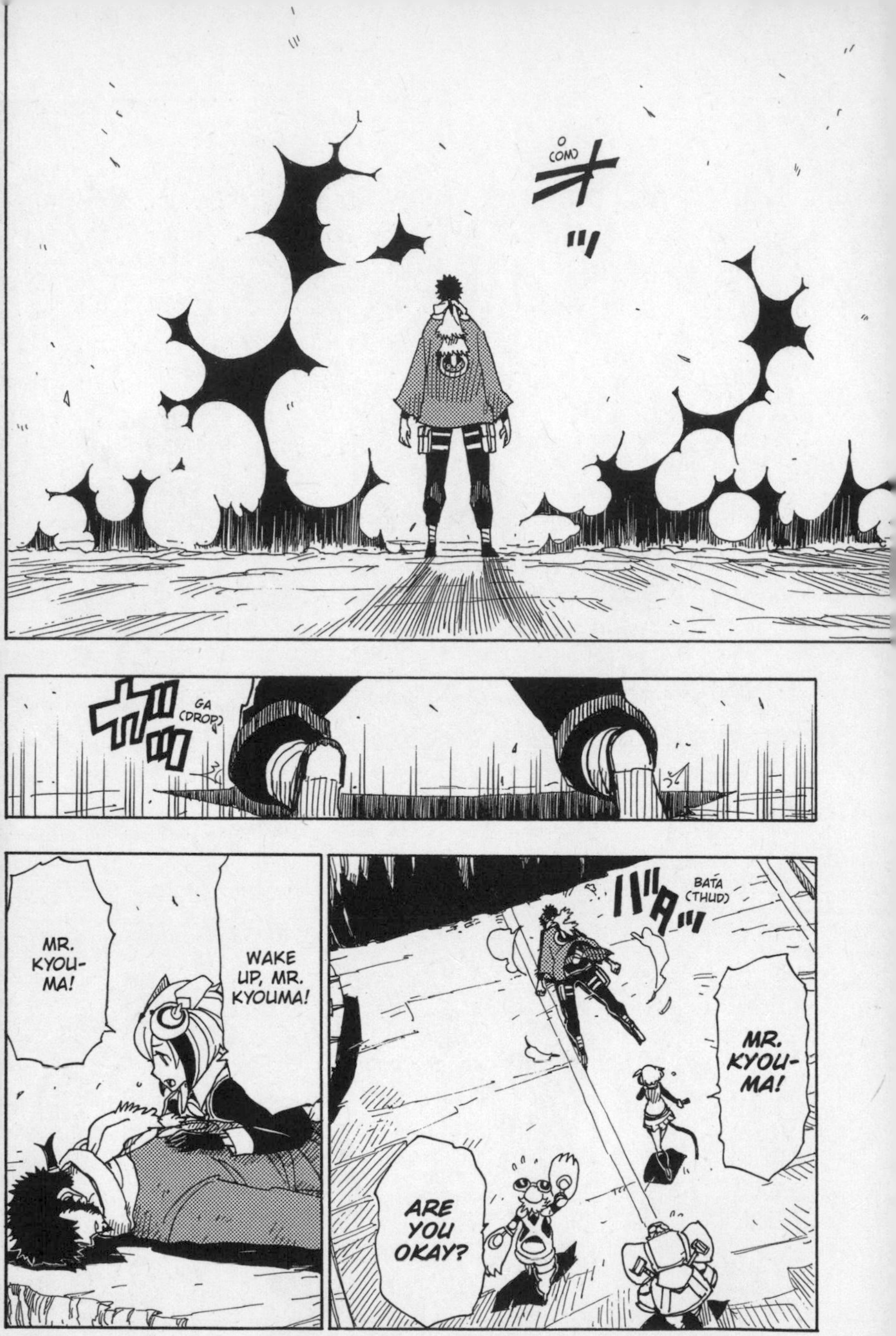
O
(OM)
GA
(DROP)
BATA
(THUD)
MR. KYOU-MA!
ARE YOU OKAY?
WAKE UP, MR. KYOUMA!
MR. KYOU-MA!

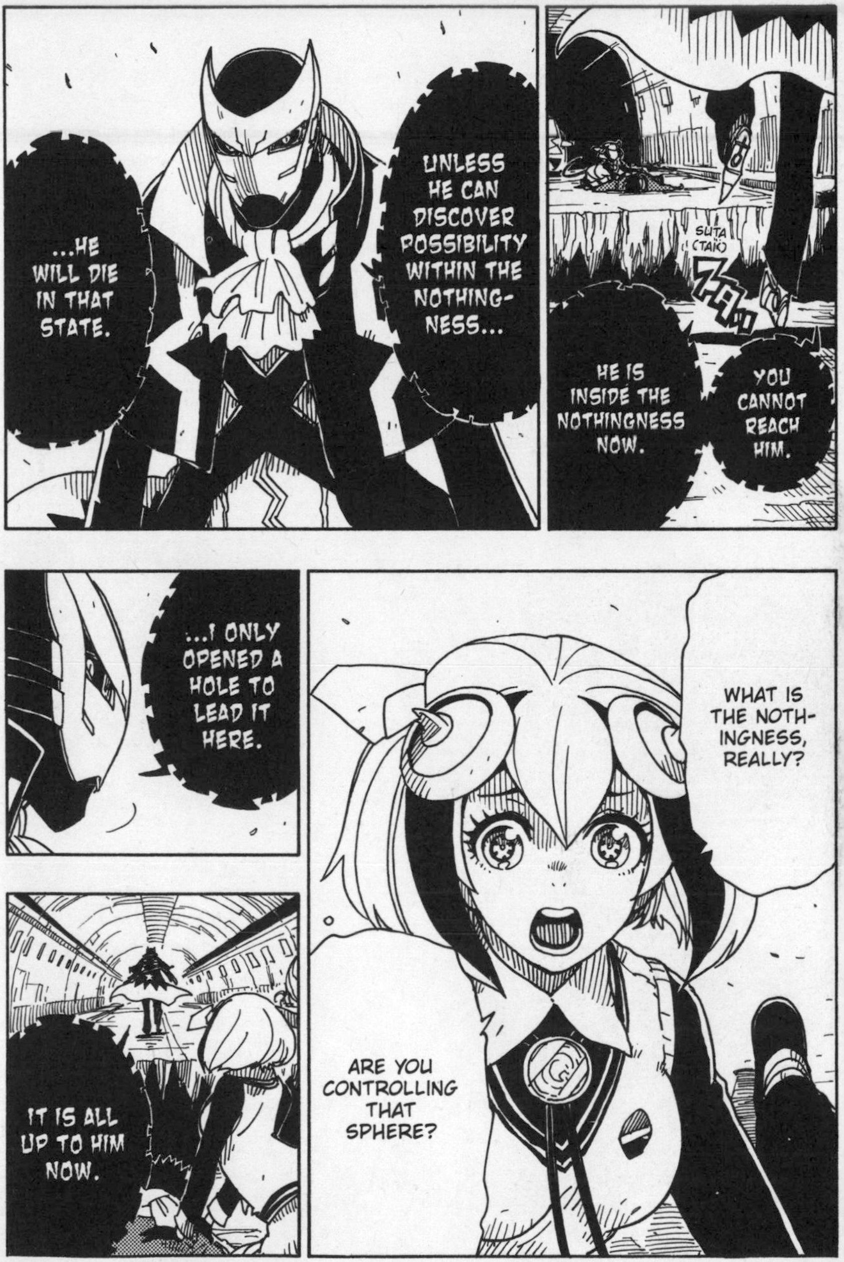
SUTA (TAK)
HE IS INSIDE THE NOTHINGNESS NOW.
YOU CANNOT REACH HIM.
UNLESS HE CAN DISCOVER POSSIBILITY WITHIN THE NOTHING-NESS...
...HE WILL DIE IN THAT STATE.
WHAT IS THE NOTH-INGNESS, REALLY?
ARE YOU CONTROLLING THAT SPHERE?
...I ONLY OPENED A HOLE TO LEAD IT HERE.
IT IS ALL UP TO HIM NOW.

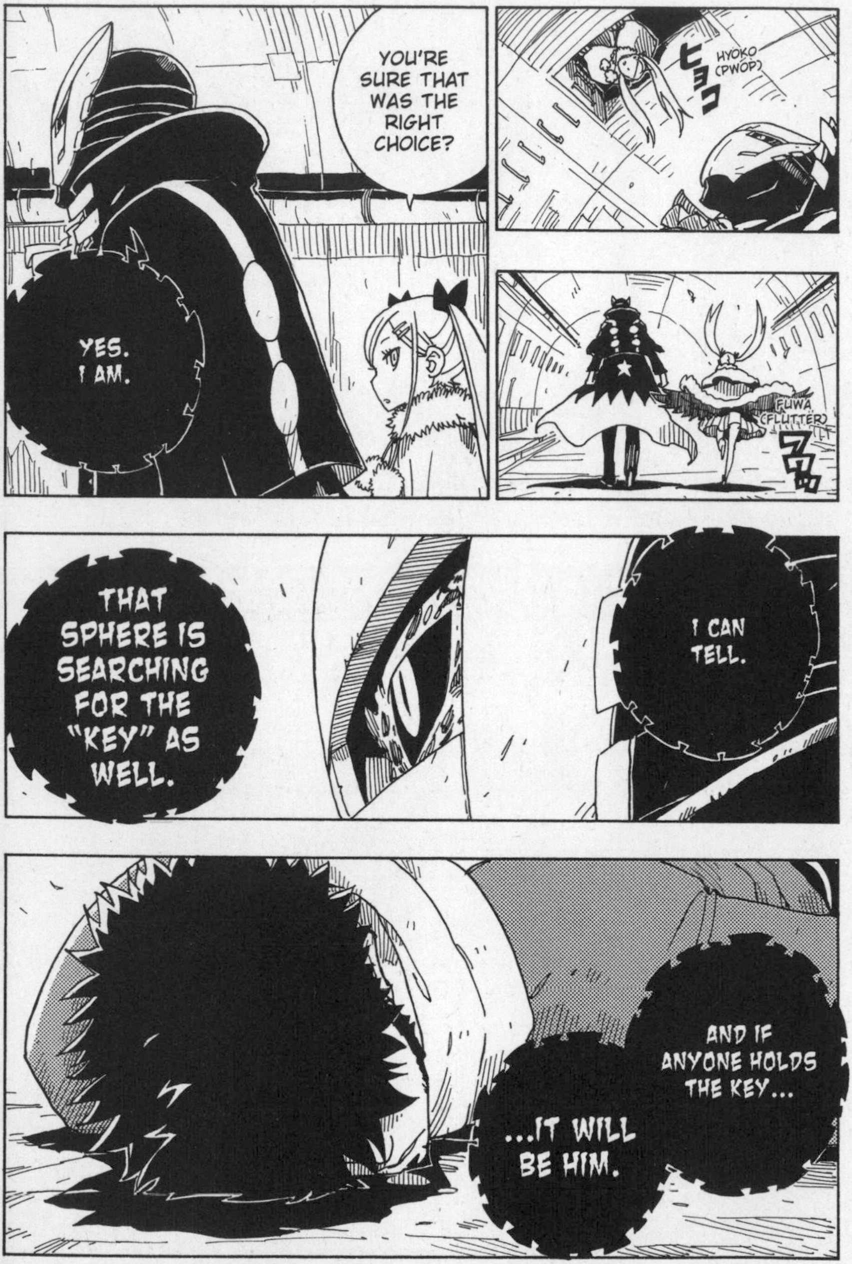
ヒョコ
HYOKO (PWOP)
FUWA (FLUTTER)
フワ
YOU'RE SURE THAT WAS THE RIGHT CHOICE?
YES. I AM.
I CAN TELL.
THAT SPHERE IS SEARCHING FOR THE "KEY" AS WELL.
AND IF ANYONE HOLDS THE KEY...
...IT WILL BE HIM.

FILE.51
MEMORIES OF THE PAST

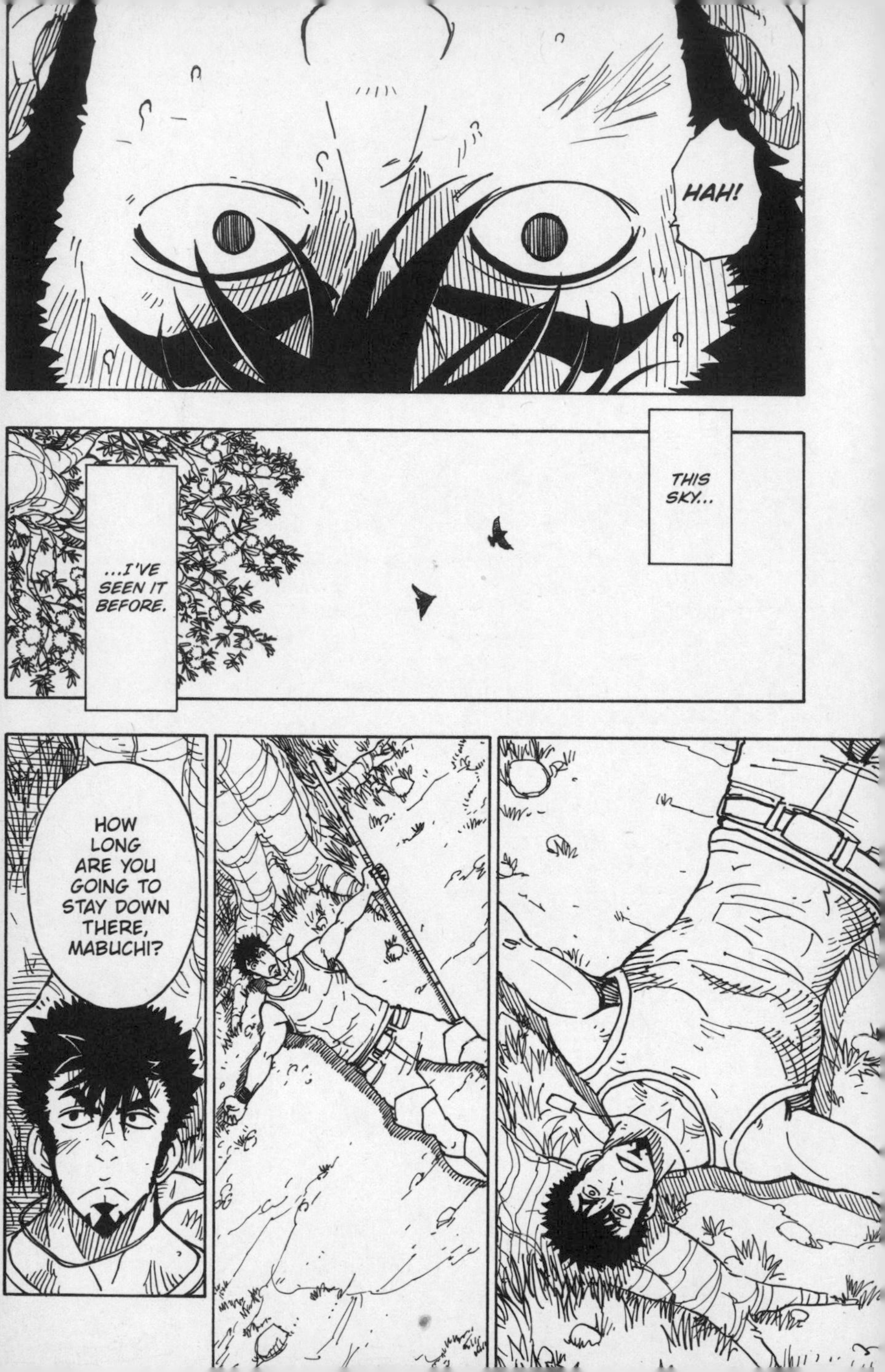
HAH!
THIS SKY...
...I'VE SEEN IT BEFORE.
HOW LONG ARE YOU GOING TO STAY DOWN THERE, MABUCHI?

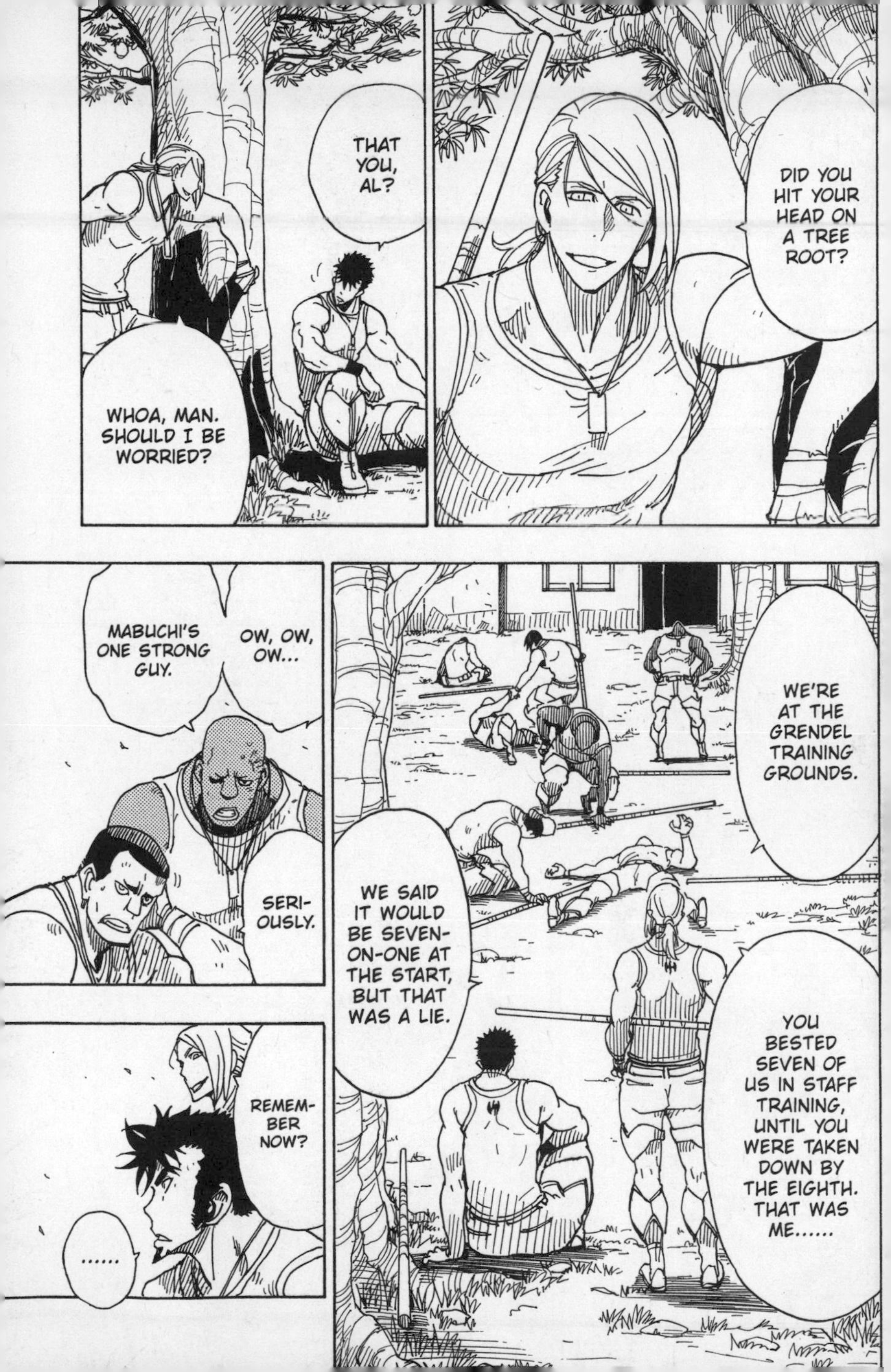
DID YOU HIT YOUR HEAD ON A TREE ROOT?
THAT YOU, AL?
WHOA, MAN. SHOULD I BE WORRIED?
WE'RE AT THE GRENDEL TRAINING GROUNDS.
YOU BESTED SEVEN OF US IN STAFF TRAINING, UNTIL YOU WERE TAKEN DOWN BY THE EIGHTH. THAT WAS ME......
WE SAID IT WOULD BE SEVEN-ON-ONE AT THE START, BUT THAT WAS A LIE.
OW, OW, OW...
MABUCHI'S ONE STRONG GUY.
SERIOUSLY.
REMEMBER NOW?
......

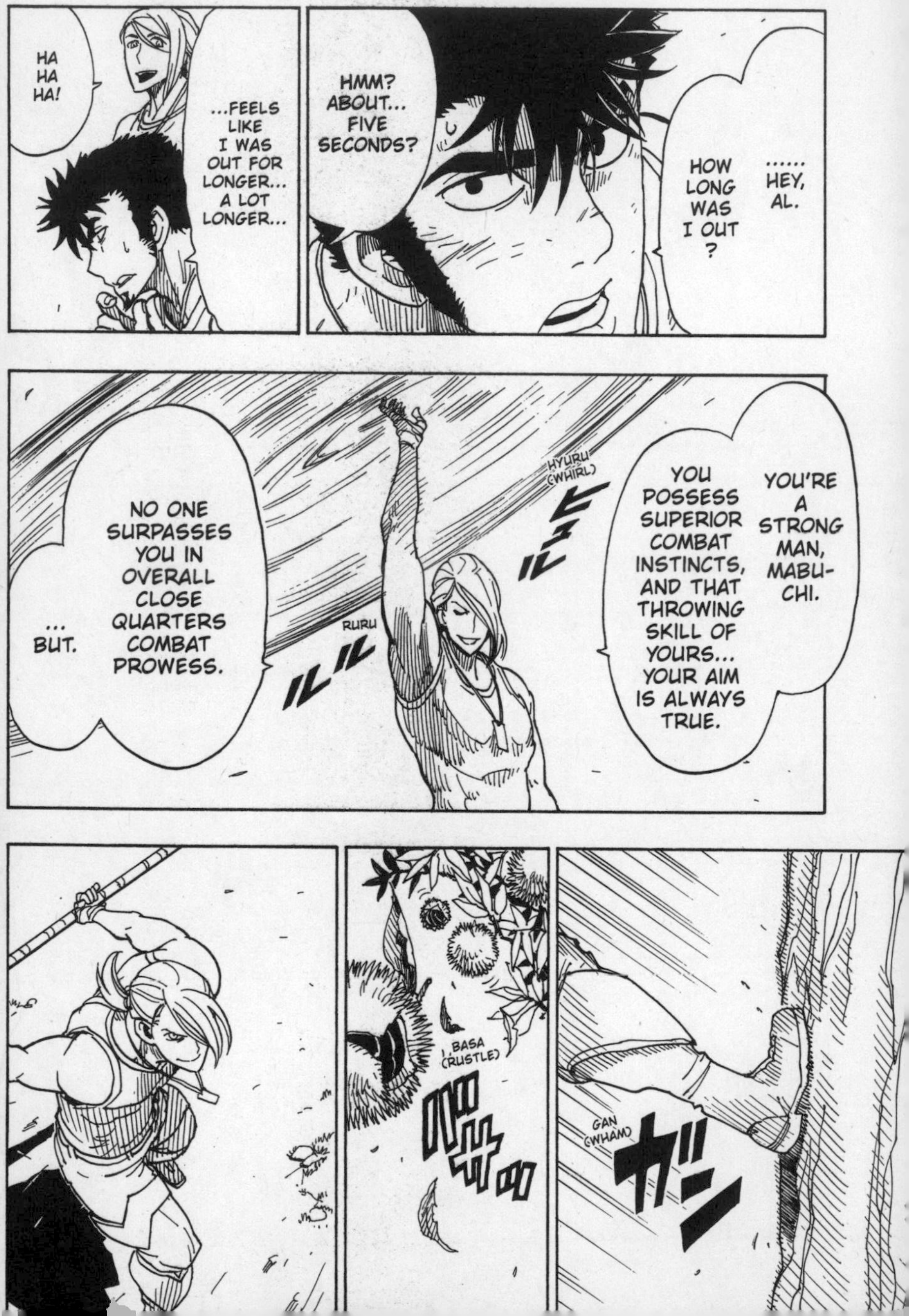
......HEY, AL.
HOW LONG WAS I OUT?
HMM? ABOUT... FIVE SECONDS?
...FEELS LIKE I WAS OUT FOR LONGER... A LOT LONGER...
HA HA HA!
YOU'RE A STRONG MAN, MABUCHI.
YOU POSSESS SUPERIOR COMBAT INSTINCTS, AND THAT THROWING SKILL OF YOURS... YOUR AIM IS ALWAYS TRUE.
HYURU (WHIRL)
RURU
NO ONE SURPASSES YOU IN OVERALL CLOSE QUARTERS COMBAT PROWESS.
...BUT.
GAN (WHAM)
BASA (RUSTLE)

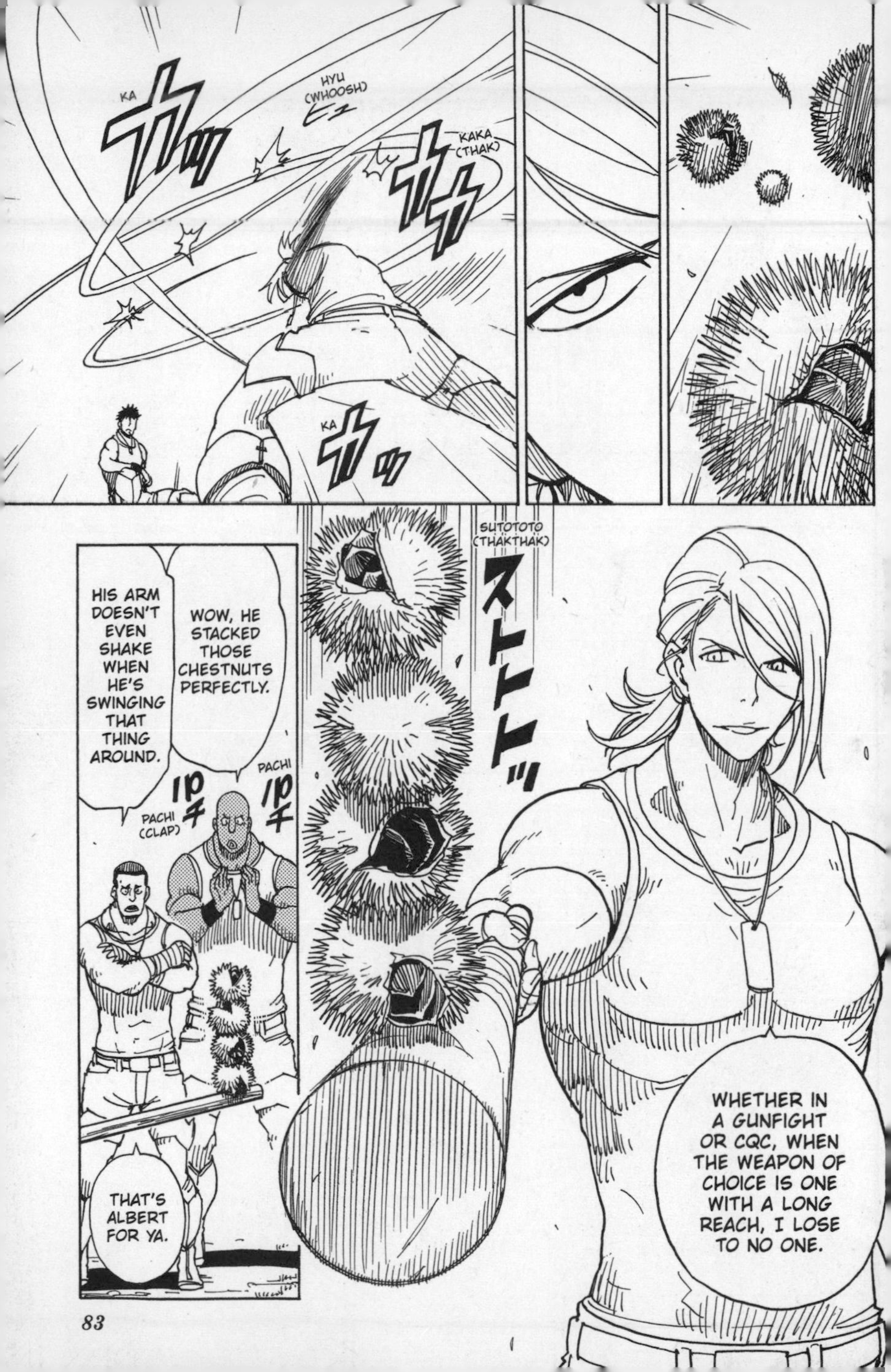
KAKA (THAK)
HYU (WHOOSH)
KA
KA
SUTOTOTO (THAKTHAK)
WHETHER IN A GUNFIGHT OR CQC, WHEN THE WEAPON OF CHOICE IS ONE WITH A LONG REACH, I LOSE TO NO ONE.
WOW, HE STACKED THOSE CHESTNUTS PERFECTLY.
HIS ARM DOESN'T EVEN SHAKE WHEN HE'S SWINGING THAT THING AROUND.
PACHI
PACHI (CLAP)
THAT'S ALBERT FOR YA.

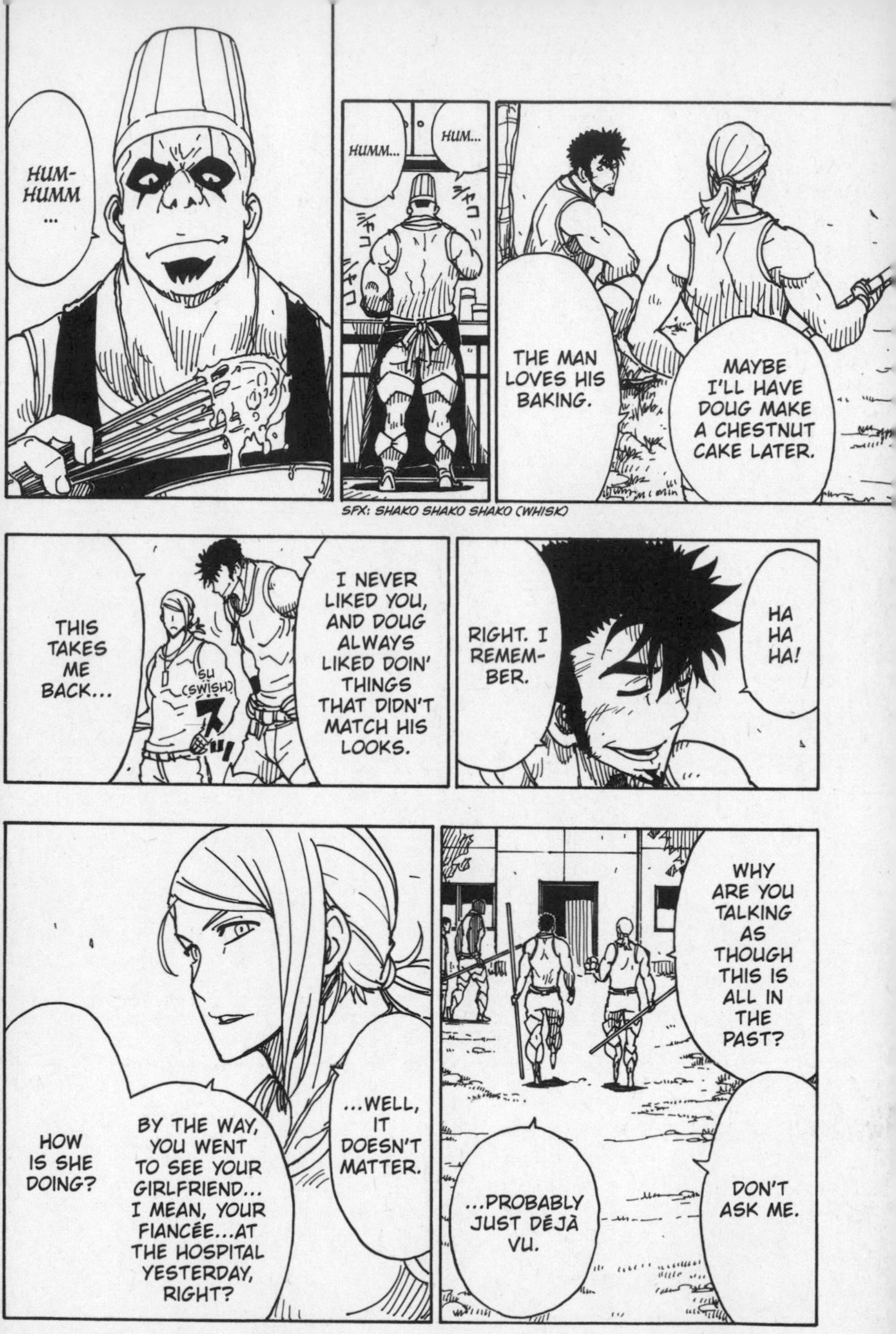
MAYBE I'LL HAVE DOUG MAKE A CHESTNUT CAKE LATER.
THE MAN LOVES HIS BAKING.
HUM...
HUMM...
HUM-HUMM ...
SFX: SHAKO SHAKO SHAKO (WHISK)
HA HA HA!
RIGHT. I REMEMBER.
I NEVER LIKED YOU, AND DOUG ALWAYS LIKED DOIN' THINGS THAT DIDN'T MATCH HIS LOOKS.
THIS TAKES ME BACK...
SU (SWISH)
WHY ARE YOU TALKING AS THOUGH THIS IS ALL IN THE PAST?
DON'T ASK ME.
...PROBABLY JUST DÉJÀ VU.
...WELL, IT DOESN'T MATTER.
BY THE WAY, YOU WENT TO SEE YOUR GIRLFRIEND... I MEAN, YOUR FIANCÉE...AT THE HOSPITAL YESTERDAY, RIGHT?
HOW IS SHE DOING?

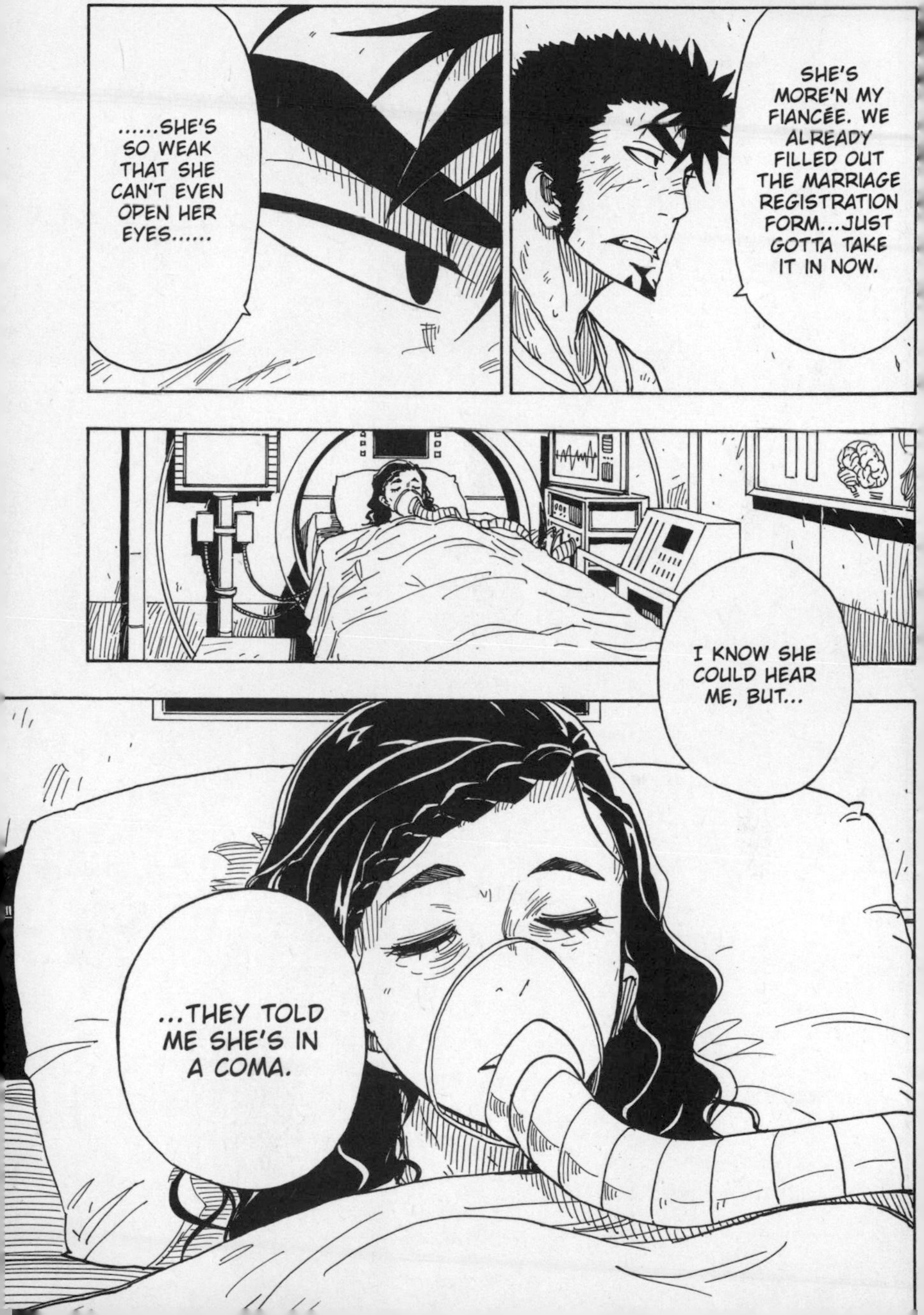
SHE'S MORE'N MY FIANCÉE. WE ALREADY FILLED OUT THE MARRIAGE REGISTRATION FORM...JUST GOTTA TAKE IT IN NOW.
......SHE'S SO WEAK THAT SHE CAN'T EVEN OPEN HER EYES......
I KNOW SHE COULD HEAR ME, BUT...
...THEY TOLD ME SHE'S IN A COMA.

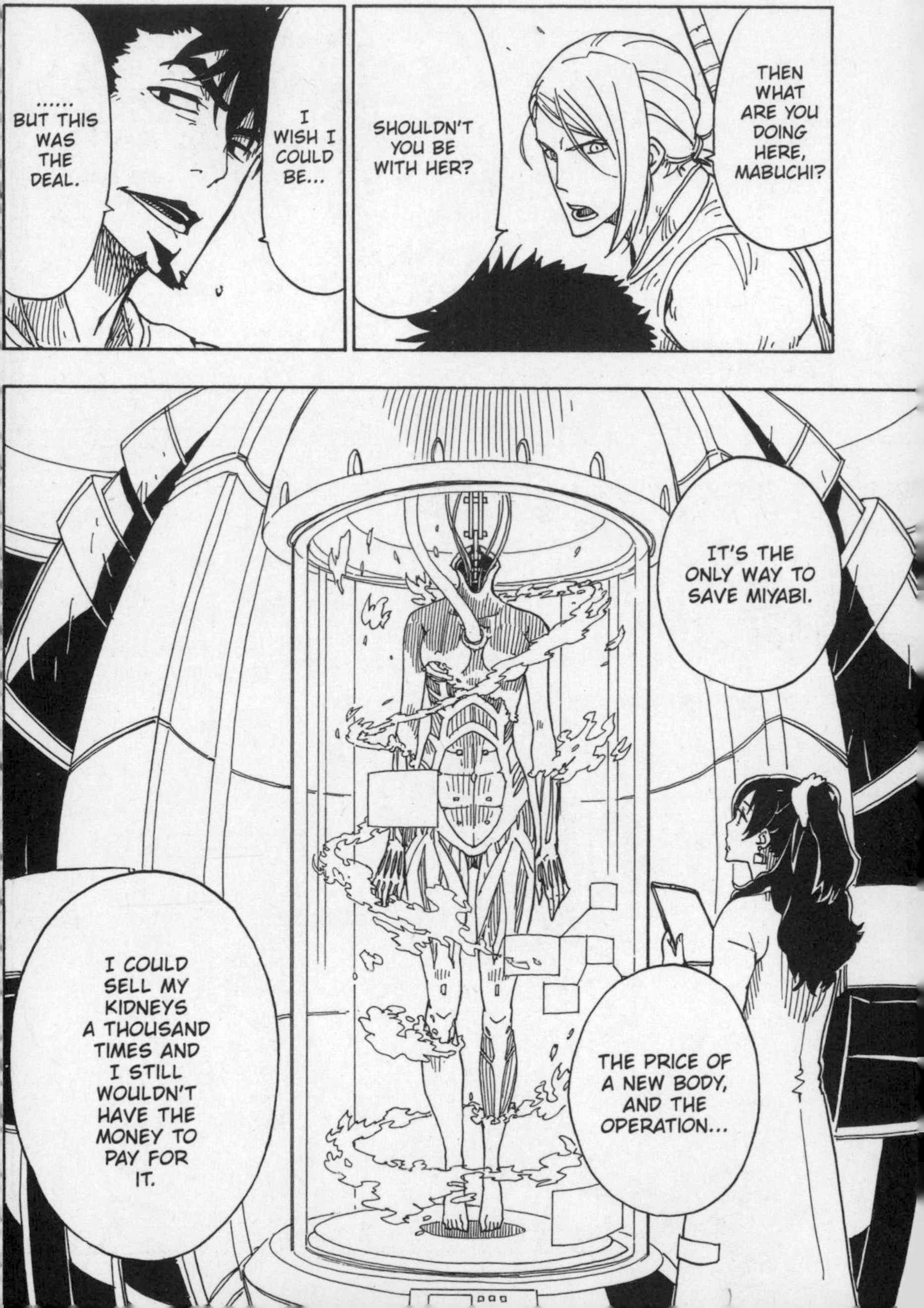
THEN WHAT ARE YOU DOING HERE, MABUCHI?
SHOULDN'T YOU BE WITH HER?
I WISH I COULD BE...
...... BUT THIS WAS THE DEAL.
IT'S THE ONLY WAY TO SAVE MIYABI.
THE PRICE OF A NEW BODY, AND THE OPERATION...
I COULD SELL MY KIDNEYS A THOUSAND TIMES AND I STILL WOULDN'T HAVE THE MONEY TO PAY FOR IT.

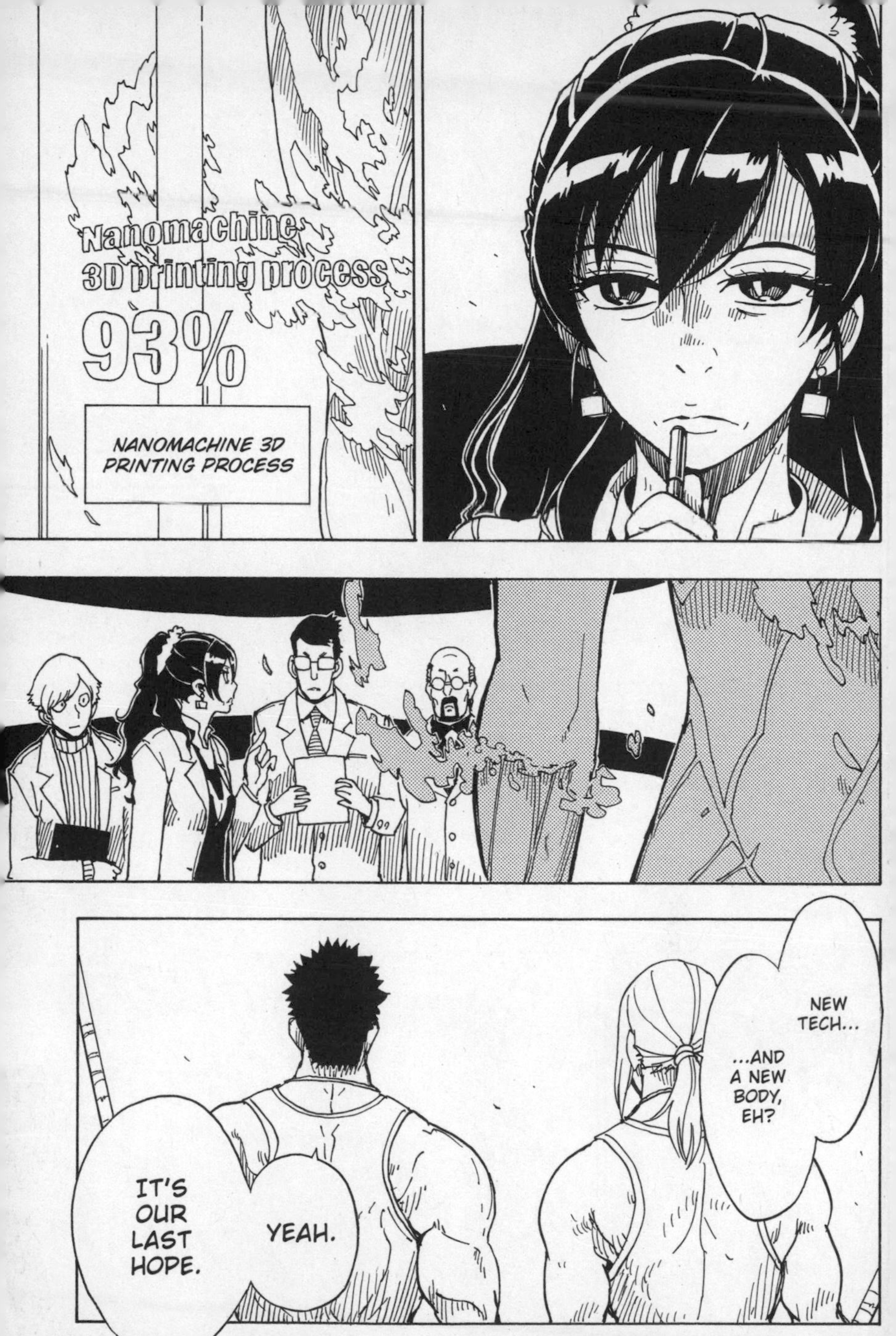
Nanomachine 3D printing process
93%
NANOMACHINE 3D PRINTING PROCESS
NEW TECH...
...AND A NEW BODY, EH?
YEAH.
IT'S OUR LAST HOPE.

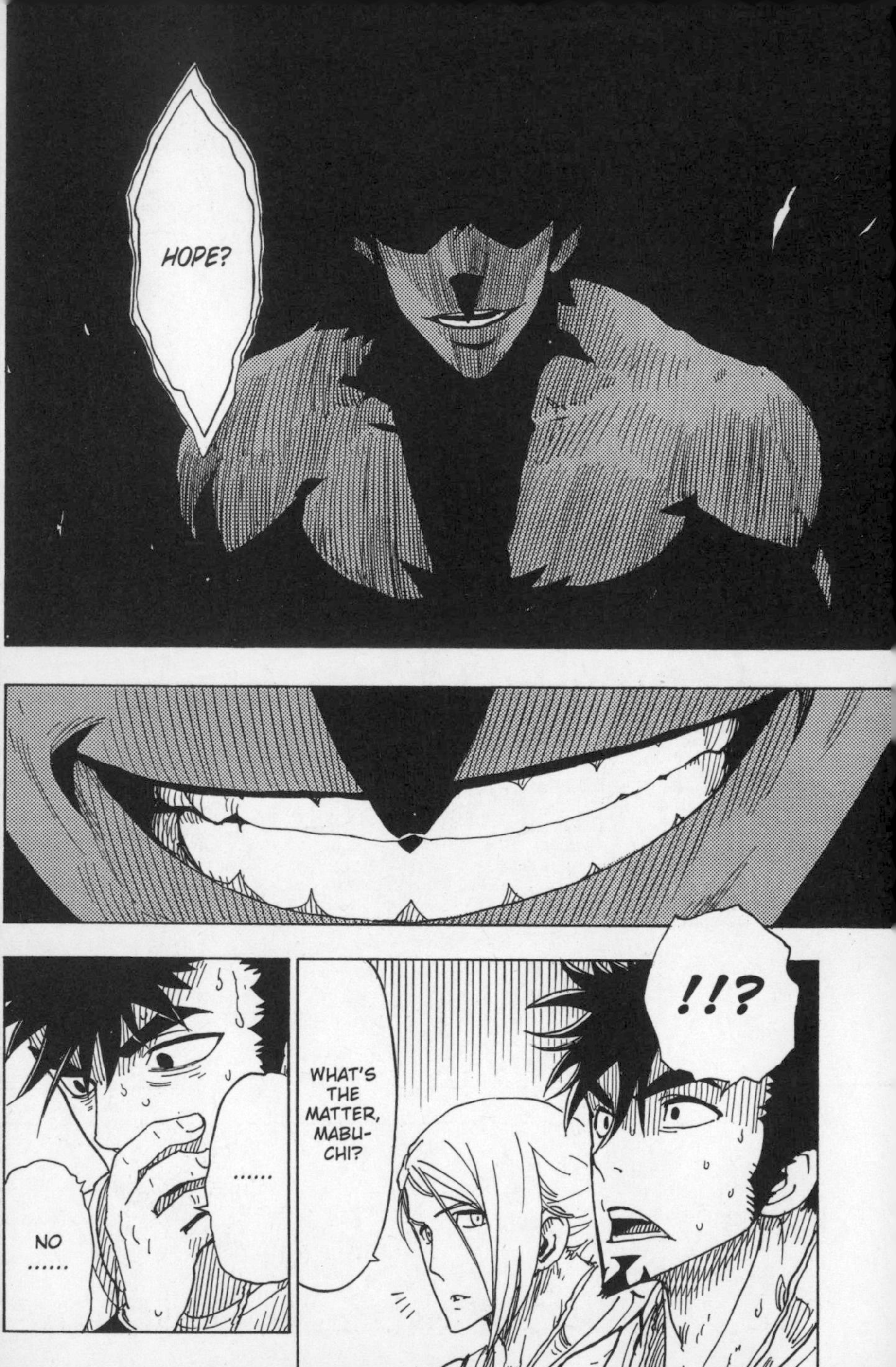
HOPE?
!!?
WHAT'S THE MATTER, MABU-CHI?
......
NO ......

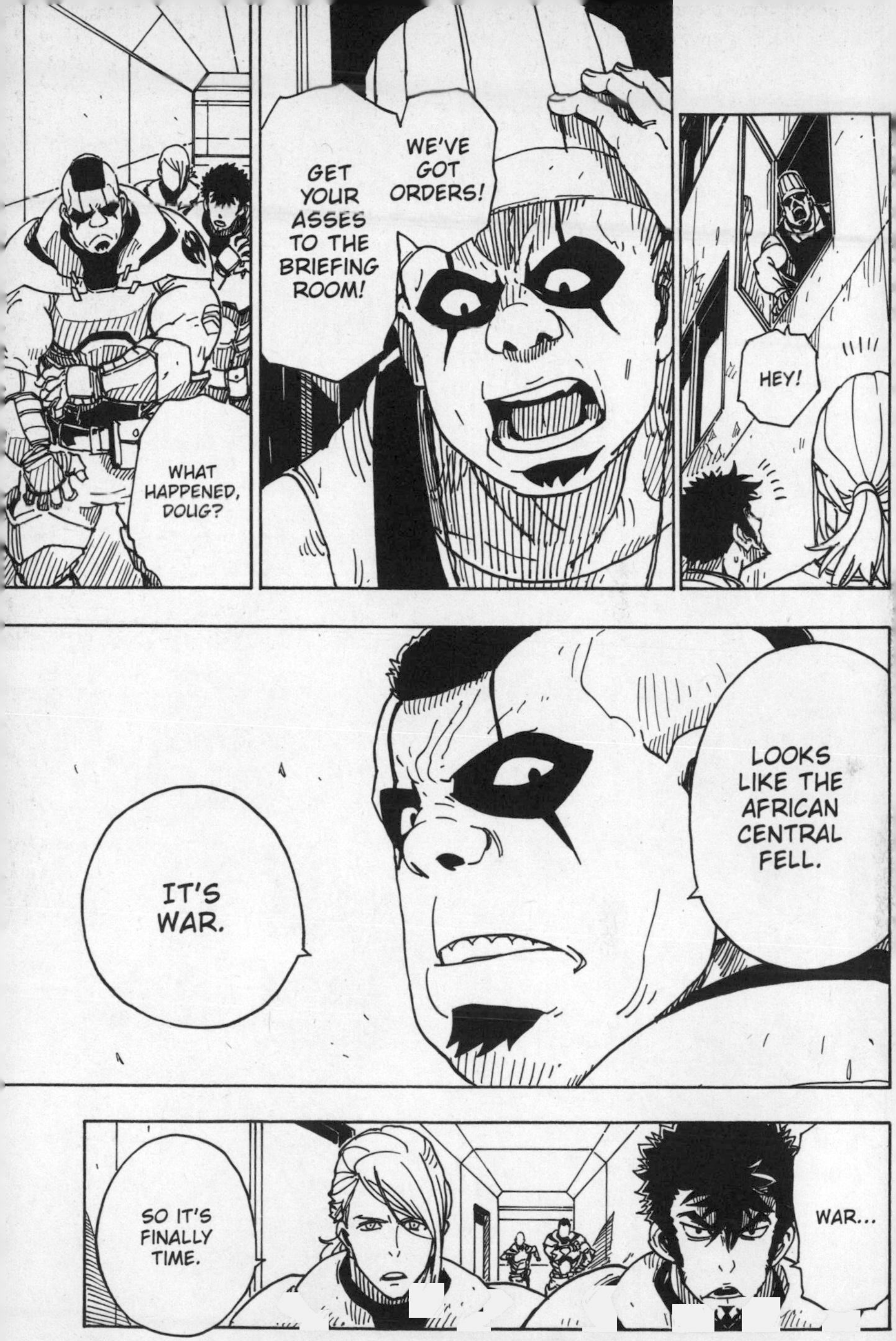
HEY!
WE'VE GOT ORDERS!
GET YOUR ASSES TO THE BRIEFING ROOM!
WHAT HAPPENED, DOUG?
LOOKS LIKE THE AFRICAN CENTRAL FELL.
IT'S WAR.
WAR...
SO IT'S FINALLY TIME.

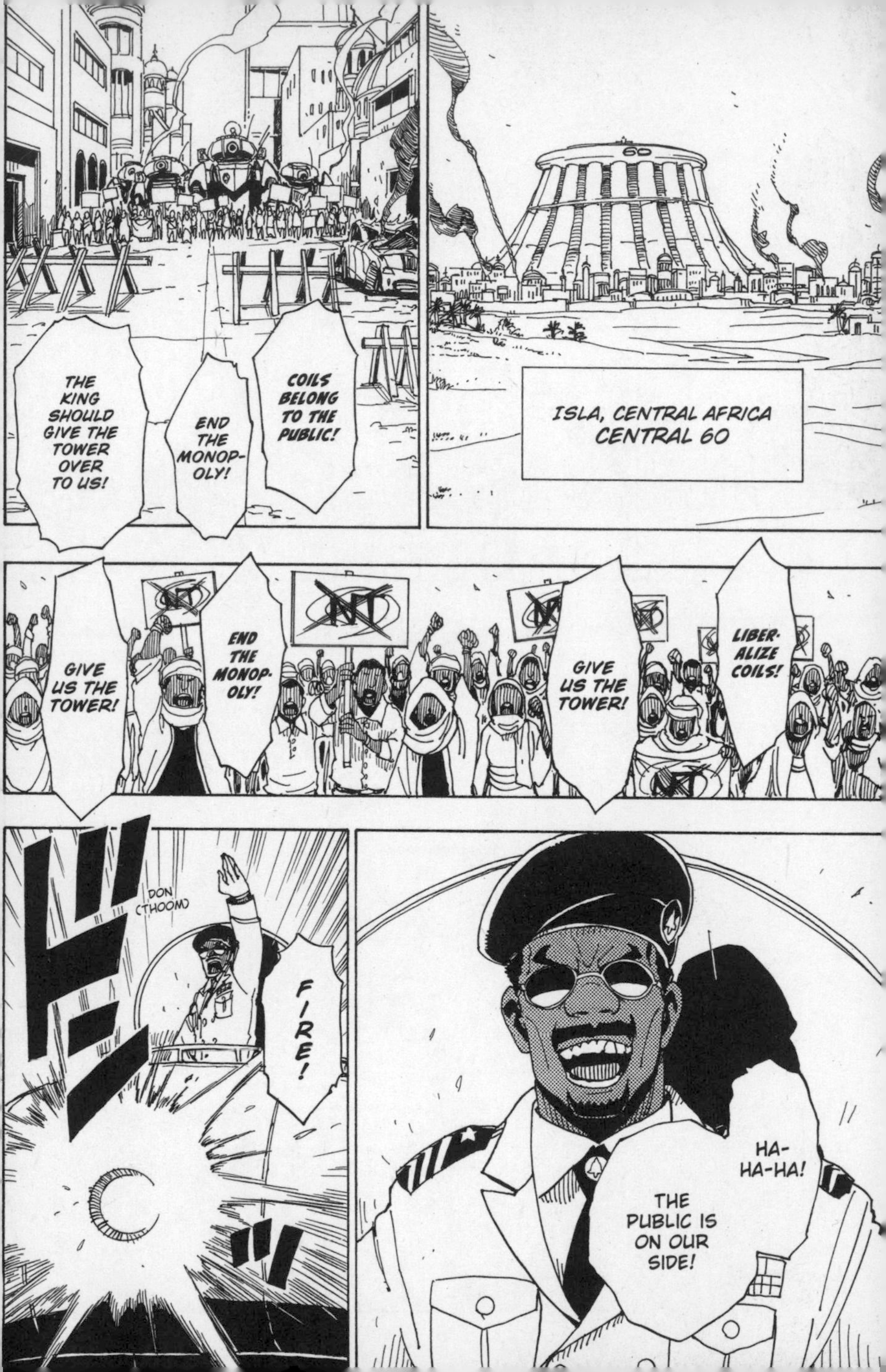
ISLA, CENTRAL AFRICA
CENTRAL 60
COILS BELONG TO THE PUBLIC!
END THE MONOPOLY!
THE KING SHOULD GIVE THE TOWER OVER TO US!
LIBERALIZE COILS!
GIVE US THE TOWER!
END THE MONOPOLY!
GIVE US THE TOWER!
HA-HA-HA!
THE PUBLIC IS ON OUR SIDE!
FIRE!
DON (THOOM)

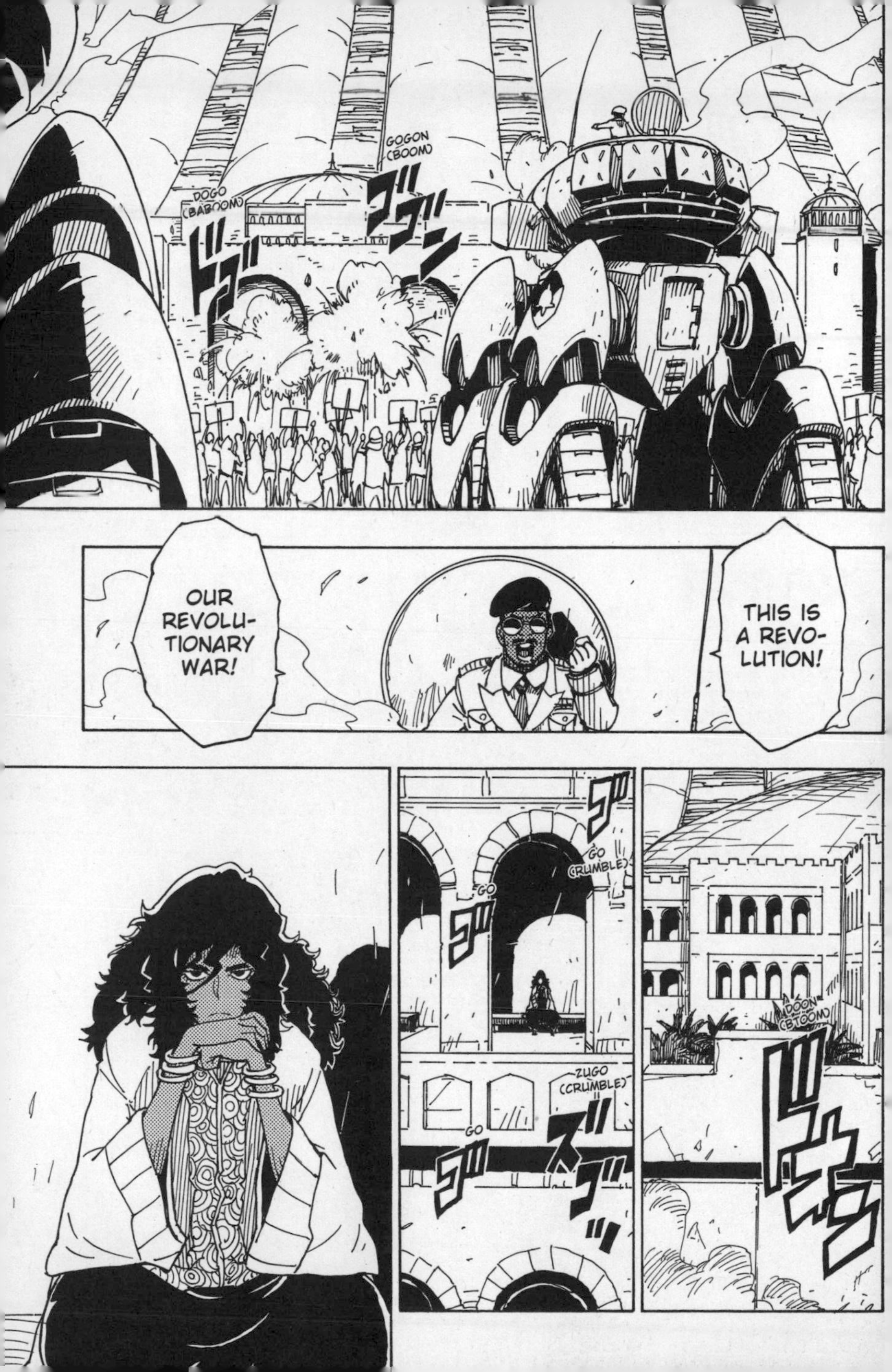
GOGON (BOOM)
DOGO (BABOOM)
THIS IS A REVOLUTION!
OUR REVOLUTIONARY WAR!
DOON (BTOOM)
GO (CRUMBLE)
GO
ZUGO (CRUMBLE)
GO

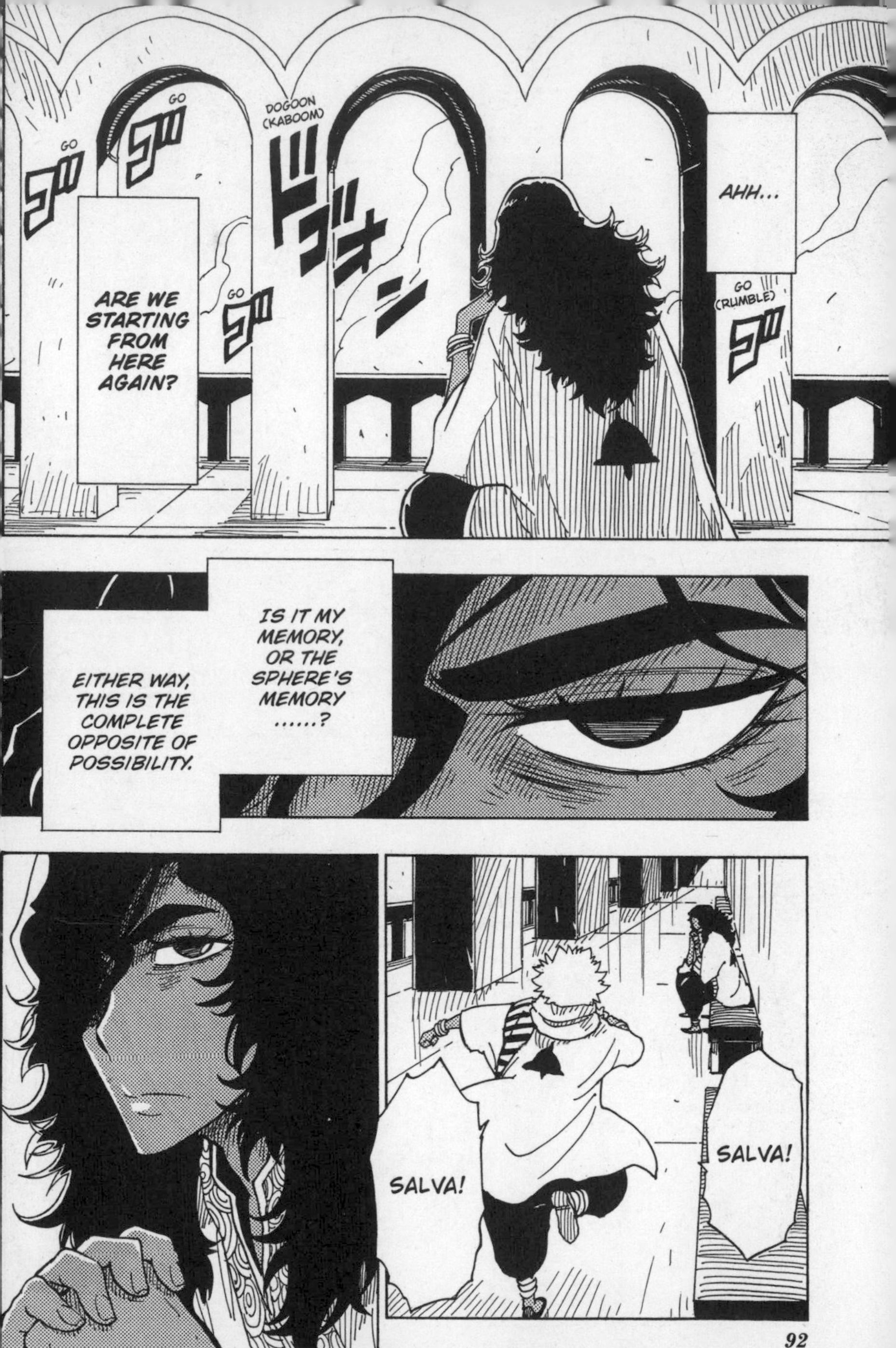
AHH...
GO (RUMBLE)
DOGOON (KABOOM)
GO
GO
ARE WE STARTING FROM HERE AGAIN?
GO
IS IT MY MEMORY, OR THE SPHERE'S MEMORY ......?
EITHER WAY, THIS IS THE COMPLETE OPPOSITE OF POSSIBILITY.
SALVA!
SALVA!

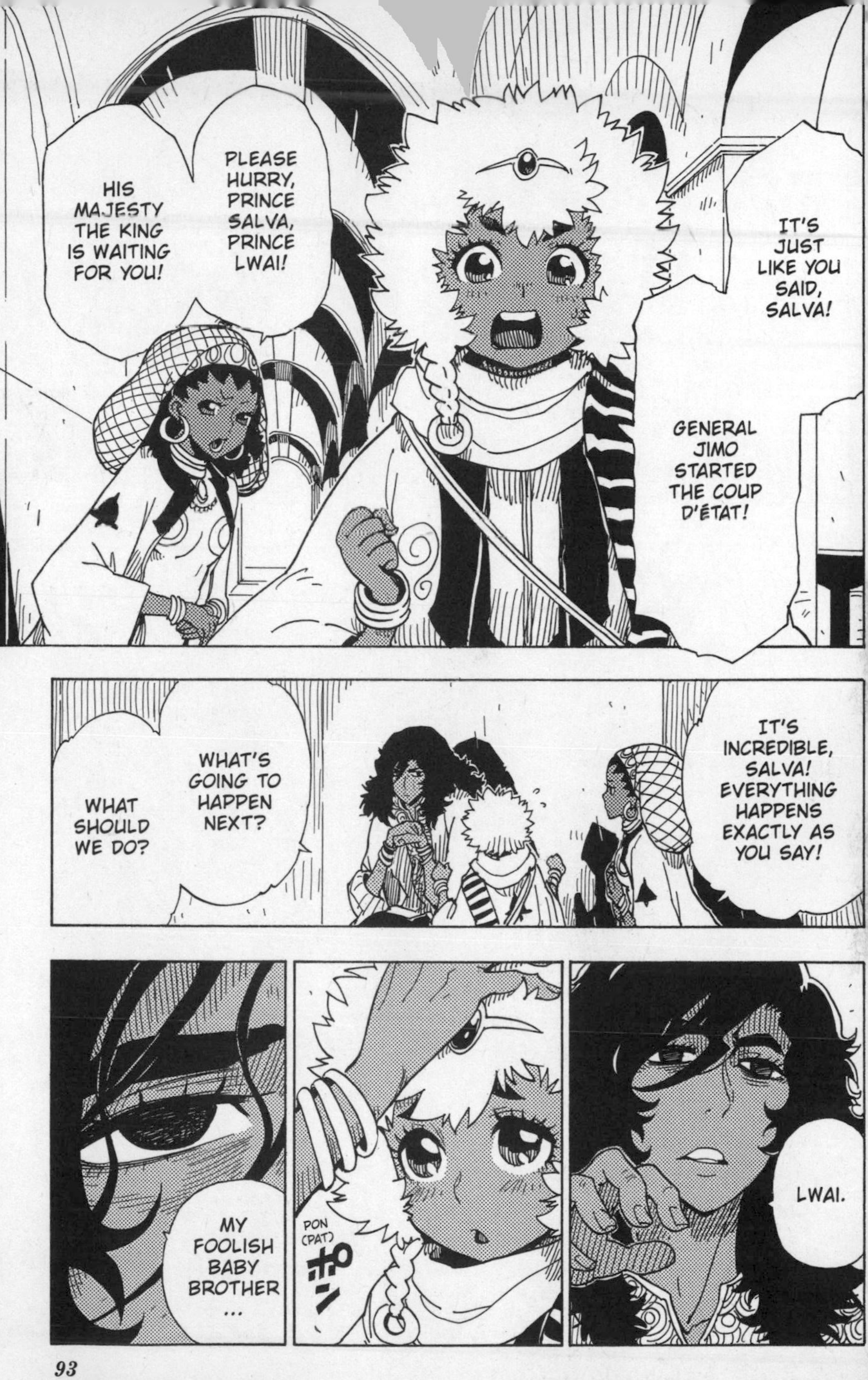

IT'S JUST LIKE YOU SAID, SALVA!
GENERAL JIMO STARTED THE COUP D'ÉTAT!
PLEASE HURRY, PRINCE SALVA, PRINCE LWAI!
HIS MAJESTY THE KING IS WAITING FOR YOU!
IT'S INCREDIBLE, SALVA! EVERYTHING HAPPENS EXACTLY AS YOU SAY!
WHAT'S GOING TO HAPPEN NEXT?
WHAT SHOULD WE DO?
LWAI.
PON (PAT)
MY FOOLISH BABY BROTHER ...

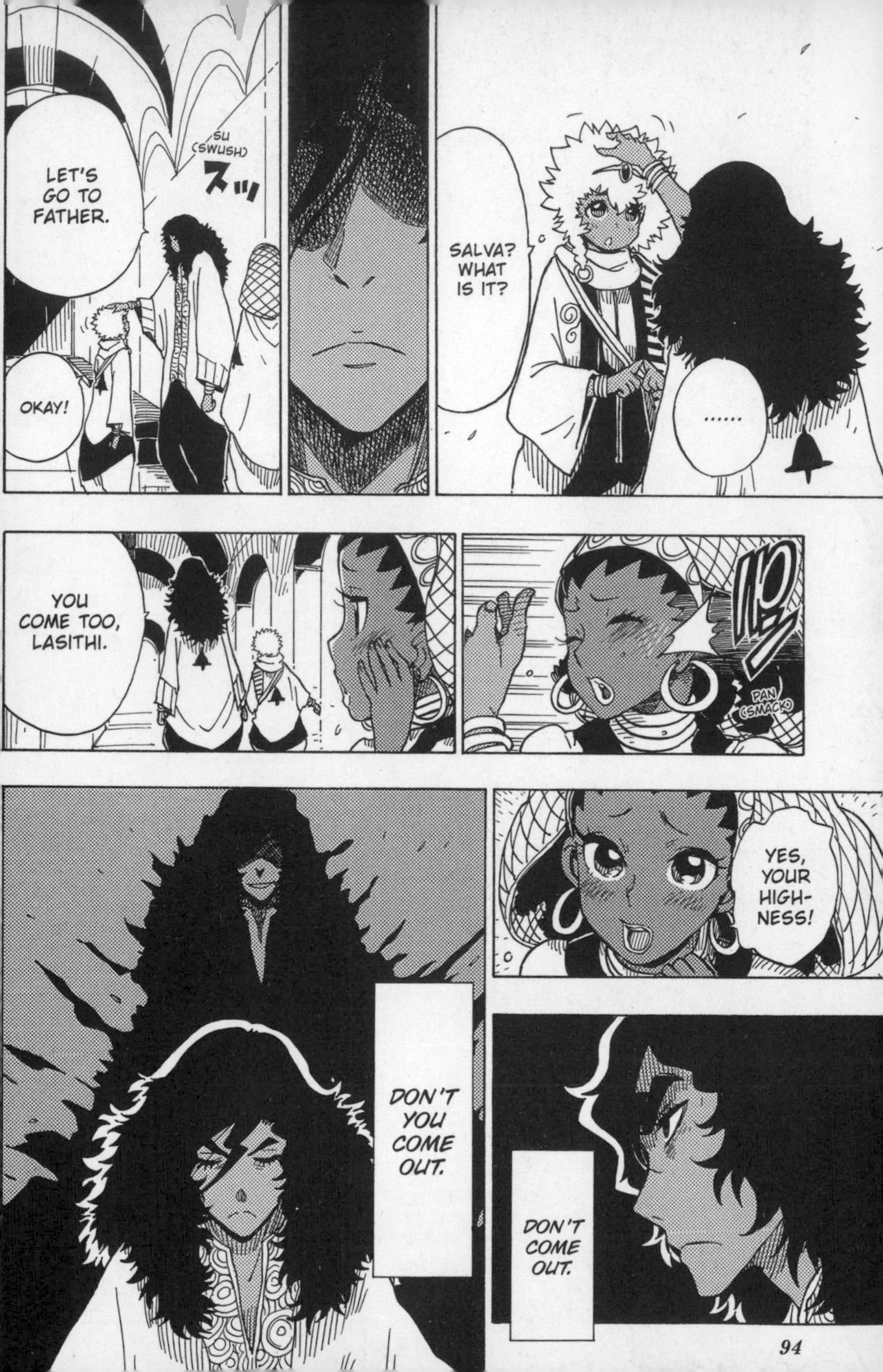
SALVA? WHAT IS IT?
......
SU (SWUSH)
スッ
LET'S GO TO FATHER.
OKAY!
PAN (SMACK)
YOU COME TOO, LASITHI.
YES, YOUR HIGH-NESS!
DON'T COME OUT.
DON'T YOU COME OUT.

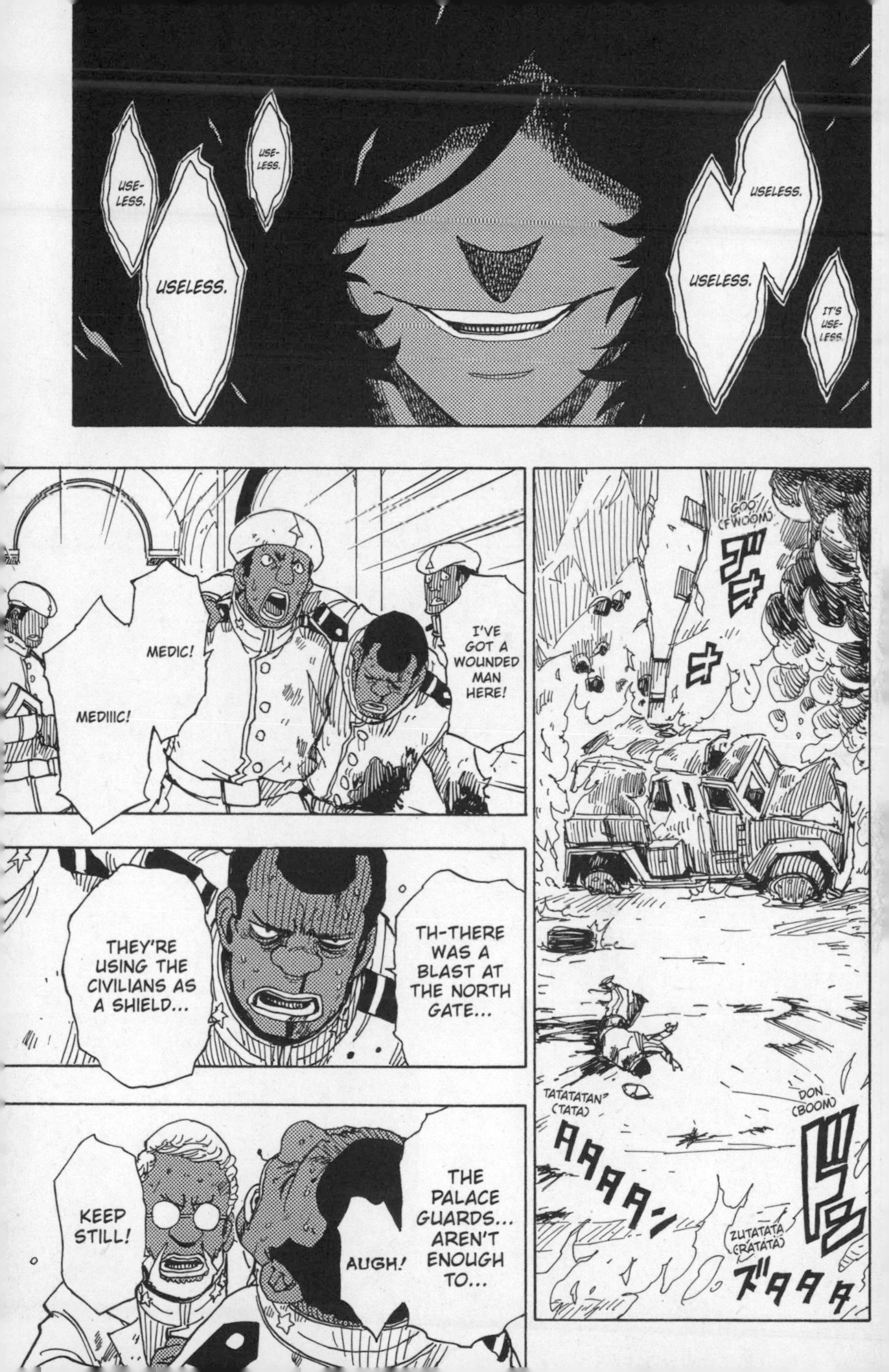
USELESS.
USELESS.
IT'S USE-LESS.
USE-LESS.
USE-LESS.
USELESS.
GOO (FWOOM)
DON (BOOM)
TATATATAN (TATA)
ZUTATATA (RATATA)
I'VE GOT A WOUNDED MAN HERE!
MEDIC!
MEDIIIC!
TH-THERE WAS A BLAST AT THE NORTH GATE...
THEY'RE USING THE CIVILIANS AS A SHIELD...
THE PALACE GUARDS... AREN'T ENOUGH TO...
AUGH!
KEEP STILL!

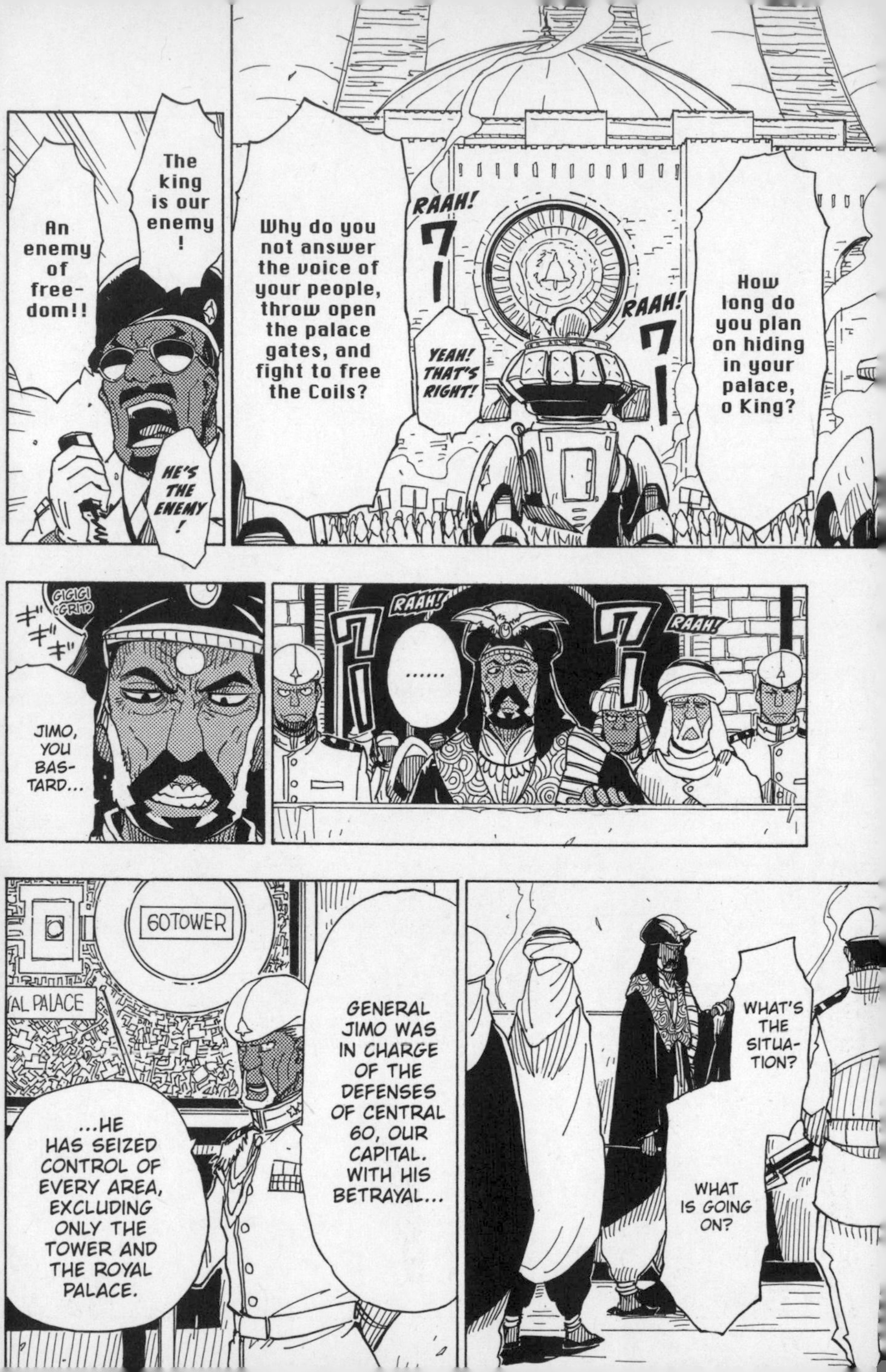
How long do you plan on hiding in your palace, o King?
RAAH!
YEAH! THAT'S RIGHT!
RAAH!
Why do you not answer the voice of your people, throw open the palace gates, and fight to free the Coils?
The king is our enemy!
An enemy of free-dom!!
HE'S THE ENEMY!
RAAH!
RAAH!
......
GIGIGI (GRIT)
JIMO, YOU BAS-TARD...
WHAT'S THE SITUA-TION?
WHAT IS GOING ON?
60TOWER
YAL PALACE
GENERAL JIMO WAS IN CHARGE OF THE DEFENSES OF CENTRAL 60, OUR CAPITAL. WITH HIS BETRAYAL...
...HE HAS SEIZED CONTROL OF EVERY AREA, EXCLUDING ONLY THE TOWER AND THE ROYAL PALACE.

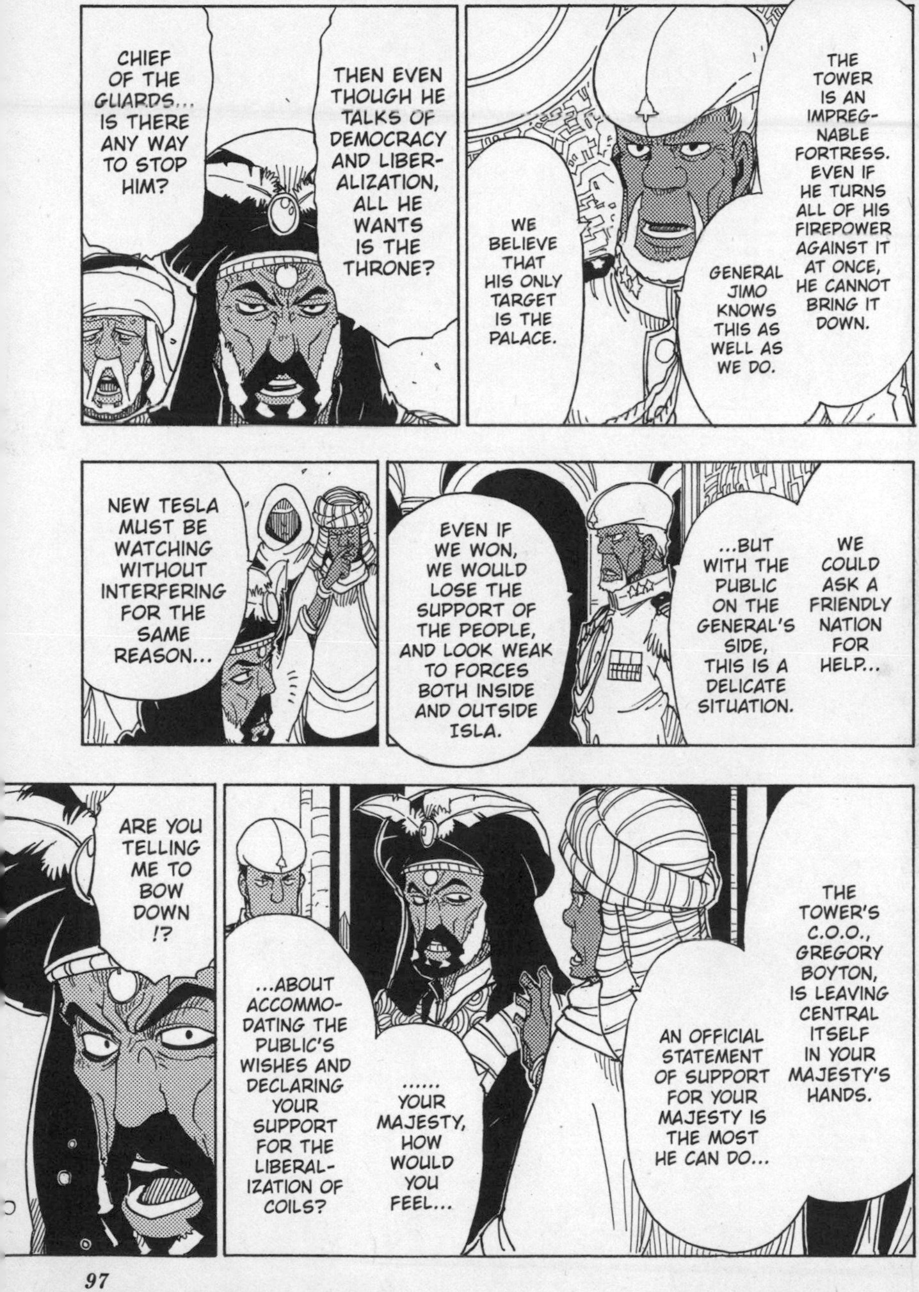
THE TOWER IS AN IMPREGNABLE FORTRESS. EVEN IF HE TURNS ALL OF HIS FIREPOWER AGAINST IT AT ONCE, HE CANNOT BRING IT DOWN.
GENERAL JIMO KNOWS THIS AS WELL AS WE DO.
WE BELIEVE THAT HIS ONLY TARGET IS THE PALACE.
THEN EVEN THOUGH HE TALKS OF DEMOCRACY AND LIBERALIZATION, ALL HE WANTS IS THE THRONE?
CHIEF OF THE GUARDS... IS THERE ANY WAY TO STOP HIM?
WE COULD ASK A FRIENDLY NATION FOR HELP...
...BUT WITH THE PUBLIC ON THE GENERAL'S SIDE, THIS IS A DELICATE SITUATION.
EVEN IF WE WON, WE WOULD LOSE THE SUPPORT OF THE PEOPLE, AND LOOK WEAK TO FORCES BOTH INSIDE AND OUTSIDE ISLA.
NEW TESLA MUST BE WATCHING WITHOUT INTERFERING FOR THE SAME REASON...
THE TOWER'S C.O.O., GREGORY BOYTON, IS LEAVING CENTRAL ITSELF IN YOUR MAJESTY'S HANDS.
AN OFFICIAL STATEMENT OF SUPPORT FOR YOUR MAJESTY IS THE MOST HE CAN DO...
......YOUR MAJESTY, HOW WOULD YOU FEEL...
...ABOUT ACCOMMODATING THE PUBLIC'S WISHES AND DECLARING YOUR SUPPORT FOR THE LIBERALIZATION OF COILS?
ARE YOU TELLING ME TO BOW DOWN!?

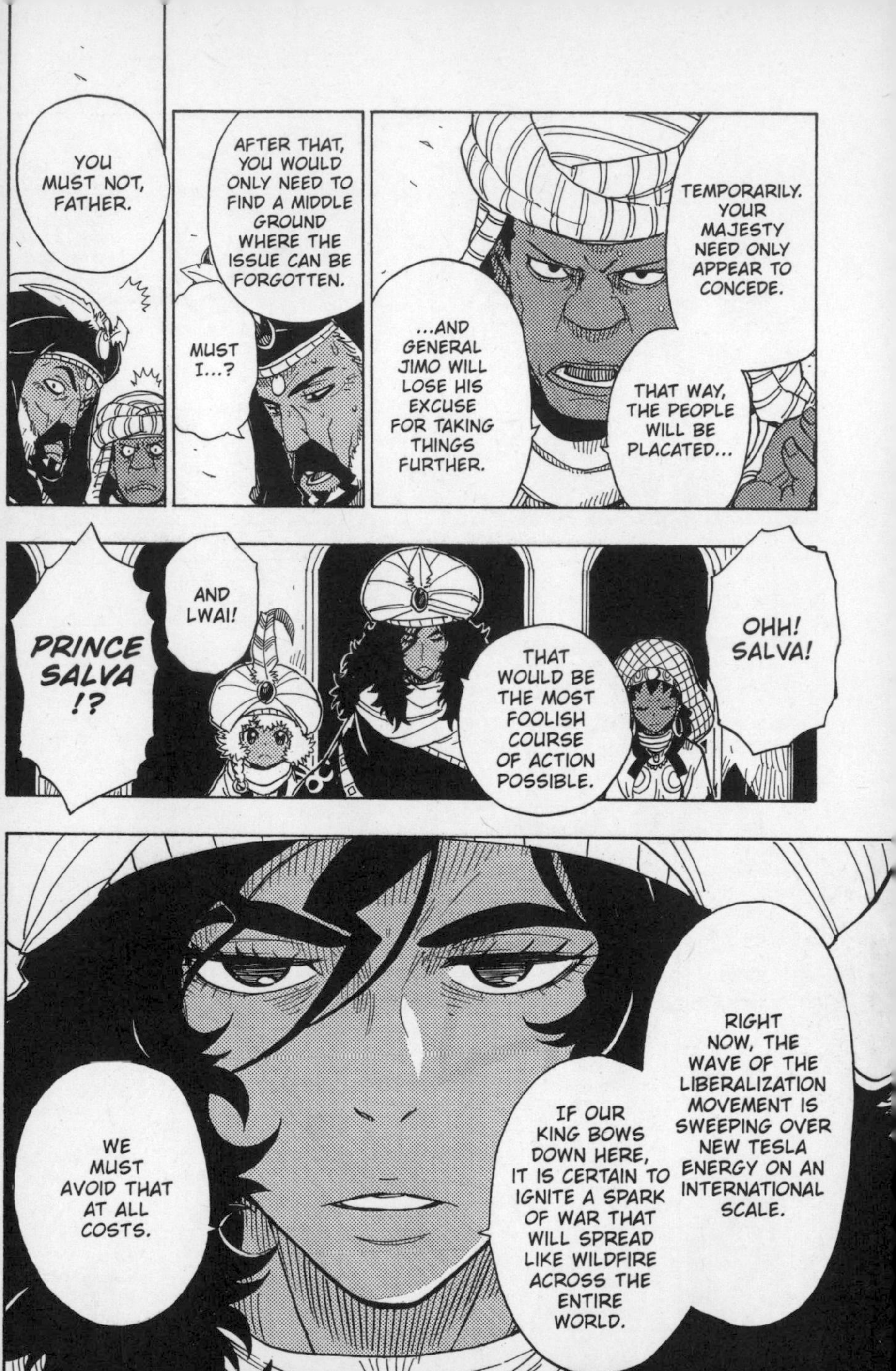
TEMPORARILY. YOUR MAJESTY NEED ONLY APPEAR TO CONCEDE.
THAT WAY, THE PEOPLE WILL BE PLACATED...
...AND GENERAL JIMO WILL LOSE HIS EXCUSE FOR TAKING THINGS FURTHER.
AFTER THAT, YOU WOULD ONLY NEED TO FIND A MIDDLE GROUND WHERE THE ISSUE CAN BE FORGOTTEN.
MUST I...?
YOU MUST NOT, FATHER.
OHH! SALVA!
THAT WOULD BE THE MOST FOOLISH COURSE OF ACTION POSSIBLE.
AND LWAI!
PRINCE SALVA !?
RIGHT NOW, THE WAVE OF THE LIBERALIZATION MOVEMENT IS SWEEPING OVER NEW TESLA ENERGY ON AN INTERNATIONAL SCALE.
IF OUR KING BOWS DOWN HERE, IT IS CERTAIN TO IGNITE A SPARK OF WAR THAT WILL SPREAD LIKE WILDFIRE ACROSS THE ENTIRE WORLD.
WE MUST AVOID THAT AT ALL COSTS.

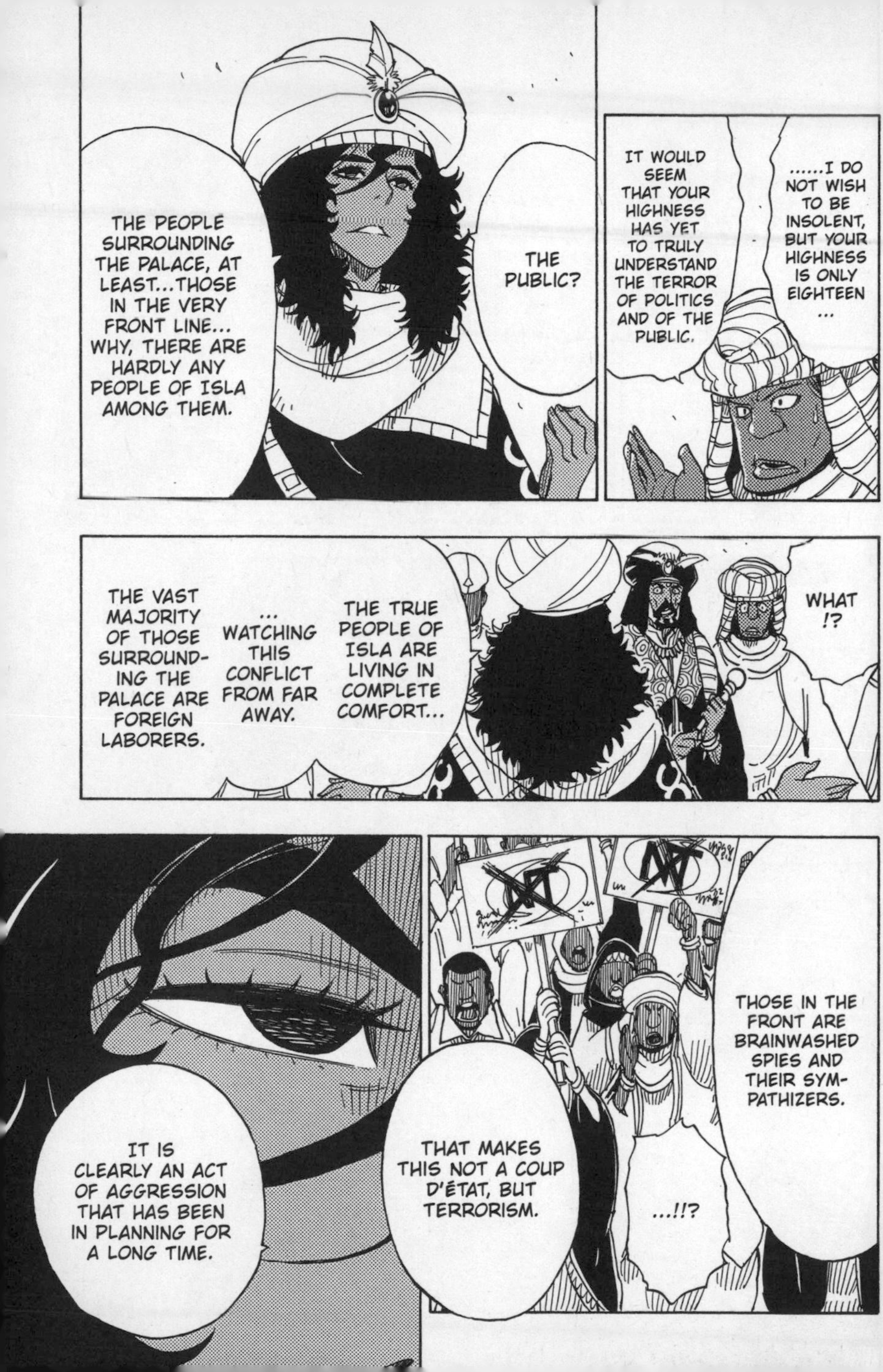
......I DO NOT WISH TO BE INSOLENT, BUT YOUR HIGHNESS IS ONLY EIGHTEEN ...
IT WOULD SEEM THAT YOUR HIGHNESS HAS YET TO TRULY UNDERSTAND THE TERROR OF POLITICS AND OF THE PUBLIC.
THE PUBLIC?
THE PEOPLE SURROUNDING THE PALACE, AT LEAST...THOSE IN THE VERY FRONT LINE... WHY, THERE ARE HARDLY ANY PEOPLE OF ISLA AMONG THEM.
WHAT !?
THE TRUE PEOPLE OF ISLA ARE LIVING IN COMPLETE COMFORT...
... WATCHING THIS CONFLICT FROM FAR AWAY.
THE VAST MAJORITY OF THOSE SURROUNDING THE PALACE ARE FOREIGN LABORERS.
THOSE IN THE FRONT ARE BRAINWASHED SPIES AND THEIR SYMPATHIZERS.
...!!?
IT IS CLEARLY AN ACT OF AGGRESSION THAT HAS BEEN IN PLANNING FOR A LONG TIME.
THAT MAKES THIS NOT A COUP D'ÉTAT, BUT TERRORISM.

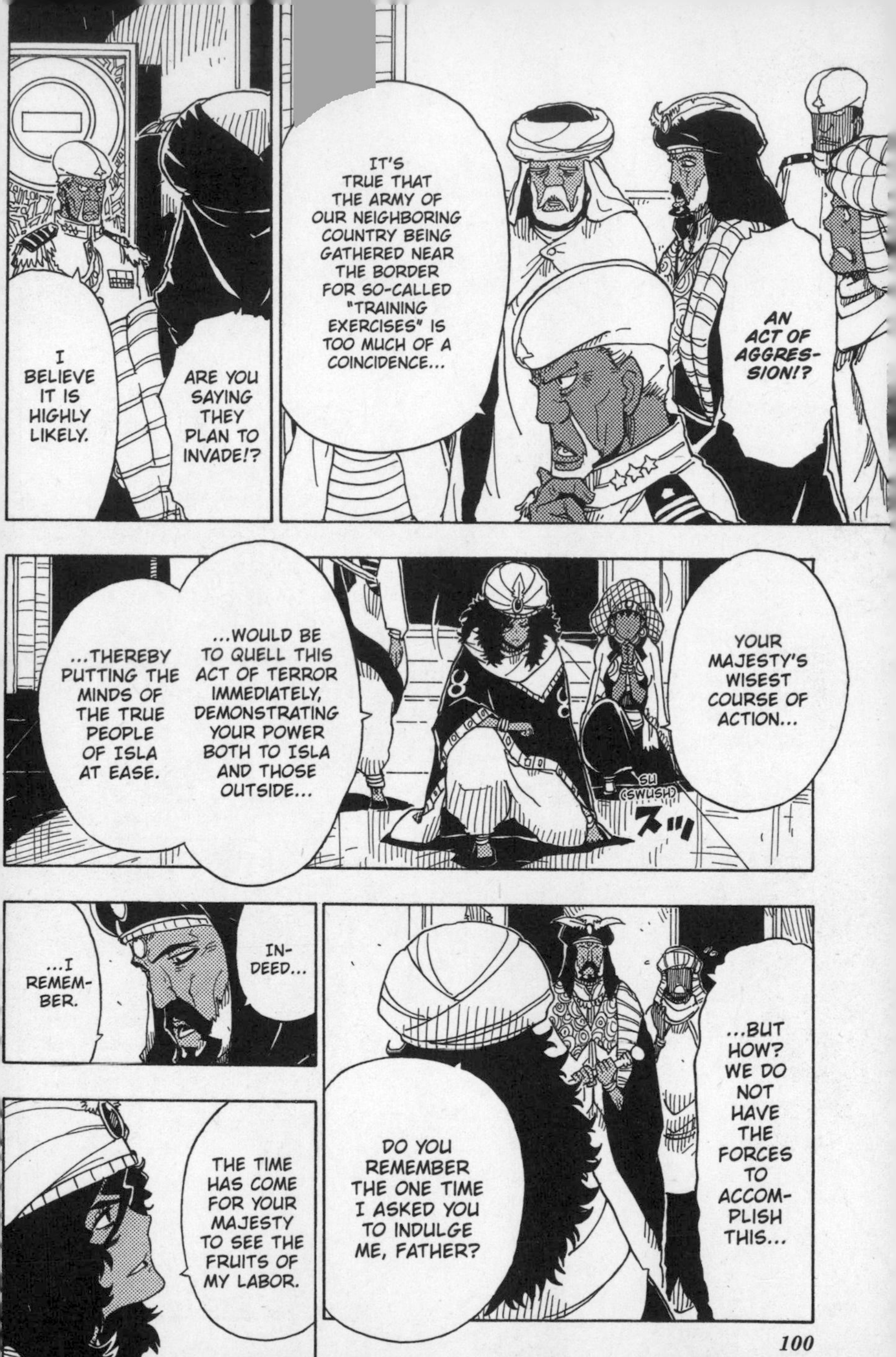
IT'S TRUE THAT THE ARMY OF OUR NEIGHBORING COUNTRY BEING GATHERED NEAR THE BORDER FOR SO-CALLED "TRAINING EXERCISES" IS TOO MUCH OF A COINCIDENCE...
AN ACT OF AGGRESSION!?
ARE YOU SAYING THEY PLAN TO INVADE!?
I BELIEVE IT IS HIGHLY LIKELY.
YOUR MAJESTY'S WISEST COURSE OF ACTION...
SU (SWUSH)
ズッ
...WOULD BE TO QUELL THIS ACT OF TERROR IMMEDIATELY, DEMONSTRATING YOUR POWER BOTH TO ISLA AND THOSE OUTSIDE...
...THEREBY PUTTING THE MINDS OF THE TRUE PEOPLE OF ISLA AT EASE.
...BUT HOW? WE DO NOT HAVE THE FORCES TO ACCOMPLISH THIS...
DO YOU REMEMBER THE ONE TIME I ASKED YOU TO INDULGE ME, FATHER?
IN-DEED...
...I REMEMBER.
THE TIME HAS COME FOR YOUR MAJESTY TO SEE THE FRUITS OF MY LABOR.

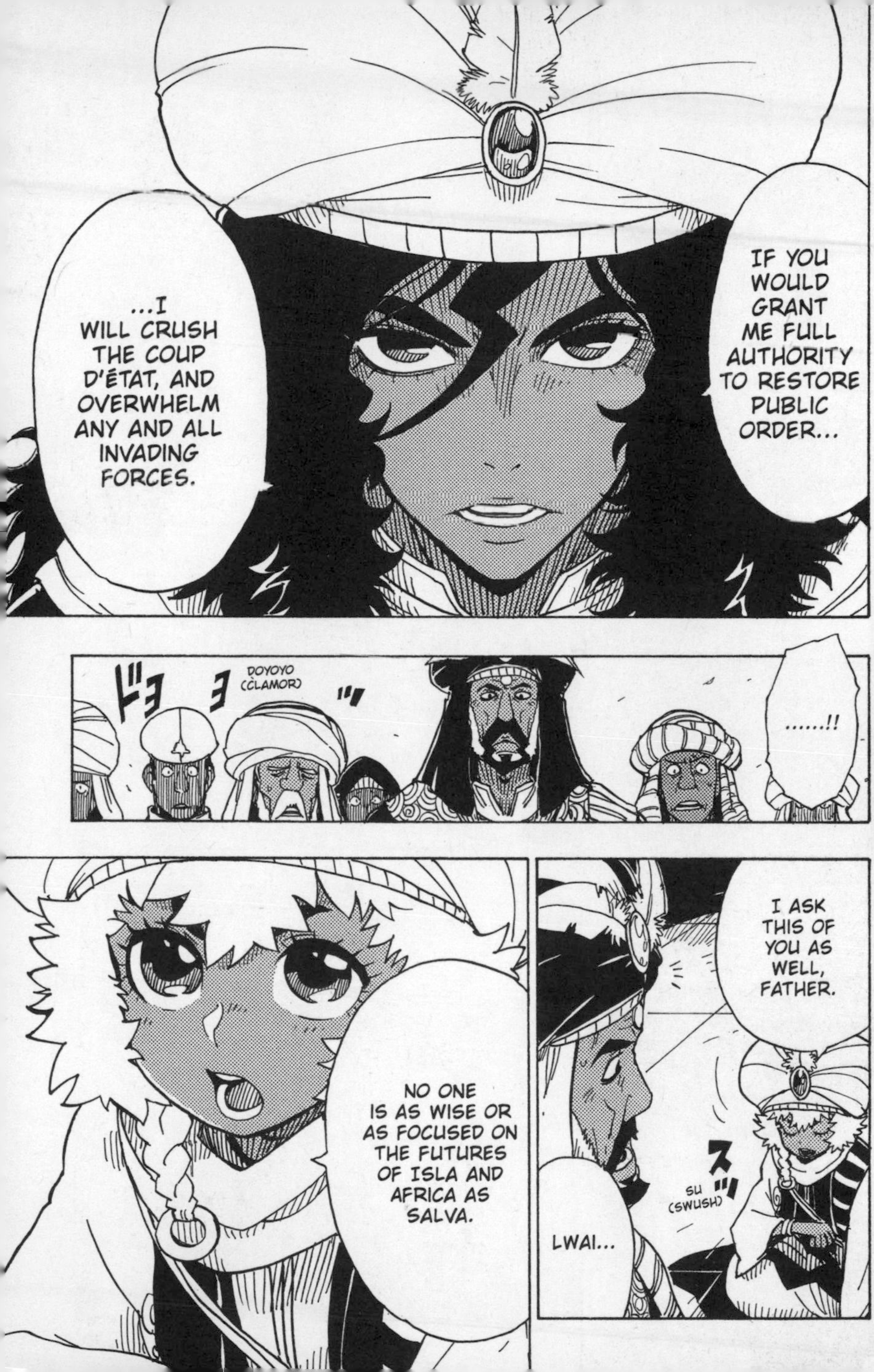
IF YOU WOULD GRANT ME FULL AUTHORITY TO RESTORE PUBLIC ORDER...
...I WILL CRUSH THE COUP D'ÉTAT, AND OVERWHELM ANY AND ALL INVADING FORCES.
......!!
DOYOYO (CLAMOR)
I ASK THIS OF YOU AS WELL, FATHER.
SU (SWUSH)
LWAI...
NO ONE IS AS WISE OR AS FOCUSED ON THE FUTURES OF ISLA AND AFRICA AS SALVA.

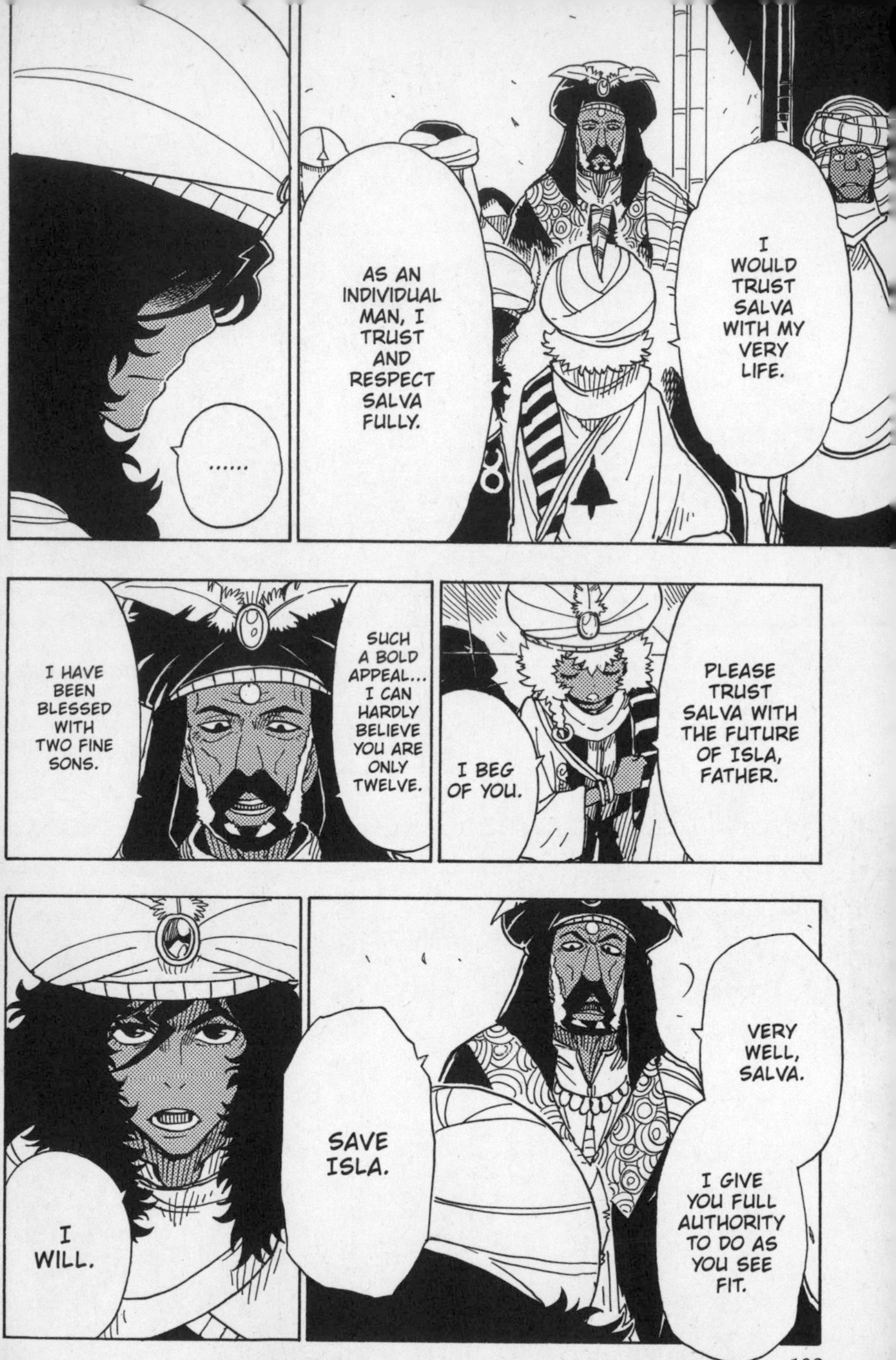
I WOULD TRUST SALVA WITH MY VERY LIFE.
AS AN INDIVIDUAL MAN, I TRUST AND RESPECT SALVA FULLY.
......
PLEASE TRUST SALVA WITH THE FUTURE OF ISLA, FATHER.
I BEG OF YOU.
SUCH A BOLD APPEAL... I CAN HARDLY BELIEVE YOU ARE ONLY TWELVE.
I HAVE BEEN BLESSED WITH TWO FINE SONS.
VERY WELL, SALVA.
I GIVE YOU FULL AUTHORITY TO DO AS YOU SEE FIT.
SAVE ISLA.
I WILL.

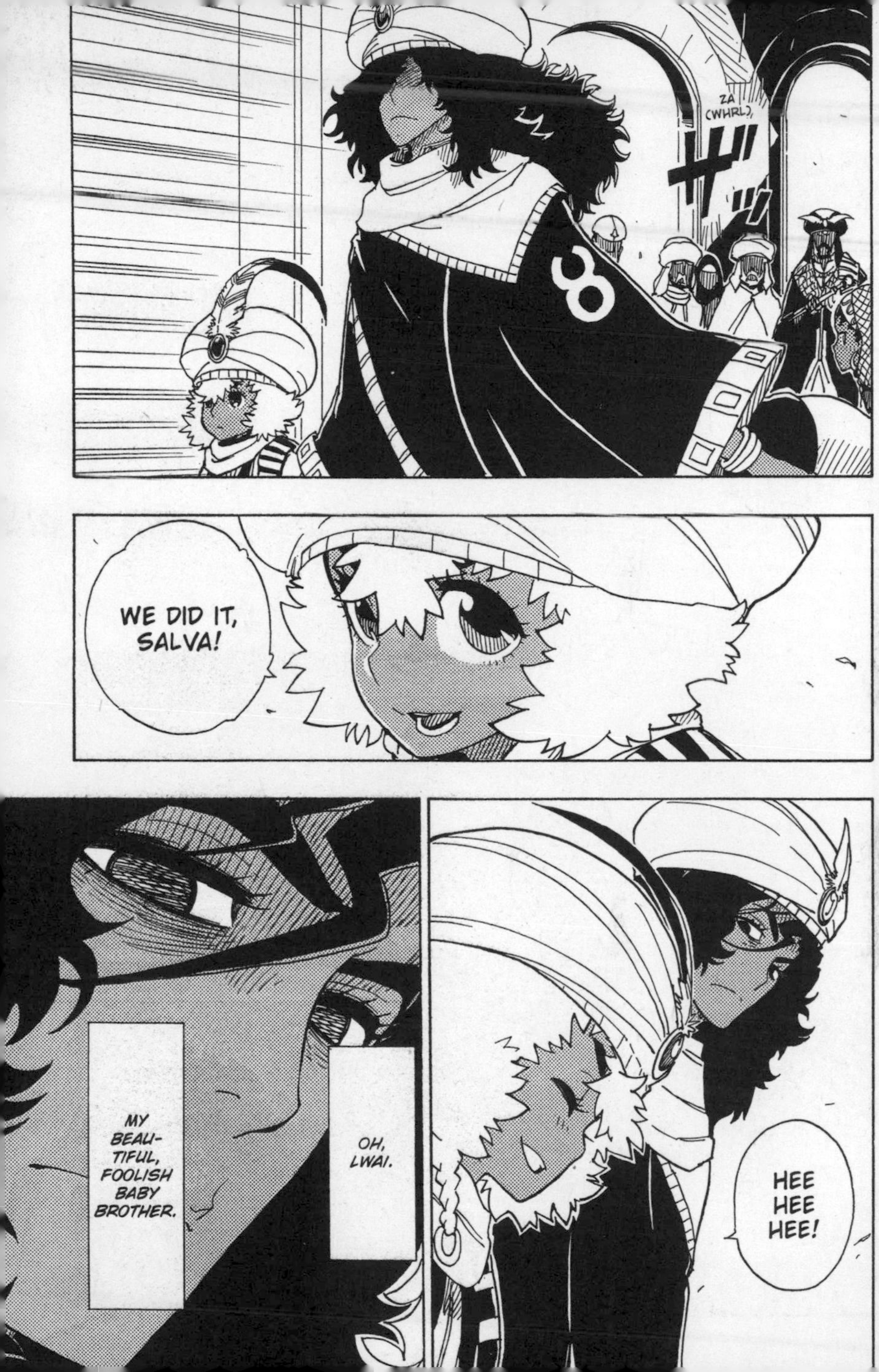
ZA (WHRL)
ザッ
WE DID IT, SALVA!
HEE HEE HEE!
OH, LWAI.
MY BEAUTIFUL, FOOLISH BABY BROTHER.

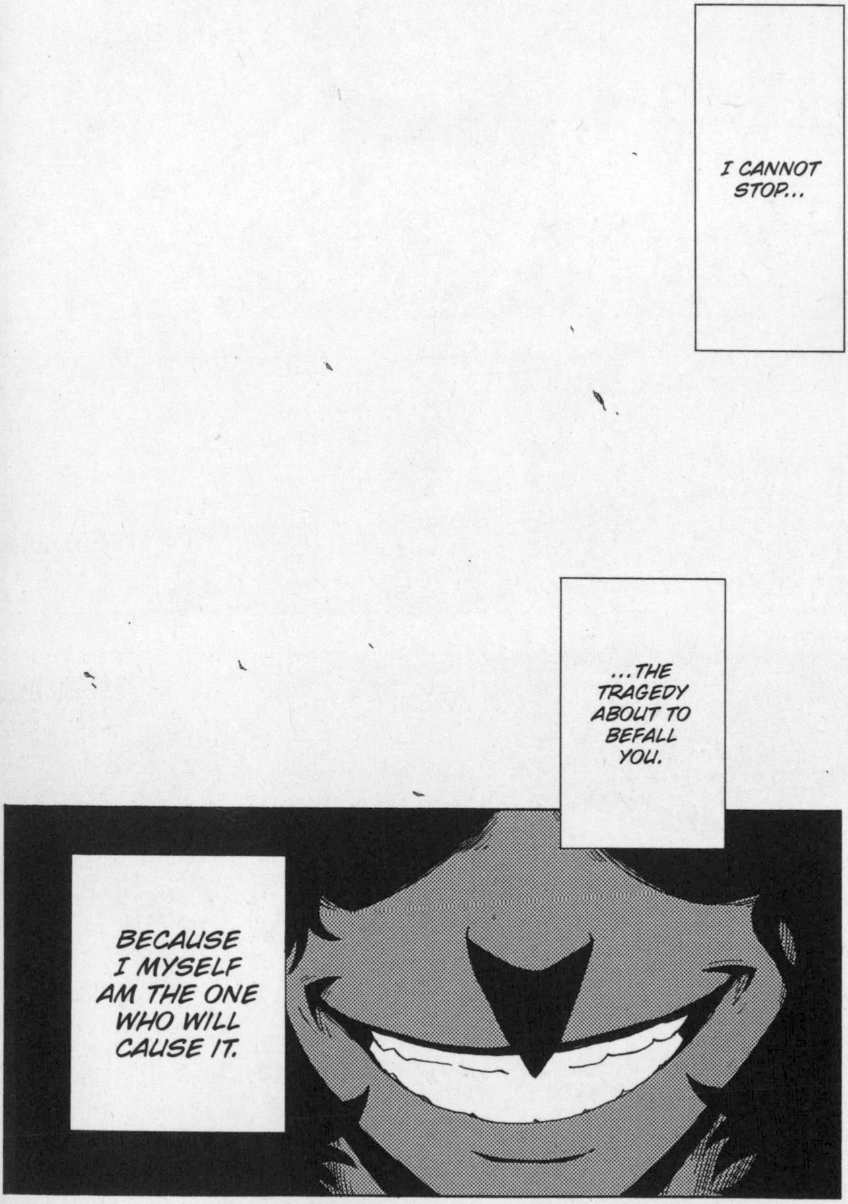
I CANNOT STOP...
...THE TRAGEDY ABOUT TO BEFALL YOU.
BECAUSE I MYSELF AM THE ONE WHO WILL CAUSE IT.

Dimension W

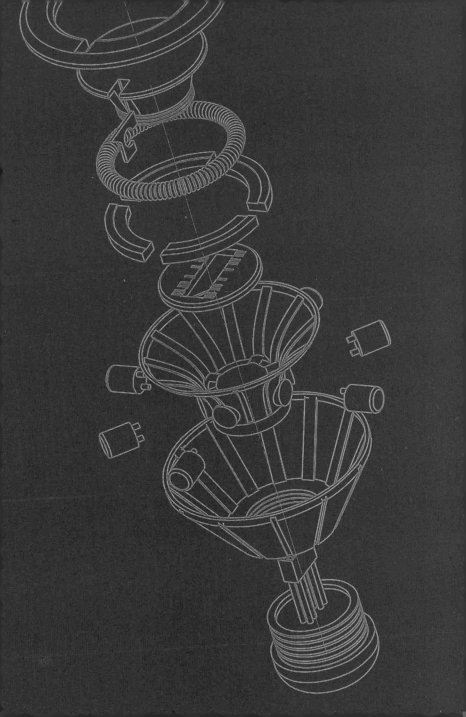

FILE.52
TWO BODIES

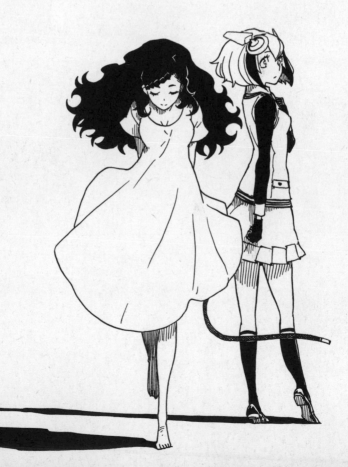

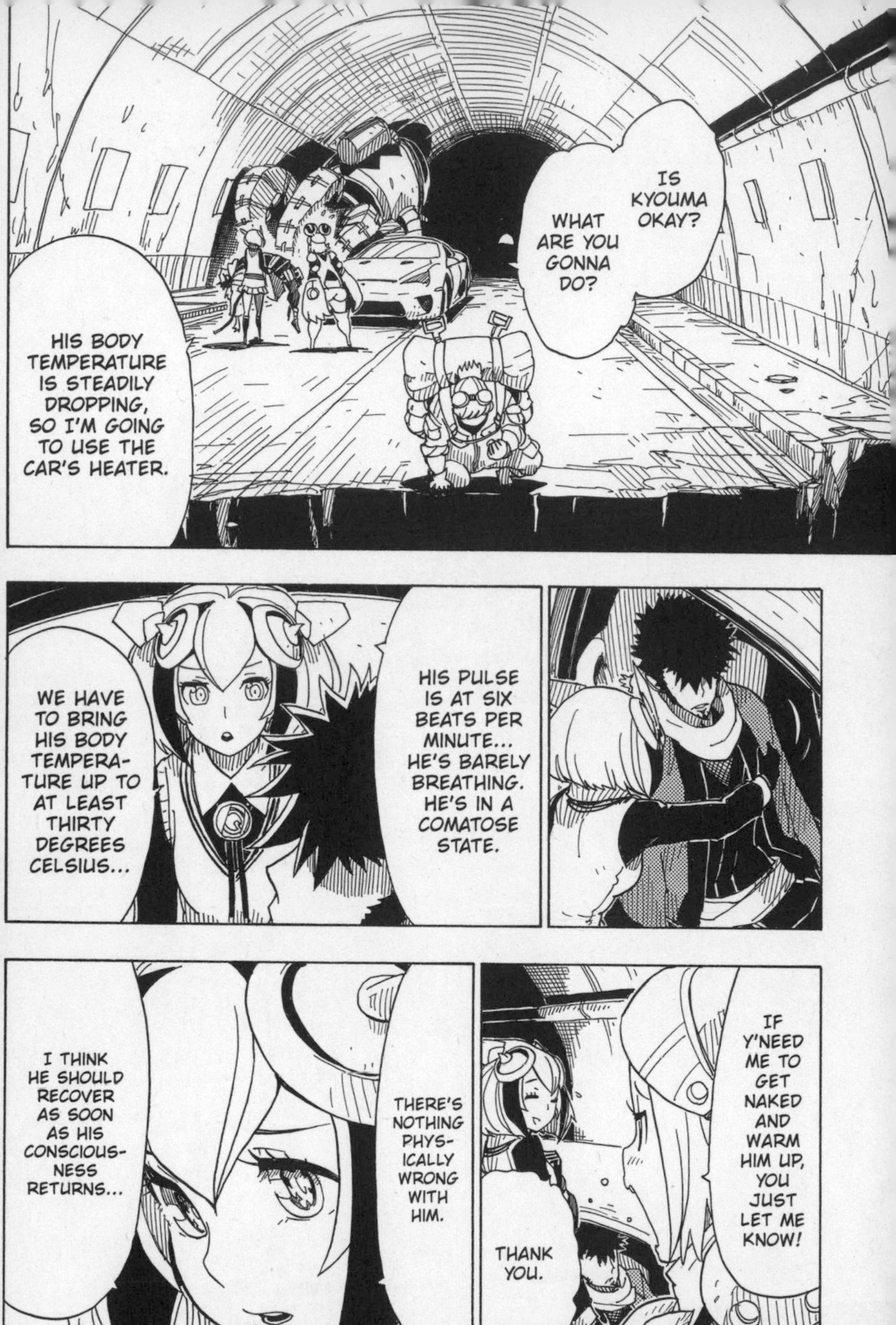
IS KYOUMA OKAY? WHAT ARE YOU GONNA DO?
HIS BODY TEMPERATURE IS STEADILY DROPPING, SO I'M GOING TO USE THE CAR'S HEATER.
HIS PULSE IS AT SIX BEATS PER MINUTE... HE'S BARELY BREATHING. HE'S IN A COMATOSE STATE.
WE HAVE TO BRING HIS BODY TEMPERATURE UP TO AT LEAST THIRTY DEGREES CELSIUS...
IF Y'NEED ME TO GET NAKED AND WARM HIM UP, YOU JUST LET ME KNOW!
THANK YOU.
THERE'S NOTHING PHYSICALLY WRONG WITH HIM.
I THINK HE SHOULD RECOVER AS SOON AS HIS CONSCIOUSNESS RETURNS...

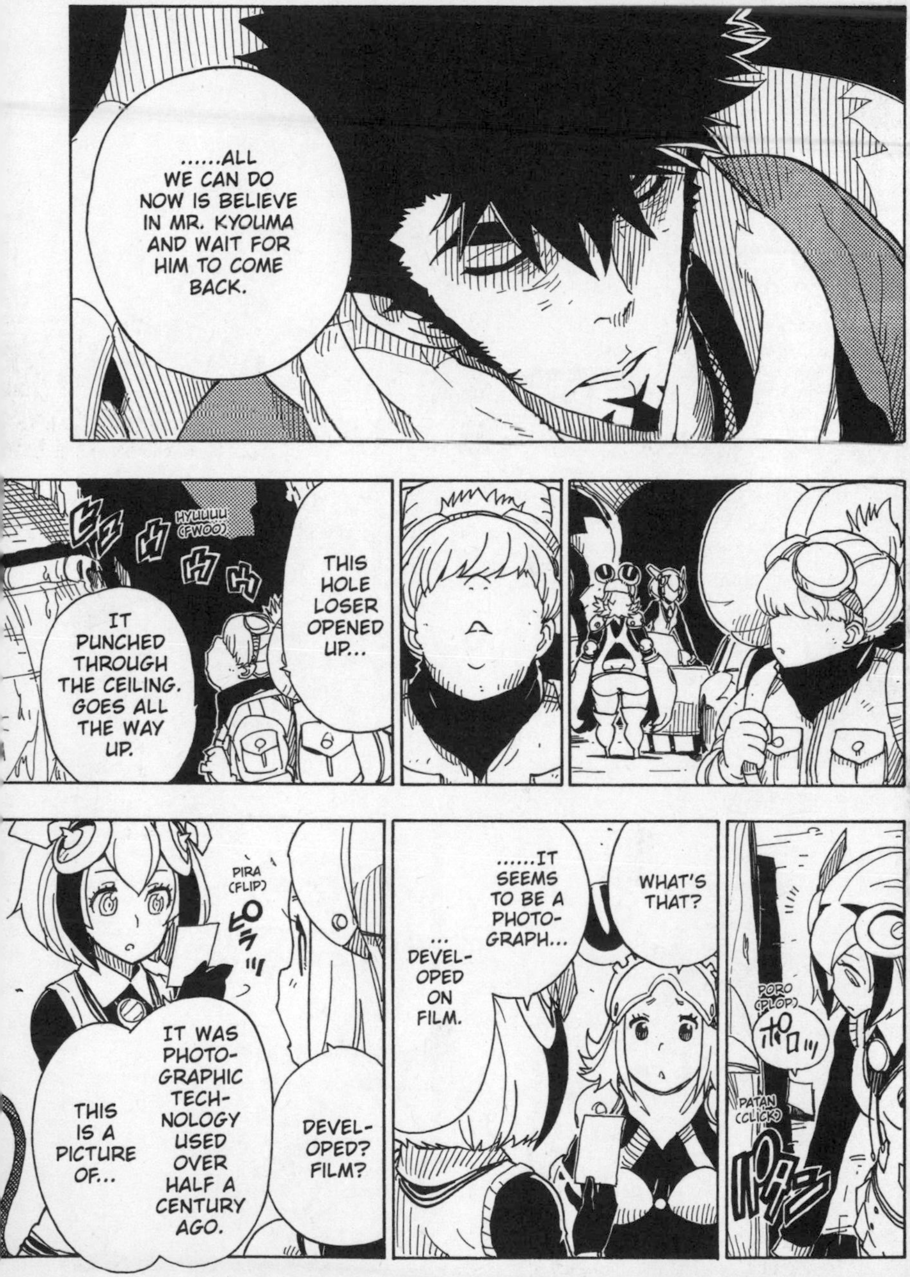
......ALL WE CAN DO NOW IS BELIEVE IN MR. KYOUMA AND WAIT FOR HIM TO COME BACK.
THIS HOLE LOSER OPENED UP...
HYUUUU (FWOO)
IT PUNCHED THROUGH THE CEILING. GOES ALL THE WAY UP.
PORO (PLOP)
PATAN (CLICK)
WHAT'S THAT?
......IT SEEMS TO BE A PHOTO-GRAPH...
... DEVEL-OPED ON FILM.
PIRA (FLIP)
DEVEL-OPED? FILM?
IT WAS PHOTO-GRAPHIC TECH-NOLOGY USED OVER HALF A CENTURY AGO.
THIS IS A PICTURE OF...

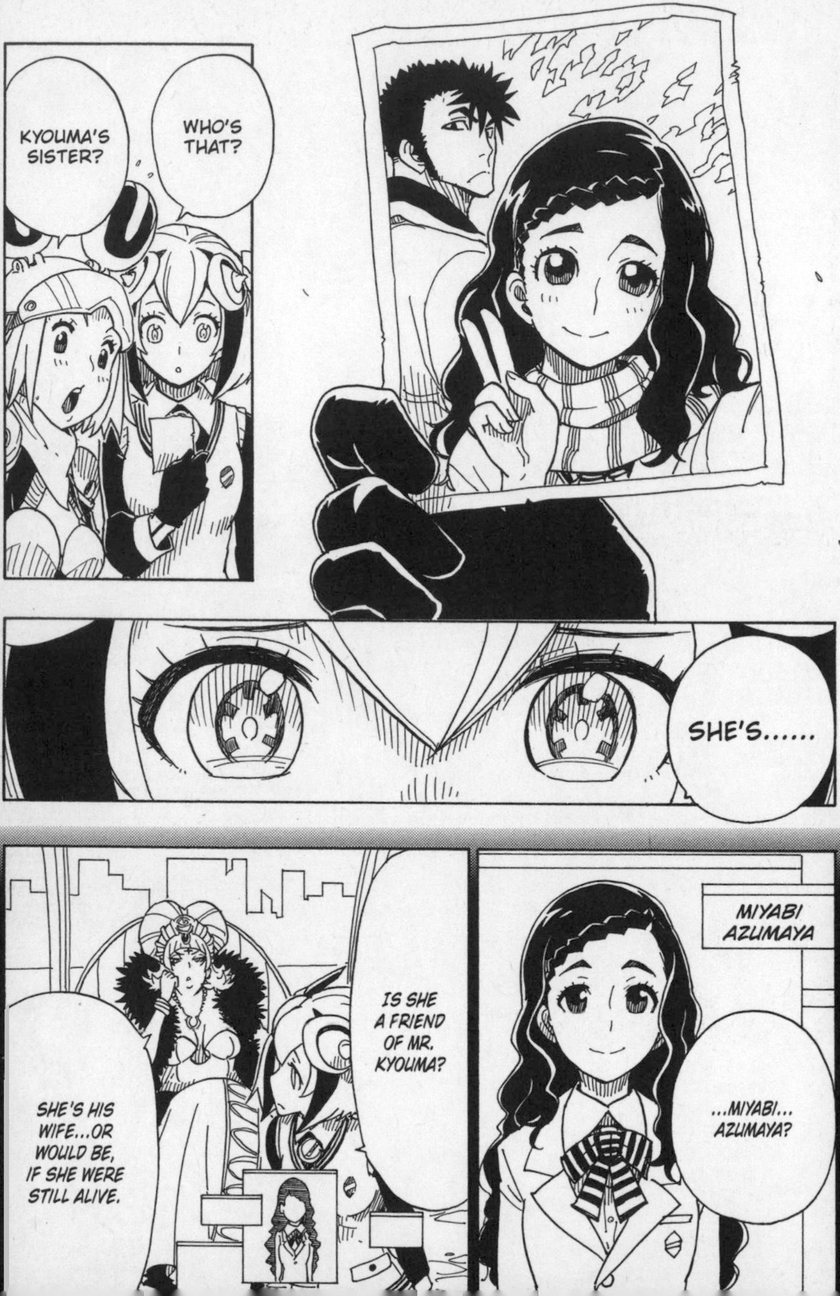
WHO'S THAT?
KYOUMA'S SISTER?
SHE'S......
MIYABI AZUMAYA
...MIYABI... AZUMAYA?
IS SHE A FRIEND OF MR. KYOUMA?
SHE'S HIS WIFE...OR WOULD BE, IF SHE WERE STILL ALIVE.

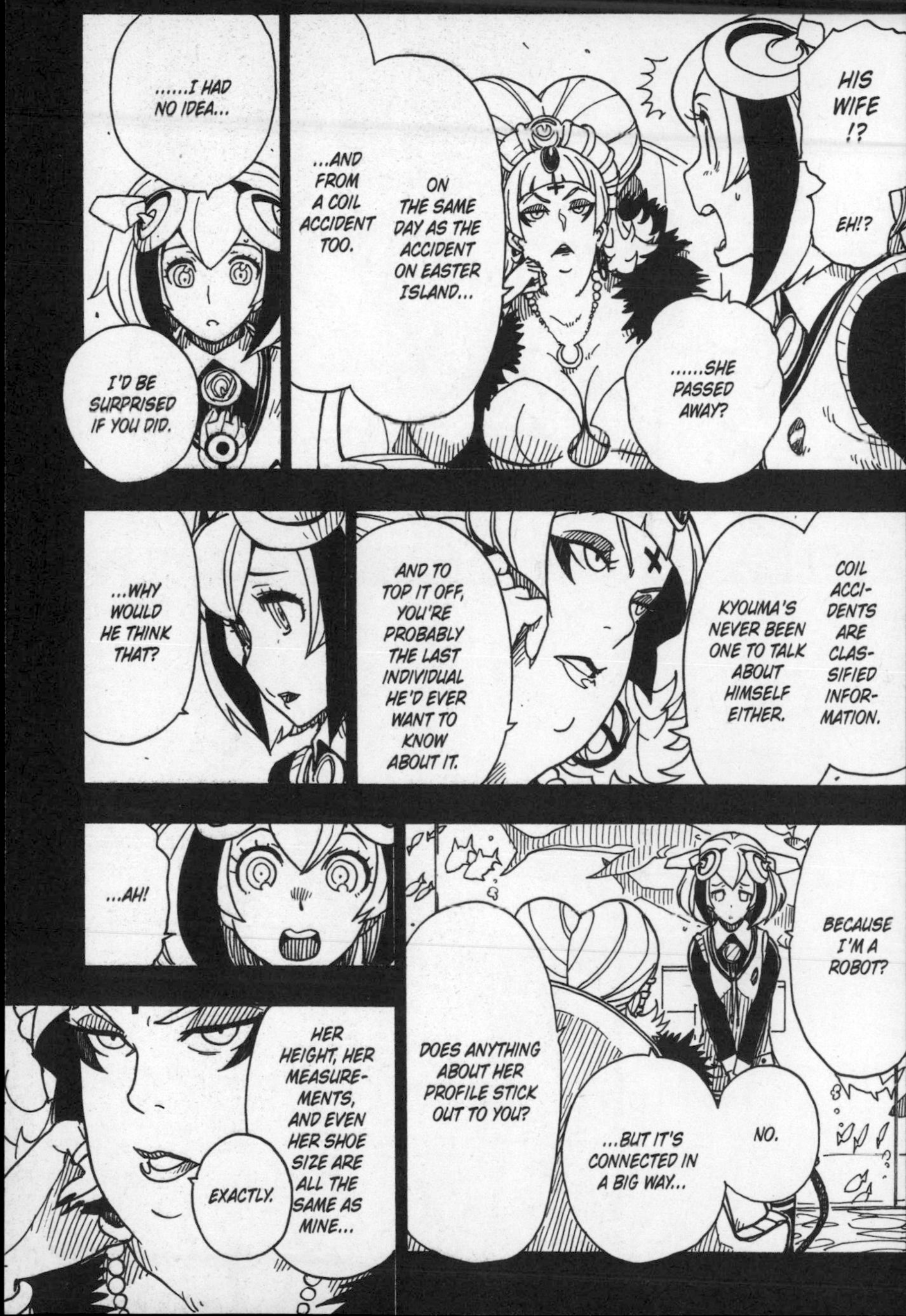
HIS WIFE !?
EH!?
......SHE PASSED AWAY?
ON THE SAME DAY AS THE ACCIDENT ON EASTER ISLAND...
...AND FROM A COIL ACCIDENT TOO.
......I HAD NO IDEA...
I'D BE SURPRISED IF YOU DID.
COIL ACCI-DENTS ARE CLAS-SIFIED INFOR-MATION.
KYOUMA'S NEVER BEEN ONE TO TALK ABOUT HIMSELF EITHER.
AND TO TOP IT OFF, YOU'RE PROBABLY THE LAST INDIVIDUAL HE'D EVER WANT TO KNOW ABOUT IT.
...WHY WOULD HE THINK THAT?
BECAUSE I'M A ROBOT?
NO.
...BUT IT'S CONNECTED IN A BIG WAY...
DOES ANYTHING ABOUT HER PROFILE STICK OUT TO YOU?
...AH!
HER HEIGHT, HER MEASURE-MENTS, AND EVEN HER SHOE SIZE ARE ALL THE SAME AS MINE...
EXACTLY.

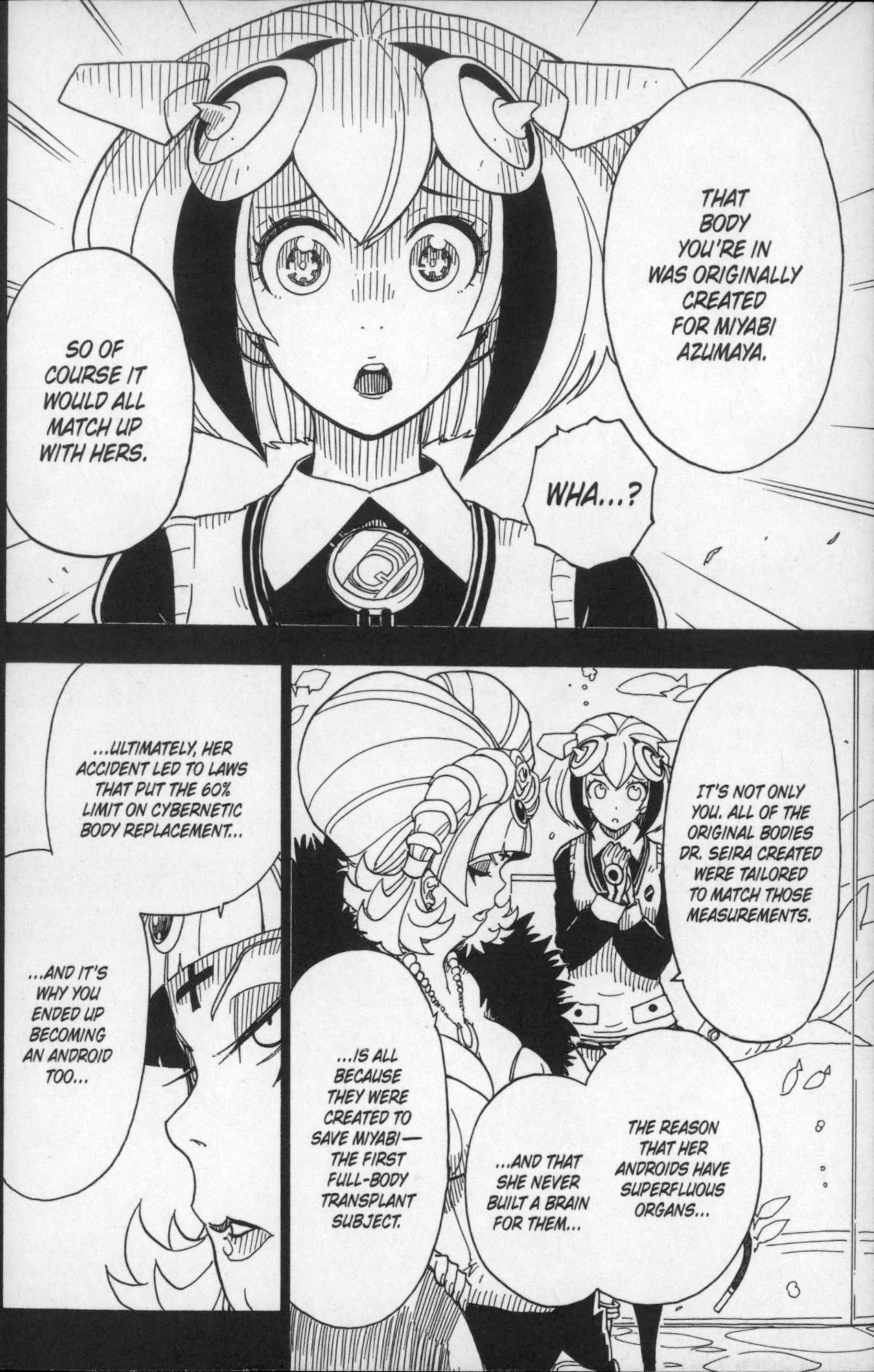
THAT BODY YOU'RE IN WAS ORIGINALLY CREATED FOR MIYABI AZUMAYA.
WHA...?
SO OF COURSE IT WOULD ALL MATCH UP WITH HERS.
IT'S NOT ONLY YOU. ALL OF THE ORIGINAL BODIES DR. SEIRA CREATED WERE TAILORED TO MATCH THOSE MEASUREMENTS.
THE REASON THAT HER ANDROIDS HAVE SUPERFLUOUS ORGANS...
...AND THAT SHE NEVER BUILT A BRAIN FOR THEM...
...IS ALL BECAUSE THEY WERE CREATED TO SAVE MIYABI—THE FIRST FULL-BODY TRANSPLANT SUBJECT.
...ULTIMATELY, HER ACCIDENT LED TO LAWS THAT PUT THE 60% LIMIT ON CYBERNETIC BODY REPLACEMENT...
...AND IT'S WHY YOU ENDED UP BECOMING AN ANDROID TOO...

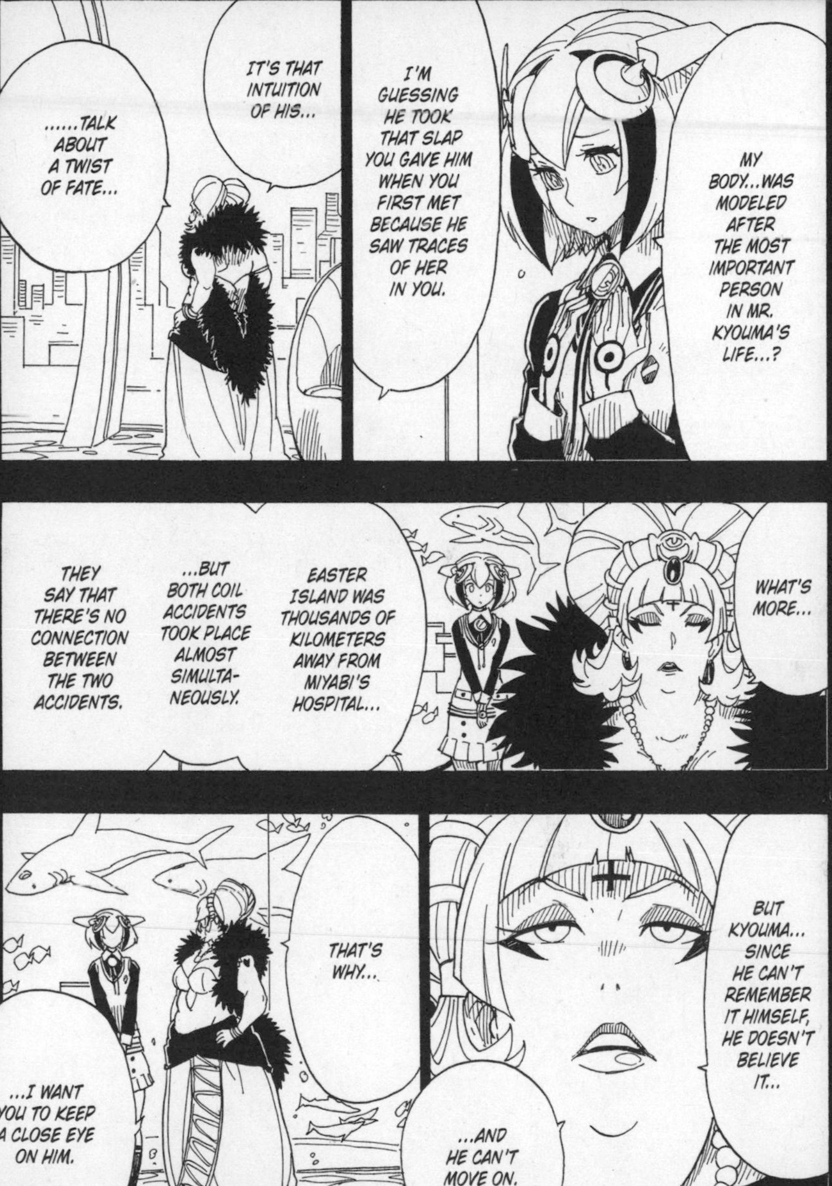
MY BODY...WAS MODELED AFTER THE MOST IMPORTANT PERSON IN MR. KYOUMA'S LIFE...?
I'M GUESSING HE TOOK THAT SLAP YOU GAVE HIM WHEN YOU FIRST MET BECAUSE HE SAW TRACES OF HER IN YOU.
IT'S THAT INTUITION OF HIS...
......TALK ABOUT A TWIST OF FATE...
WHAT'S MORE...
EASTER ISLAND WAS THOUSANDS OF KILOMETERS AWAY FROM MIYABI'S HOSPITAL...
...BUT BOTH COIL ACCIDENTS TOOK PLACE ALMOST SIMULTA-NEOUSLY.
THEY SAY THAT THERE'S NO CONNECTION BETWEEN THE TWO ACCIDENTS.
BUT KYOUMA... SINCE HE CAN'T REMEMBER IT HIMSELF, HE DOESN'T BELIEVE IT...
...AND HE CAN'T MOVE ON.
THAT'S WHY...
...I WANT YOU TO KEEP A CLOSE EYE ON HIM.

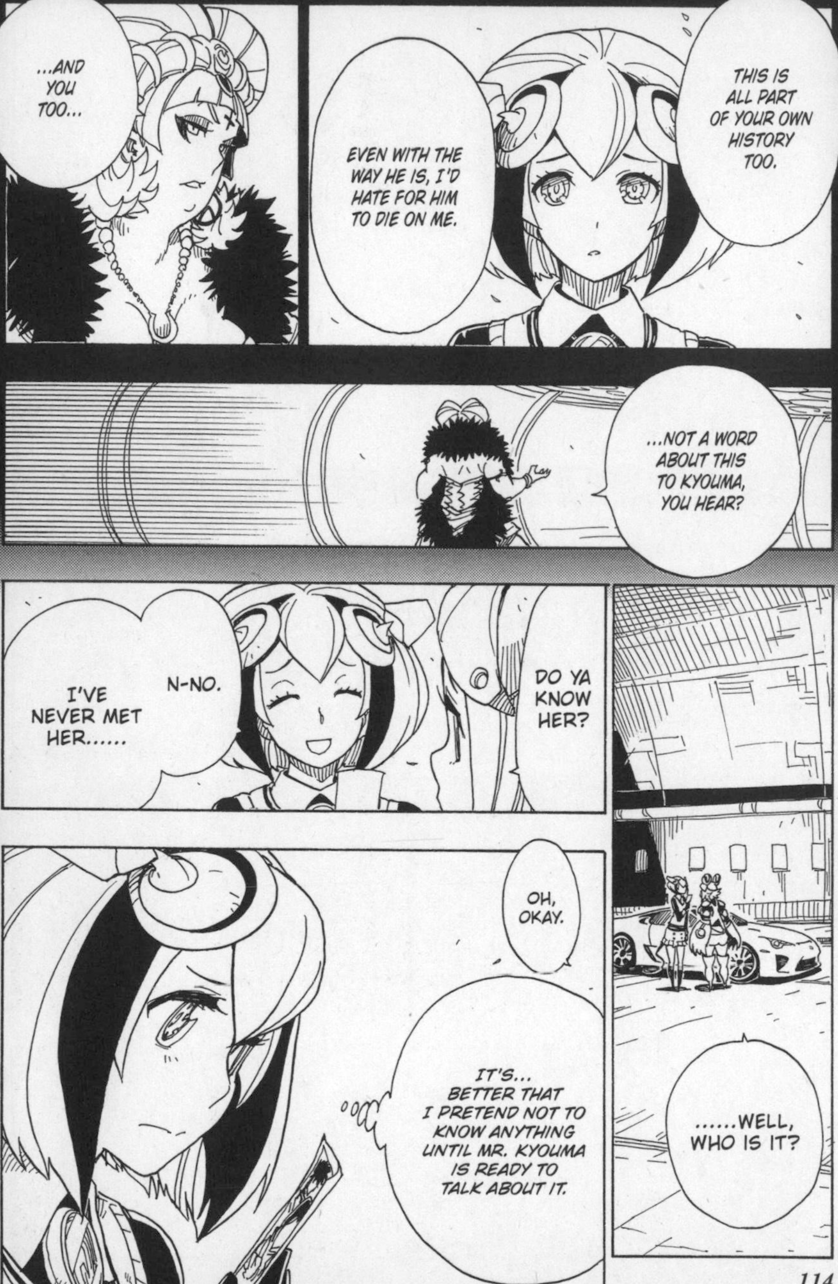
THIS IS ALL PART OF YOUR OWN HISTORY TOO.
EVEN WITH THE WAY HE IS, I'D HATE FOR HIM TO DIE ON ME.
...AND YOU TOO...
...NOT A WORD ABOUT THIS TO KYOUMA, YOU HEAR?
......WELL, WHO IS IT?
DO YA KNOW HER?
N-NO.
I'VE NEVER MET HER......
OH, OKAY.
IT'S... BETTER THAT I PRETEND NOT TO KNOW ANYTHING UNTIL MR. KYOUMA IS READY TO TALK ABOUT IT.

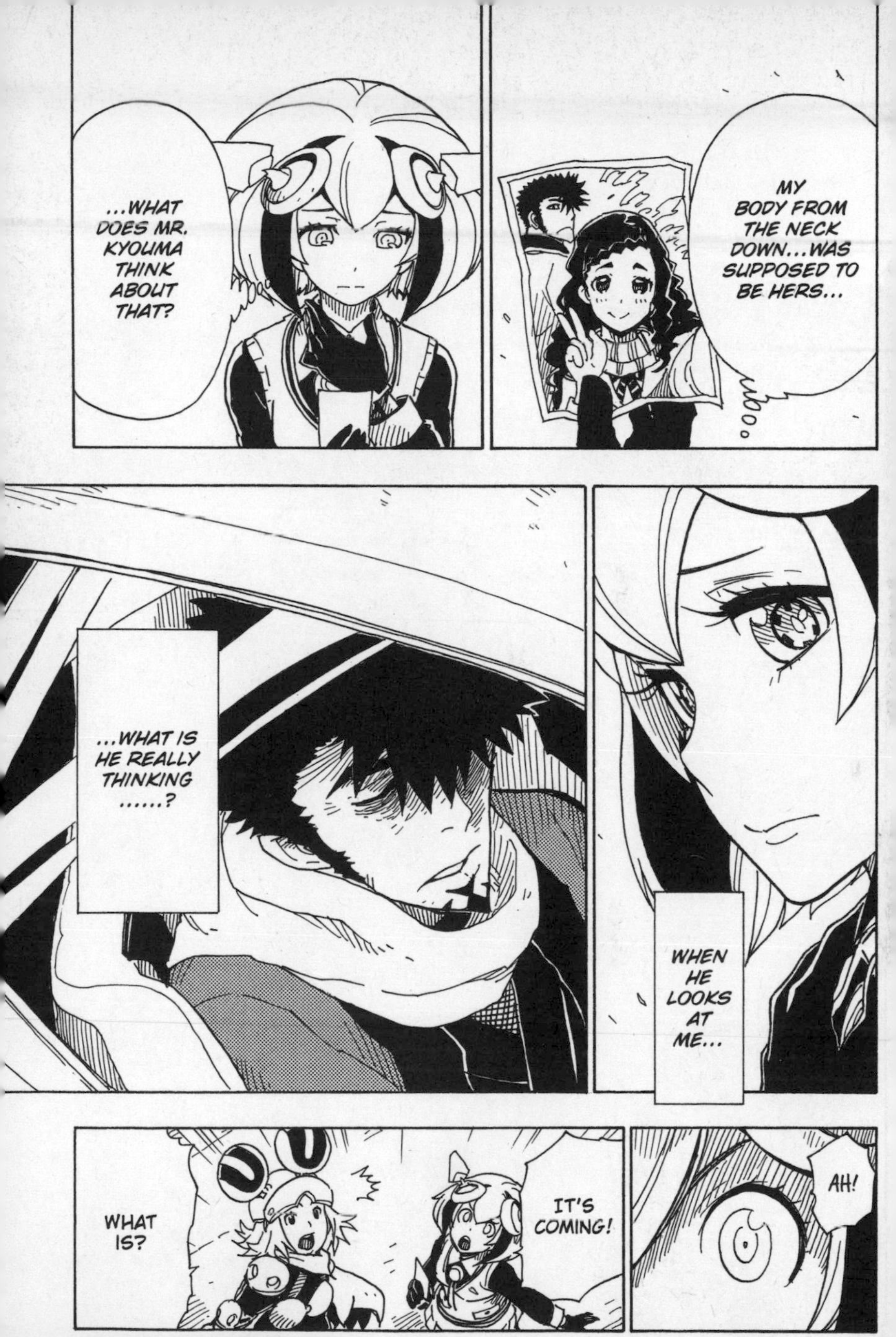
MY BODY FROM THE NECK DOWN...WAS SUPPOSED TO BE HERS...
...WHAT DOES MR. KYOUMA THINK ABOUT THAT?
WHEN HE LOOKS AT ME...
...WHAT IS HE REALLY THINKING ......?
AH!
IT'S COMING!
WHAT IS?

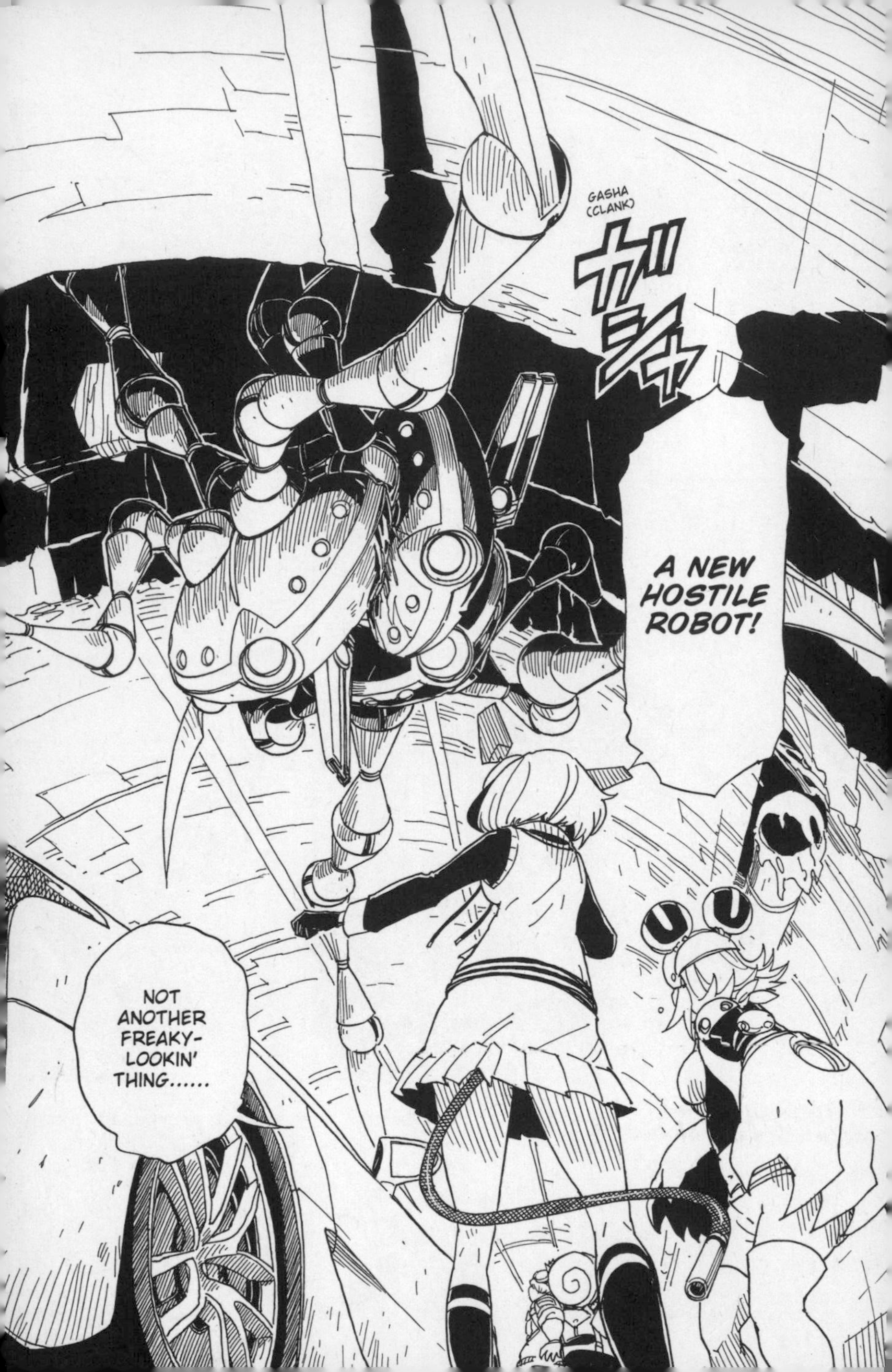
GASHA (CLANK)
ガシャ
A NEW HOSTILE ROBOT!
NOT ANOTHER FREAKY-LOOKIN' THING......

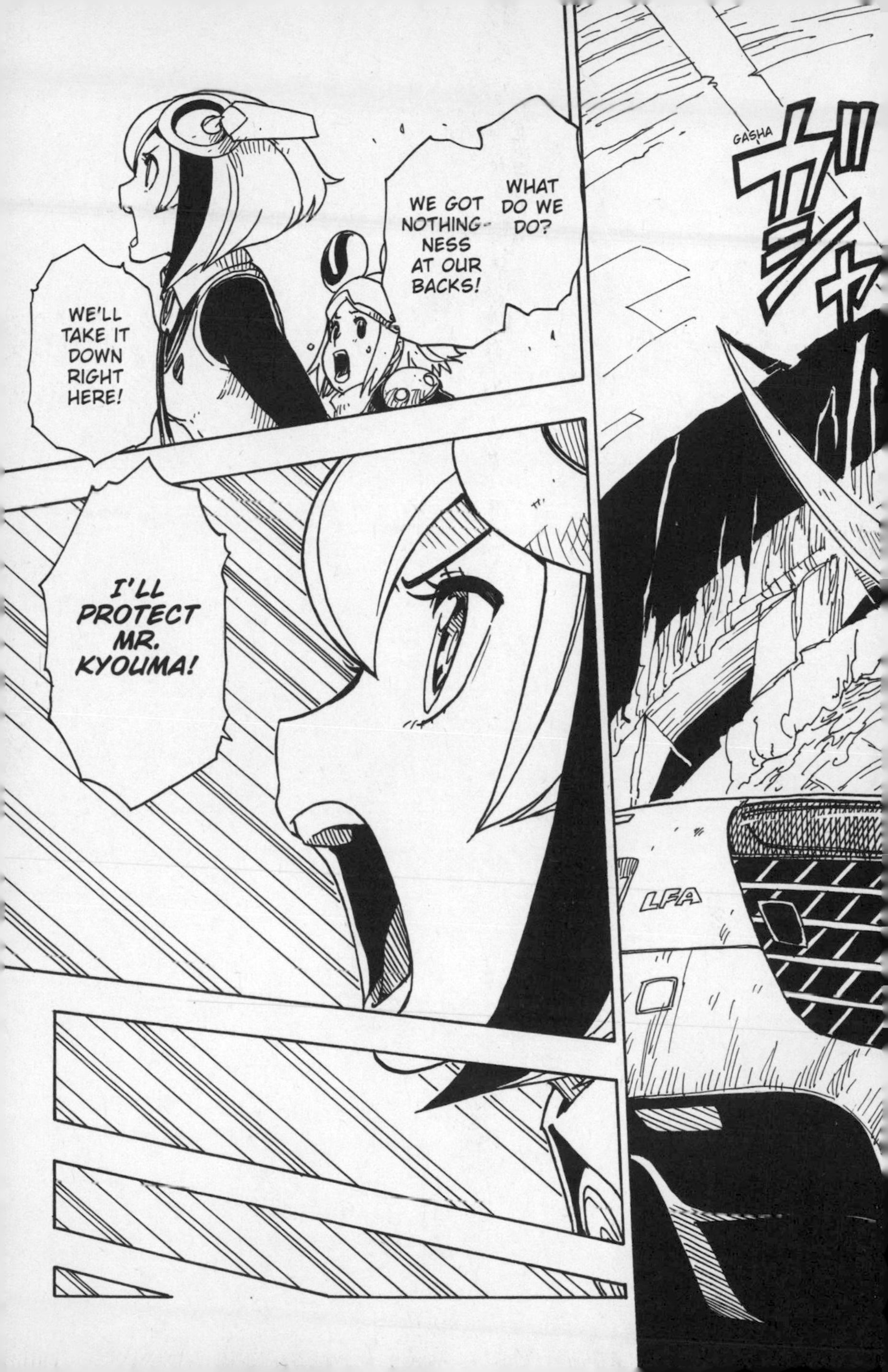
GASHA
ガシャ
LFA
WHAT DO WE DO?
WE GOT NOTHING-NESS AT OUR BACKS!
WE'LL TAKE IT DOWN RIGHT HERE!
I'LL PROTECT MR. KYOUMA!

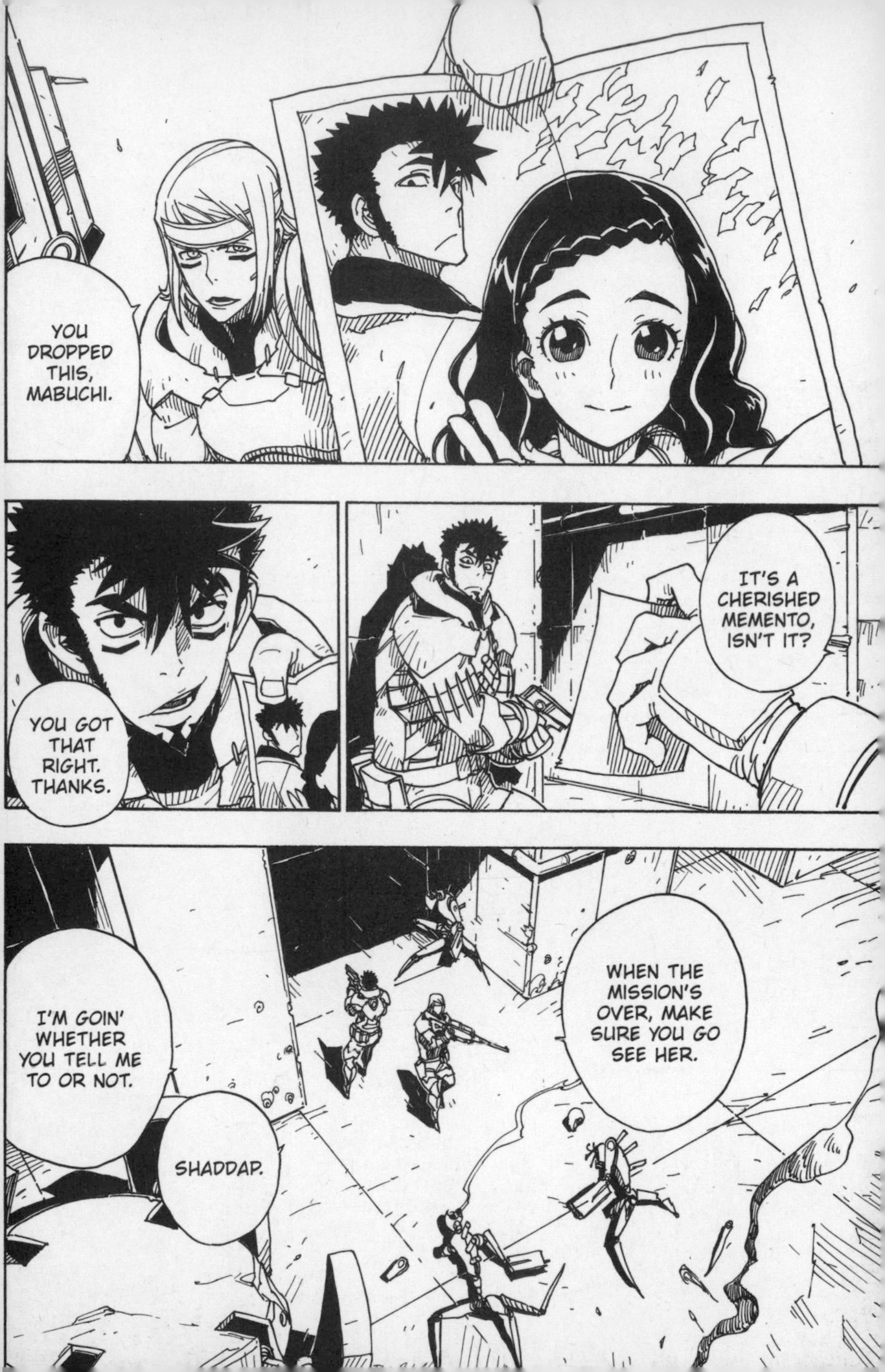
YOU DROPPED THIS, MABUCHI.
IT'S A CHERISHED MEMENTO, ISN'T IT?
YOU GOT THAT RIGHT. THANKS.
WHEN THE MISSION'S OVER, MAKE SURE YOU GO SEE HER.
I'M GOIN' WHETHER YOU TELL ME TO OR NOT.
SHADDAP.

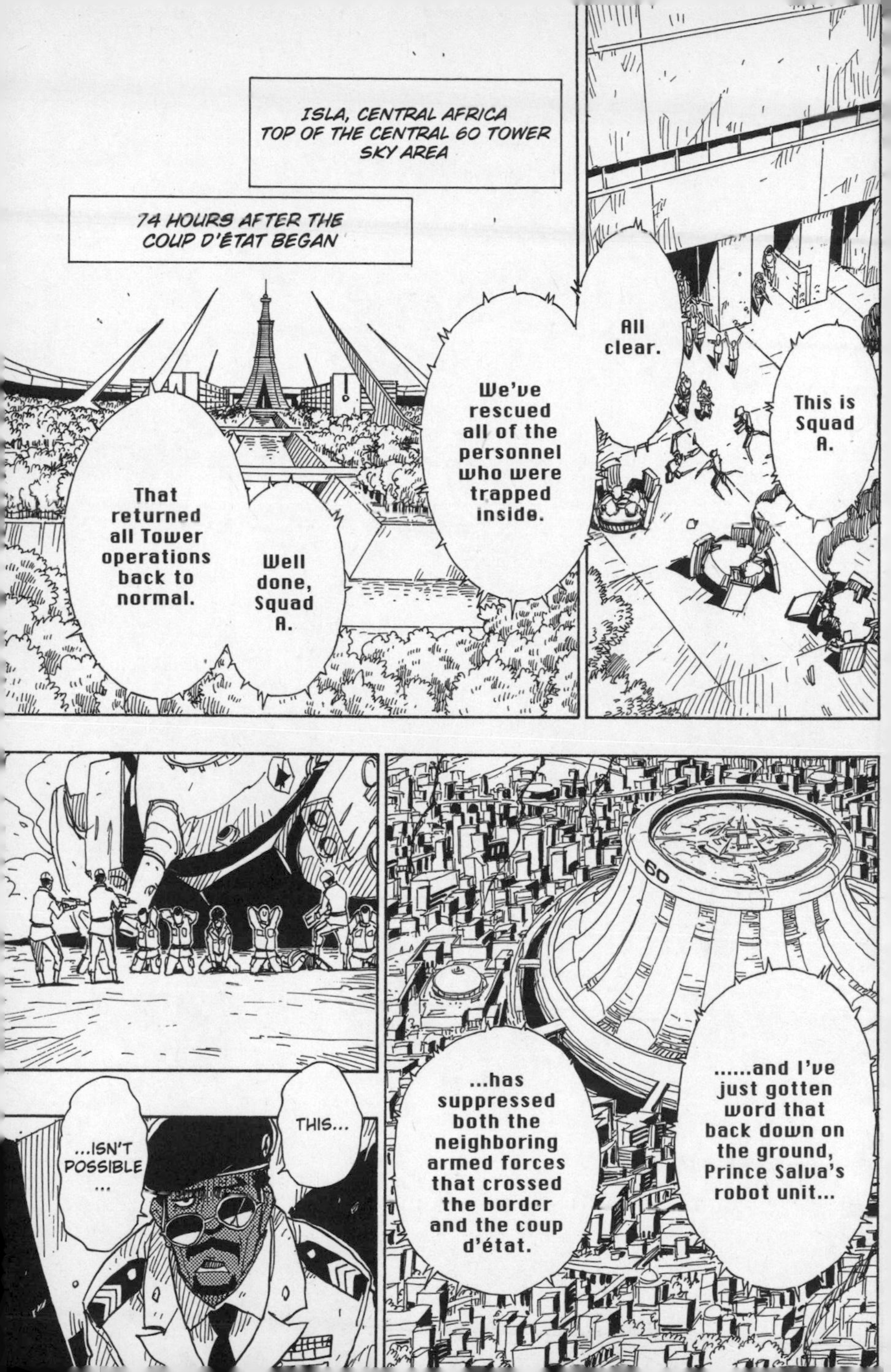

This is Squad A.
All clear.
We've rescued all of the personnel who were trapped inside.
ISLA, CENTRAL AFRICA
TOP OF THE CENTRAL 60 TOWER
SKY AREA
74 HOURS AFTER THE COUP D'ÉTAT BEGAN
Well done, Squad A.
That returned all Tower operations back to normal.
60
......and I've just gotten word that back down on the ground, Prince Salva's robot unit...
...has suppressed both the neighboring armed forces that crossed the border and the coup d'état.
THIS...
...ISN'T POSSIBLE ...

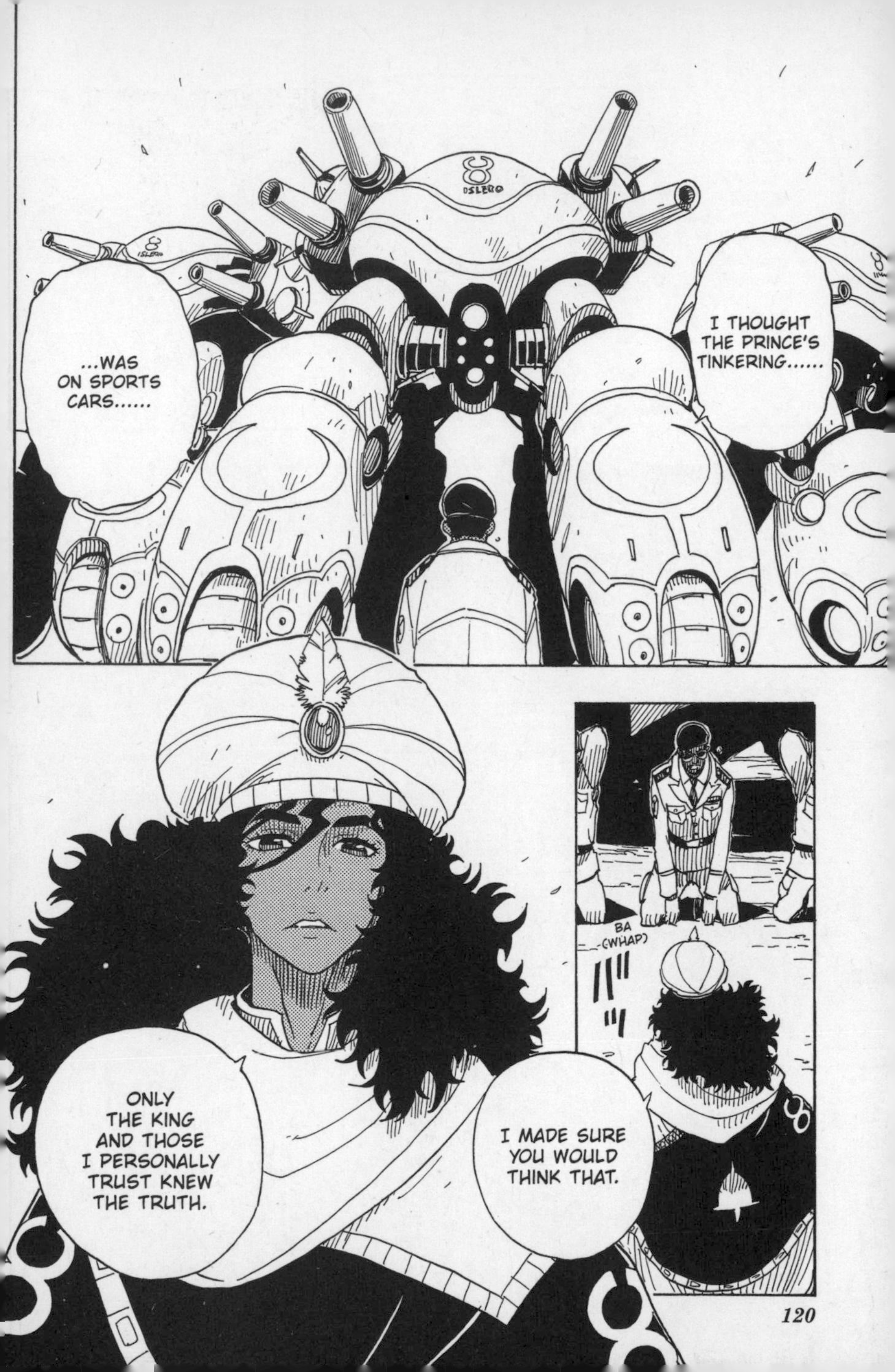
I THOUGHT THE PRINCE'S TINKERING......
...WAS ON SPORTS CARS......
BA (WHAP)
I MADE SURE YOU WOULD THINK THAT.
ONLY THE KING AND THOSE I PERSONALLY TRUST KNEW THE TRUTH.

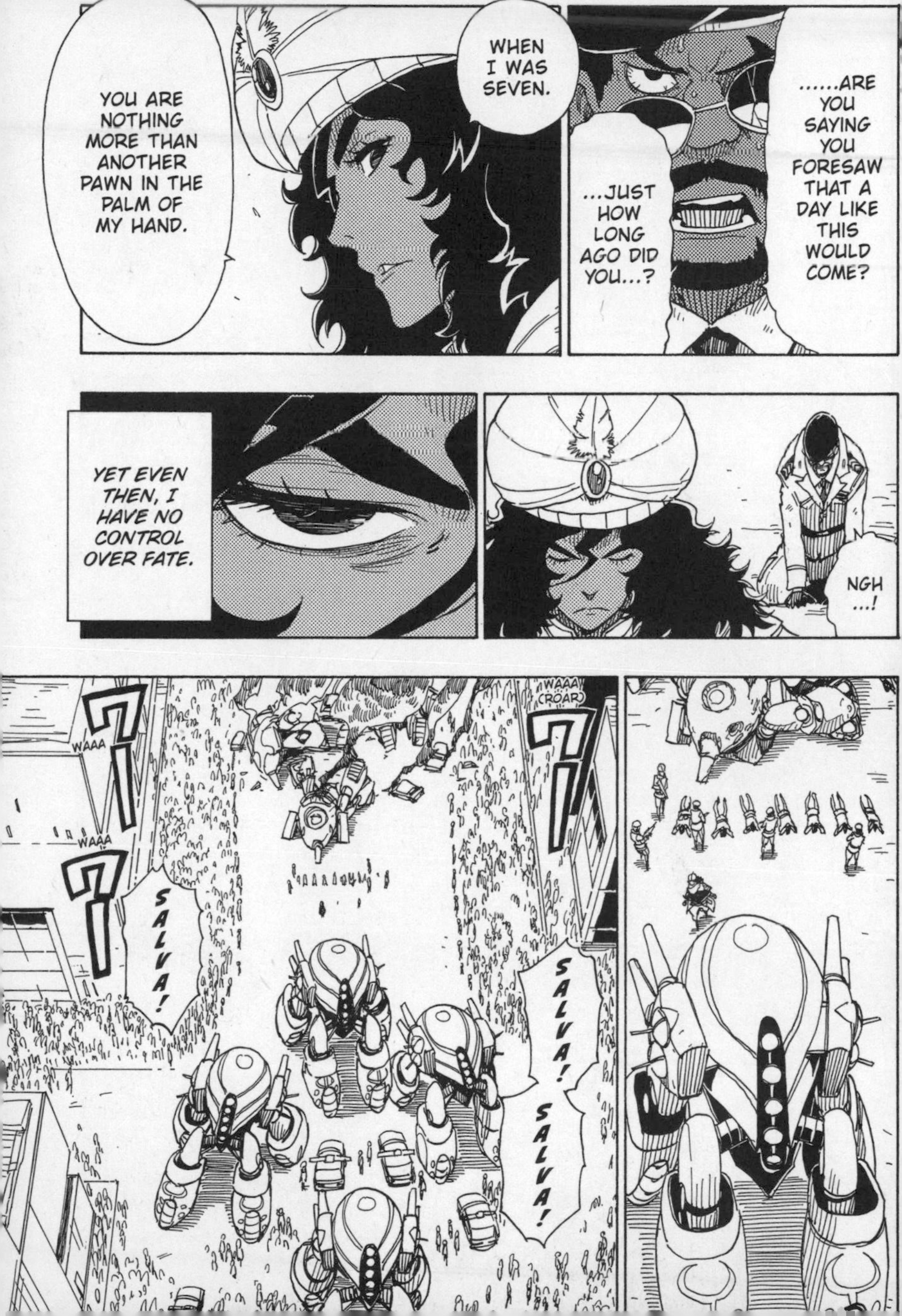
......ARE YOU SAYING YOU FORESAW THAT A DAY LIKE THIS WOULD COME?
...JUST HOW LONG AGO DID YOU...?
WHEN I WAS SEVEN.
YOU ARE NOTHING MORE THAN ANOTHER PAWN IN THE PALM OF MY HAND.
NGH ...!
YET EVEN THEN, I HAVE NO CONTROL OVER FATE.
WAAA (ROAR)
SALVA!
SALVA!
SALVA!
WAAA
WAAA
SALVA!

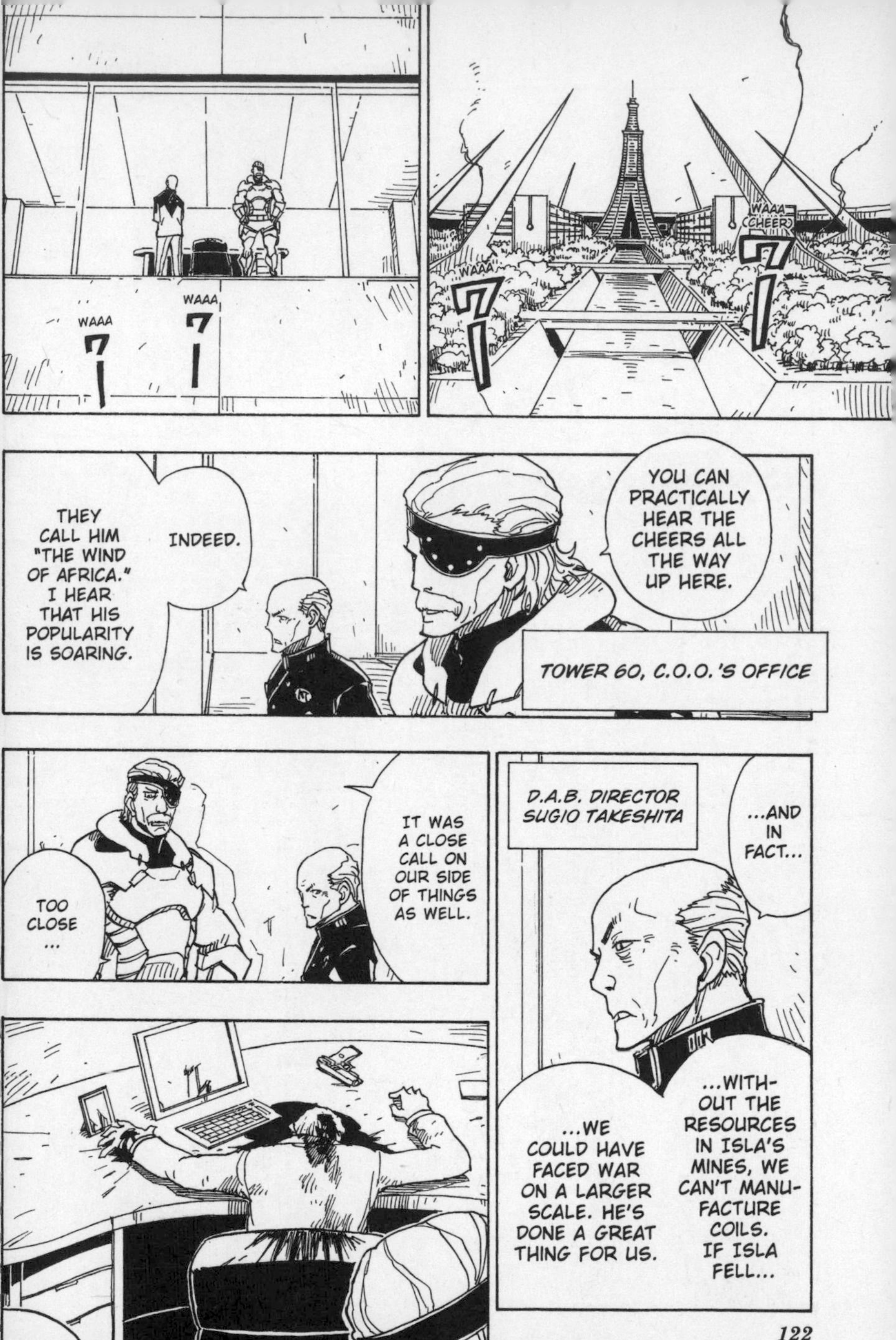
WAAA
(CHEER)
WAAA
WAAA
WAAA
YOU CAN PRACTICALLY HEAR THE CHEERS ALL THE WAY UP HERE.
TOWER 60, C.O.O.'S OFFICE
INDEED.
THEY CALL HIM "THE WIND OF AFRICA." I HEAR THAT HIS POPULARITY IS SOARING.
D.A.B. DIRECTOR SUGIO TAKESHITA
...AND IN FACT...
...WITHOUT THE RESOURCES IN ISLA'S MINES, WE CAN'T MANUFACTURE COILS. IF ISLA FELL...
...WE COULD HAVE FACED WAR ON A LARGER SCALE. HE'S DONE A GREAT THING FOR US.
IT WAS A CLOSE CALL ON OUR SIDE OF THINGS AS WELL.
TOO CLOSE ...

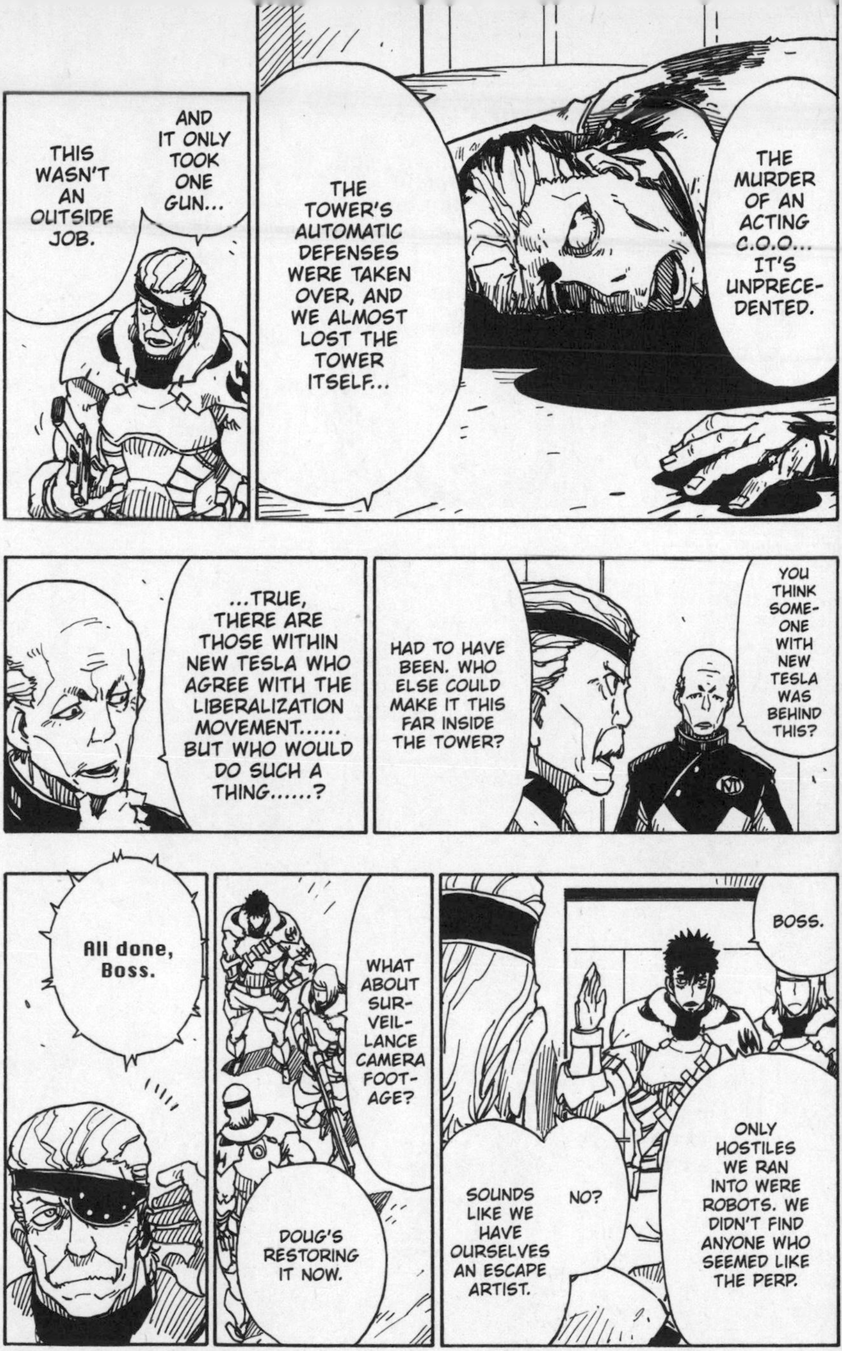
THE MURDER OF AN ACTING C.O.O... IT'S UNPRECE-DENTED.
THE TOWER'S AUTOMATIC DEFENSES WERE TAKEN OVER, AND WE ALMOST LOST THE TOWER ITSELF...
AND IT ONLY TOOK ONE GUN...
THIS WASN'T AN OUTSIDE JOB.
YOU THINK SOME-ONE WITH NEW TESLA WAS BEHIND THIS?
HAD TO HAVE BEEN. WHO ELSE COULD MAKE IT THIS FAR INSIDE THE TOWER?
...TRUE, THERE ARE THOSE WITHIN NEW TESLA WHO AGREE WITH THE LIBERALIZATION MOVEMENT...... BUT WHO WOULD DO SUCH A THING......?
BOSS.
ONLY HOSTILES WE RAN INTO WERE ROBOTS. WE DIDN'T FIND ANYONE WHO SEEMED LIKE THE PERP.
NO?
SOUNDS LIKE WE HAVE OURSELVES AN ESCAPE ARTIST.
WHAT ABOUT SUR-VEIL-LANCE CAMERA FOOT-AGE?
DOUG'S RESTORING IT NOW.
All done, Boss.

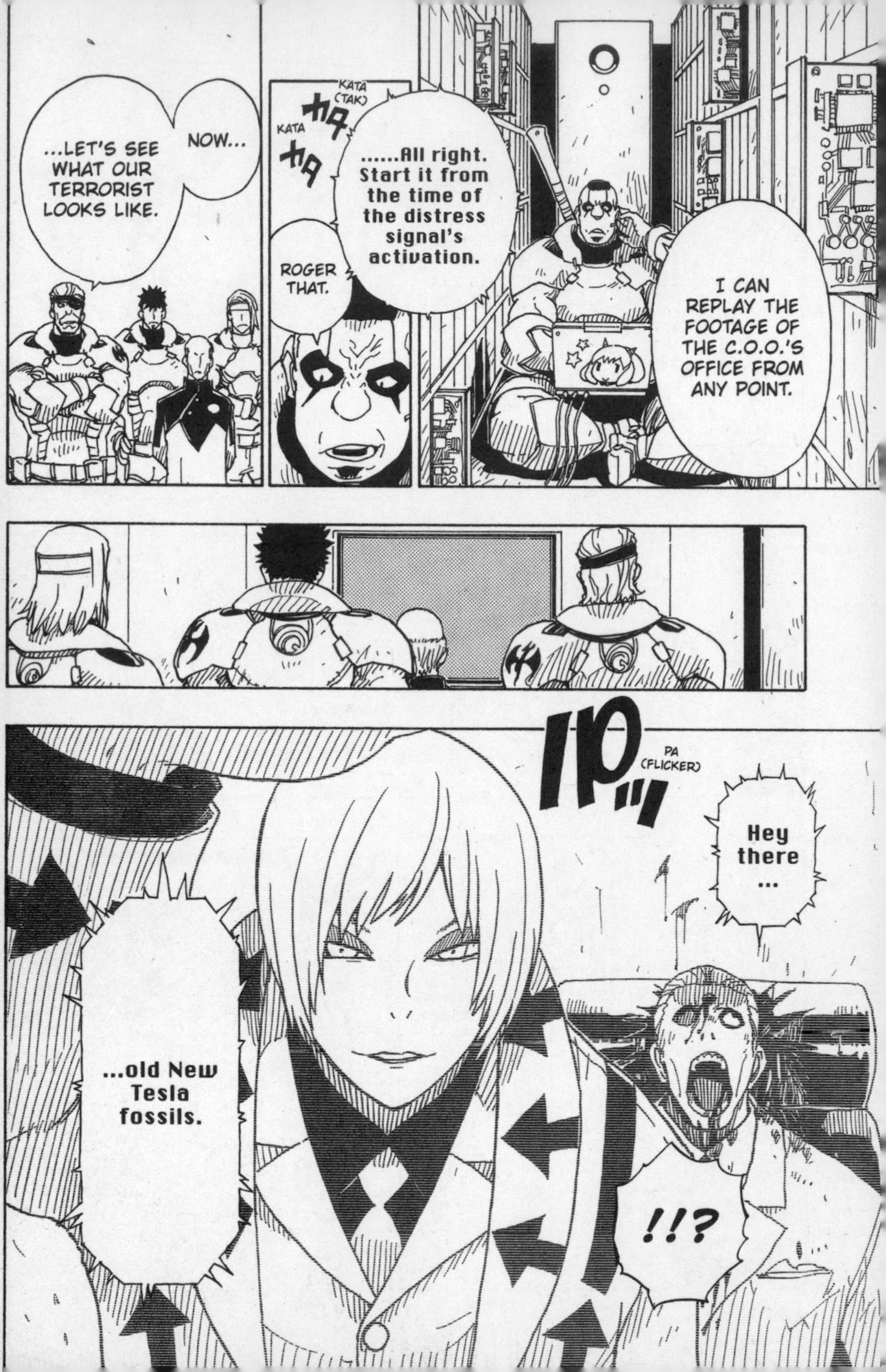
I CAN REPLAY THE FOOTAGE OF THE C.O.O.'S OFFICE FROM ANY POINT.
......All right. Start it from the time of the distress signal's activation.
カタ KATA (TAK)
カタ KATA
ROGER THAT.
NOW...
...LET'S SEE WHAT OUR TERRORIST LOOKS LIKE.
PA (FLICKER)
Hey there ...
...old New Tesla fossils.
!!?

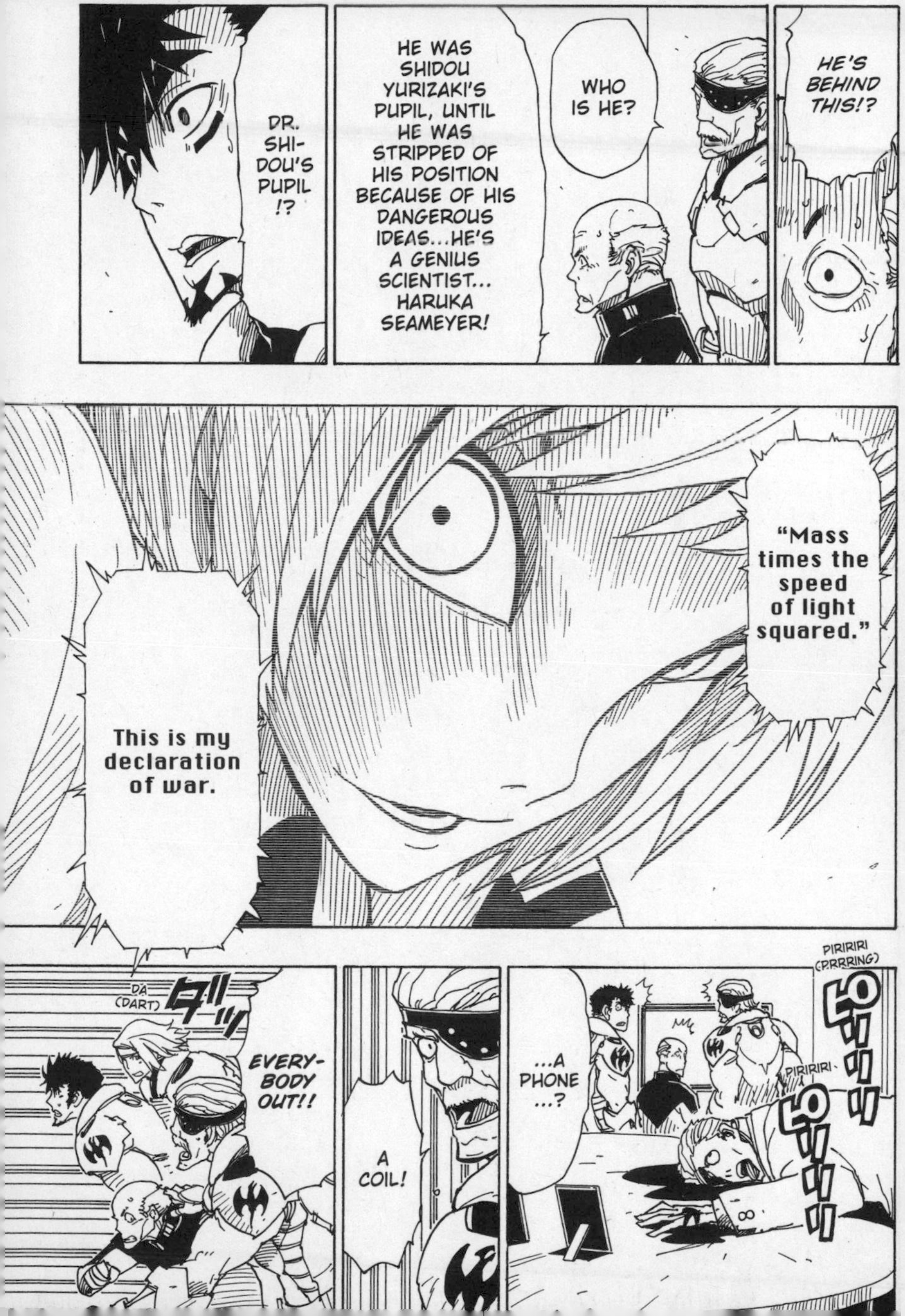
HE'S BEHIND THIS!?
WHO IS HE?
HE WAS SHIDOU YURIZAKI'S PUPIL, UNTIL HE WAS STRIPPED OF HIS POSITION BECAUSE OF HIS DANGEROUS IDEAS...HE'S A GENIUS SCIENTIST... HARUKA SEAMEYER!
DR. SHIDOU'S PUPIL!?
"Mass times the speed of light squared."
This is my declaration of war.
PIRIRIRI (PRRRING)
PIRIRIRI
...A PHONE...?
A COIL!
DA (DART)
EVERYBODY OUT!!

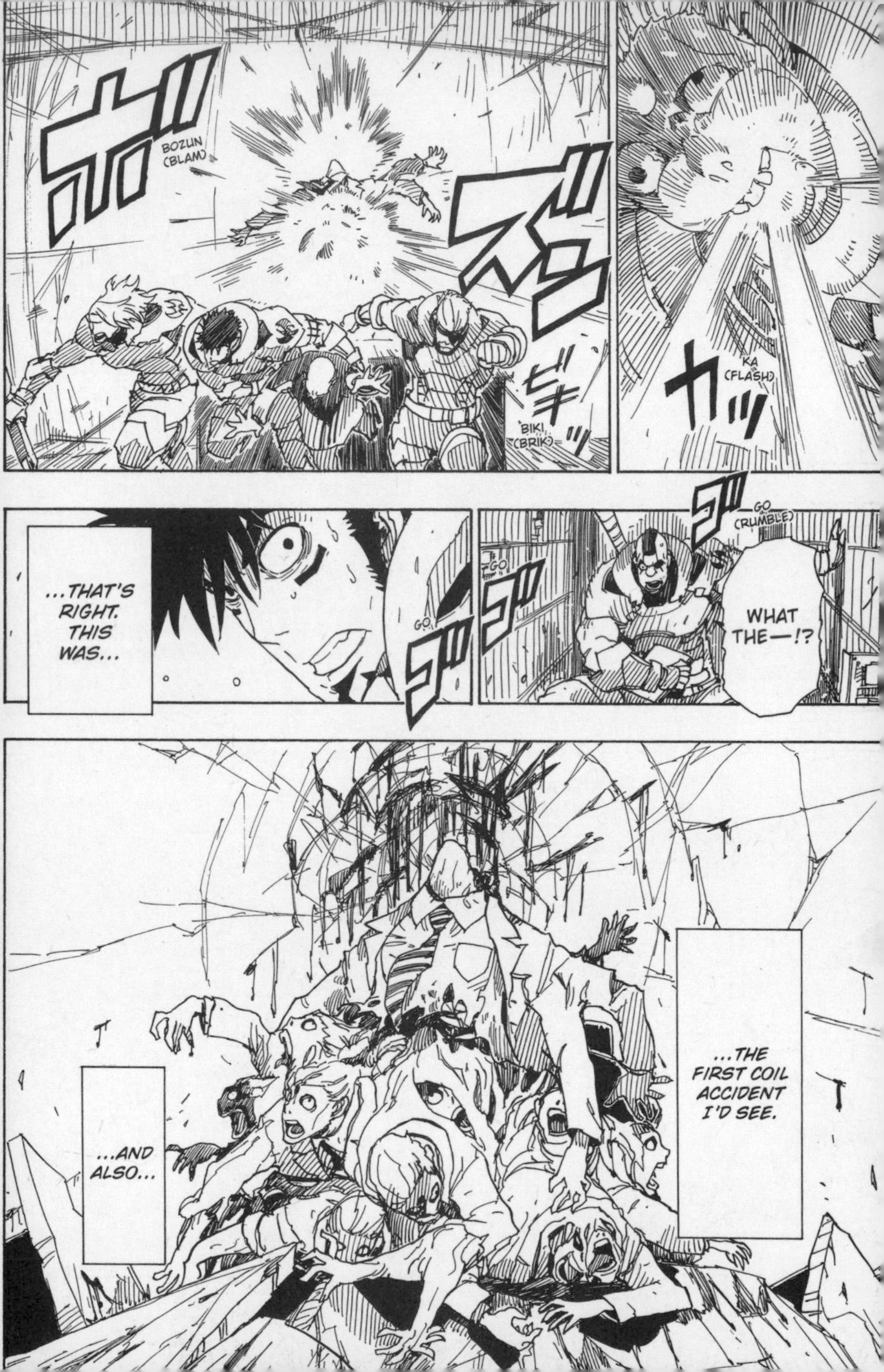
KA
(FLASH)
BOZUN
(BLAM)
BIKI
(BRIK)
GO
(RUMBLE)
WHAT THE—!?
GO
GO
...THAT'S RIGHT. THIS WAS...
...THE FIRST COIL ACCIDENT I'D SEE.
...AND ALSO...

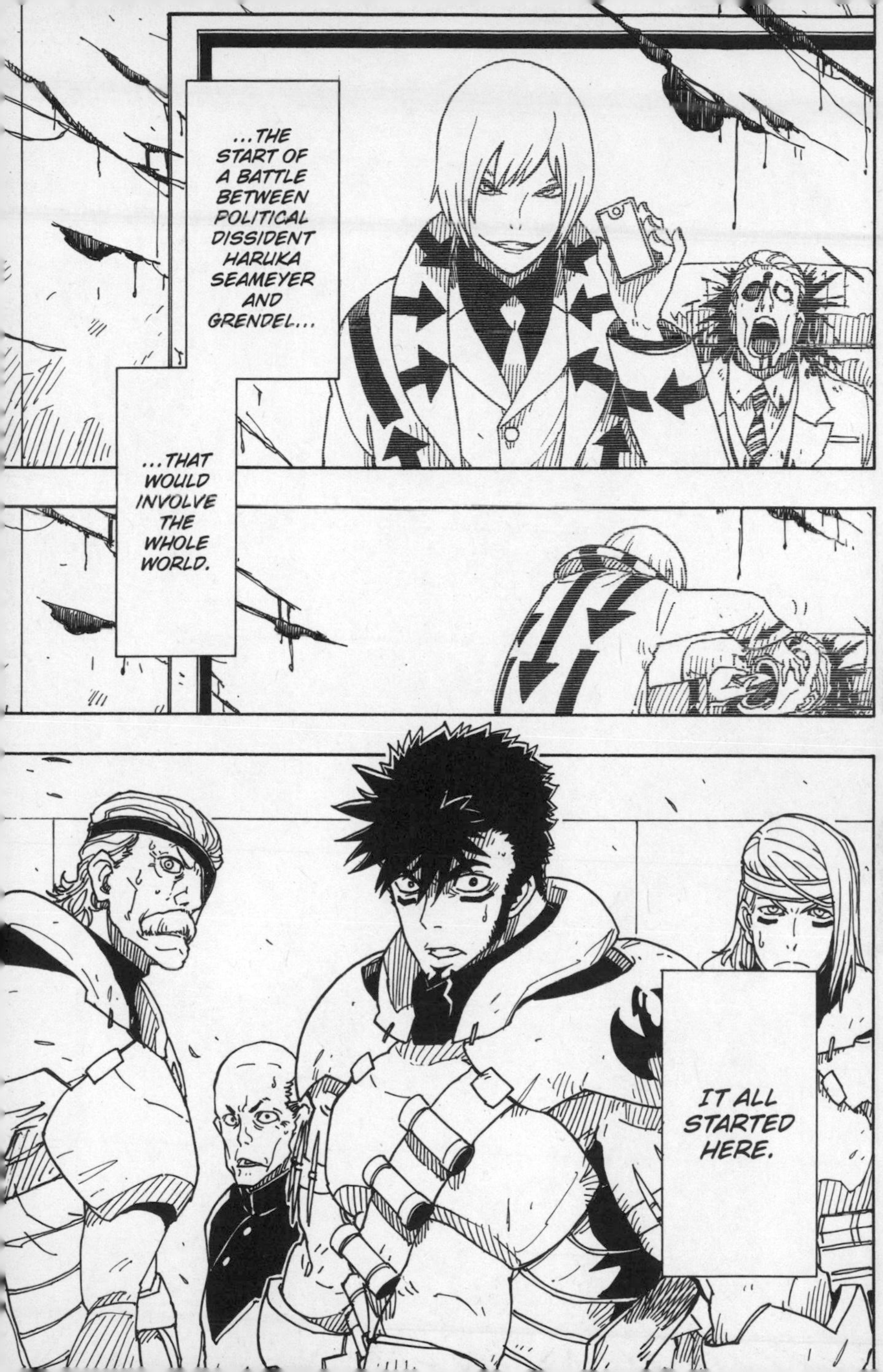
...THE START OF A BATTLE BETWEEN POLITICAL DISSIDENT HARUKA SEAMEYER AND GRENDEL...
...THAT WOULD INVOLVE THE WHOLE WORLD.
IT ALL STARTED HERE.

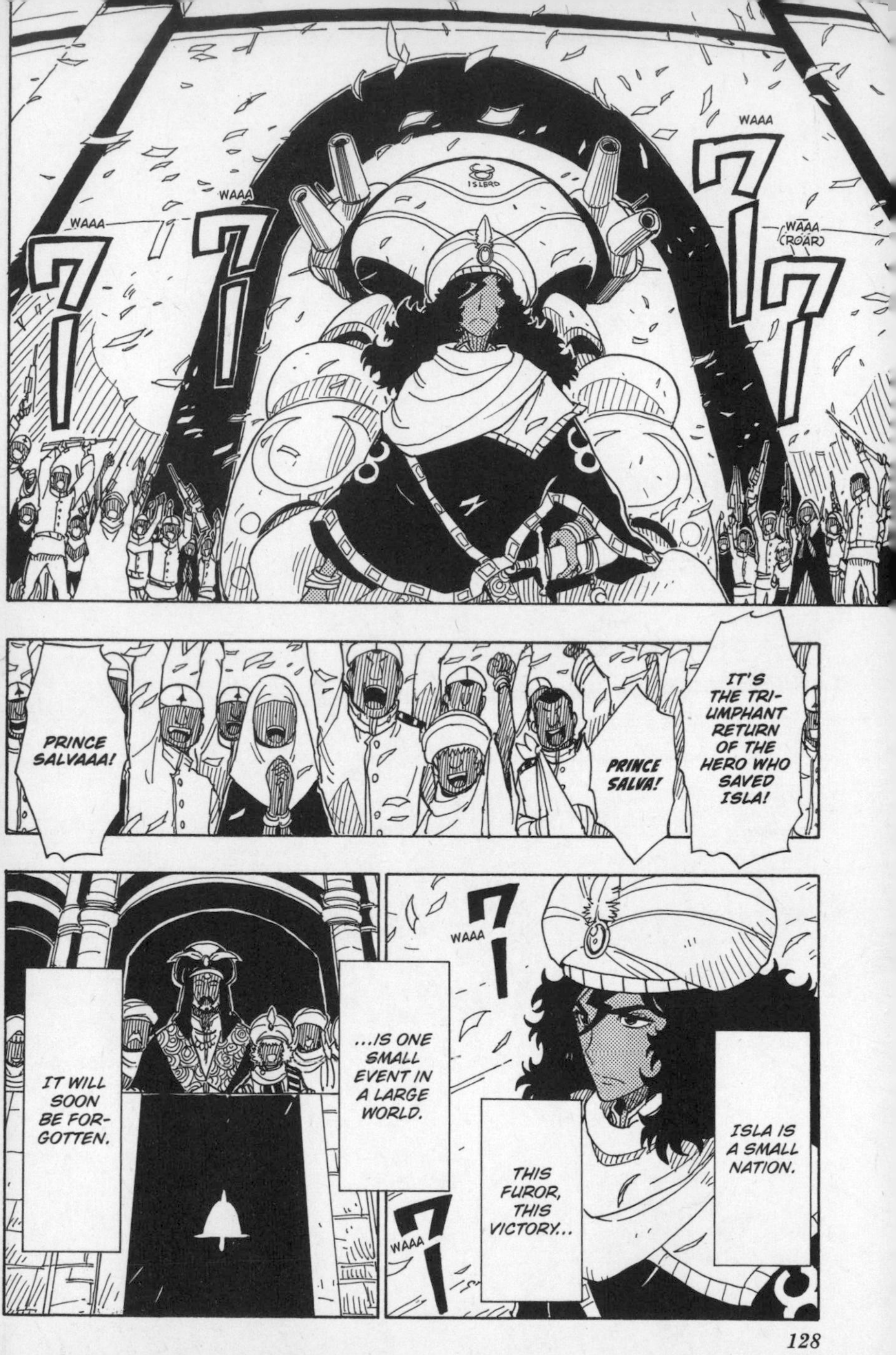
WAAA
WAAA
(ROAR)
WAAA
WAAA
IT'S THE TRI-UMPHANT RETURN OF THE HERO WHO SAVED ISLA!
PRINCE SALVA!
PRINCE SALVAAA!
ISLA IS A SMALL NATION.
THIS FUROR, THIS VICTORY...
WAAA
WAAA
...IS ONE SMALL EVENT IN A LARGE WORLD.
IT WILL SOON BE FORGOTTEN.

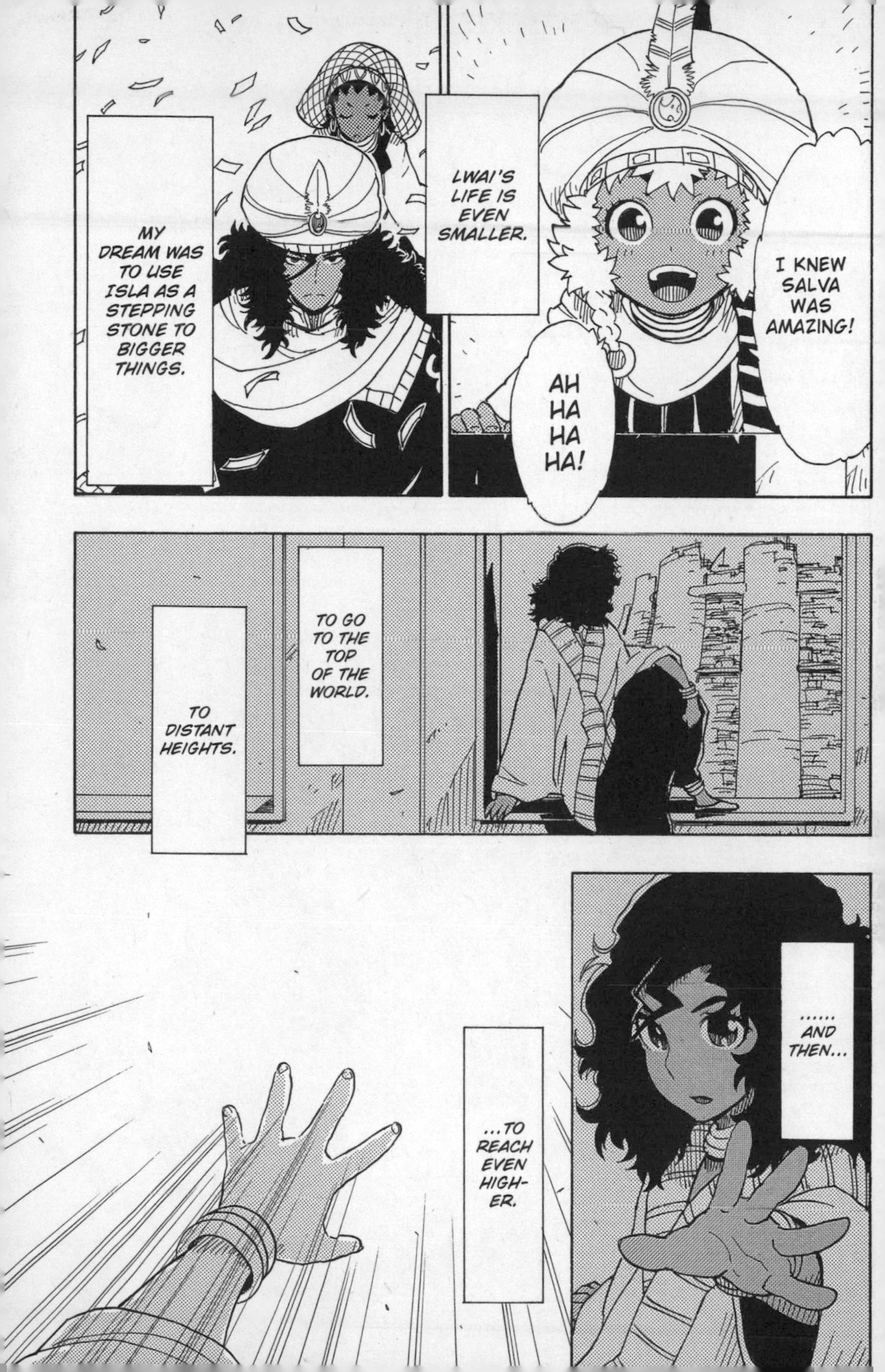
I KNEW SALVA WAS AMAZING!
AH HA HA HA!
LWAI'S LIFE IS EVEN SMALLER.
MY DREAM WAS TO USE ISLA AS A STEPPING STONE TO BIGGER THINGS.
TO GO TO THE TOP OF THE WORLD.
TO DISTANT HEIGHTS.
......AND THEN...
...TO REACH EVEN HIGH-ER.

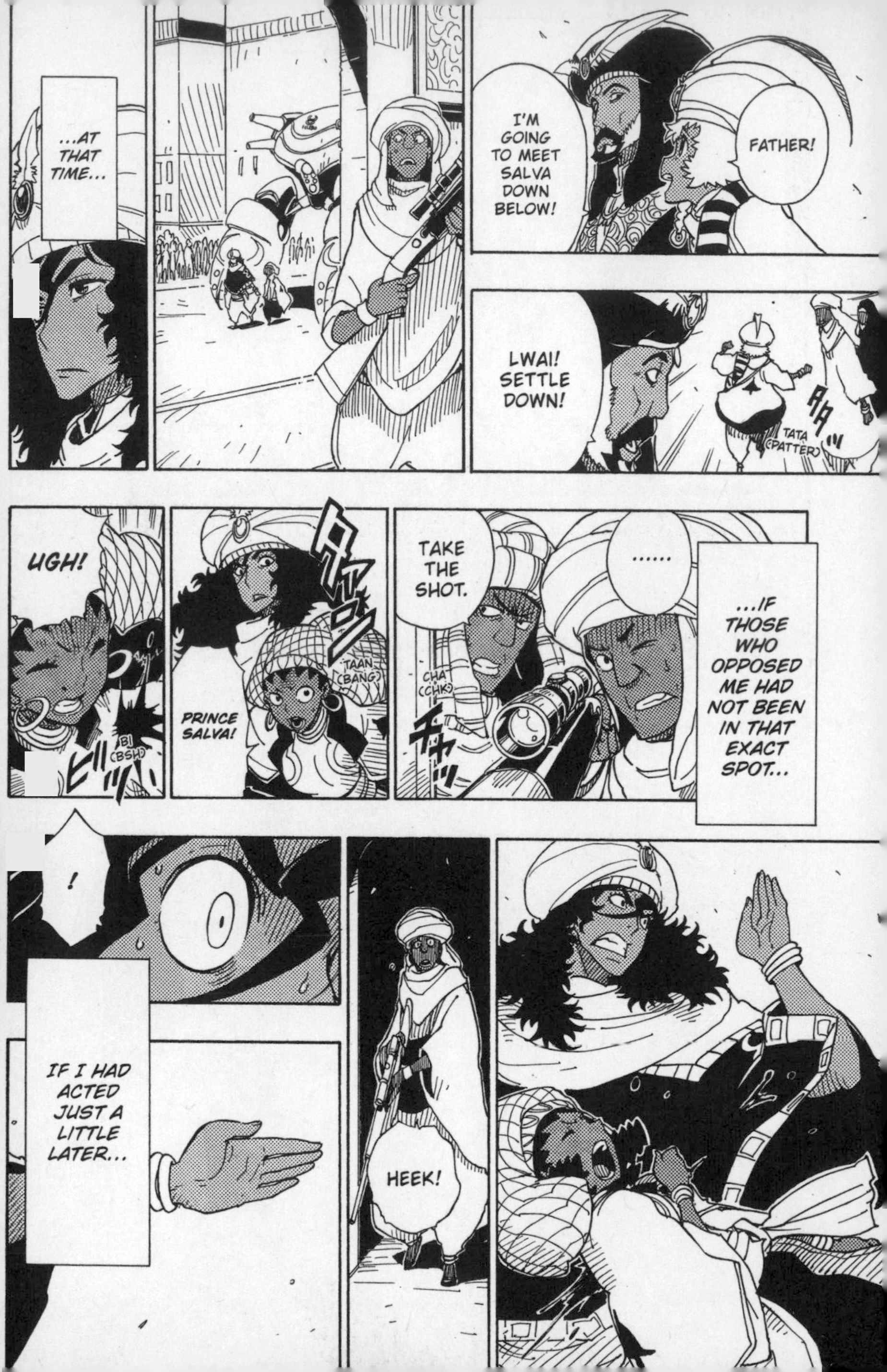
FATHER!
I'M GOING TO MEET SALVA DOWN BELOW!
LWAI! SETTLE DOWN!
TATA (PATTER)
...AT THAT TIME...
...IF THOSE WHO OPPOSED ME HAD NOT BEEN IN THAT EXACT SPOT...
......
TAKE THE SHOT.
CHA (CHK)
TAAN (BANG)
PRINCE SALVA!
UGH!
BI (BSH)
HEEK!
!
IF I HAD ACTED JUST A LITTLE LATER...

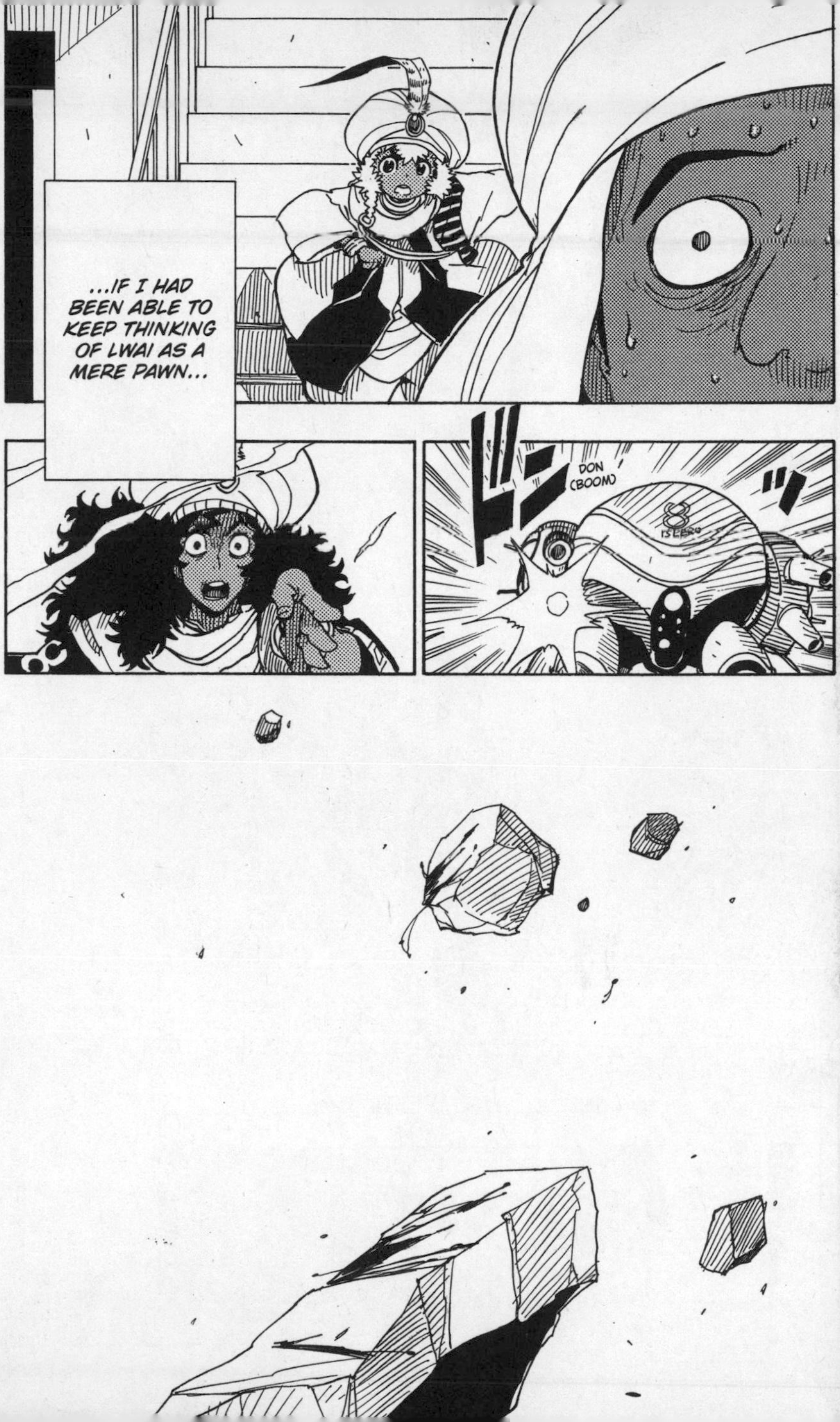
...IF I HAD BEEN ABLE TO KEEP THINKING OF LWAI AS A MERE PAWN...
DON (BOOM)

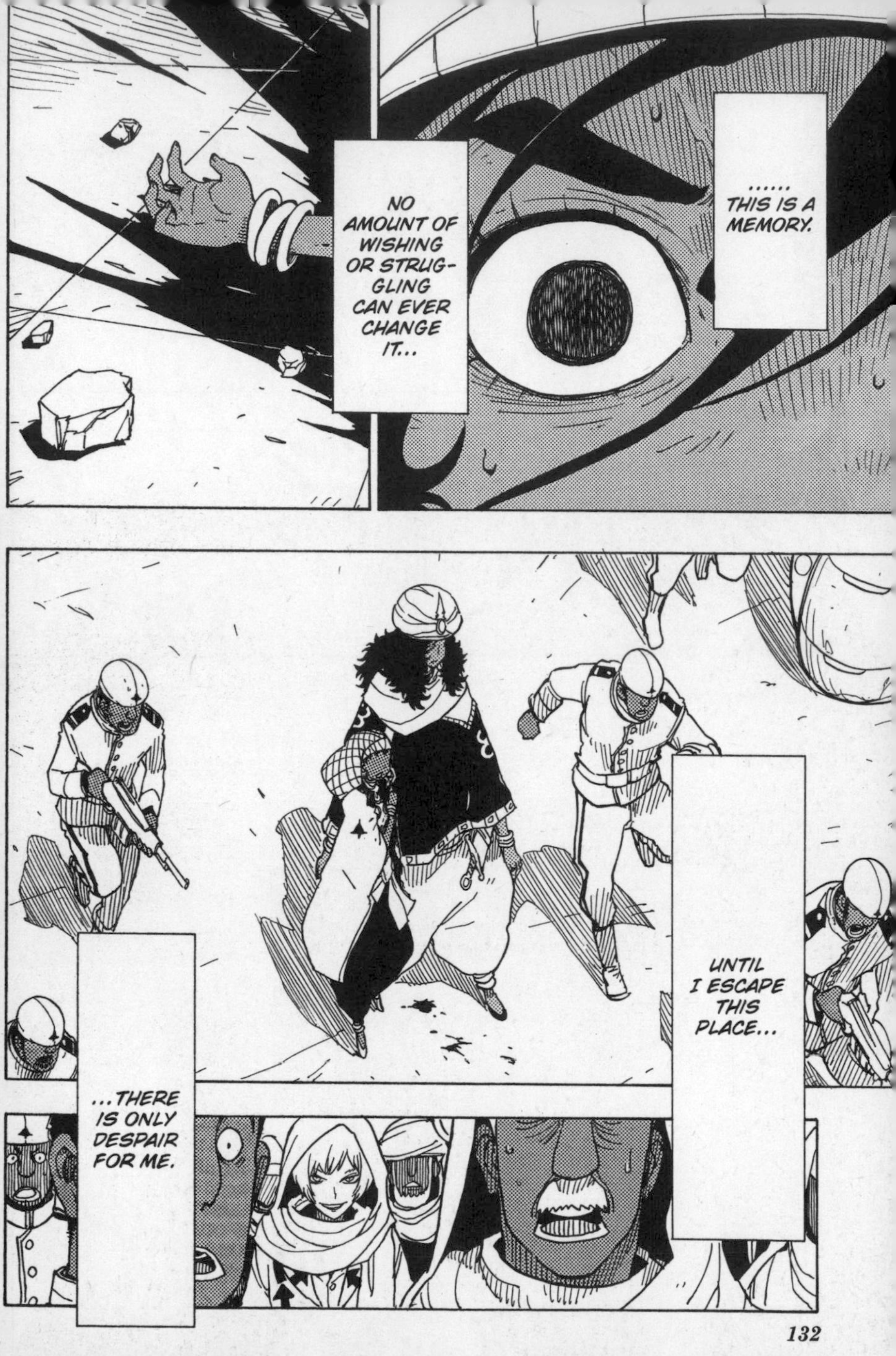

......
THIS IS A MEMORY.
NO AMOUNT OF WISHING OR STRUG-GLING CAN EVER CHANGE IT...
UNTIL I ESCAPE THIS PLACE...
...THERE IS ONLY DESPAIR FOR ME.

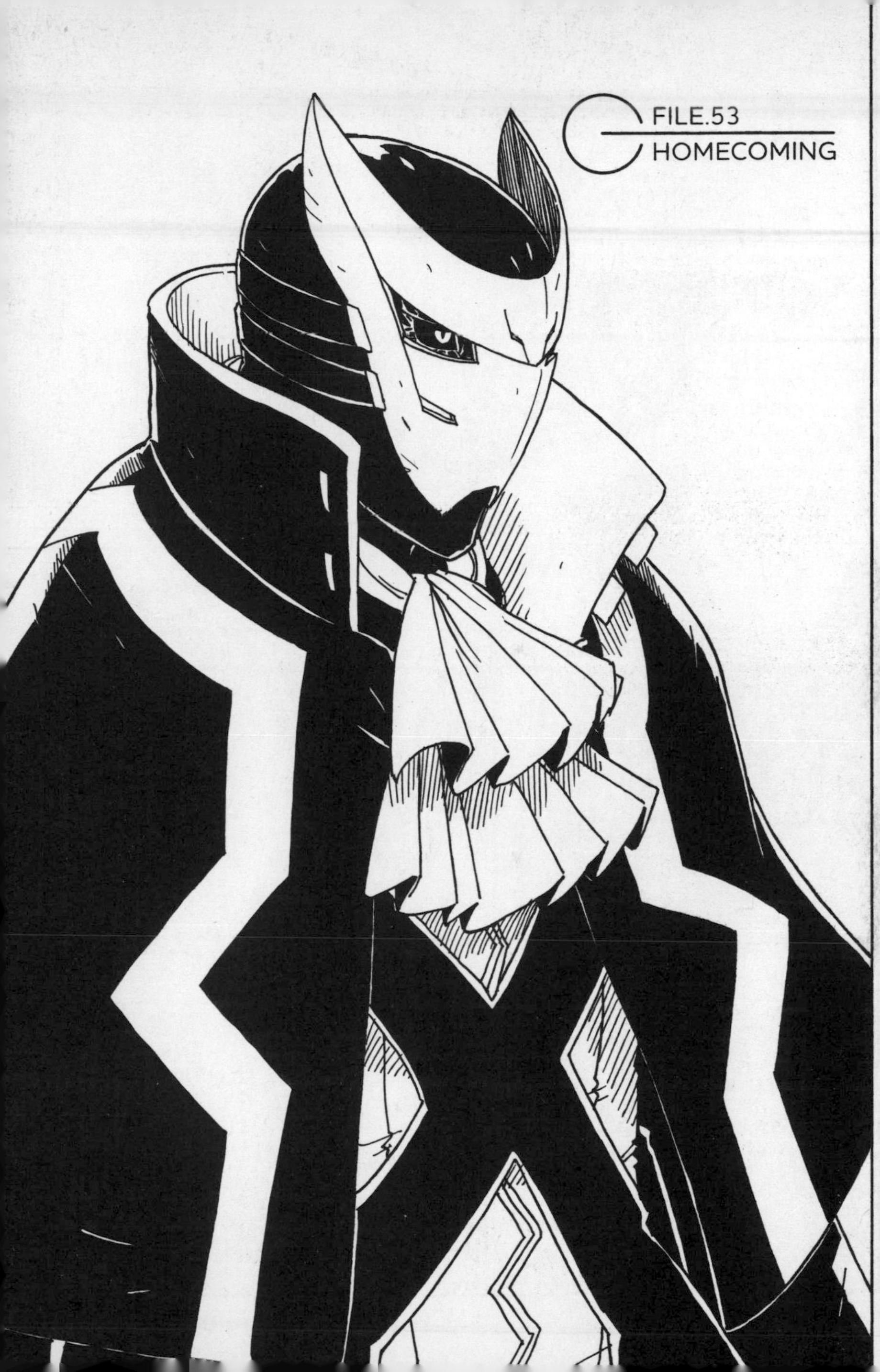
FILE.53
HOMECOMING

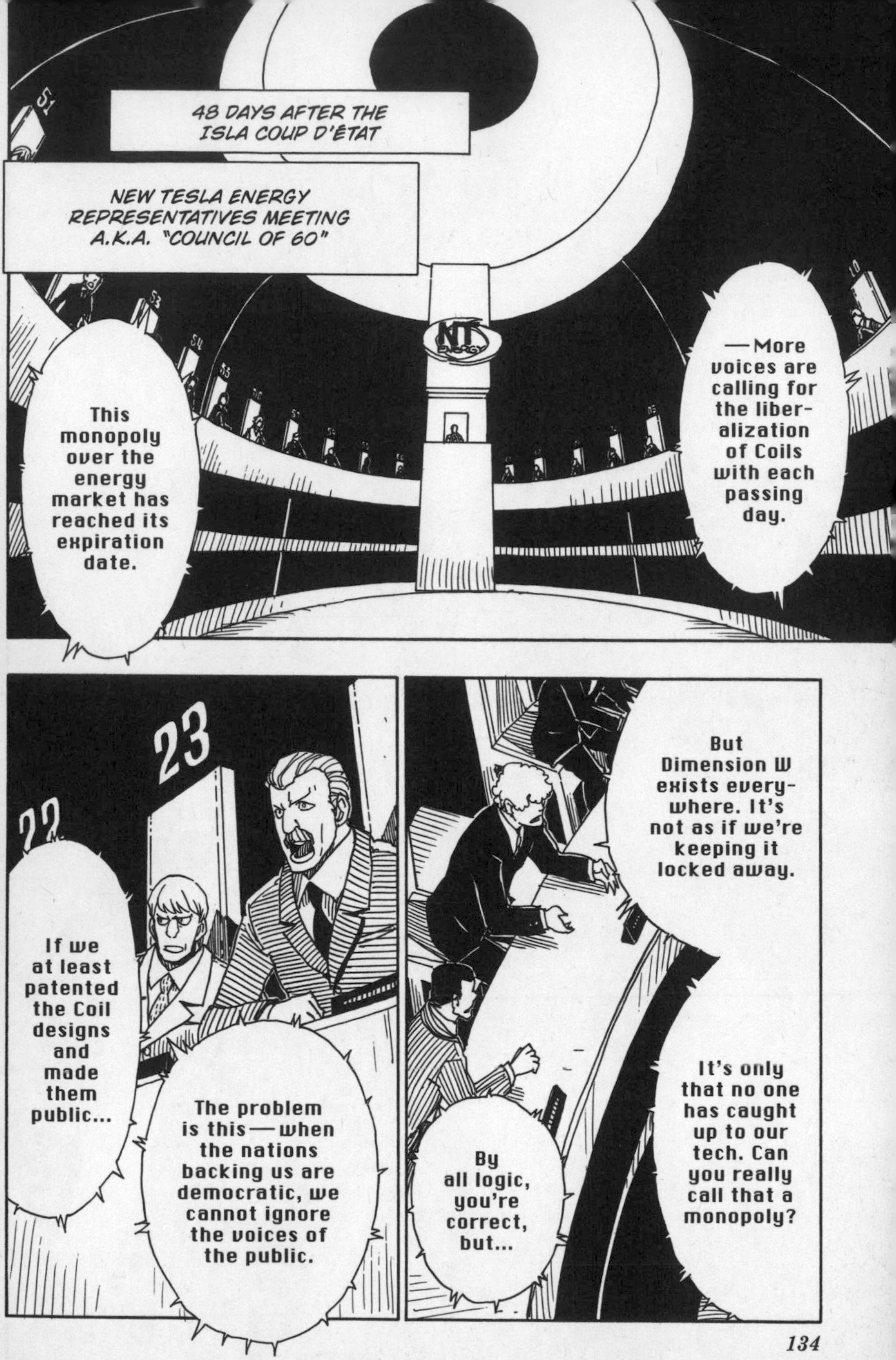
48 DAYS AFTER THE ISLA COUP D'ÉTAT
NEW TESLA ENERGY REPRESENTATIVES MEETING A.K.A. "COUNCIL OF 60"
—More voices are calling for the liberalization of Coils with each passing day.
This monopoly over the energy market has reached its expiration date.
But Dimension W exists everywhere. It's not as if we're keeping it locked away.
It's only that no one has caught up to our tech. Can you really call that a monopoly?
By all logic, you're correct, but...
If we at least patented the Coil designs and made them public...
The problem is this—when the nations backing us are democratic, we cannot ignore the voices of the public.

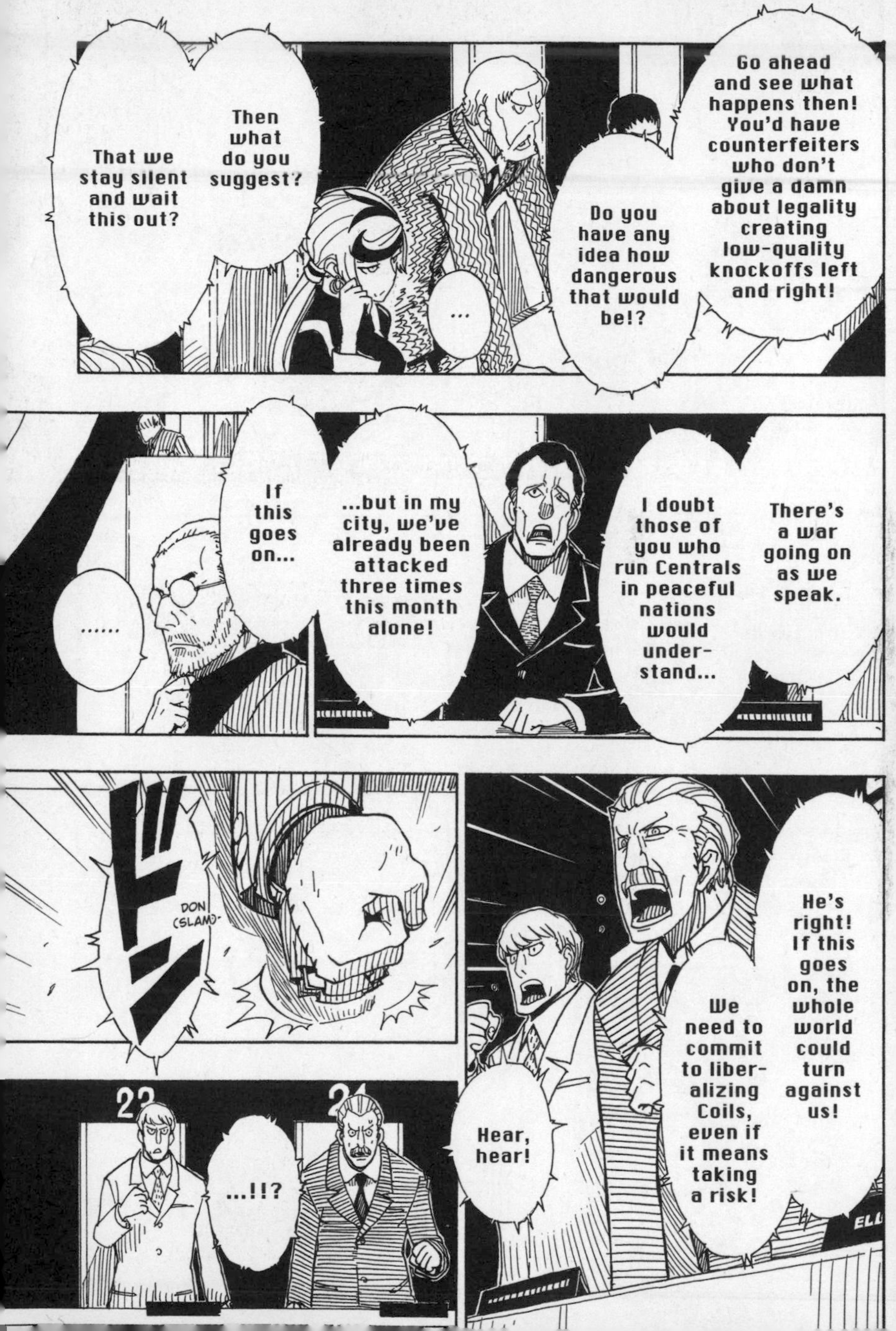

Go ahead and see what happens then! You'd have counterfeiters who don't give a damn about legality creating low-quality knockoffs left and right!
Do you have any idea how dangerous that would be!?
...
Then what do you suggest?
That we stay silent and wait this out?
There's a war going on as we speak.
I doubt those of you who run Centrals in peaceful nations would under-stand...
...but in my city, we've already been attacked three times this month alone!
If this goes on...
......
He's right! If this goes on, the whole world could turn against us!
We need to commit to liber-alizing Coils, even if it means taking a risk!
Hear, hear!
DON (SLAM)
...!!?

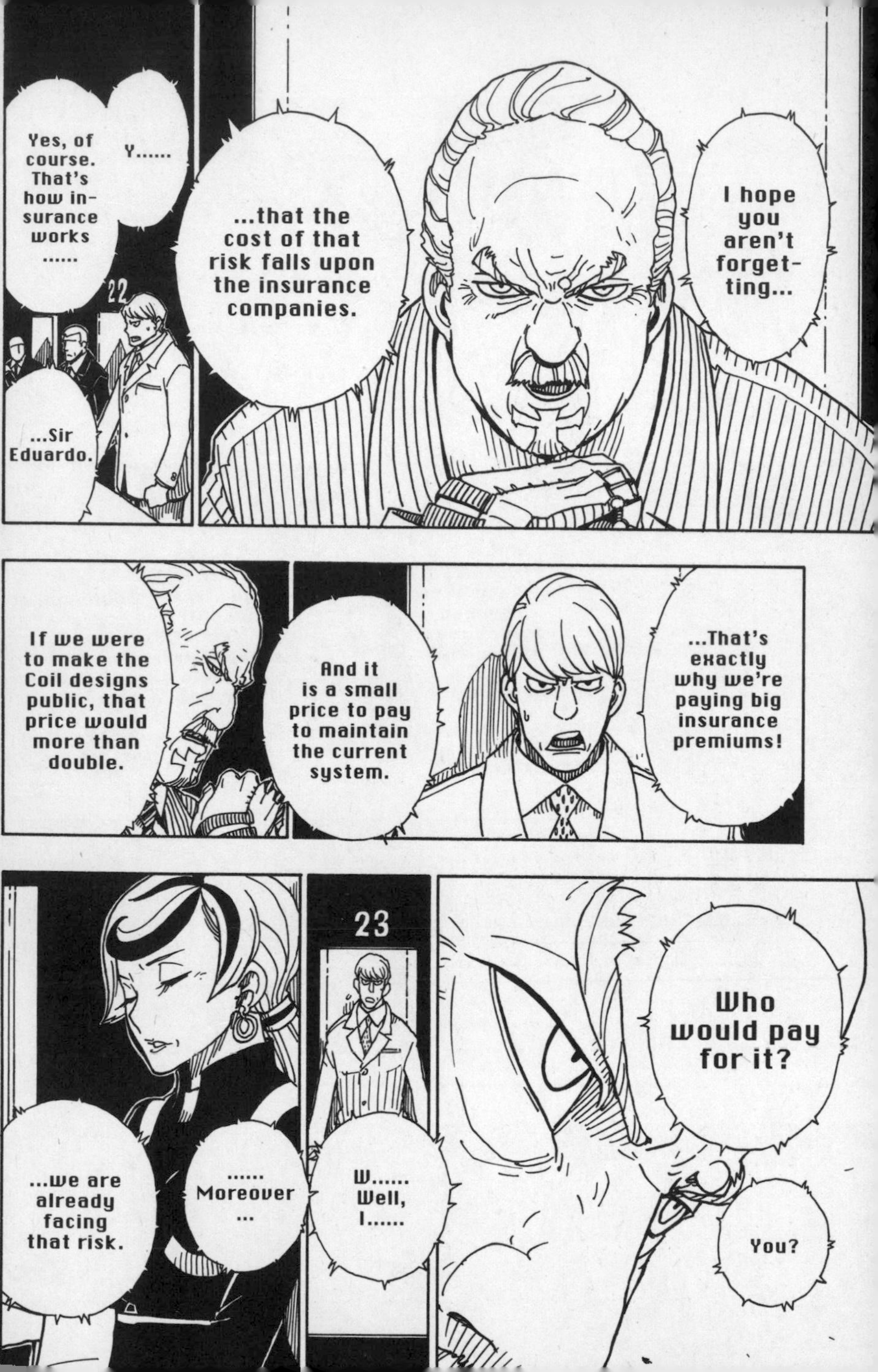
I hope you aren't forgetting...
...that the cost of that risk falls upon the insurance companies.
Y......
Yes, of course. That's how insurance works ......
...Sir Eduardo.
...That's exactly why we're paying big insurance premiums!
And it is a small price to pay to maintain the current system.
If we were to make the Coil designs public, that price would more than double.
Who would pay for it?
You?
W...... Well, I......
...... Moreover ...
...we are already facing that risk.

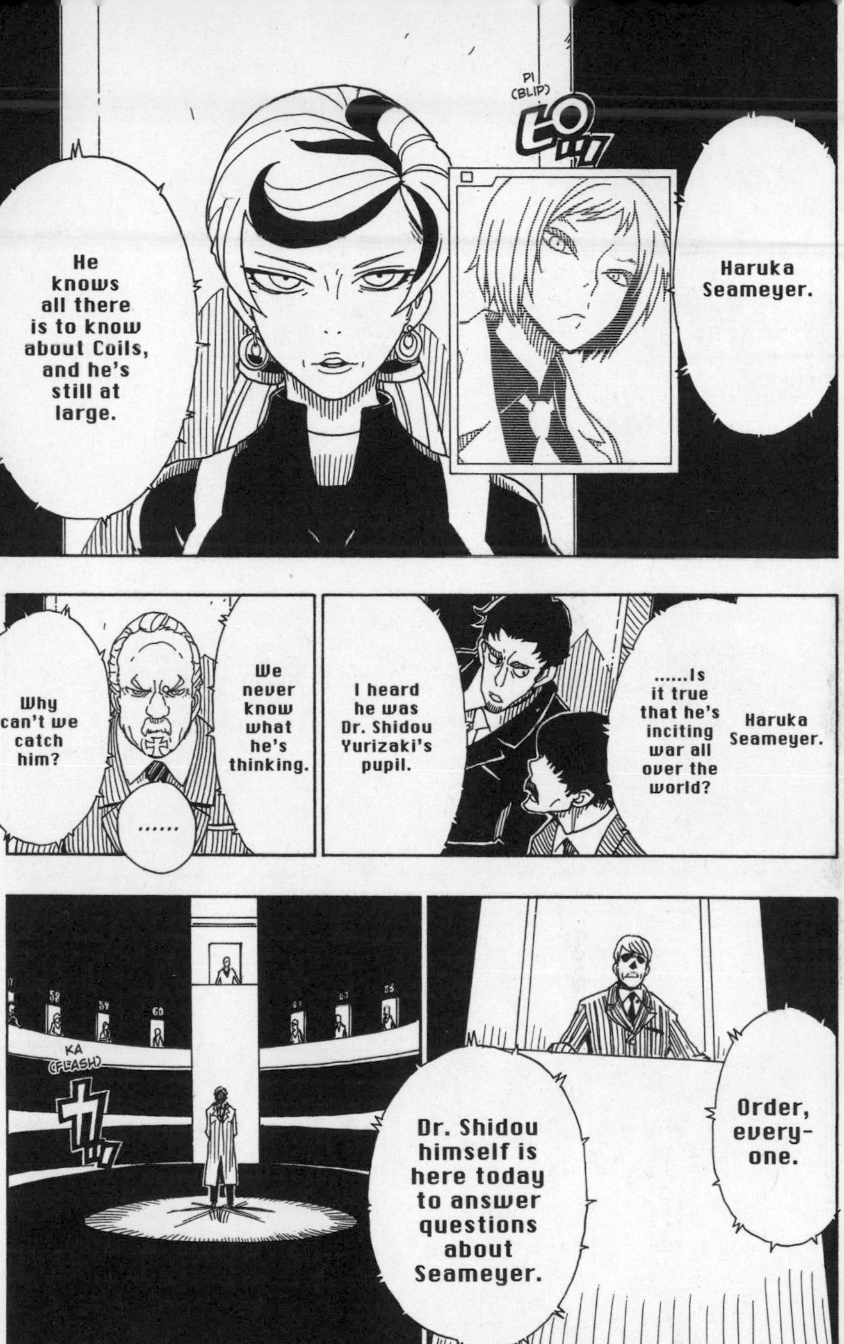
PI (BLIP)
Haruka Seameyer.
He knows all there is to know about Coils, and he's still at large.
Haruka Seameyer.
......Is it true that he's inciting war all over the world?
I heard he was Dr. Shidou Yurizaki's pupil.
We never know what he's thinking.
Why can't we catch him?
......
Order, everyone.
Dr. Shidou himself is here today to answer questions about Seameyer.
KA (FLASH)

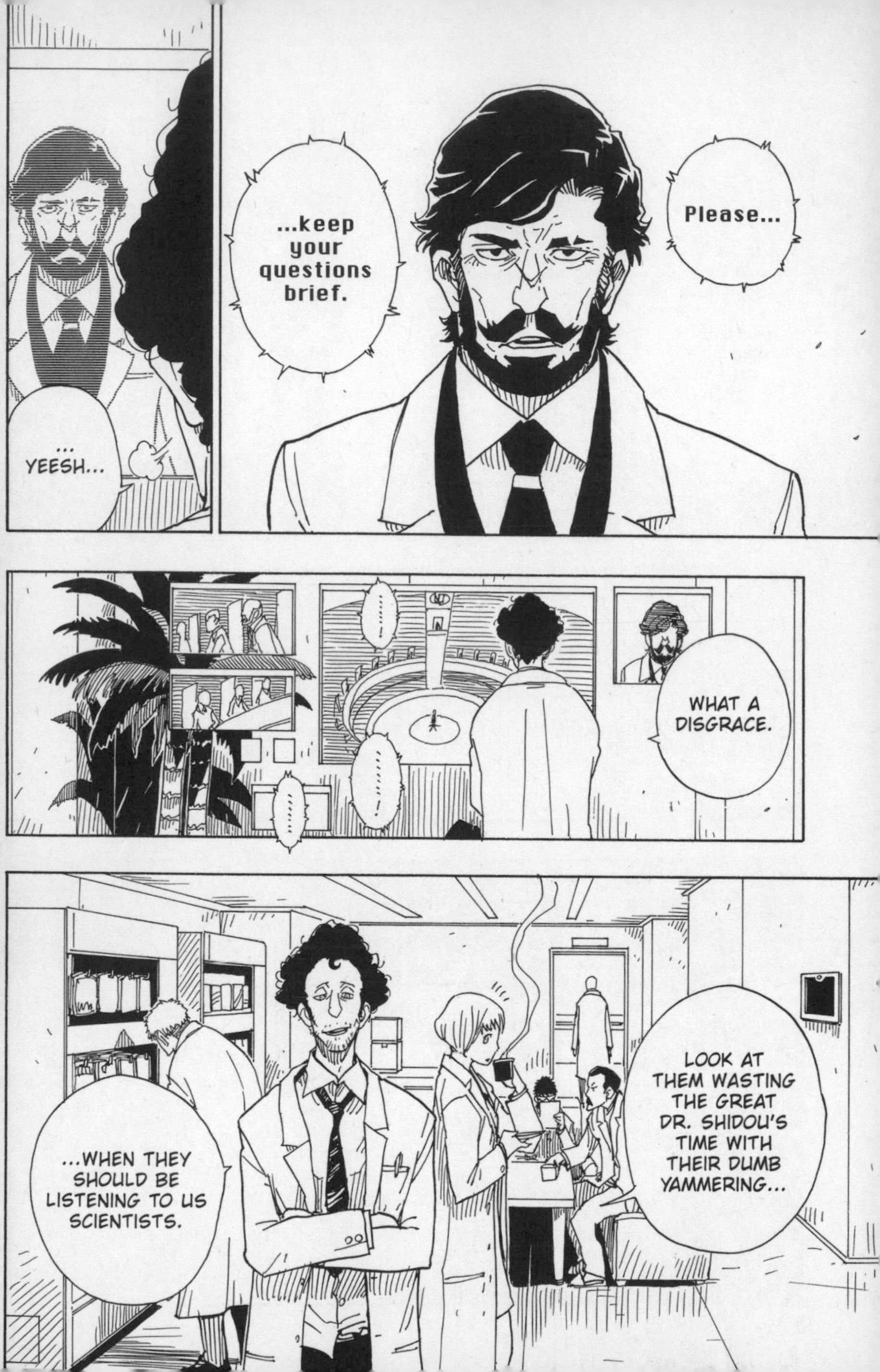
Please...
...keep your questions brief.
... YEESH...
WHAT A DISGRACE.
......
......
......
LOOK AT THEM WASTING THE GREAT DR. SHIDOU'S TIME WITH THEIR DUMB YAMMERING...
...WHEN THEY SHOULD BE LISTENING TO US SCIENTISTS.

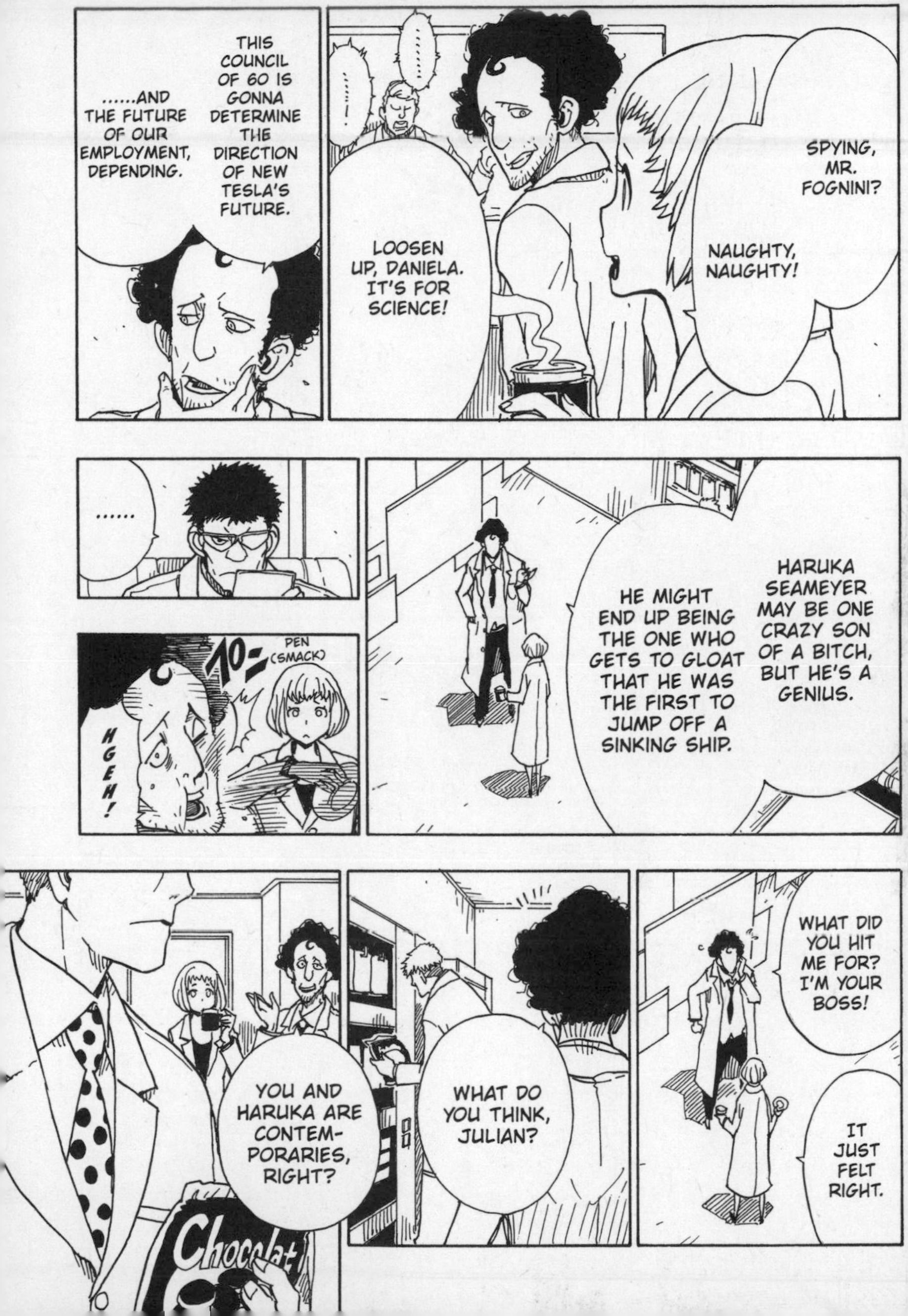
SPYING, MR. FOGNINI?
NAUGHTY, NAUGHTY!
......!
......
LOOSEN UP, DANIELA. IT'S FOR SCIENCE!
THIS COUNCIL OF 60 IS GONNA DETERMINE THE DIRECTION OF NEW TESLA'S FUTURE.
......AND THE FUTURE OF OUR EMPLOYMENT, DEPENDING.
HARUKA SEAMEYER MAY BE ONE CRAZY SON OF A BITCH, BUT HE'S A GENIUS.
HE MIGHT END UP BEING THE ONE WHO GETS TO GLOAT THAT HE WAS THE FIRST TO JUMP OFF A SINKING SHIP.
......
PEN (SMACK)
HGEH!
WHAT DID YOU HIT ME FOR? I'M YOUR BOSS!
IT JUST FELT RIGHT.
WHAT DO YOU THINK, JULIAN?
YOU AND HARUKA ARE CONTEMPORARIES, RIGHT?
Chocolat

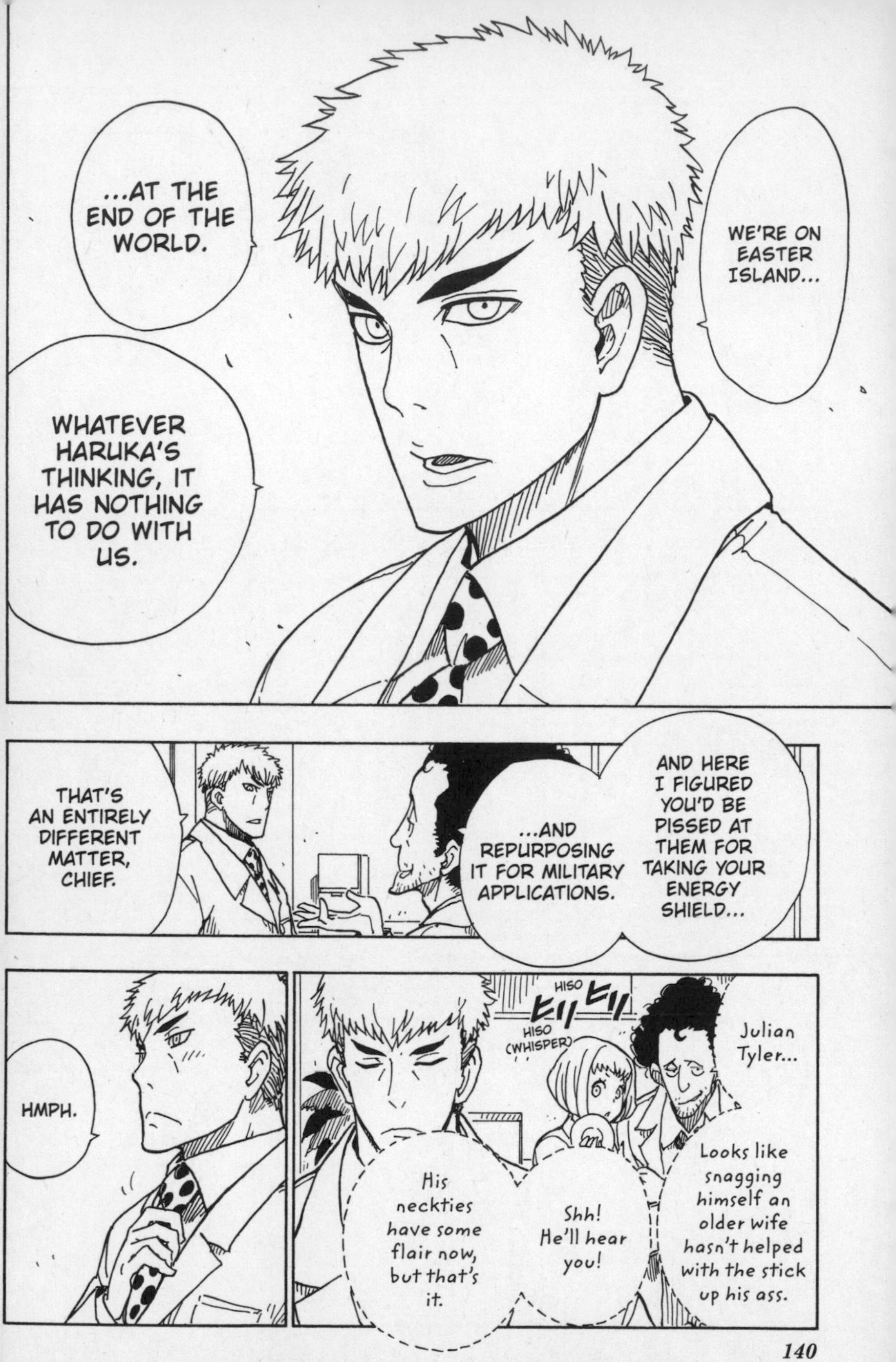
WE'RE ON EASTER ISLAND...
...AT THE END OF THE WORLD.
WHATEVER HARUKA'S THINKING, IT HAS NOTHING TO DO WITH US.
AND HERE I FIGURED YOU'D BE PISSED AT THEM FOR TAKING YOUR ENERGY SHIELD...
...AND REPURPOSING IT FOR MILITARY APPLICATIONS.
THAT'S AN ENTIRELY DIFFERENT MATTER, CHIEF.
HISO
HISO (WHISPER)
Julian Tyler...
Looks like snagging himself an older wife hasn't helped with the stick up his ass.
Shh! He'll hear you!
His neckties have some flair now, but that's it.
HMPH.

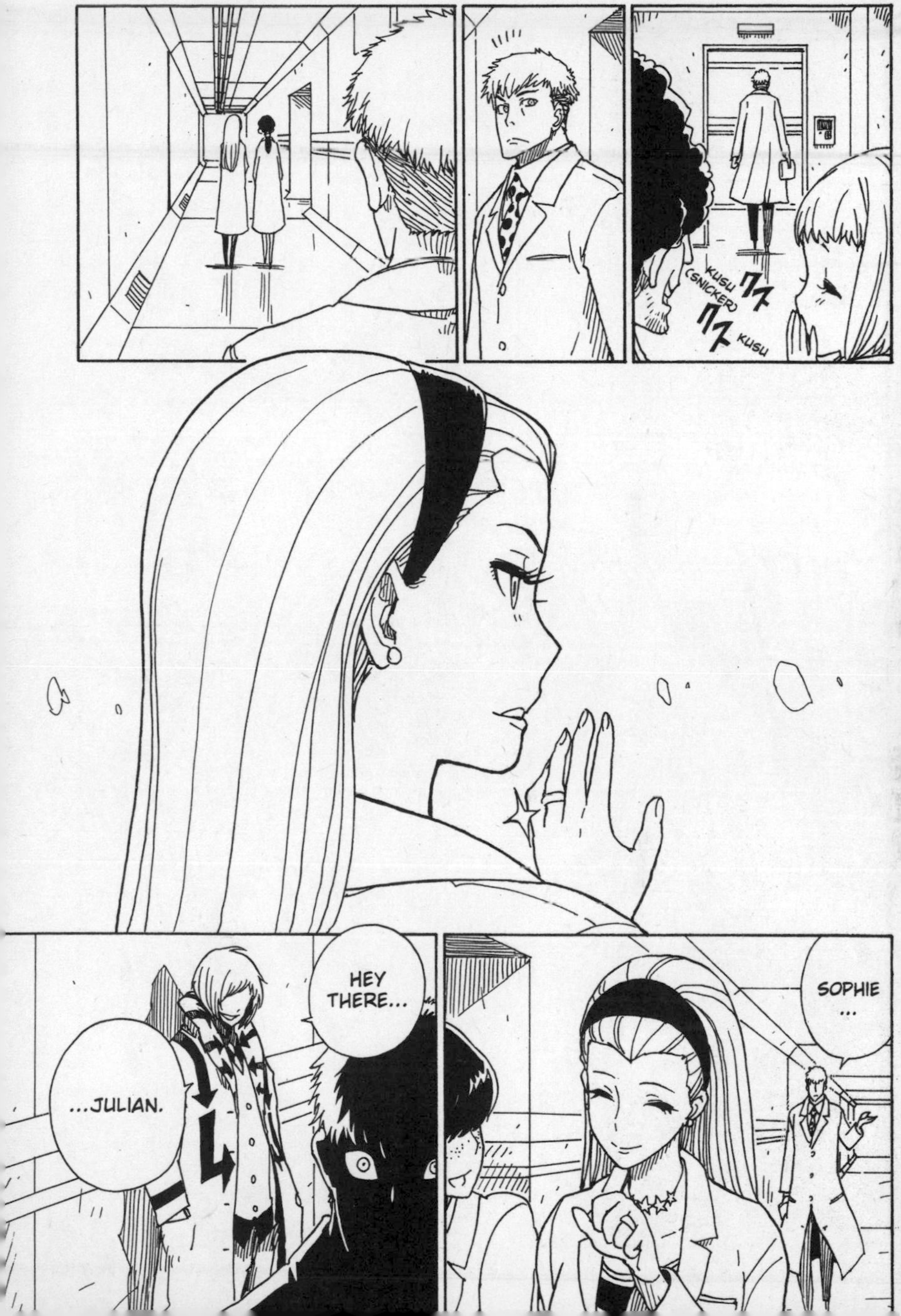
KUSU (SNICKER)
クス
クス
KUSU
SOPHIE ...
HEY THERE...
...JULIAN.

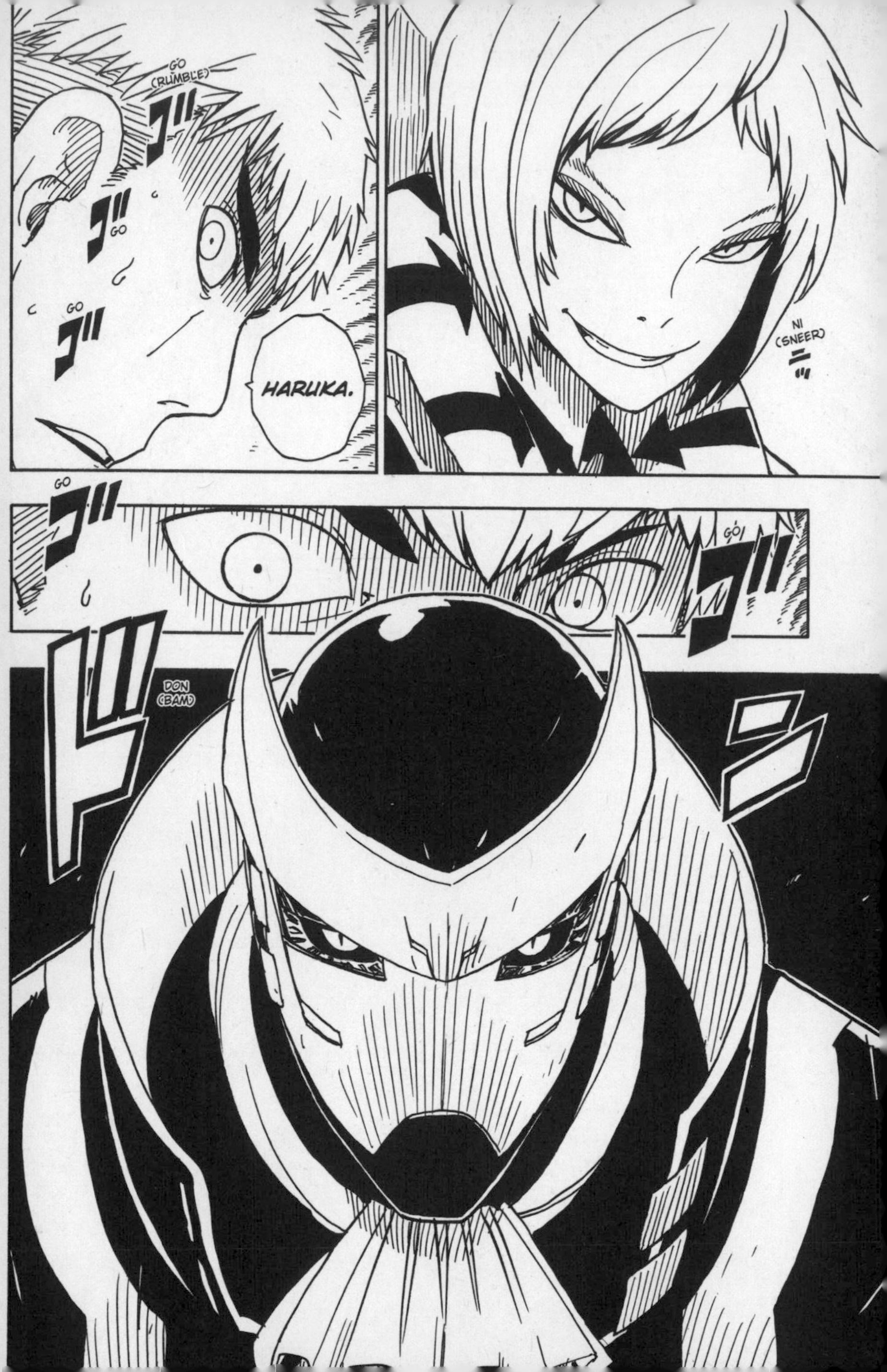
NI (SNEER)
GO (RUMBLE)
GO
GO
HARUKA.
GO
GO
DON (BAM)

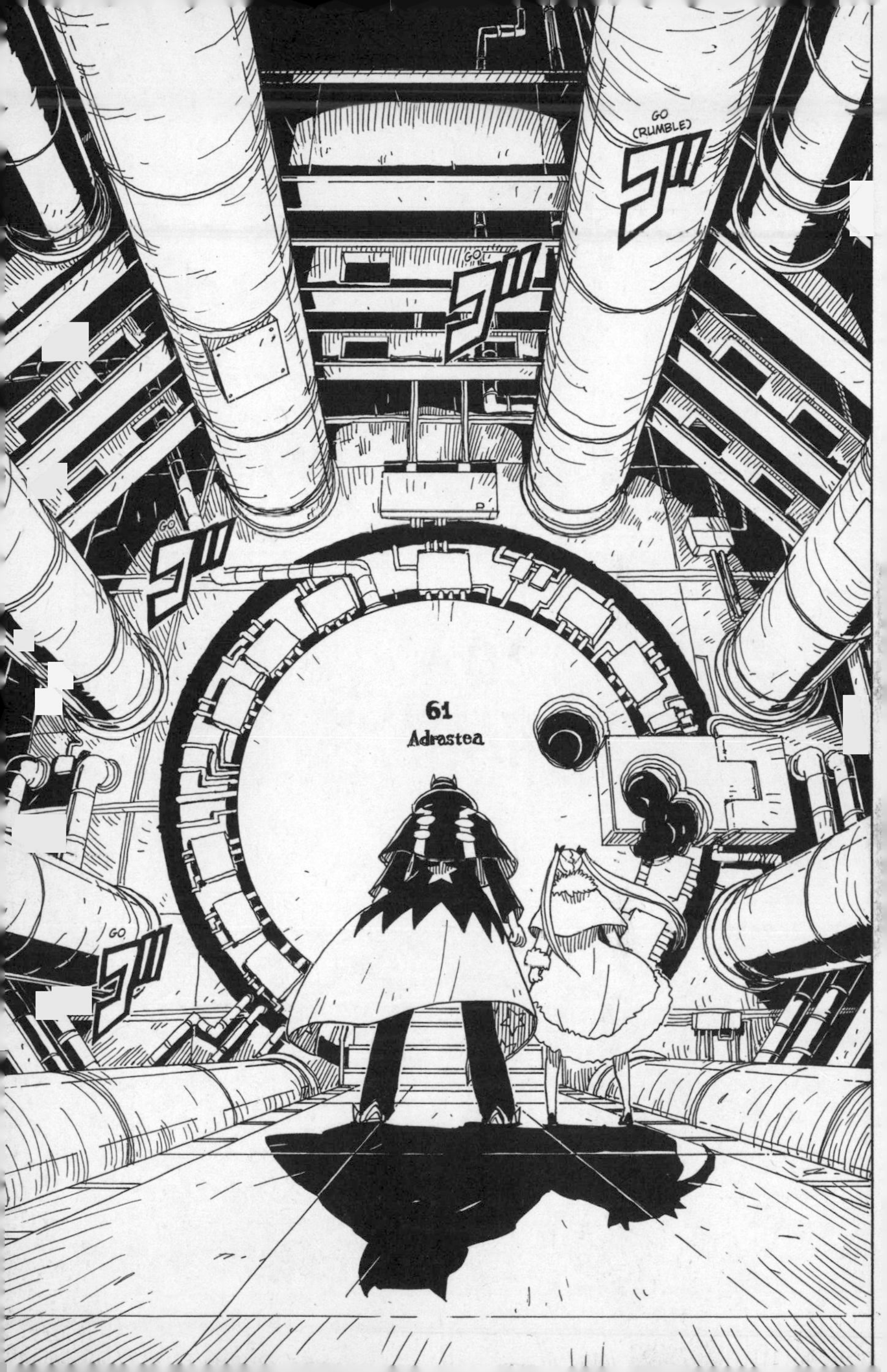
GO
(RUMBLE)
GO
GO
GO
61
Adrastea

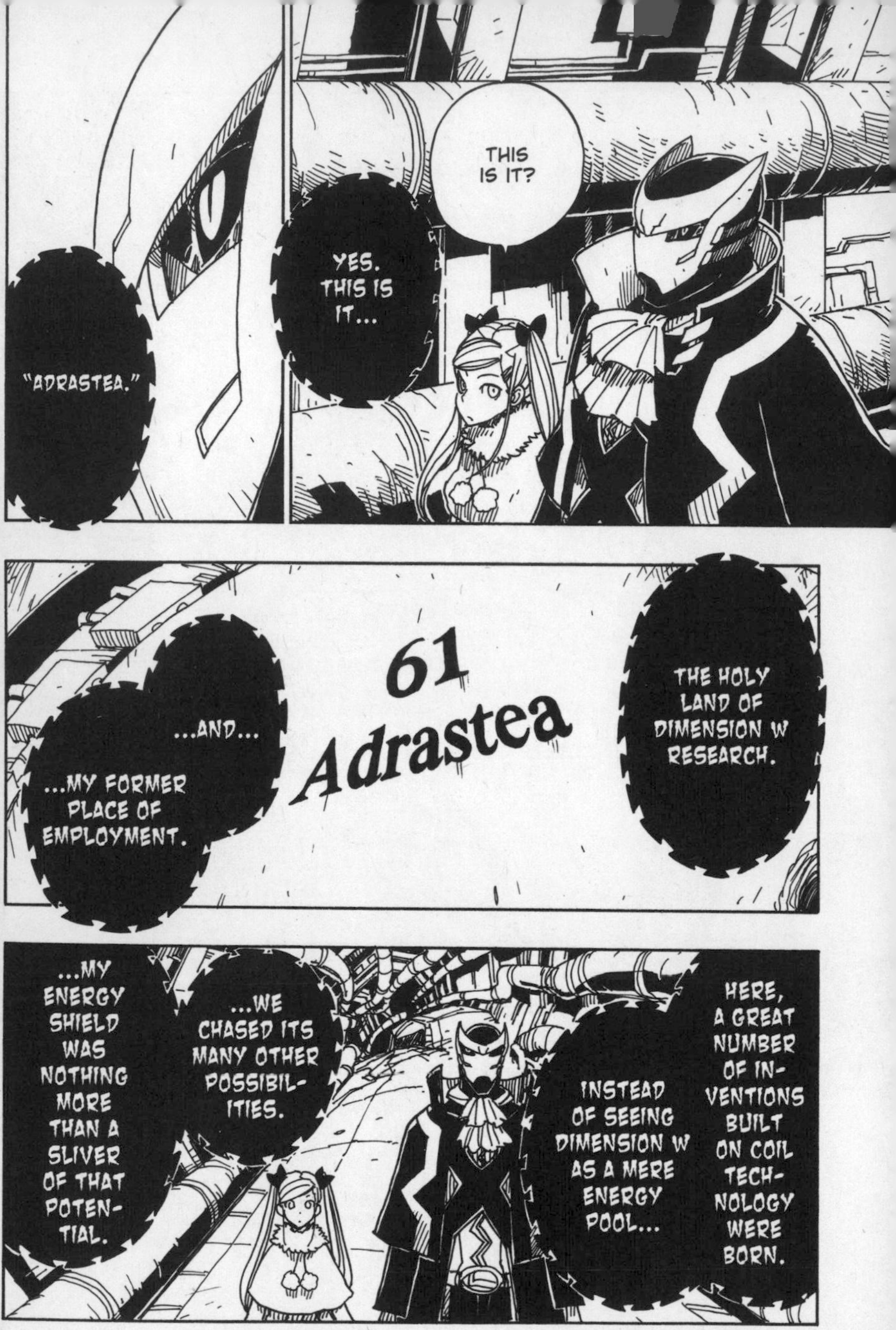
THIS IS IT?
YES. THIS IS IT...
"ADRASTEA."
THE HOLY LAND OF DIMENSION W RESEARCH.
61 Adrastea
...AND...
...MY FORMER PLACE OF EMPLOYMENT.
HERE, A GREAT NUMBER OF IN-VENTIONS BUILT ON COIL TECH-NOLOGY WERE BORN.
INSTEAD OF SEEING DIMENSION W AS A MERE ENERGY POOL...
...WE CHASED ITS MANY OTHER POSSIBIL-ITIES.
...MY ENERGY SHIELD WAS NOTHING MORE THAN A SLIVER OF THAT POTEN-TIAL.

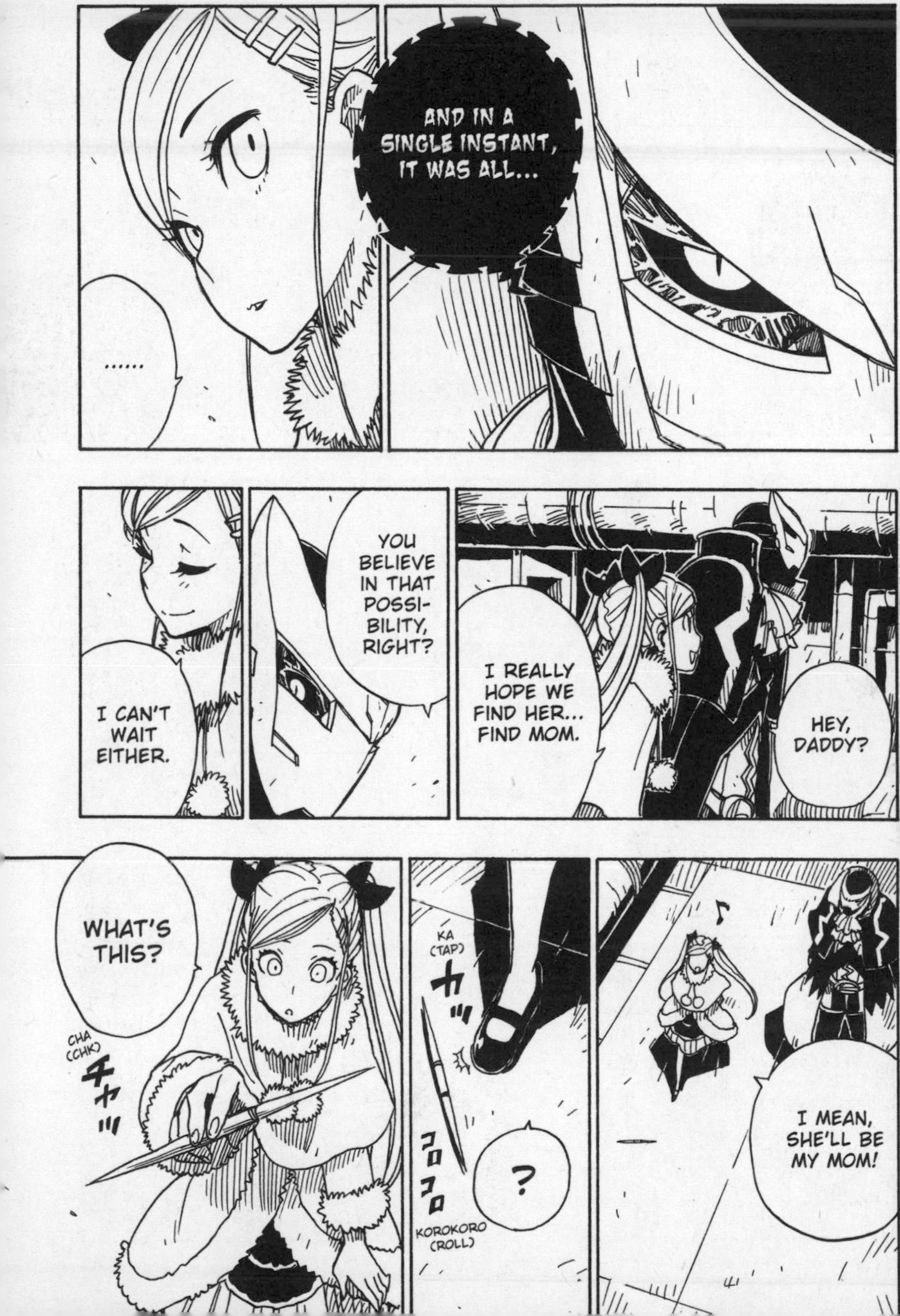
AND IN A SINGLE INSTANT, IT WAS ALL...
......
HEY, DADDY?
I REALLY HOPE WE FIND HER... FIND MOM.
YOU BELIEVE IN THAT POSSIBILITY, RIGHT?
I CAN'T WAIT EITHER.
I MEAN, SHE'LL BE MY MOM!
KA (TAP)
カッ
?
コロコロ
KOROKORO (ROLL)
WHAT'S THIS?
CHA (CHK)
チャッ

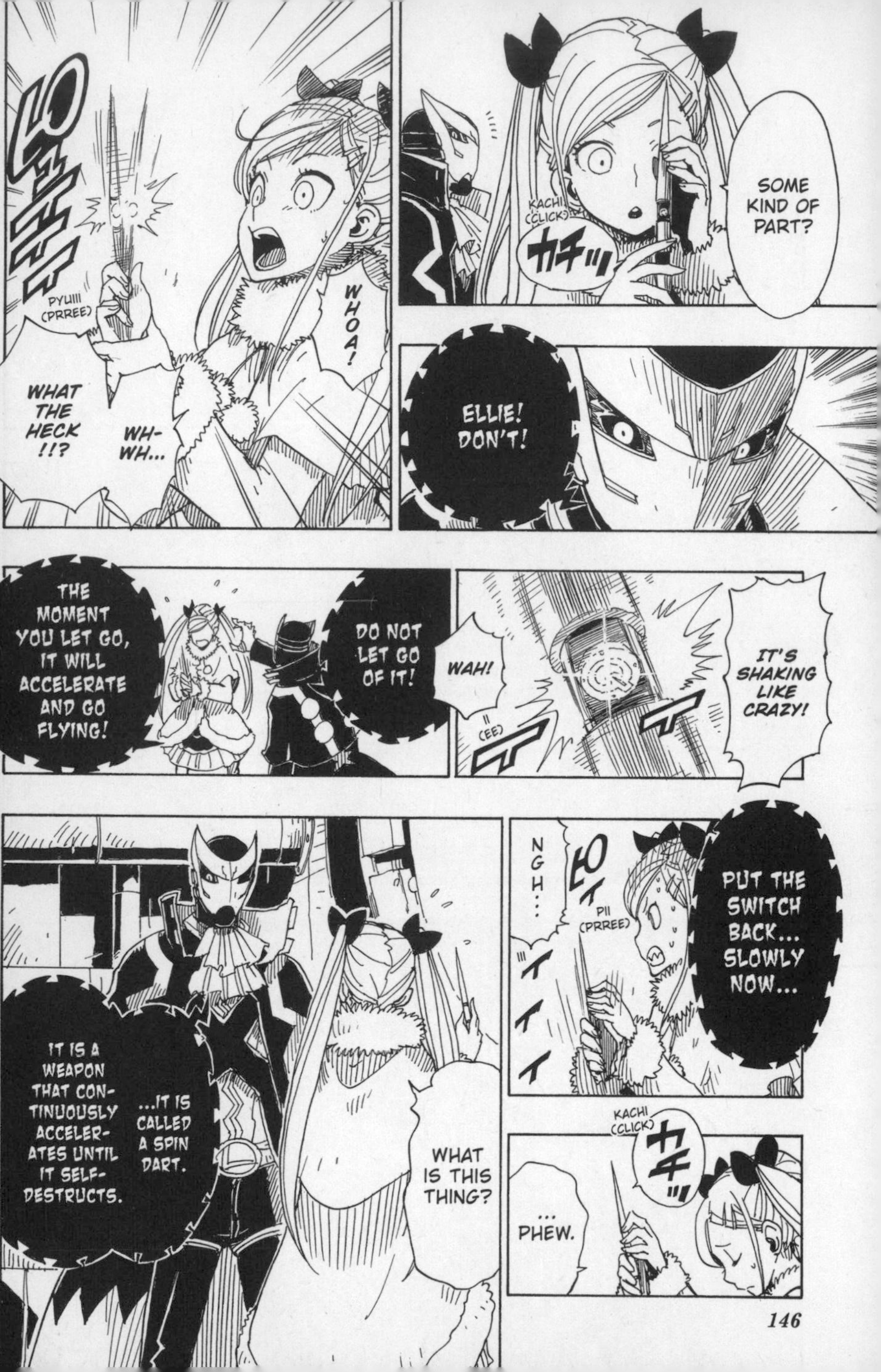
SOME KIND OF PART?
KACHI (CLICK)
カチッ
ELLIE! DON'T!
PYUIII (PRREE)
WHOA!
WH-WH...
WHAT THE HECK!!?
IT'S SHAKING LIKE CRAZY!
WAH!
II (EE)
DO NOT LET GO OF IT!
THE MOMENT YOU LET GO, IT WILL ACCELERATE AND GO FLYING!
PUT THE SWITCH BACK... SLOWLY NOW...
NGH...
PII (PRREE)
KACHI (CLICK)
...PHEW.
WHAT IS THIS THING?
...IT IS CALLED A SPIN DART.
IT IS A WEAPON THAT CONTINUOUSLY ACCELERATES UNTIL IT SELF-DESTRUCTS.

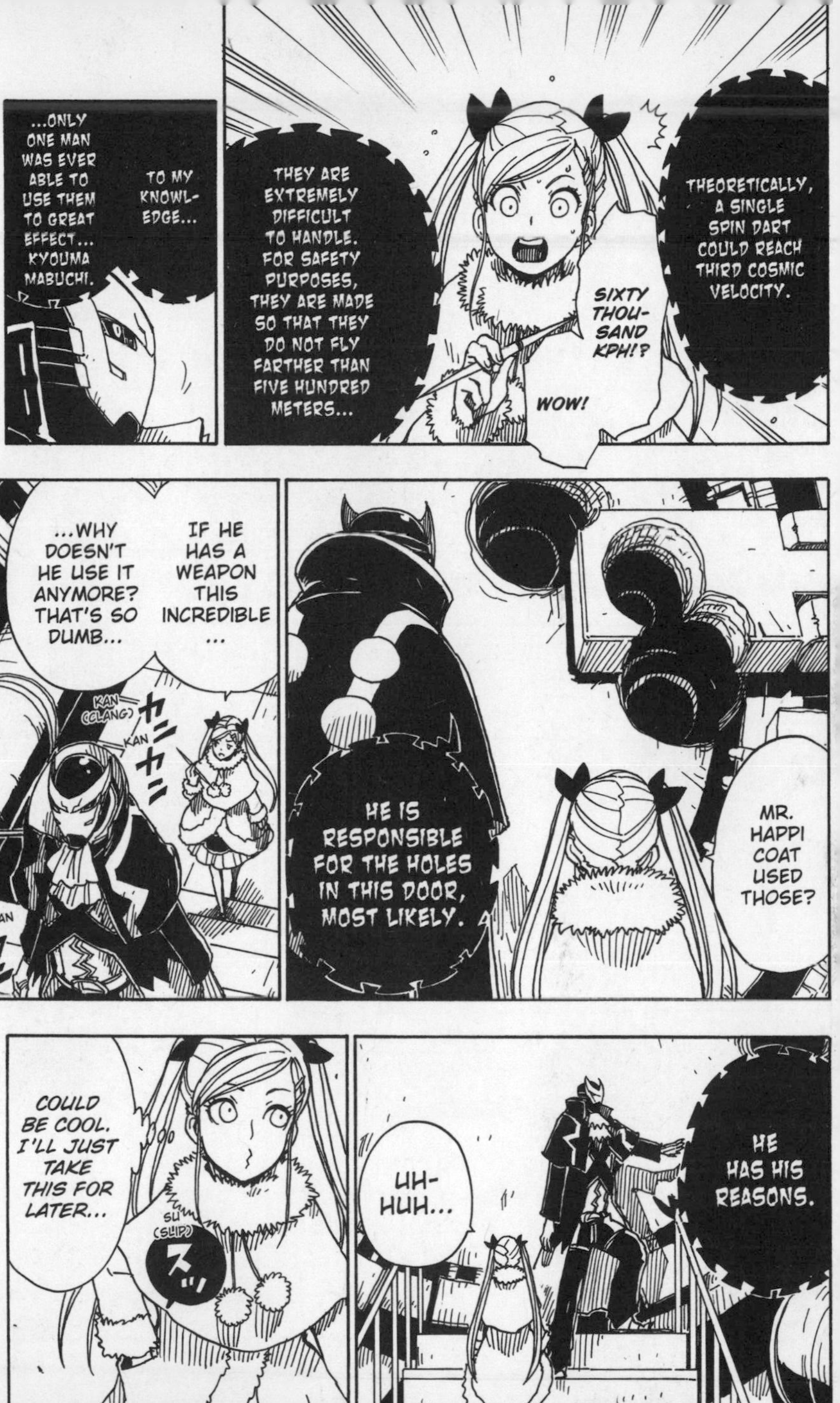
THEORETICALLY, A SINGLE SPIN DART COULD REACH THIRD COSMIC VELOCITY.
SIXTY THOUSAND KPH!?
WOW!
THEY ARE EXTREMELY DIFFICULT TO HANDLE. FOR SAFETY PURPOSES, THEY ARE MADE SO THAT THEY DO NOT FLY FARTHER THAN FIVE HUNDRED METERS...
TO MY KNOWLEDGE...
...ONLY ONE MAN WAS EVER ABLE TO USE THEM TO GREAT EFFECT... KYOUMA MABUCHI.
MR. HAPPI COAT USED THOSE?
HE IS RESPONSIBLE FOR THE HOLES IN THIS DOOR, MOST LIKELY.
IF HE HAS A WEAPON THIS INCREDIBLE...
...WHY DOESN'T HE USE IT ANYMORE? THAT'S SO DUMB...
KAN (CLANG) カン
KAN カン
KAN カン
HE HAS HIS REASONS.
UH-HUH...
COULD BE COOL. I'LL JUST TAKE THIS FOR LATER...
SU (SLIP) スッ

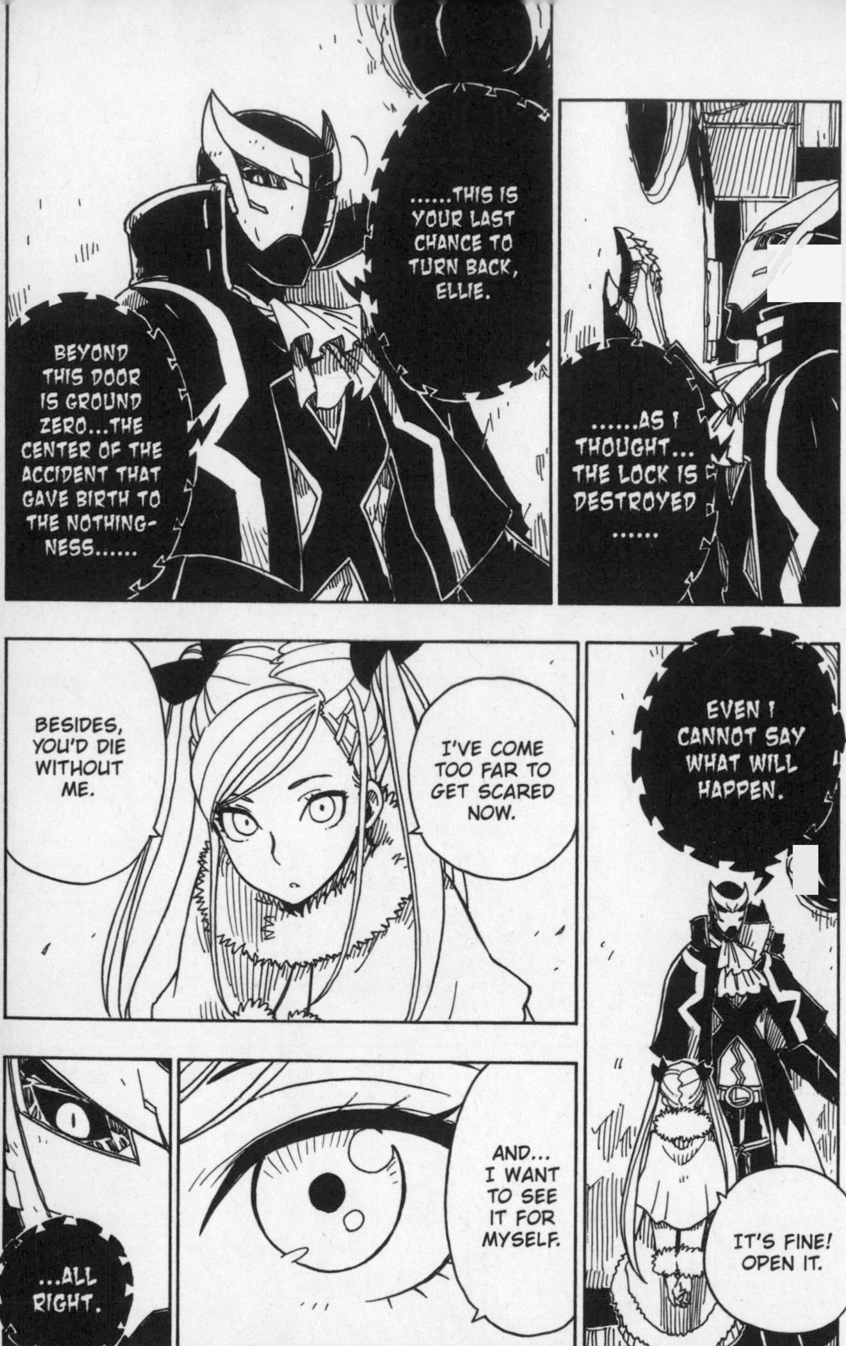

......AS I THOUGHT... THE LOCK IS DESTROYED ......
......THIS IS YOUR LAST CHANCE TO TURN BACK, ELLIE.
BEYOND THIS DOOR IS GROUND ZERO...THE CENTER OF THE ACCIDENT THAT GAVE BIRTH TO THE NOTHING-NESS......
EVEN I CANNOT SAY WHAT WILL HAPPEN.
IT'S FINE! OPEN IT.
I'VE COME TOO FAR TO GET SCARED NOW.
BESIDES, YOU'D DIE WITHOUT ME.
AND... I WANT TO SEE IT FOR MYSELF.
...ALL RIGHT.

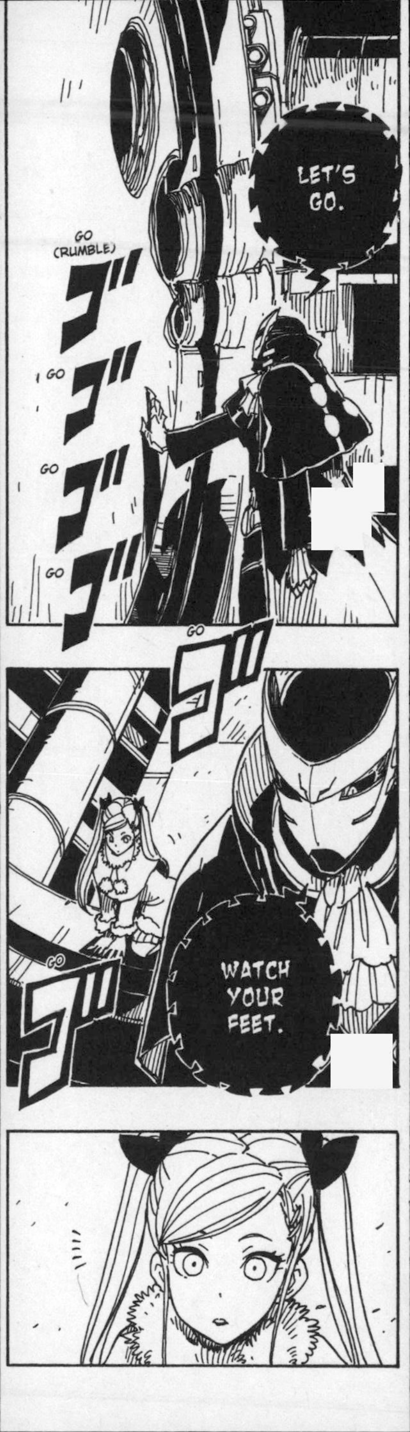
LET'S GO.
GO (RUMBLE)
ゴ
GO
ゴ
GO
ゴ
GO
ゴ
GO
ゴ
WATCH YOUR FEET.
GO
ゴ

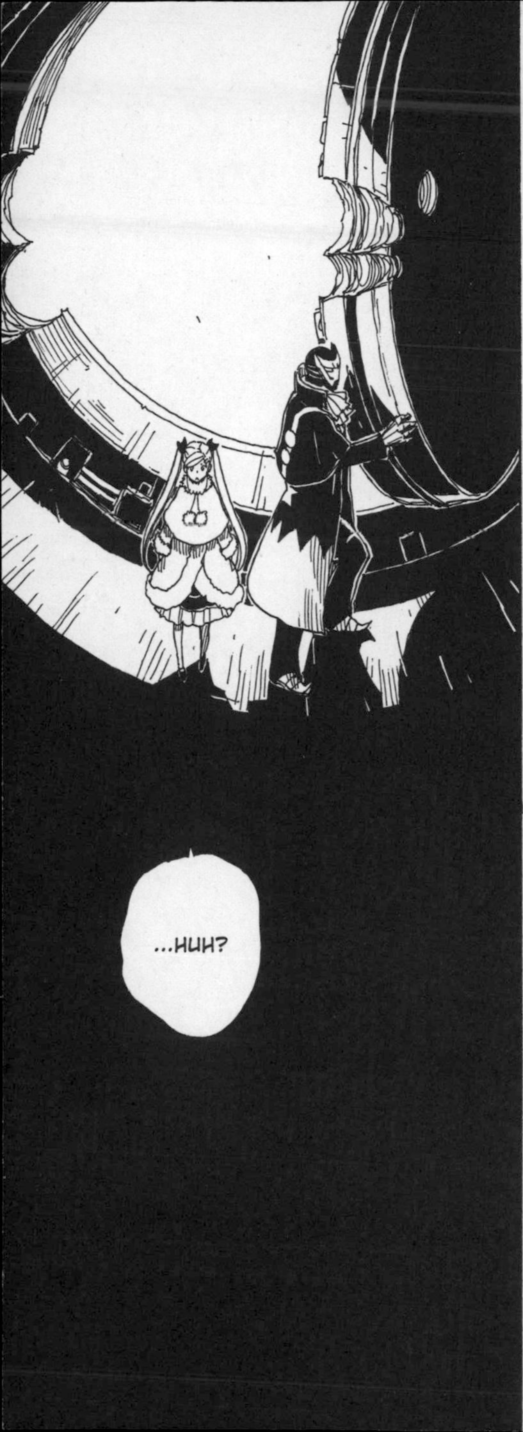
...HUH?

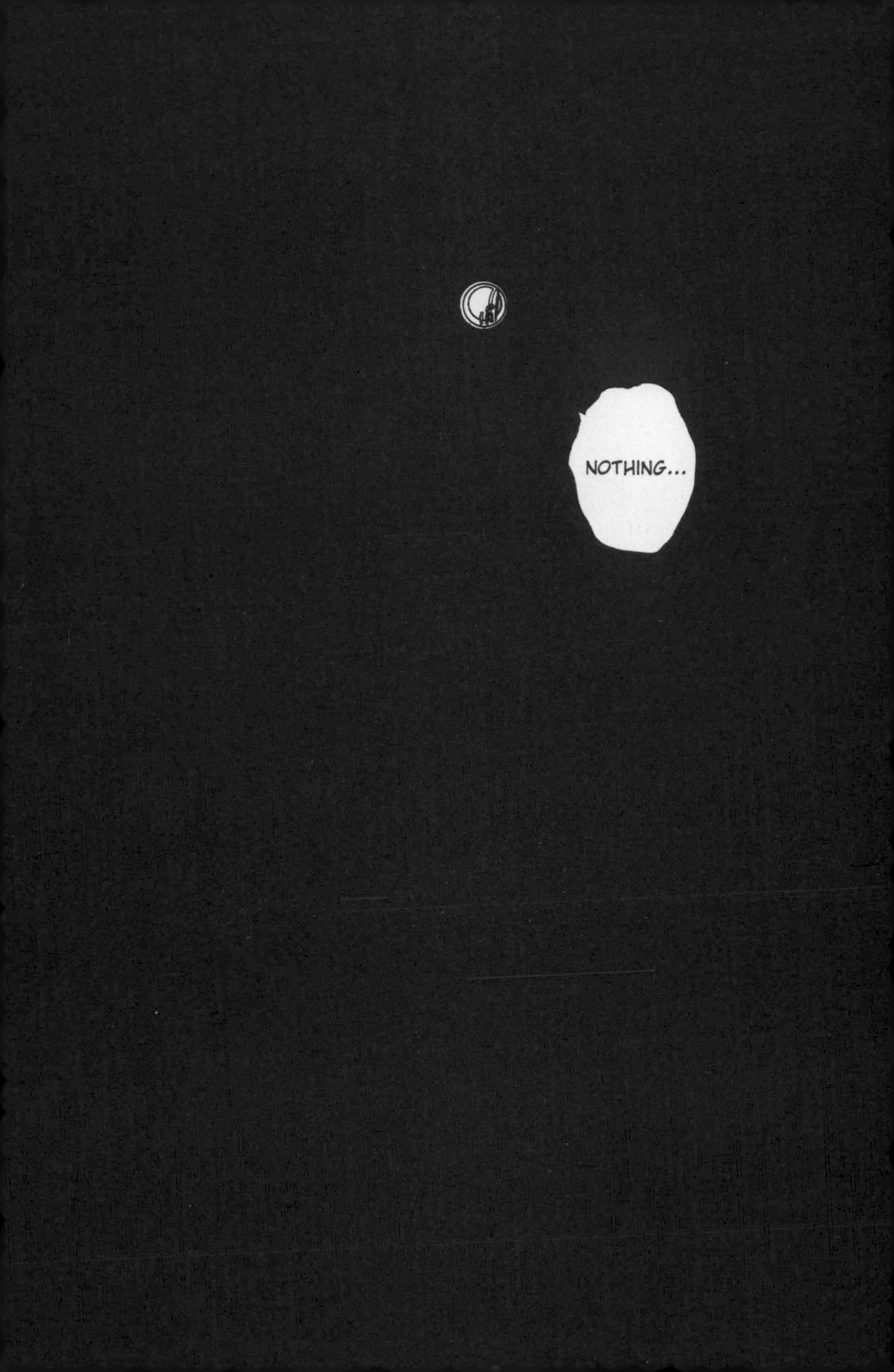
NOTHING...

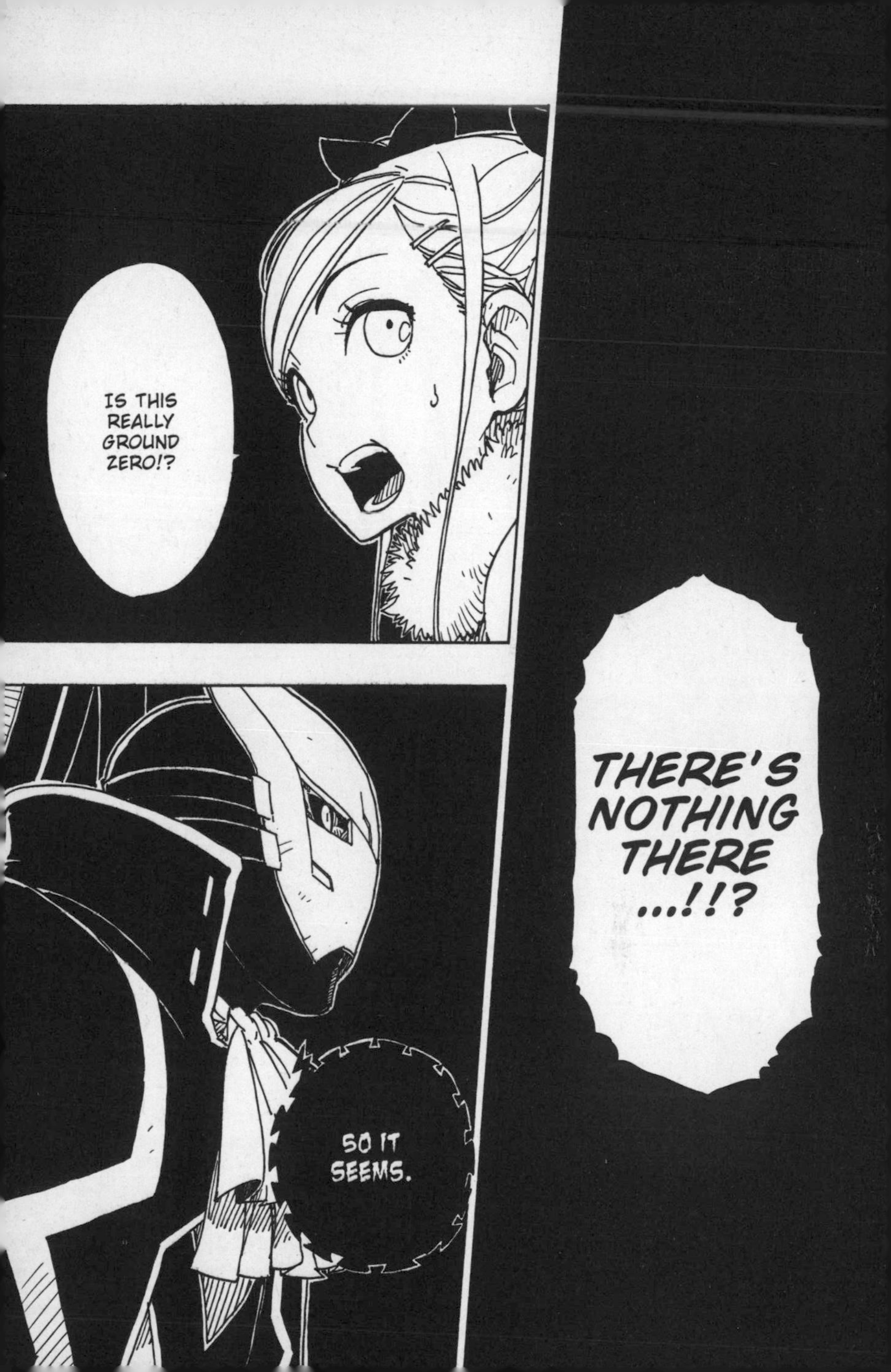
THERE'S NOTHING THERE ...!!?
IS THIS REALLY GROUND ZERO!?
SO IT SEEMS.

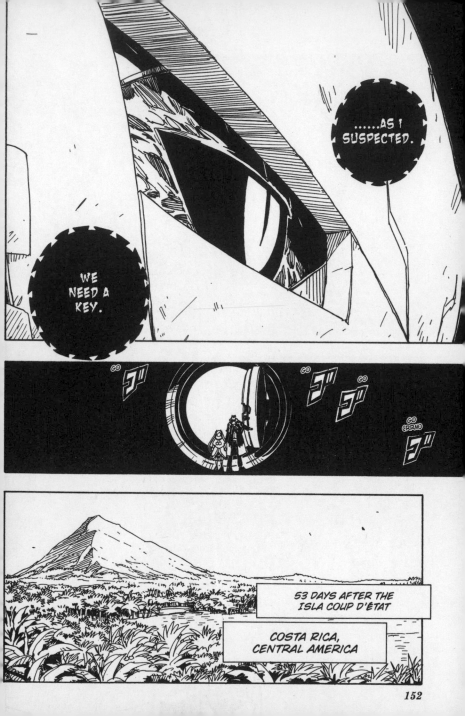

......AS I SUSPECTED.

WE NEED A KEY.

53 DAYS AFTER THE ISLA COUP D'ÉTAT

COSTA RICA, CENTRAL AMERICA

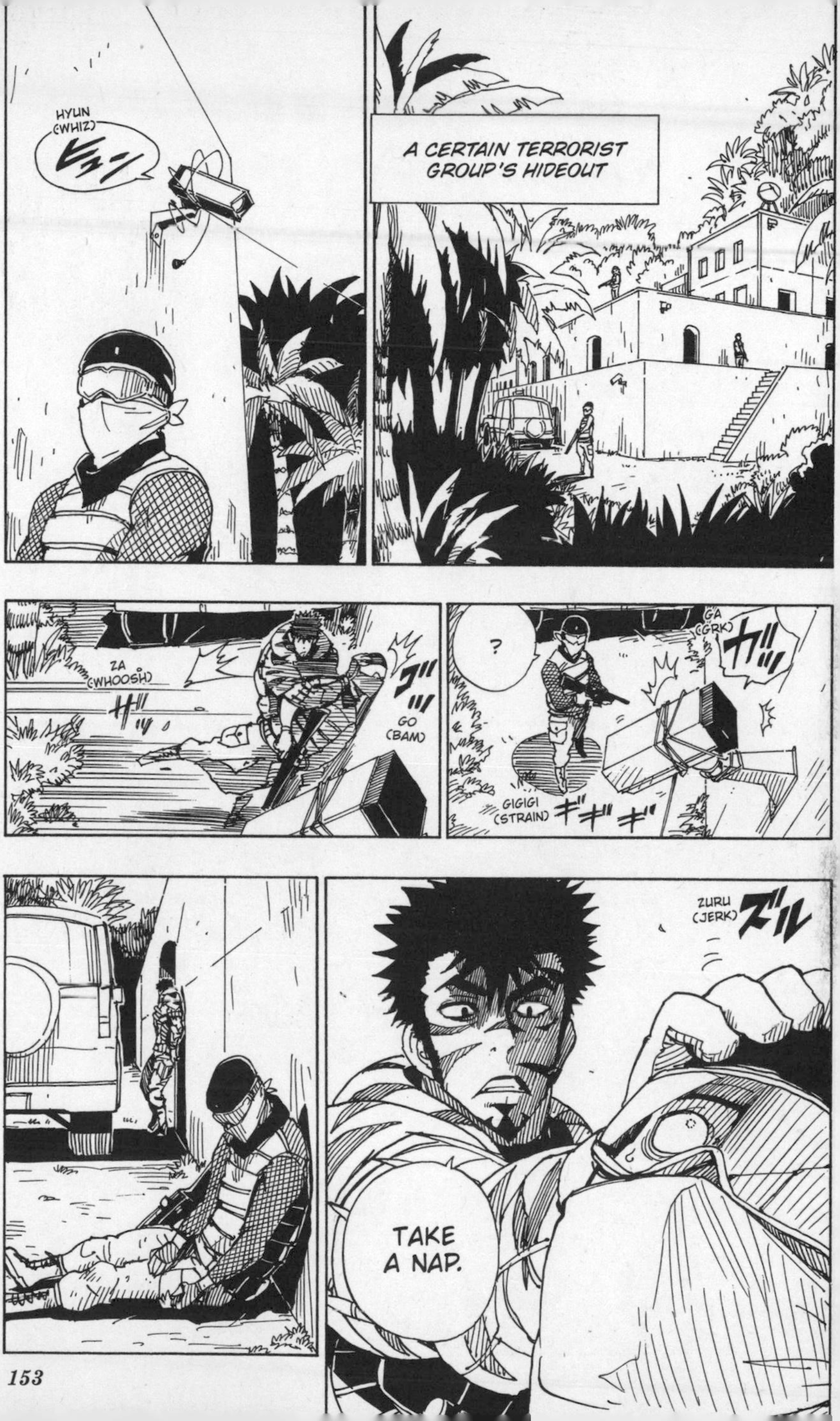

A CERTAIN TERRORIST GROUP'S HIDEOUT
HYUN (WHIZ)
ヒュン
GA (GRK)
ガッ
?
GIGIGI (STRAIN)
ギギギ
ZA (WHOOSH)
ザッ
GO (BAM)
ゴッ
ZURU (JERK)
ズル
TAKE A NAP.

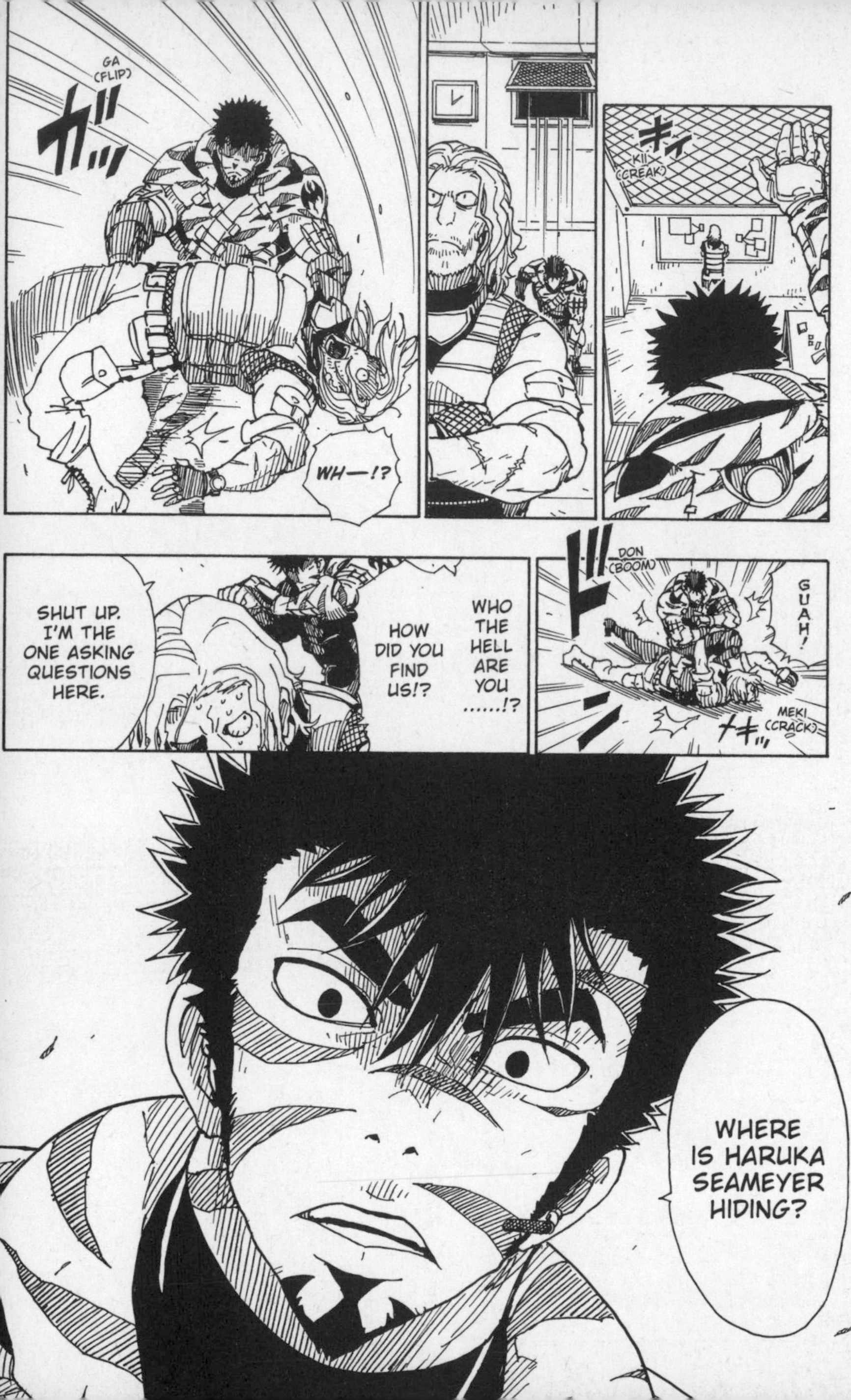

KII (CREAK)
GA (FLIP)
WH—!?
DON (BOOM)
GUAH!
MEKI (CRACK)
WHO THE HELL ARE YOU ......!?
HOW DID YOU FIND US!?
SHUT UP. I'M THE ONE ASKING QUESTIONS HERE.
WHERE IS HARUKA SEAMEYER HIDING?

Dimension W

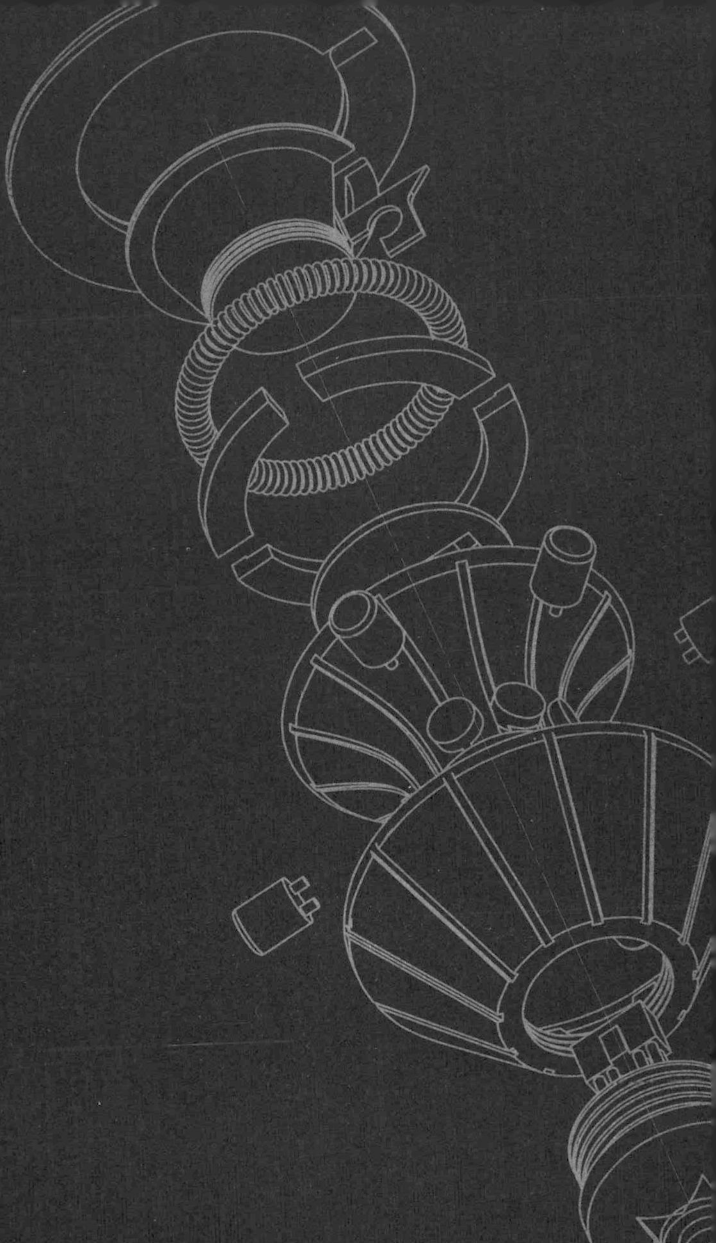

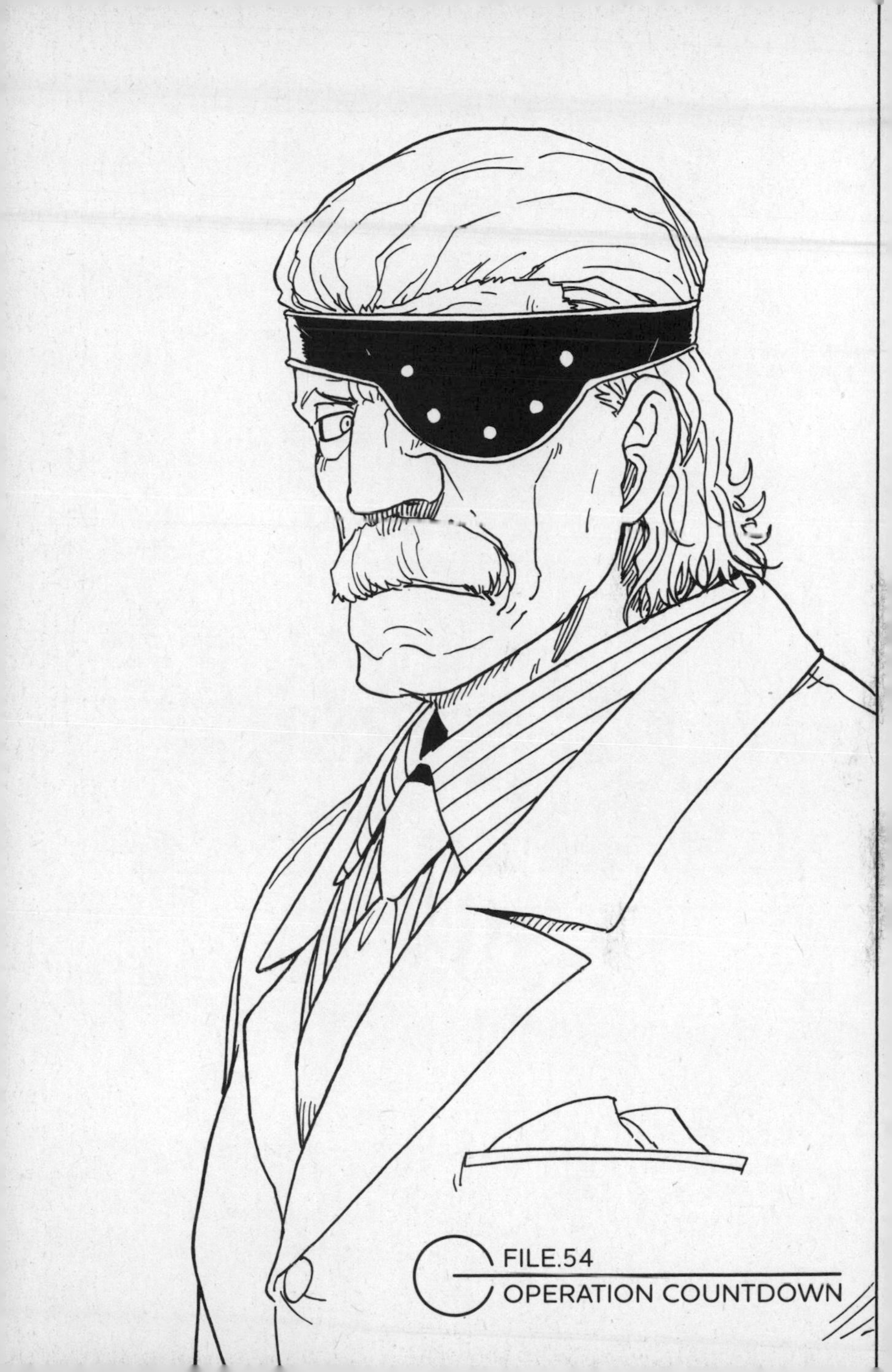
FILE.54
OPERATION COUNTDOWN

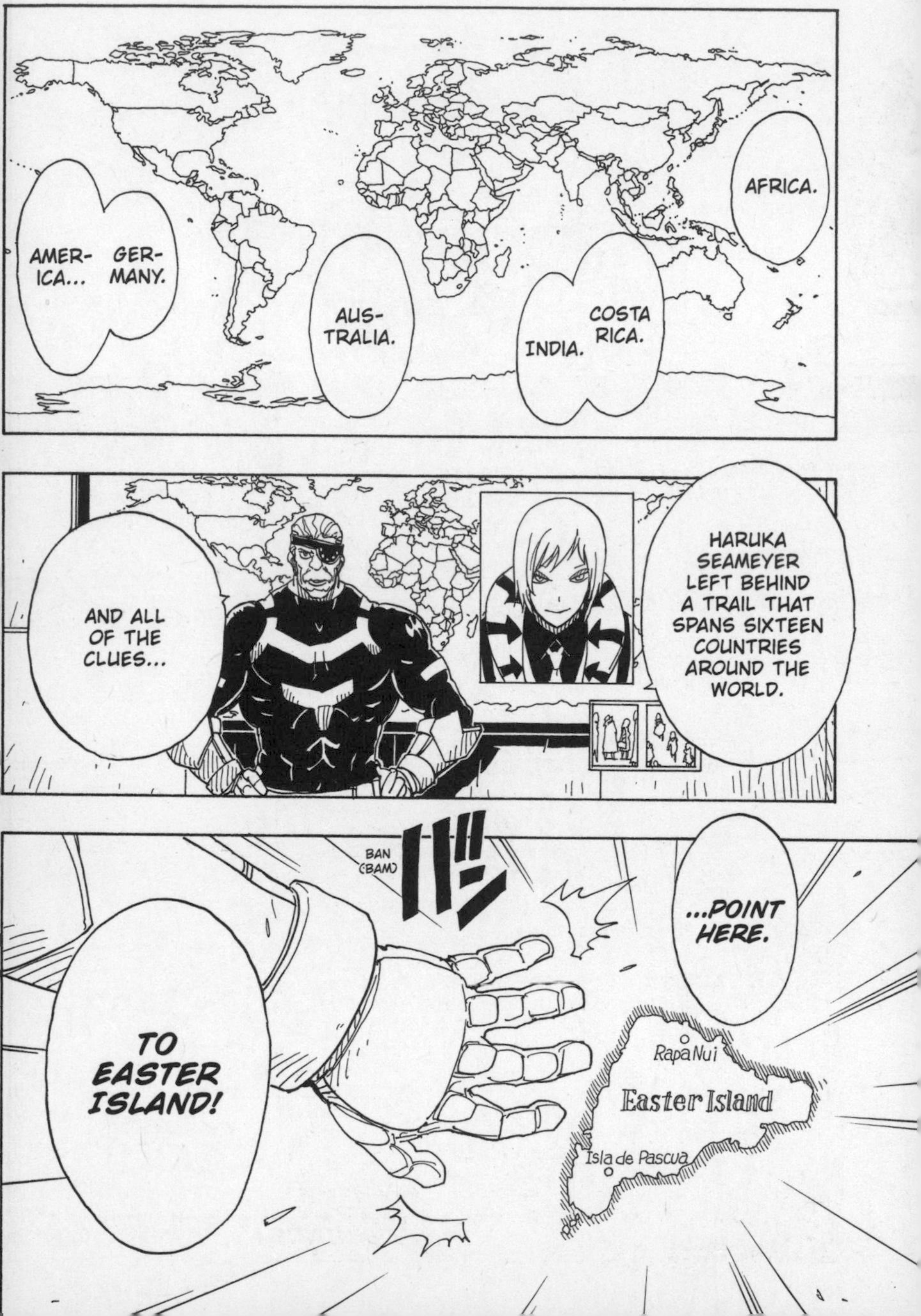
AFRICA.
COSTA RICA.
INDIA.
AUSTRALIA.
GERMANY.
AMERICA...
HARUKA SEAMEYER LEFT BEHIND A TRAIL THAT SPANS SIXTEEN COUNTRIES AROUND THE WORLD.
AND ALL OF THE CLUES...
...POINT HERE.
BAN (BAM)
TO EASTER ISLAND!
Rapa Nui
Easter Island
Isla de Pascua

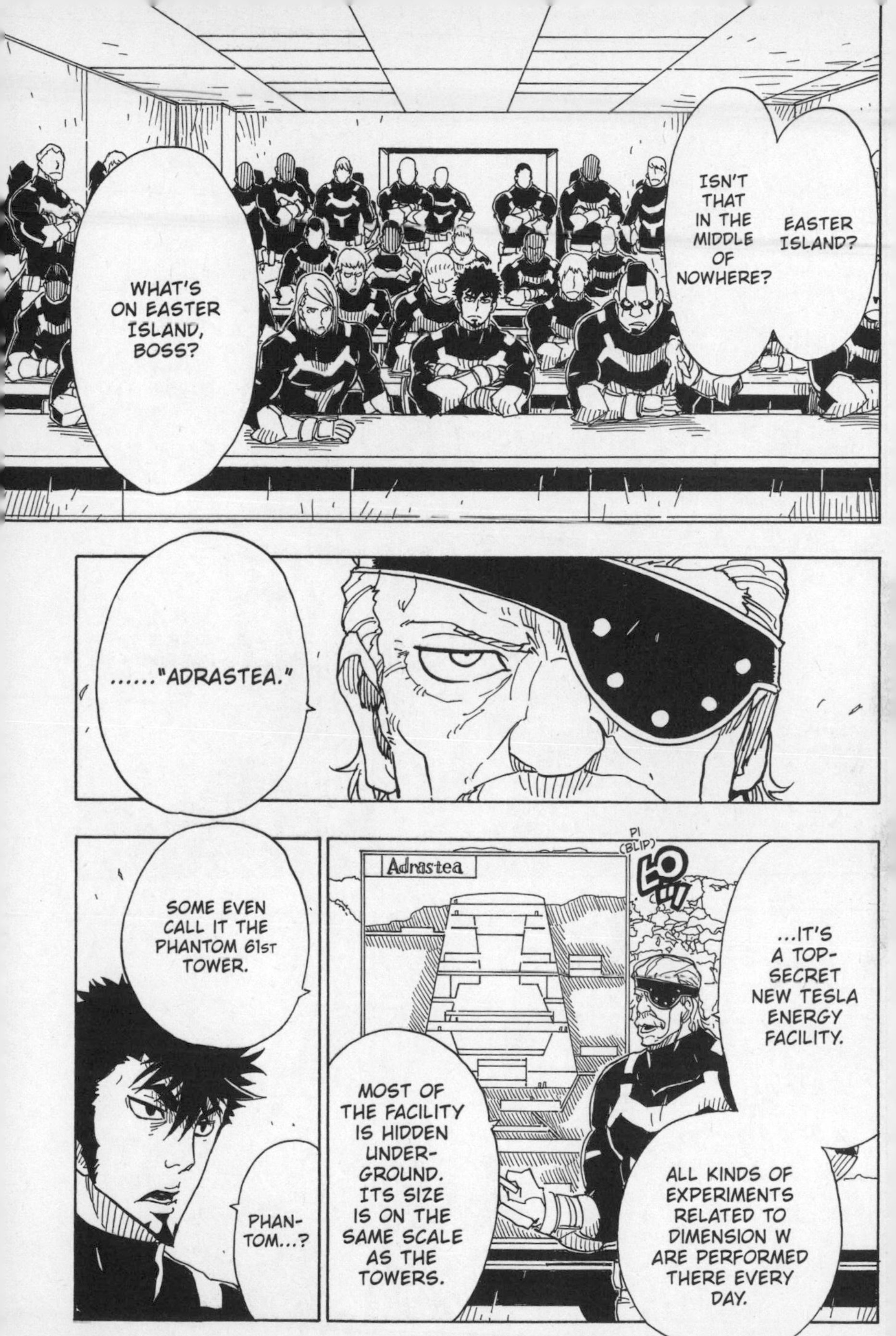
EASTER ISLAND?
ISN'T THAT IN THE MIDDLE OF NOWHERE?
WHAT'S ON EASTER ISLAND, BOSS?
......"ADRASTEA."
PI (BLIP)
Adrastea
...IT'S A TOP-SECRET NEW TESLA ENERGY FACILITY.
MOST OF THE FACILITY IS HIDDEN UNDER-GROUND. ITS SIZE IS ON THE SAME SCALE AS THE TOWERS.
ALL KINDS OF EXPERIMENTS RELATED TO DIMENSION W ARE PERFORMED THERE EVERY DAY.
SOME EVEN CALL IT THE PHANTOM 61ST TOWER.
PHAN-TOM...?

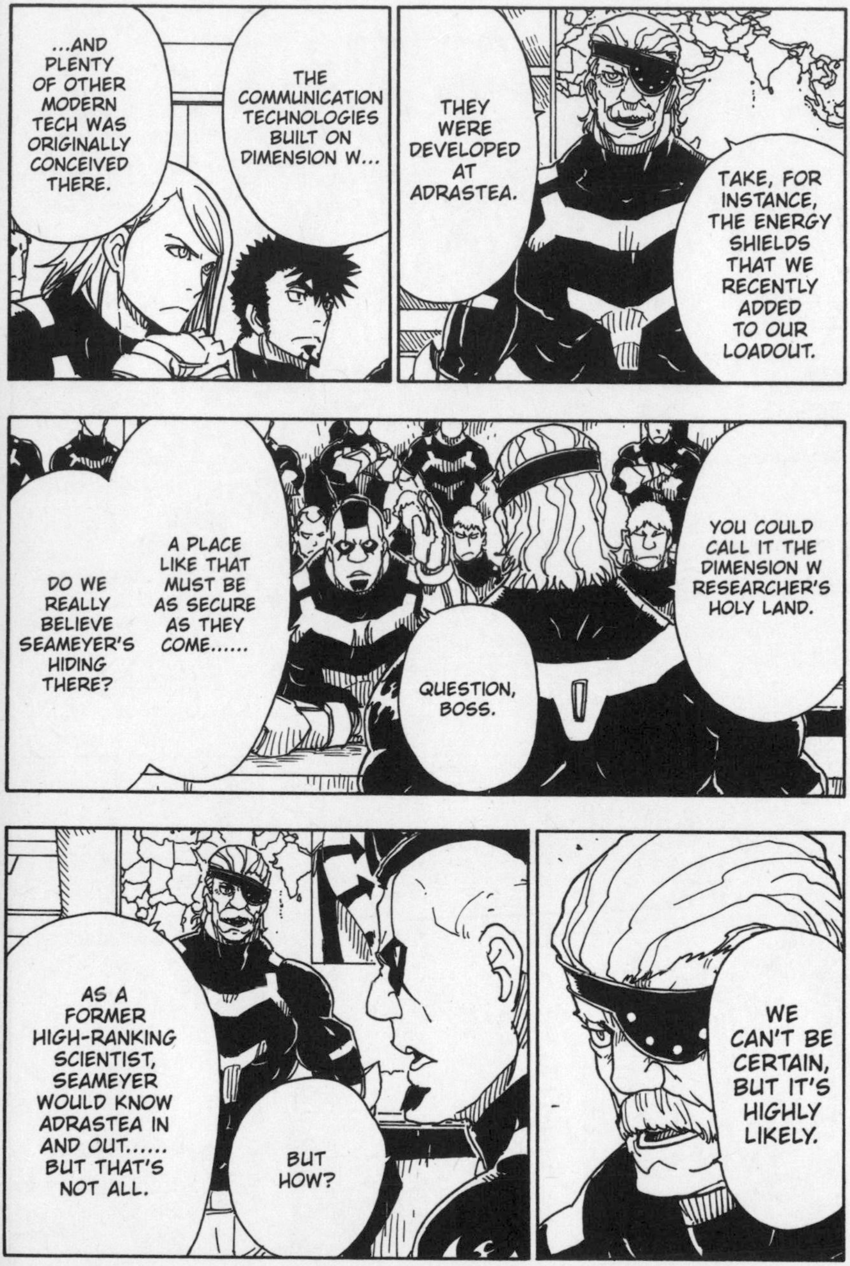
TAKE, FOR INSTANCE, THE ENERGY SHIELDS THAT WE RECENTLY ADDED TO OUR LOADOUT.
THEY WERE DEVELOPED AT ADRASTEA.
THE COMMUNICATION TECHNOLOGIES BUILT ON DIMENSION W...
...AND PLENTY OF OTHER MODERN TECH WAS ORIGINALLY CONCEIVED THERE.
YOU COULD CALL IT THE DIMENSION W RESEARCHER'S HOLY LAND.
QUESTION, BOSS.
A PLACE LIKE THAT MUST BE AS SECURE AS THEY COME......
DO WE REALLY BELIEVE SEAMEYER'S HIDING THERE?
WE CAN'T BE CERTAIN, BUT IT'S HIGHLY LIKELY.
BUT HOW?
AS A FORMER HIGH-RANKING SCIENTIST, SEAMEYER WOULD KNOW ADRASTEA IN AND OUT...... BUT THAT'S NOT ALL.

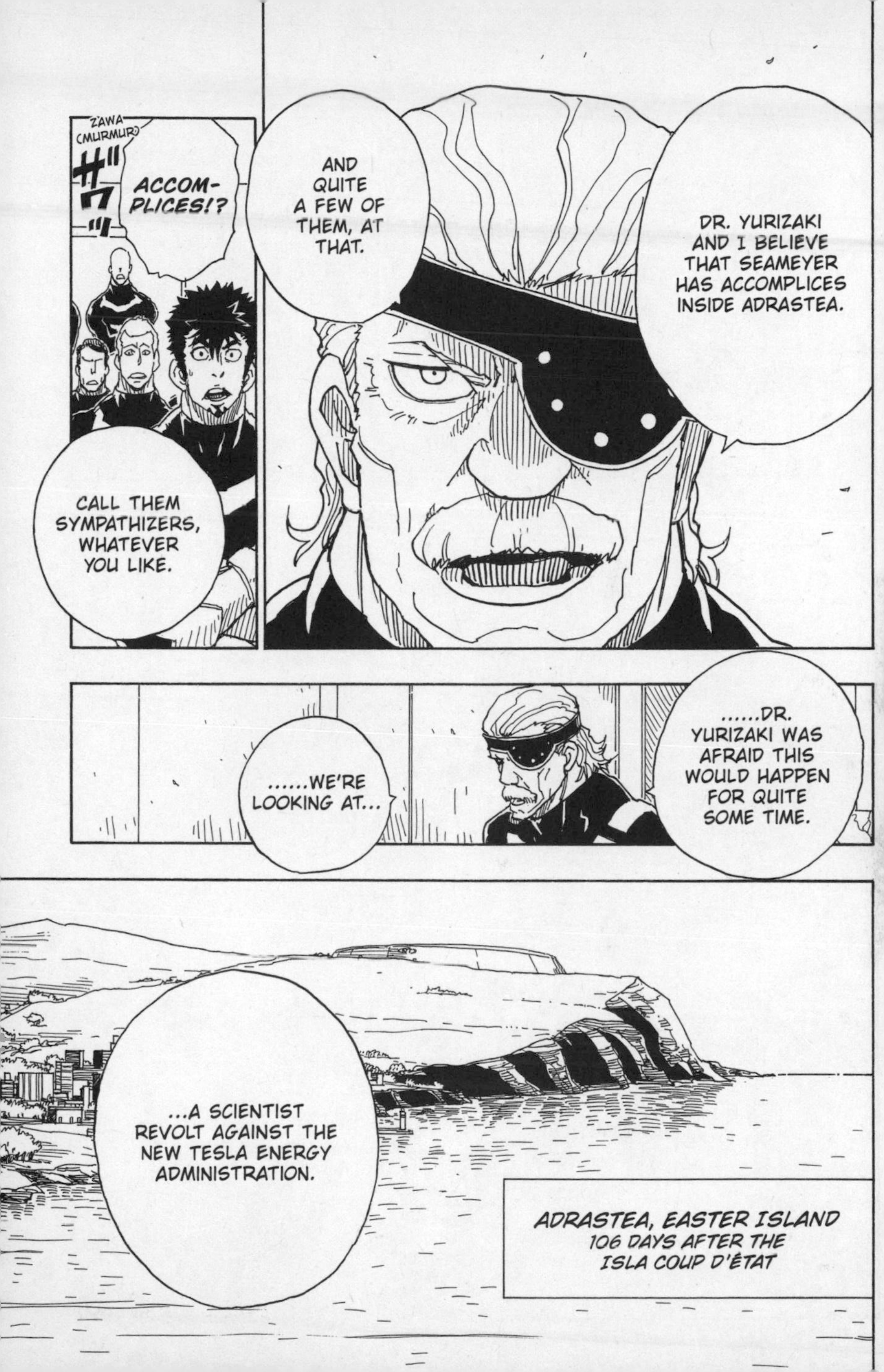
DR. YURIZAKI AND I BELIEVE THAT SEAMEYER HAS ACCOMPLICES INSIDE ADRASTEA.
AND QUITE A FEW OF THEM, AT THAT.
ザワッ
ZAWA (MURMUR)
ACCOM-PLICES!?
CALL THEM SYMPATHIZERS, WHATEVER YOU LIKE.
......DR. YURIZAKI WAS AFRAID THIS WOULD HAPPEN FOR QUITE SOME TIME.
......WE'RE LOOKING AT...
...A SCIENTIST REVOLT AGAINST THE NEW TESLA ENERGY ADMINISTRATION.
ADRASTEA, EASTER ISLAND
106 DAYS AFTER THE ISLA COUP D'ÉTAT

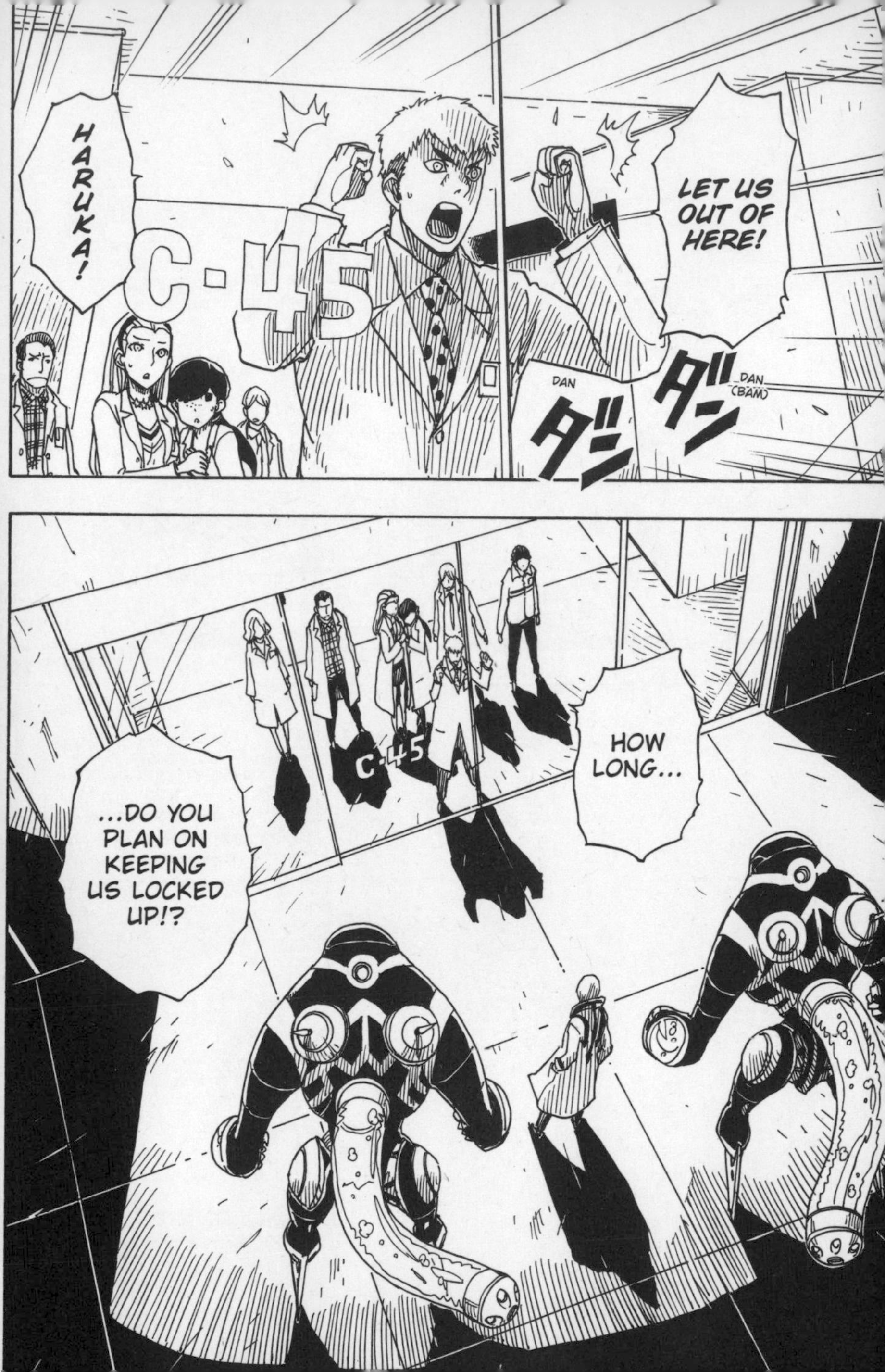
LET US OUT OF HERE!
ダン
DAN (BAM)
ダン
DAN
C-45
HARUKA!
HOW LONG...
...DO YOU PLAN ON KEEPING US LOCKED UP!?
C-45

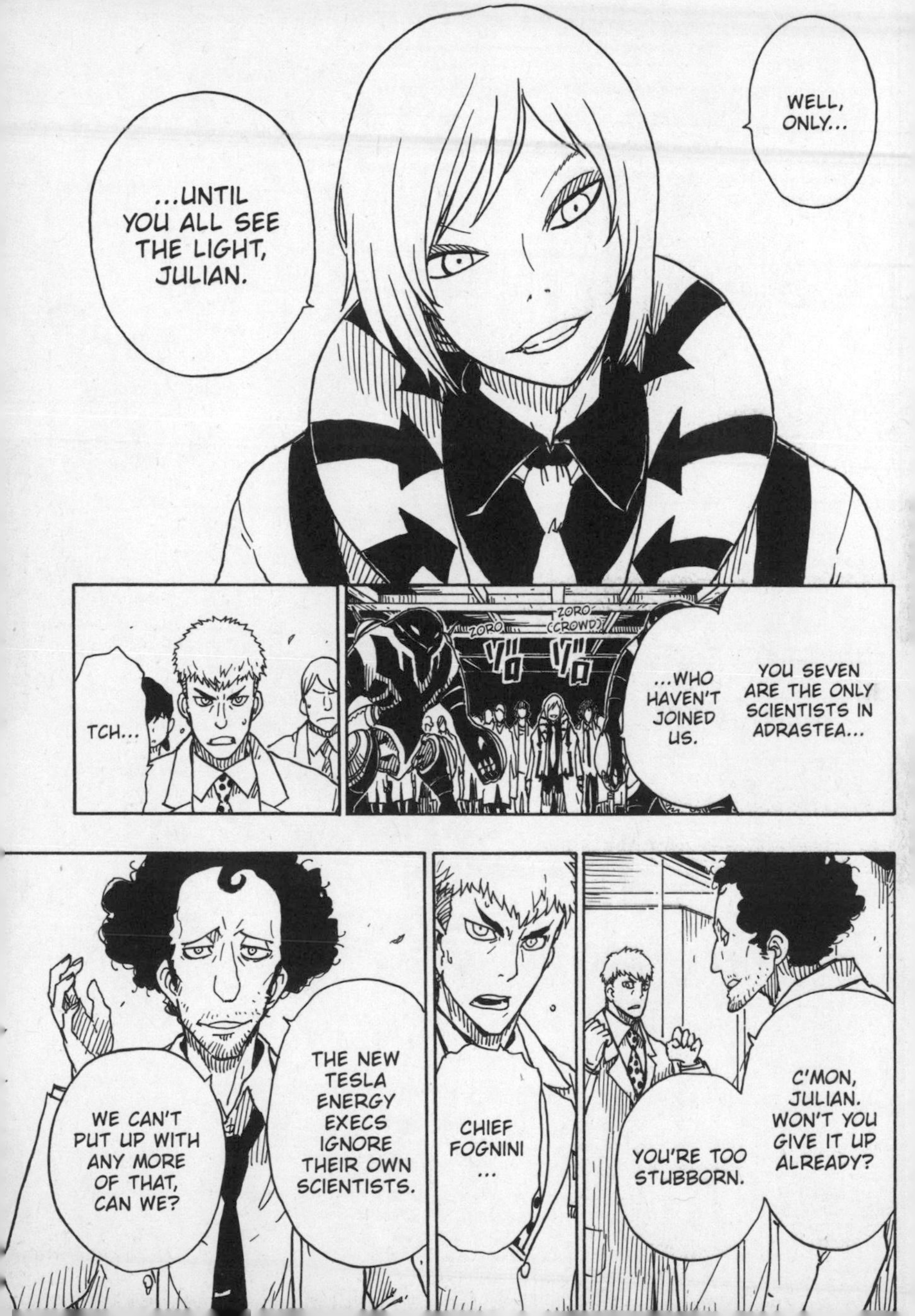
WELL, ONLY...
...UNTIL YOU ALL SEE THE LIGHT, JULIAN.
YOU SEVEN ARE THE ONLY SCIENTISTS IN ADRASTEA...
...WHO HAVEN'T JOINED US.
ZORO ZORO (CROWD)
ZORO
TCH...
C'MON, JULIAN. WON'T YOU GIVE IT UP ALREADY?
YOU'RE TOO STUBBORN.
CHIEF FOGNINI ...
THE NEW TESLA ENERGY EXECS IGNORE THEIR OWN SCIENTISTS.
WE CAN'T PUT UP WITH ANY MORE OF THAT, CAN WE?

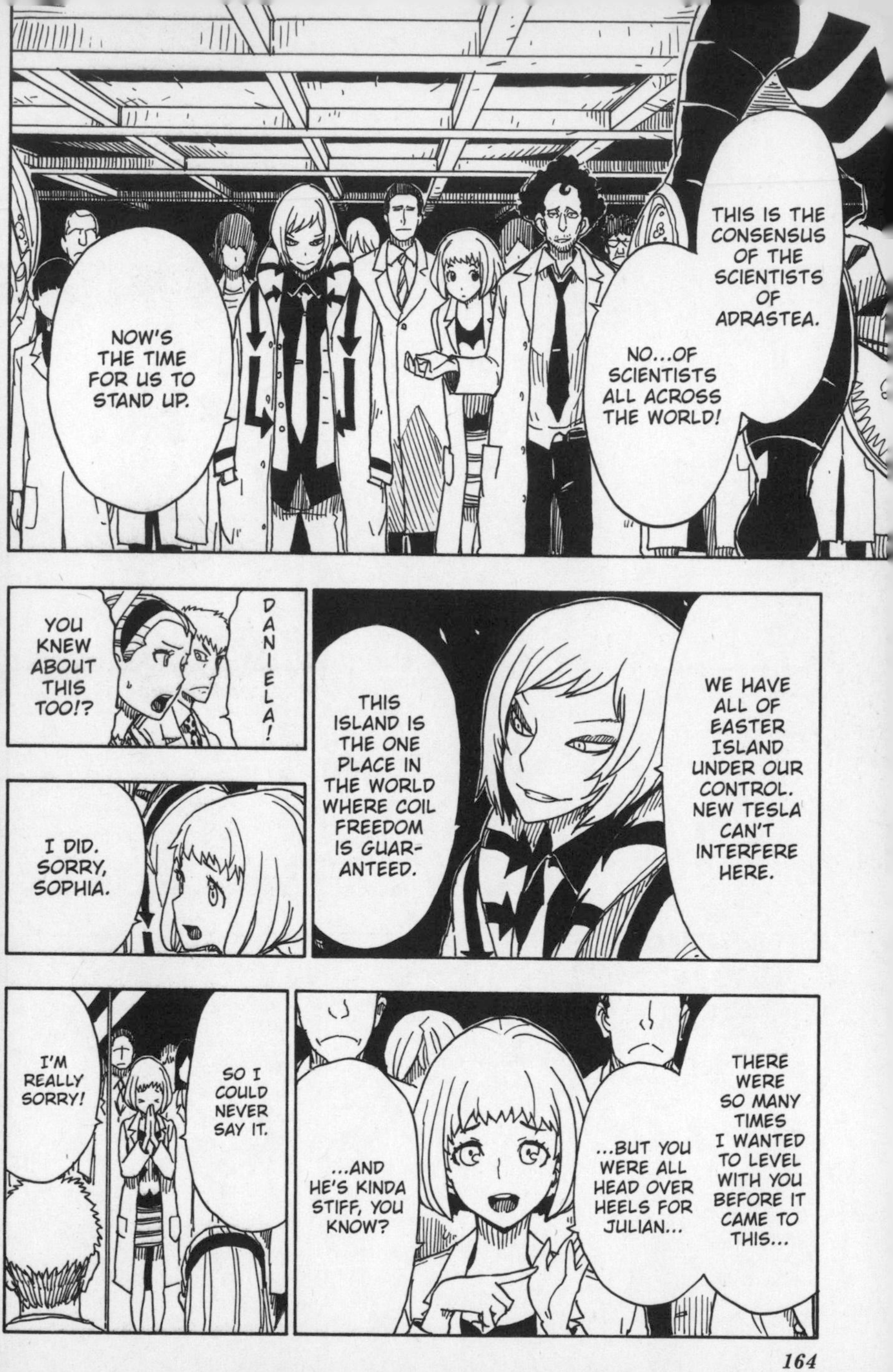
THIS IS THE CONSENSUS OF THE SCIENTISTS OF ADRASTEA.
NO...OF SCIENTISTS ALL ACROSS THE WORLD!
NOW'S THE TIME FOR US TO STAND UP.
WE HAVE ALL OF EASTER ISLAND UNDER OUR CONTROL. NEW TESLA CAN'T INTERFERE HERE.
THIS ISLAND IS THE ONE PLACE IN THE WORLD WHERE COIL FREEDOM IS GUARANTEED.
DANIELA!
YOU KNEW ABOUT THIS TOO!?
I DID. SORRY, SOPHIA.
THERE WERE SO MANY TIMES I WANTED TO LEVEL WITH YOU BEFORE IT CAME TO THIS...
...BUT YOU WERE ALL HEAD OVER HEELS FOR JULIAN...
...AND HE'S KINDA STIFF, YOU KNOW?
SO I COULD NEVER SAY IT.
I'M REALLY SORRY!

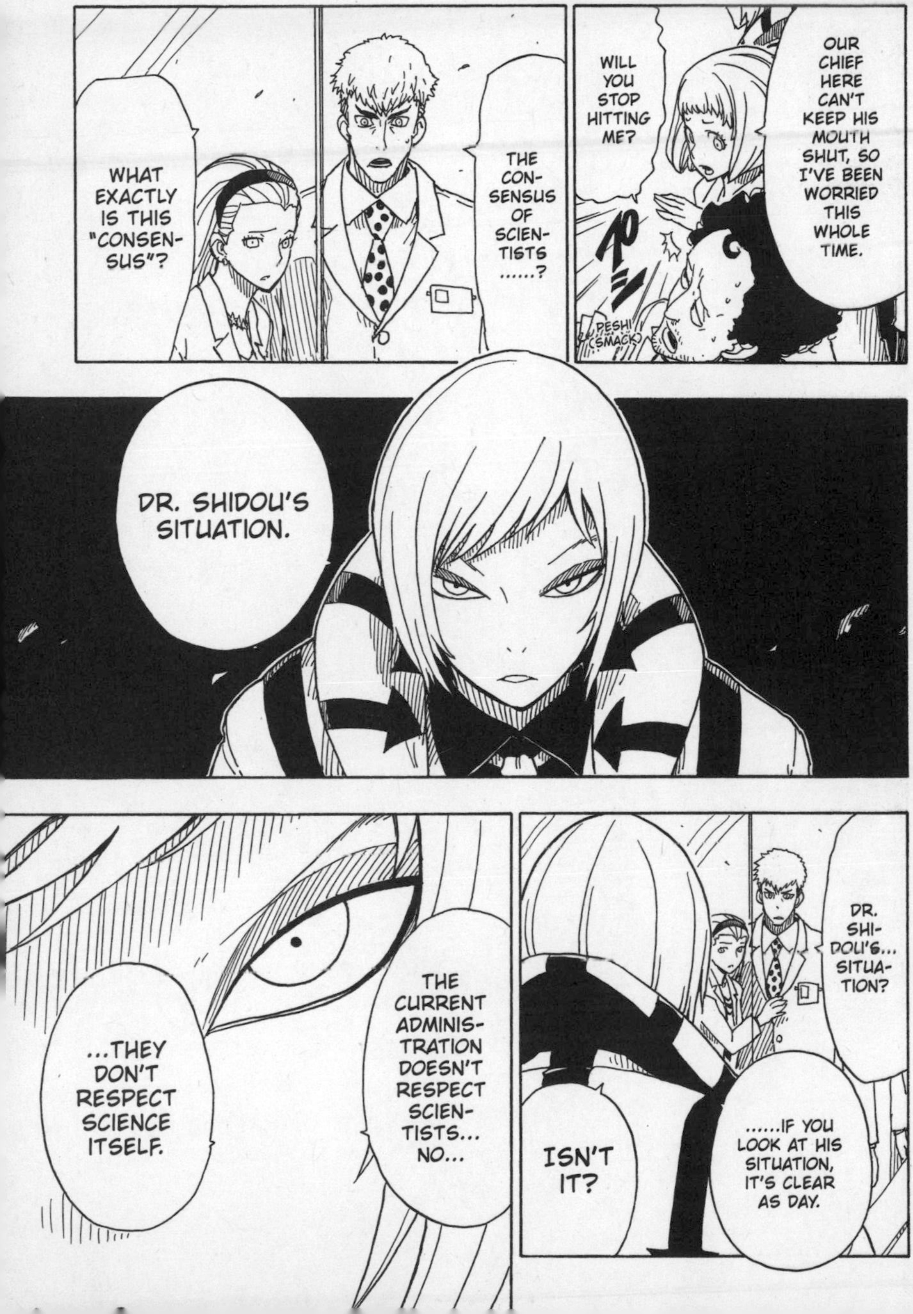
OUR CHIEF HERE CAN'T KEEP HIS MOUTH SHUT, SO I'VE BEEN WORRIED THIS WHOLE TIME.
WILL YOU STOP HITTING ME?
PESHI (SMACK)
THE CONSENSUS OF SCIENTISTS ......?
WHAT EXACTLY IS THIS "CONSENSUS"?
DR. SHIDOU'S SITUATION.
DR. SHIDOU'S... SITUATION?
......IF YOU LOOK AT HIS SITUATION, IT'S CLEAR AS DAY.
ISN'T IT?
THE CURRENT ADMINISTRATION DOESN'T RESPECT SCIENTISTS... NO...
...THEY DON'T RESPECT SCIENCE ITSELF.

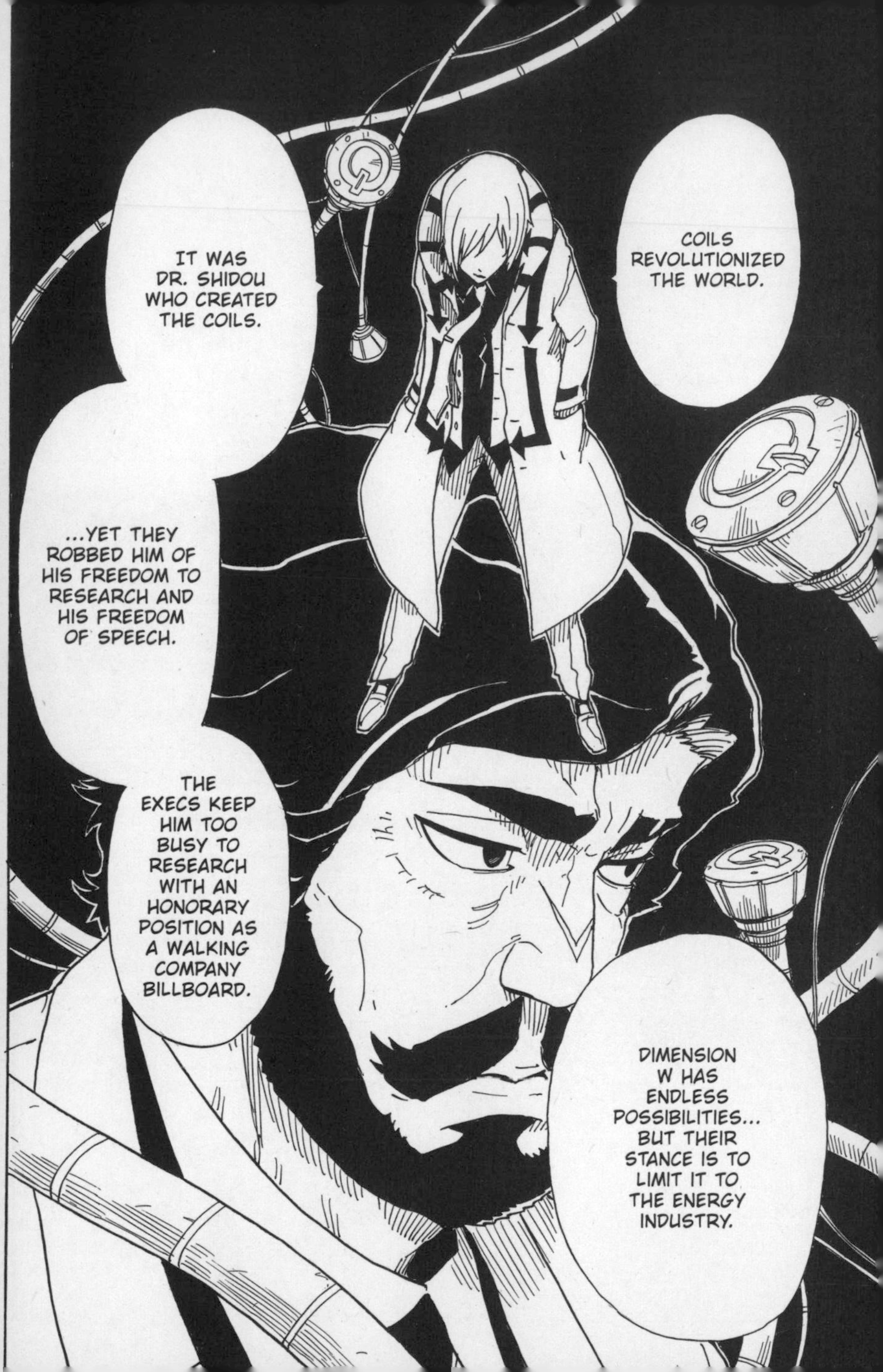
COILS REVOLUTIONIZED THE WORLD.
IT WAS DR. SHIDOU WHO CREATED THE COILS.
...YET THEY ROBBED HIM OF HIS FREEDOM TO RESEARCH AND HIS FREEDOM OF SPEECH.
THE EXECS KEEP HIM TOO BUSY TO RESEARCH WITH AN HONORARY POSITION AS A WALKING COMPANY BILLBOARD.
DIMENSION W HAS ENDLESS POSSIBILITIES... BUT THEIR STANCE IS TO LIMIT IT TO THE ENERGY INDUSTRY.

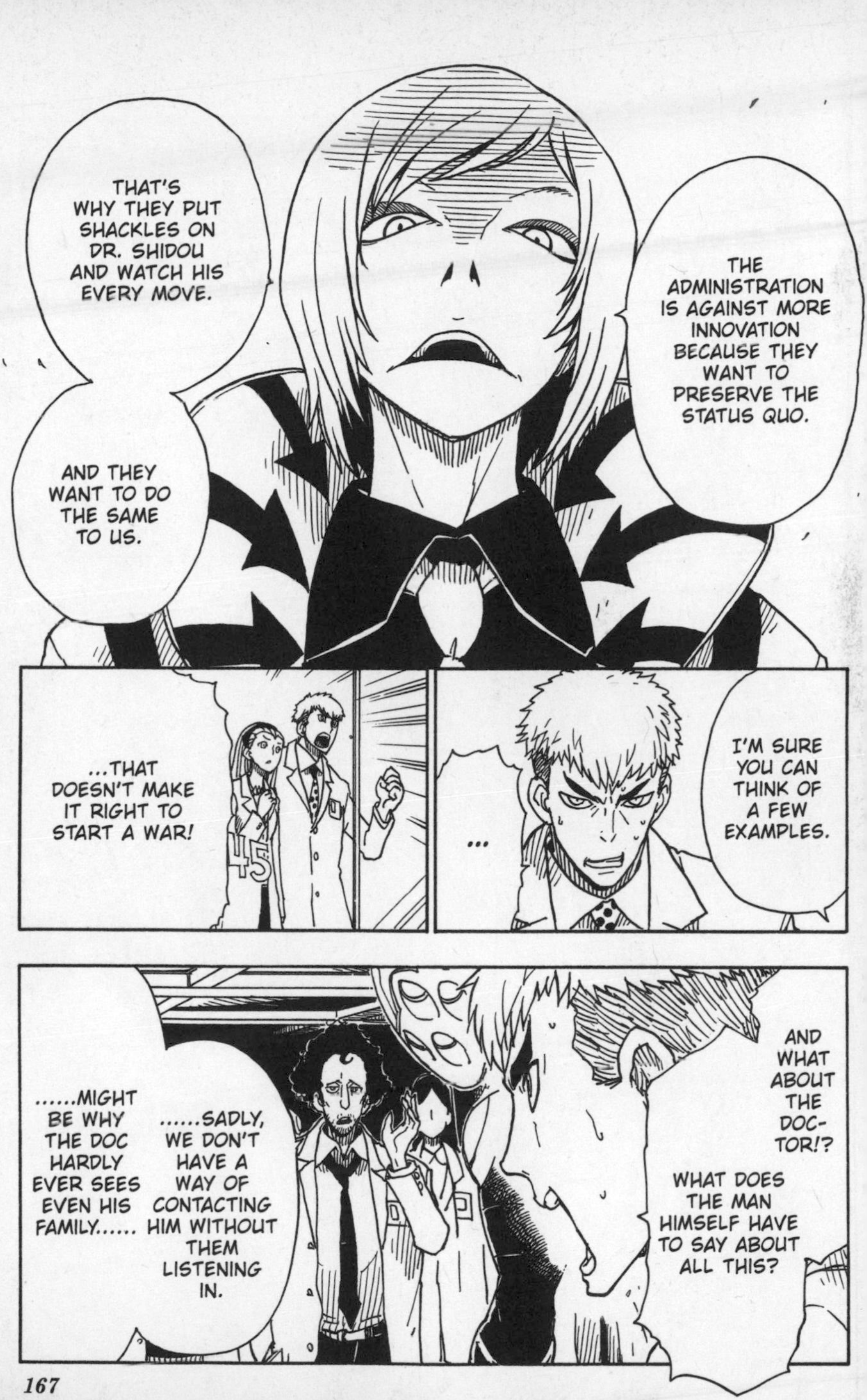
THE ADMINISTRATION IS AGAINST MORE INNOVATION BECAUSE THEY WANT TO PRESERVE THE STATUS QUO.
THAT'S WHY THEY PUT SHACKLES ON DR. SHIDOU AND WATCH HIS EVERY MOVE.
AND THEY WANT TO DO THE SAME TO US.
I'M SURE YOU CAN THINK OF A FEW EXAMPLES.
...
...THAT DOESN'T MAKE IT RIGHT TO START A WAR!
45
AND WHAT ABOUT THE DOC-TOR!?
WHAT DOES THE MAN HIMSELF HAVE TO SAY ABOUT ALL THIS?
......SADLY, WE DON'T HAVE A WAY OF CONTACTING HIM WITHOUT THEM LISTENING IN.
......MIGHT BE WHY THE DOC HARDLY EVER SEES EVEN HIS FAMILY......

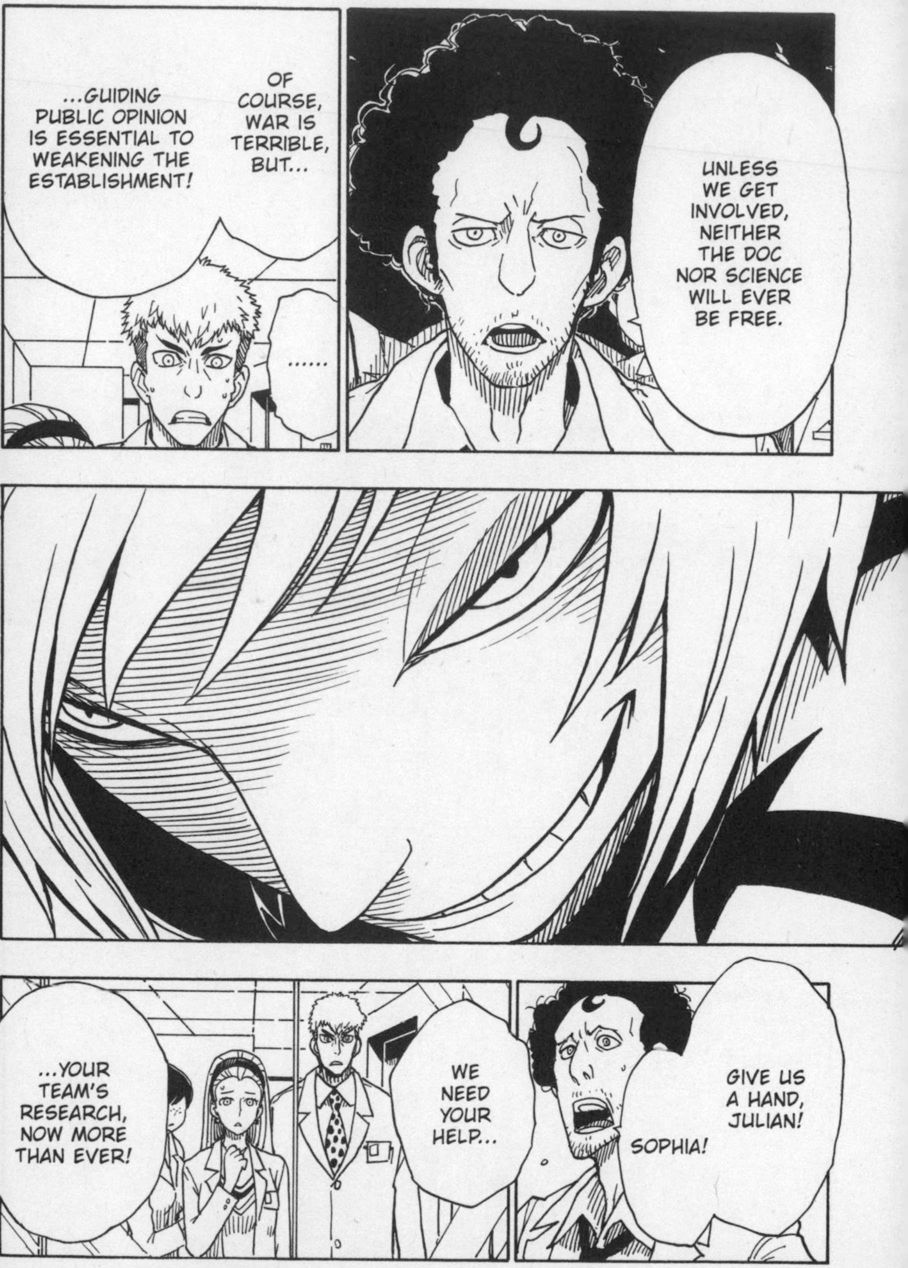
UNLESS WE GET INVOLVED, NEITHER THE DOC NOR SCIENCE WILL EVER BE FREE.
OF COURSE, WAR IS TERRIBLE, BUT...
...GUIDING PUBLIC OPINION IS ESSENTIAL TO WEAKENING THE ESTABLISHMENT!
......
GIVE US A HAND, JULIAN!
SOPHIA!
WE NEED YOUR HELP...
...YOUR TEAM'S RESEARCH, NOW MORE THAN EVER!

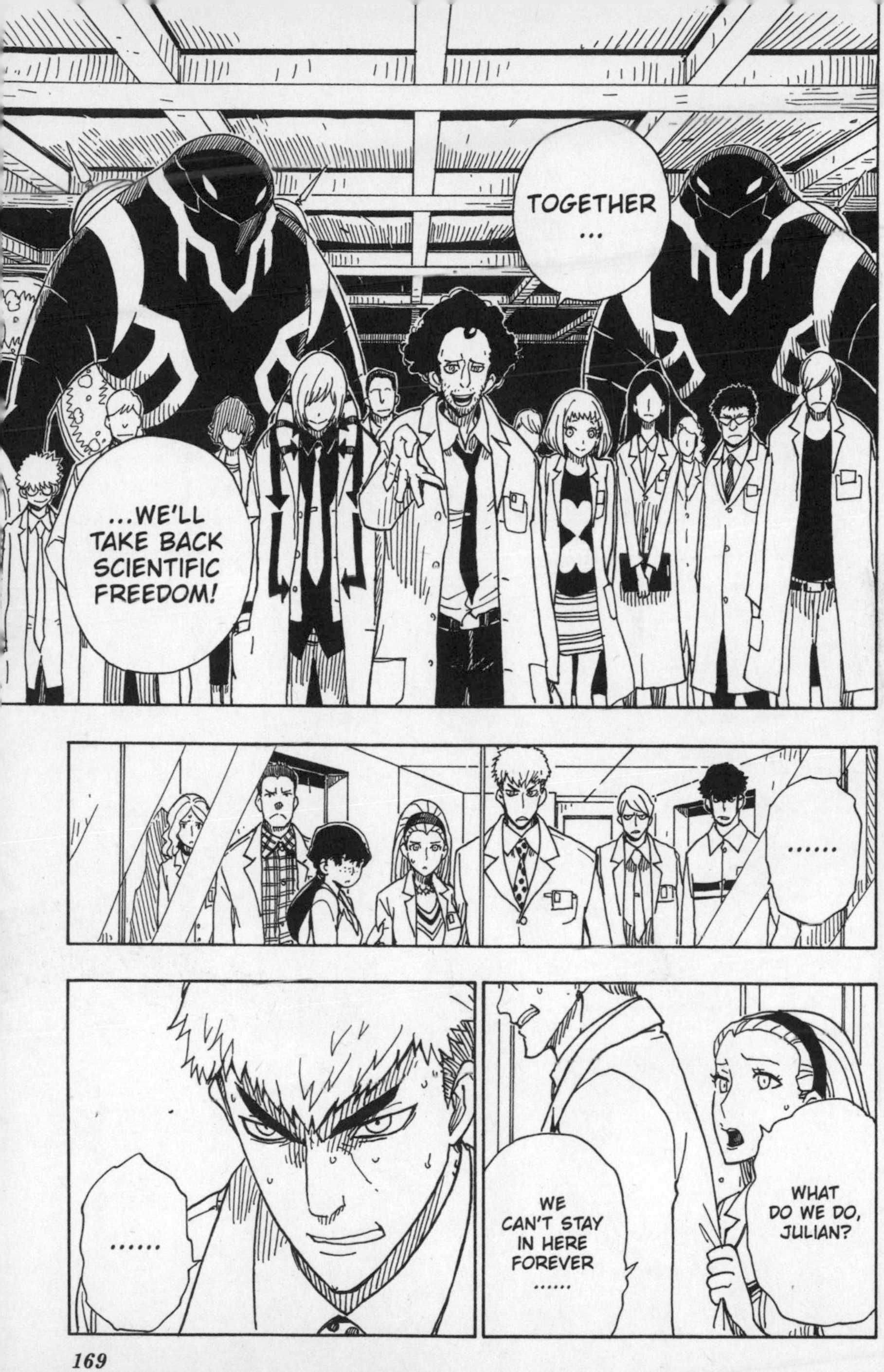
TOGETHER ...
...WE'LL TAKE BACK SCIENTIFIC FREEDOM!
......
WHAT DO WE DO, JULIAN?
WE CAN'T STAY IN HERE FOREVER ......
......

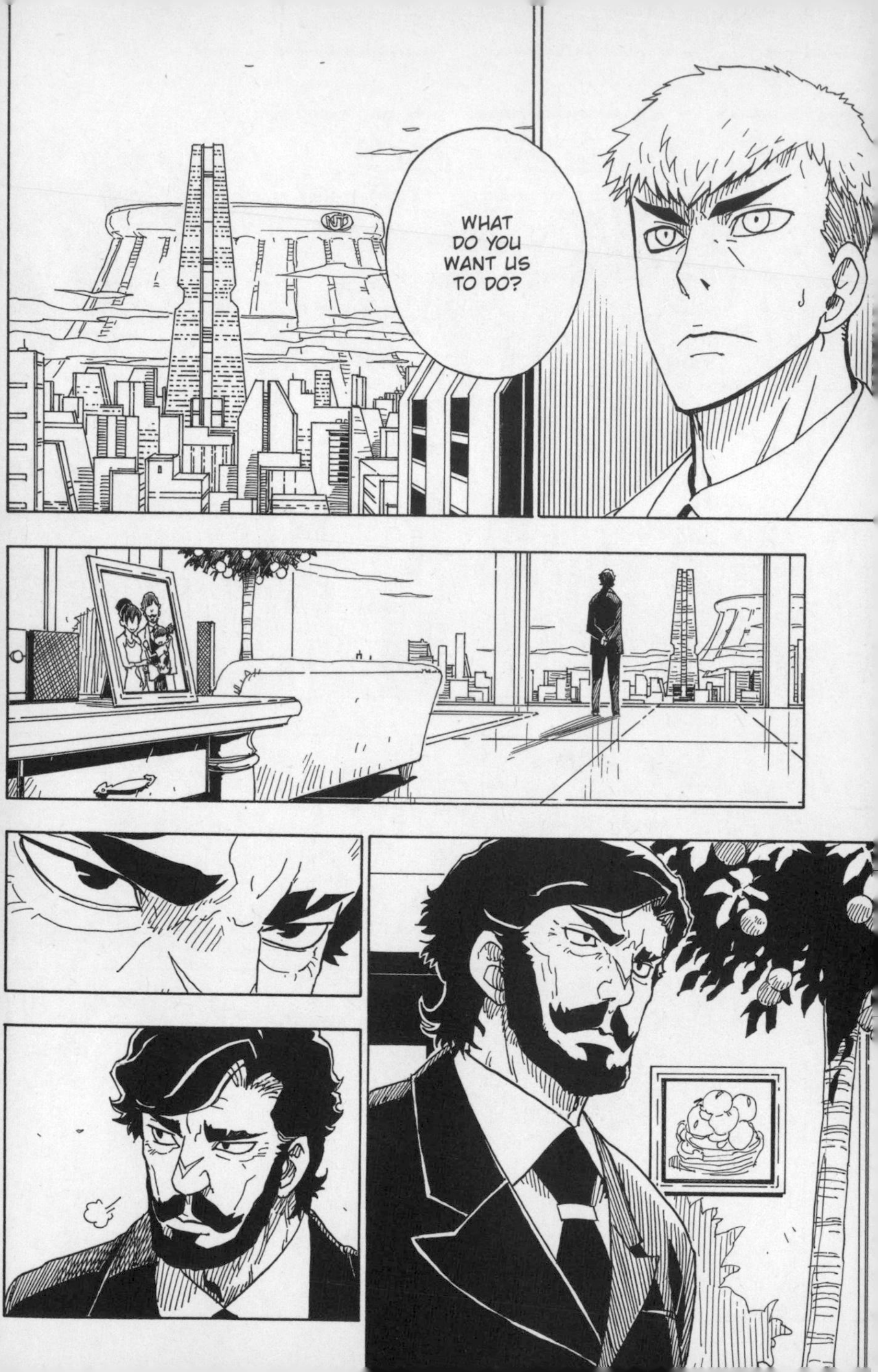
WHAT DO YOU WANT US TO DO?

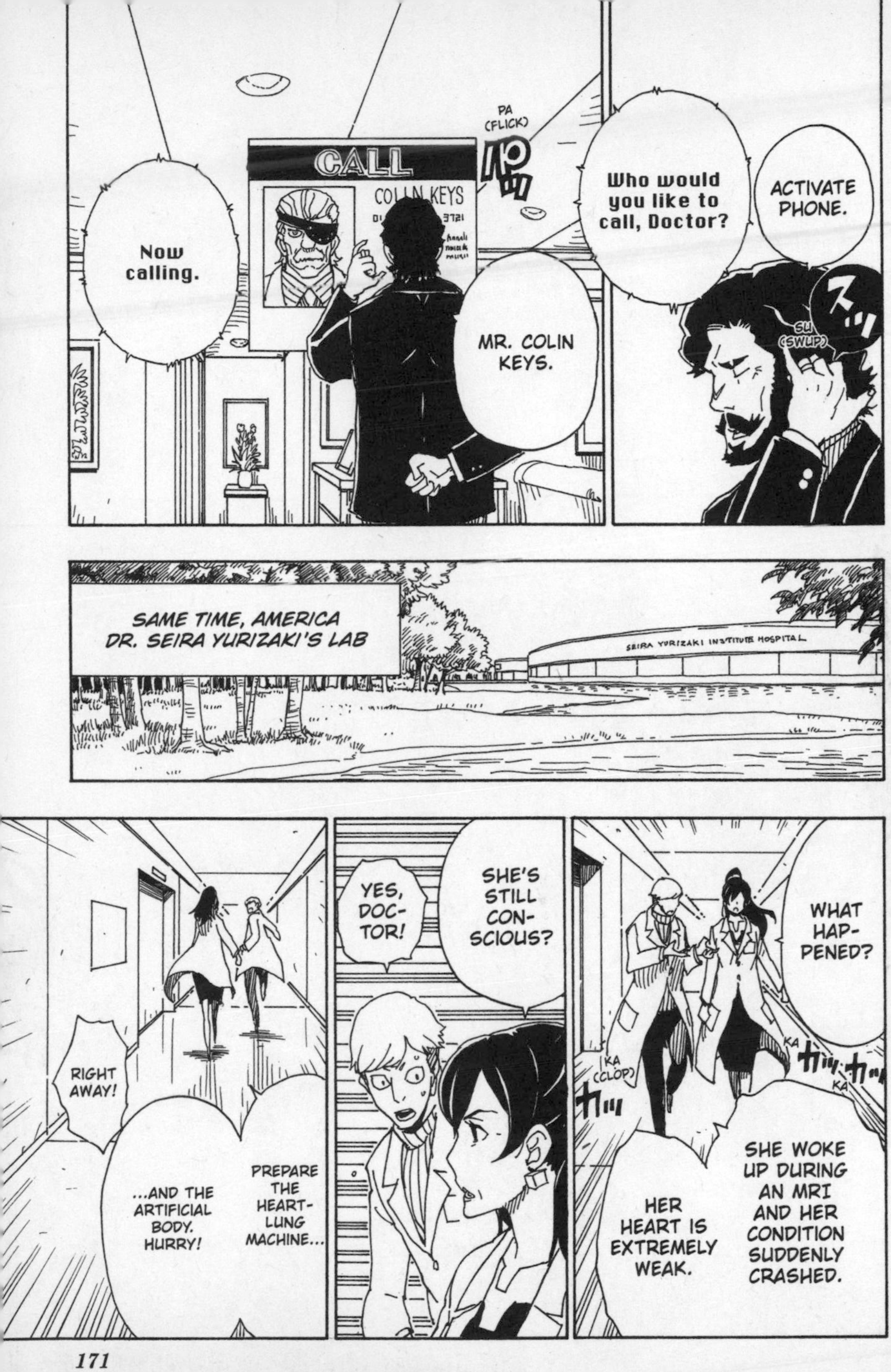

ACTIVATE PHONE.
Who would you like to call, Doctor?
SU (SWUP)
PA (FLICK)
MR. COLIN KEYS.
CALL
Now calling.
SAME TIME, AMERICA DR. SEIRA YURIZAKI'S LAB
SEIRA YURIZAKI INSTITUTE HOSPITAL
WHAT HAPPENED?
KA
KA
KA (CLOP)
SHE WOKE UP DURING AN MRI AND HER CONDITION SUDDENLY CRASHED.
HER HEART IS EXTREMELY WEAK.
SHE'S STILL CONSCIOUS?
YES, DOCTOR!
PREPARE THE HEART-LUNG MACHINE...
...AND THE ARTIFICIAL BODY. HURRY!
RIGHT AWAY!

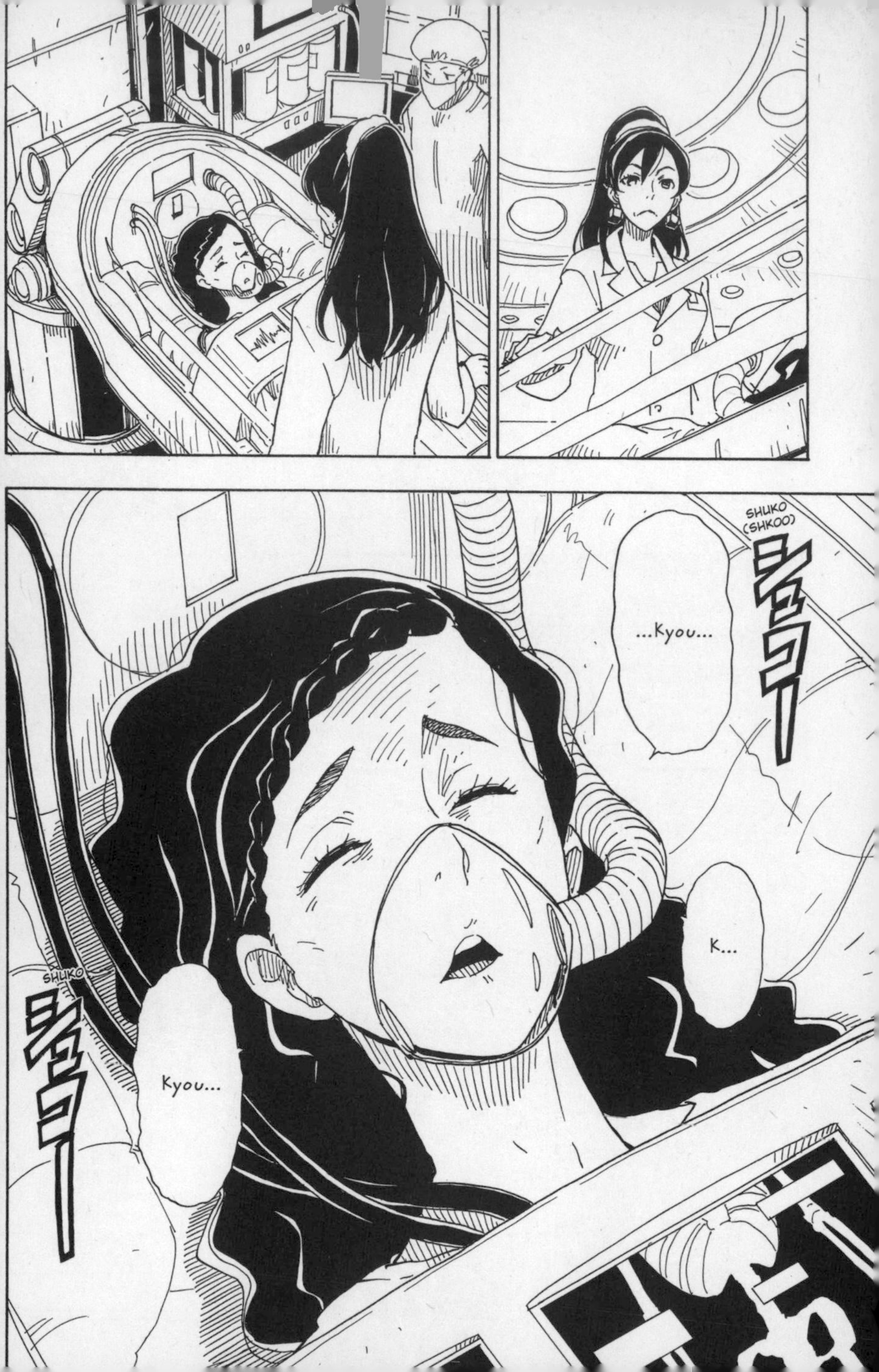

SHUKO (SHKOO)
...Kyou...
K...
SHUKO
Kyou...

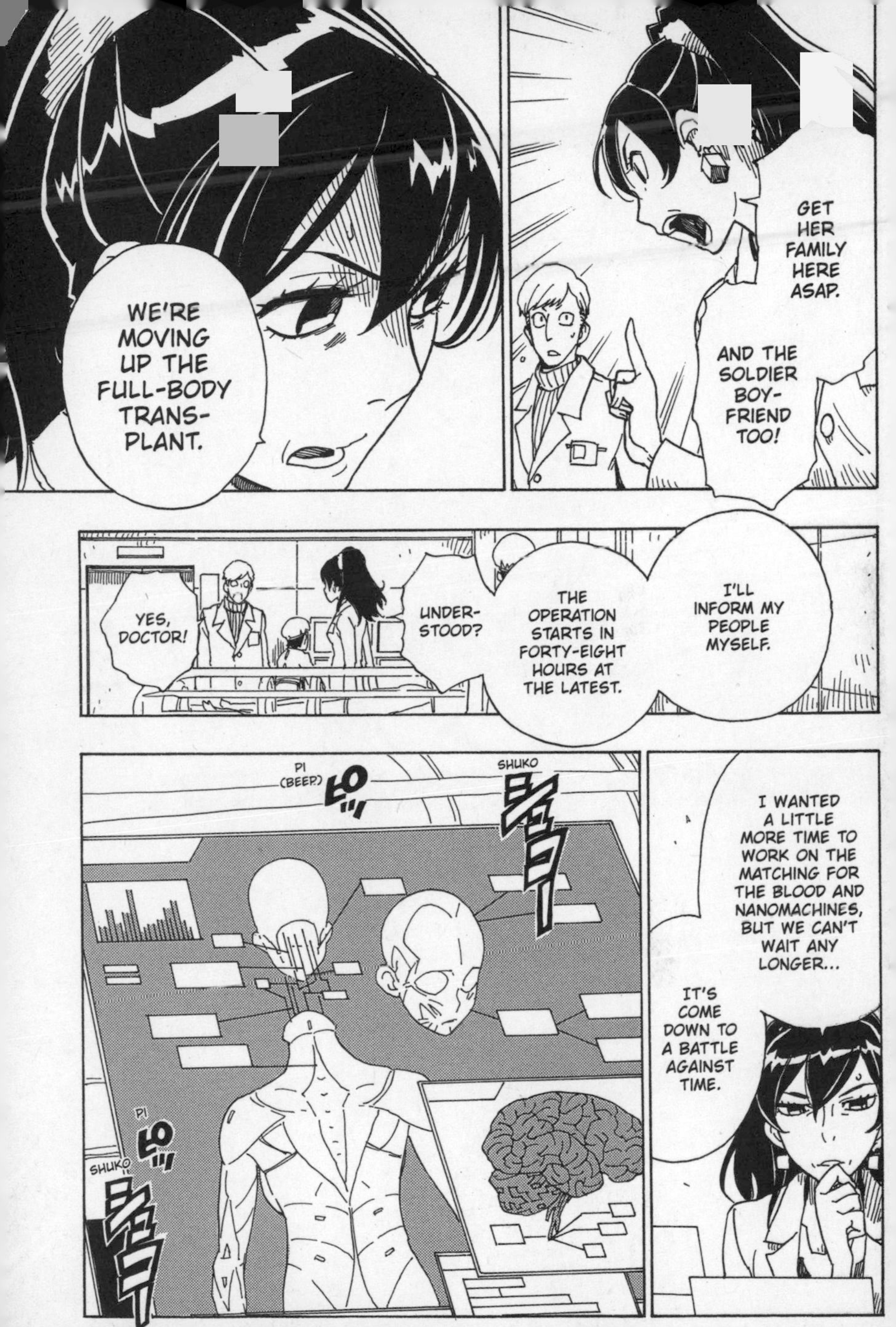
GET HER FAMILY HERE ASAP.
AND THE SOLDIER BOY-FRIEND TOO!
WE'RE MOVING UP THE FULL-BODY TRANS-PLANT.
I'LL INFORM MY PEOPLE MYSELF.
THE OPERATION STARTS IN FORTY-EIGHT HOURS AT THE LATEST.
UNDER-STOOD?
YES, DOCTOR!
I WANTED A LITTLE MORE TIME TO WORK ON THE MATCHING FOR THE BLOOD AND NANOMACHINES, BUT WE CAN'T WAIT ANY LONGER...
IT'S COME DOWN TO A BATTLE AGAINST TIME.
PI (BEEP)
SHUKO
PI
SHUKO

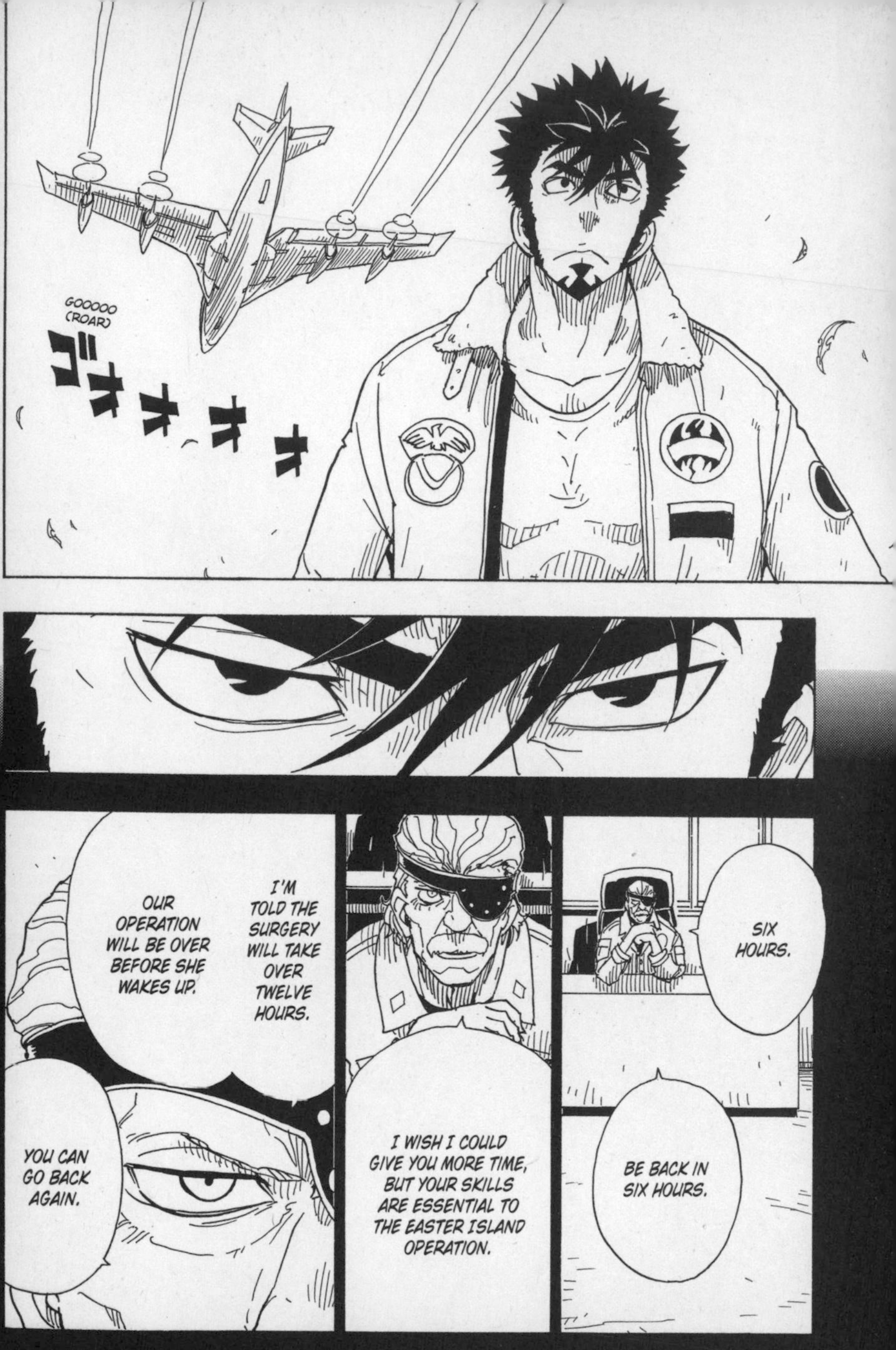
GOOOOO (ROAR)
ゴオオオオ
SIX HOURS.
BE BACK IN SIX HOURS.
I WISH I COULD GIVE YOU MORE TIME, BUT YOUR SKILLS ARE ESSENTIAL TO THE EASTER ISLAND OPERATION.
I'M TOLD THE SURGERY WILL TAKE OVER TWELVE HOURS.
OUR OPERATION WILL BE OVER BEFORE SHE WAKES UP.
YOU CAN GO BACK AGAIN.

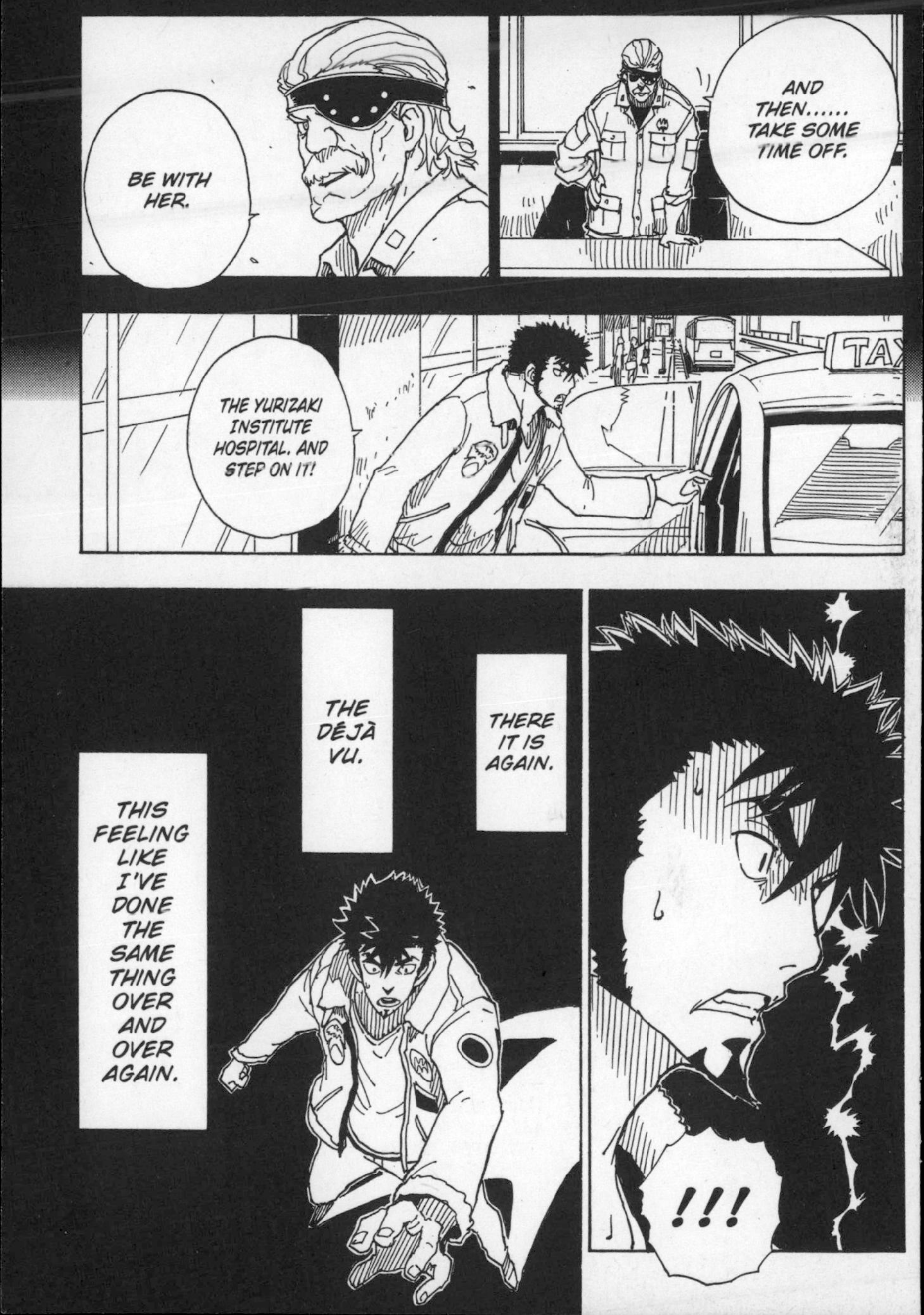
AND THEN...... TAKE SOME TIME OFF.
BE WITH HER.
THE YURIZAKI INSTITUTE HOSPITAL. AND STEP ON IT!
TAX
!!!
THERE IT IS AGAIN.
THE DÉJÀ VU.
THIS FEELING LIKE I'VE DONE THE SAME THING OVER AND OVER AGAIN.

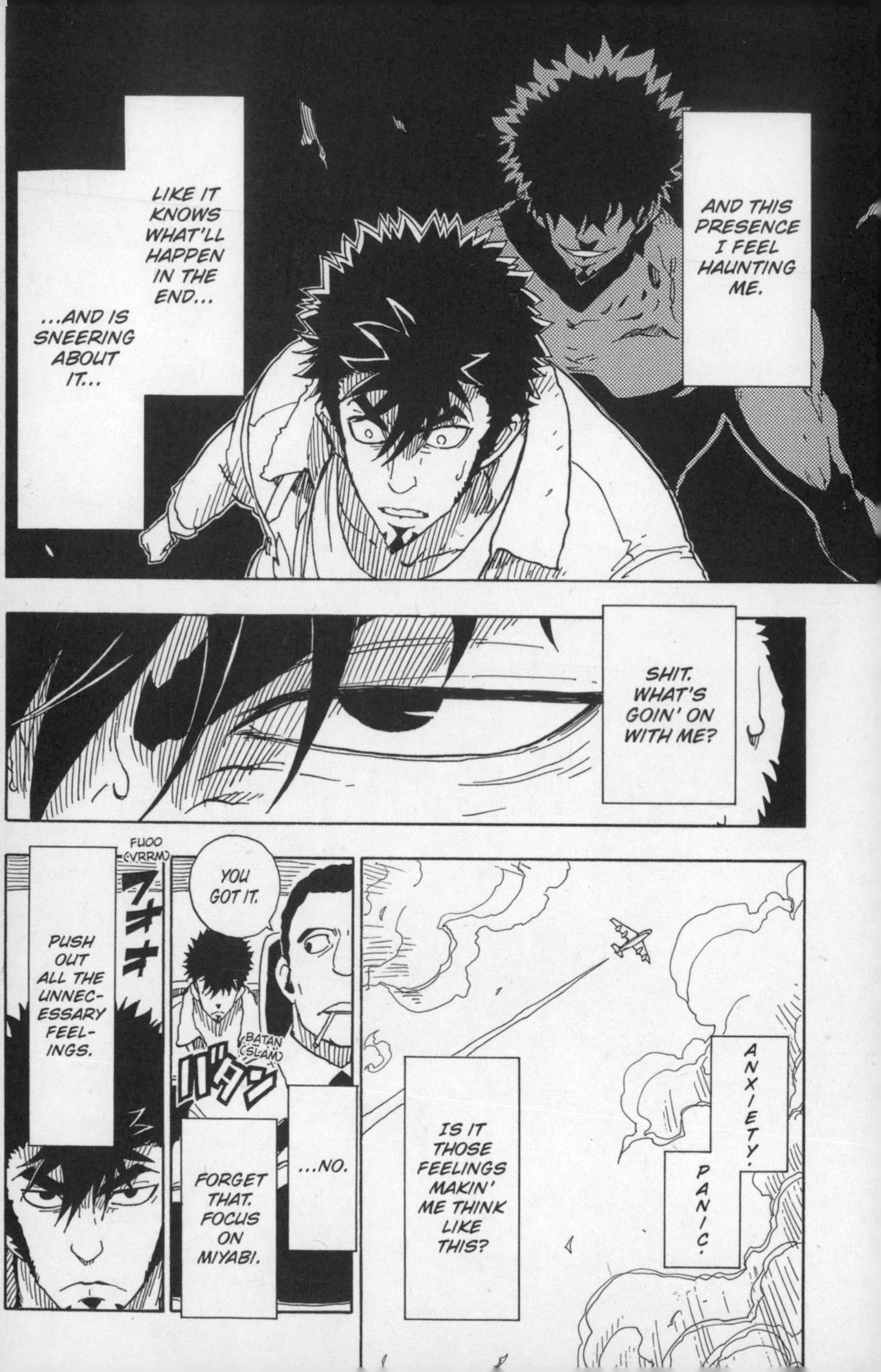
AND THIS PRESENCE I FEEL HAUNTING ME.
LIKE IT KNOWS WHAT'LL HAPPEN IN THE END...
...AND IS SNEERING ABOUT IT...
SHIT. WHAT'S GOIN' ON WITH ME?
ANXIETY.
PANIC.
IS IT THOSE FEELINGS MAKIN' ME THINK LIKE THIS?
YOU GOT IT.
バタン
BATAN (SLAM)
...NO.
FORGET THAT. FOCUS ON MIYABI.
フオオ
FUOO (VRRM)
PUSH OUT ALL THE UNNEC-ESSARY FEEL-INGS.

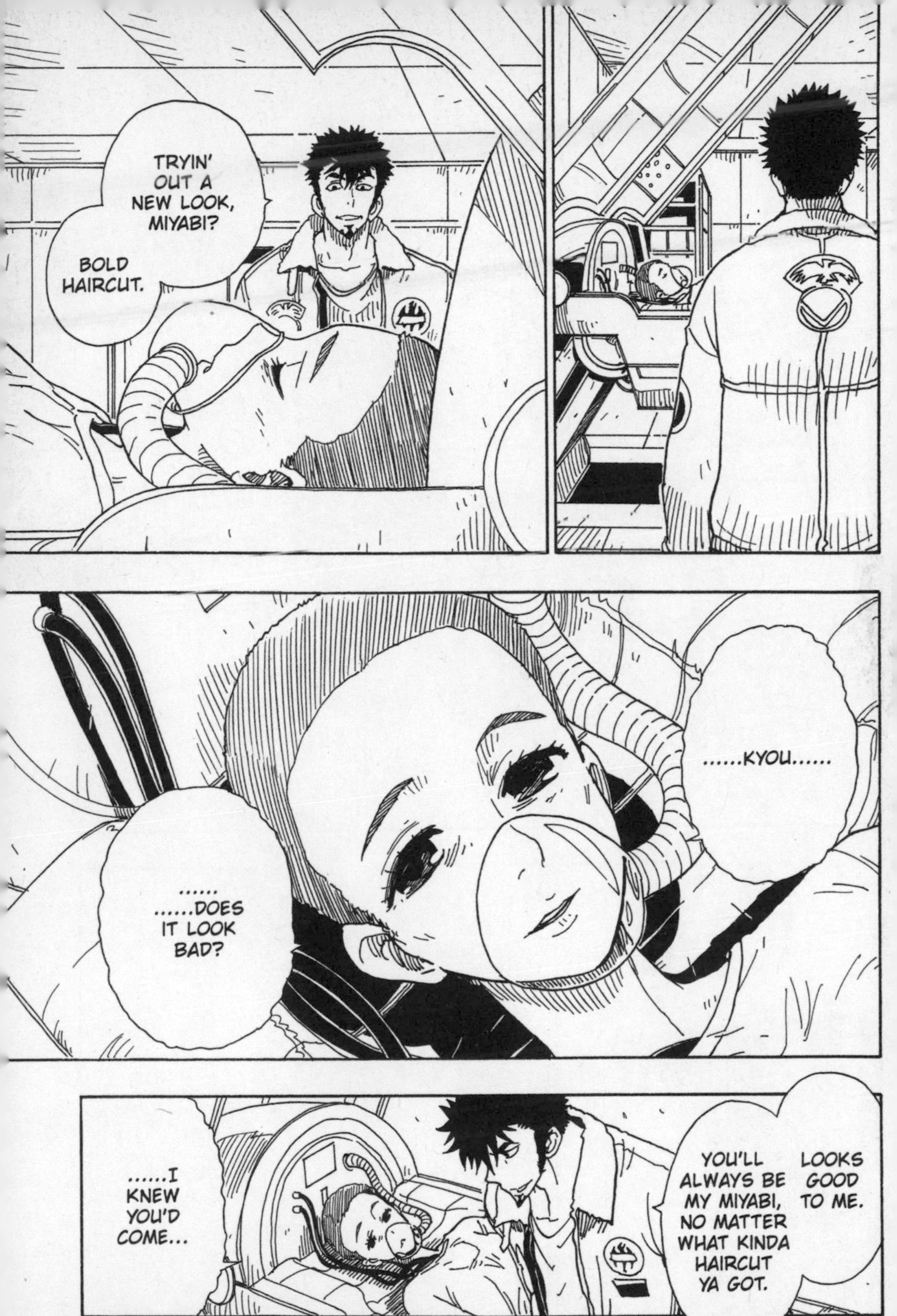
TRYIN' OUT A NEW LOOK, MIYABI?
BOLD HAIRCUT.
......KYOU......
....DOES IT LOOK BAD?
LOOKS GOOD TO ME.
YOU'LL ALWAYS BE MY MIYABI, NO MATTER WHAT KINDA HAIRCUT YA GOT.
......I KNEW YOU'D COME...

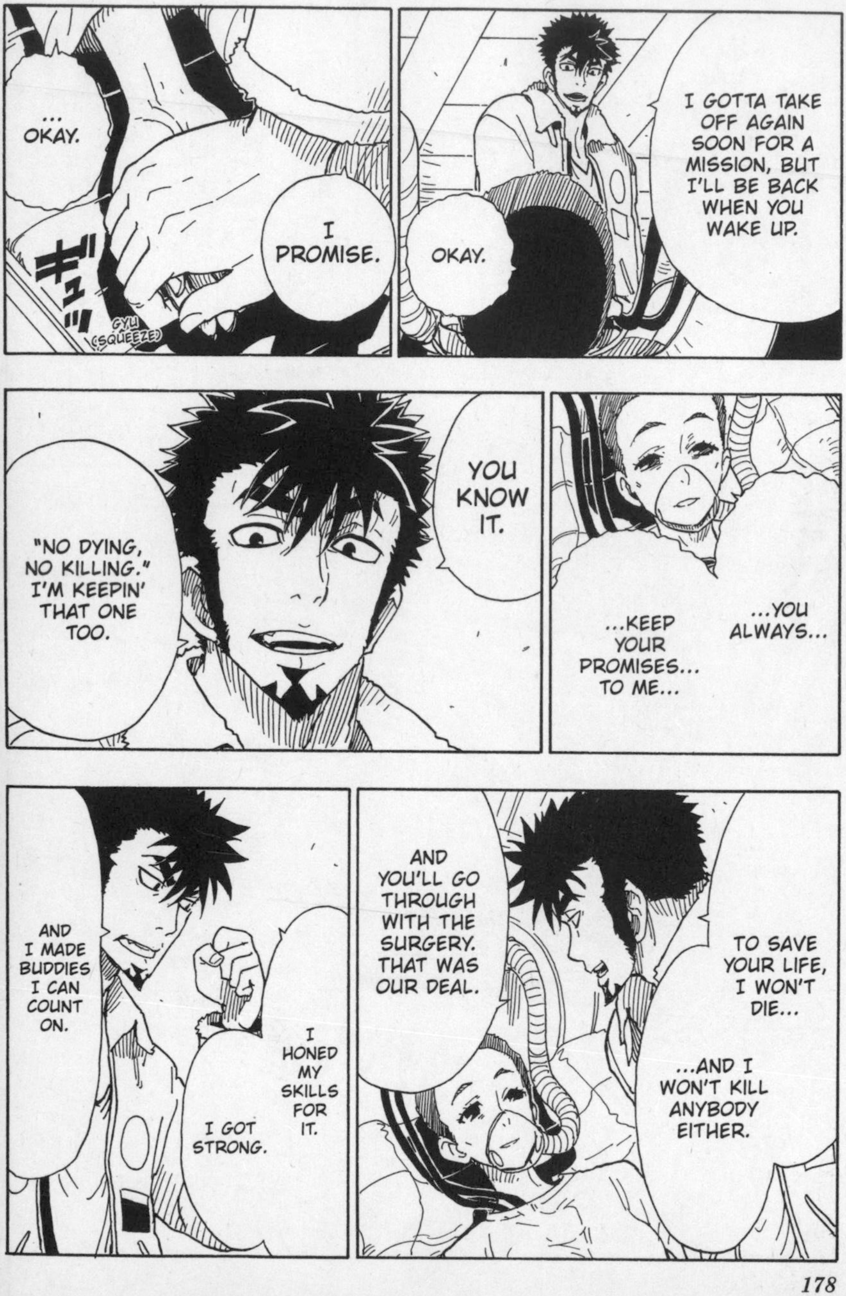
I GOTTA TAKE OFF AGAIN SOON FOR A MISSION, BUT I'LL BE BACK WHEN YOU WAKE UP.
OKAY.
I PROMISE.
... OKAY.
ギュッ
GYU (SQUEEZE)
...YOU ALWAYS...
...KEEP YOUR PROMISES... TO ME...
YOU KNOW IT.
"NO DYING, NO KILLING." I'M KEEPIN' THAT ONE TOO.
TO SAVE YOUR LIFE, I WON'T DIE...
...AND I WON'T KILL ANYBODY EITHER.
AND YOU'LL GO THROUGH WITH THE SURGERY. THAT WAS OUR DEAL.
I HONED MY SKILLS FOR IT.
I GOT STRONG.
AND I MADE BUDDIES I CAN COUNT ON.

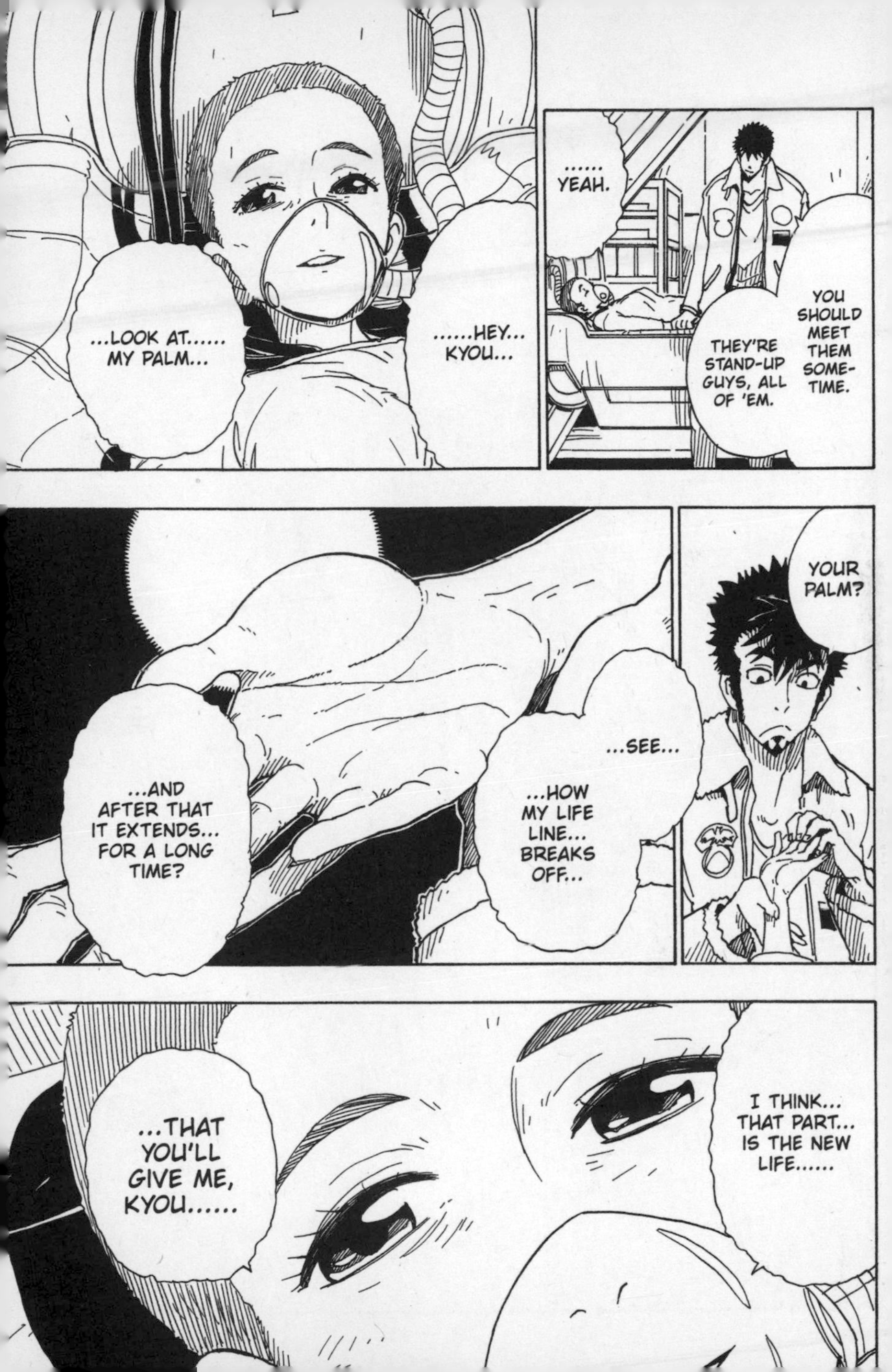

YOU SHOULD MEET THEM SOMETIME.
THEY'RE STAND-UP GUYS, ALL OF 'EM.
......YEAH.
......HEY... KYOU...
...LOOK AT...... MY PALM...
YOUR PALM?
...SEE...
...HOW MY LIFE LINE... BREAKS OFF...
...AND AFTER THAT IT EXTENDS... FOR A LONG TIME?
I THINK... THAT PART... IS THE NEW LIFE......
...THAT YOU'LL GIVE ME, KYOU......

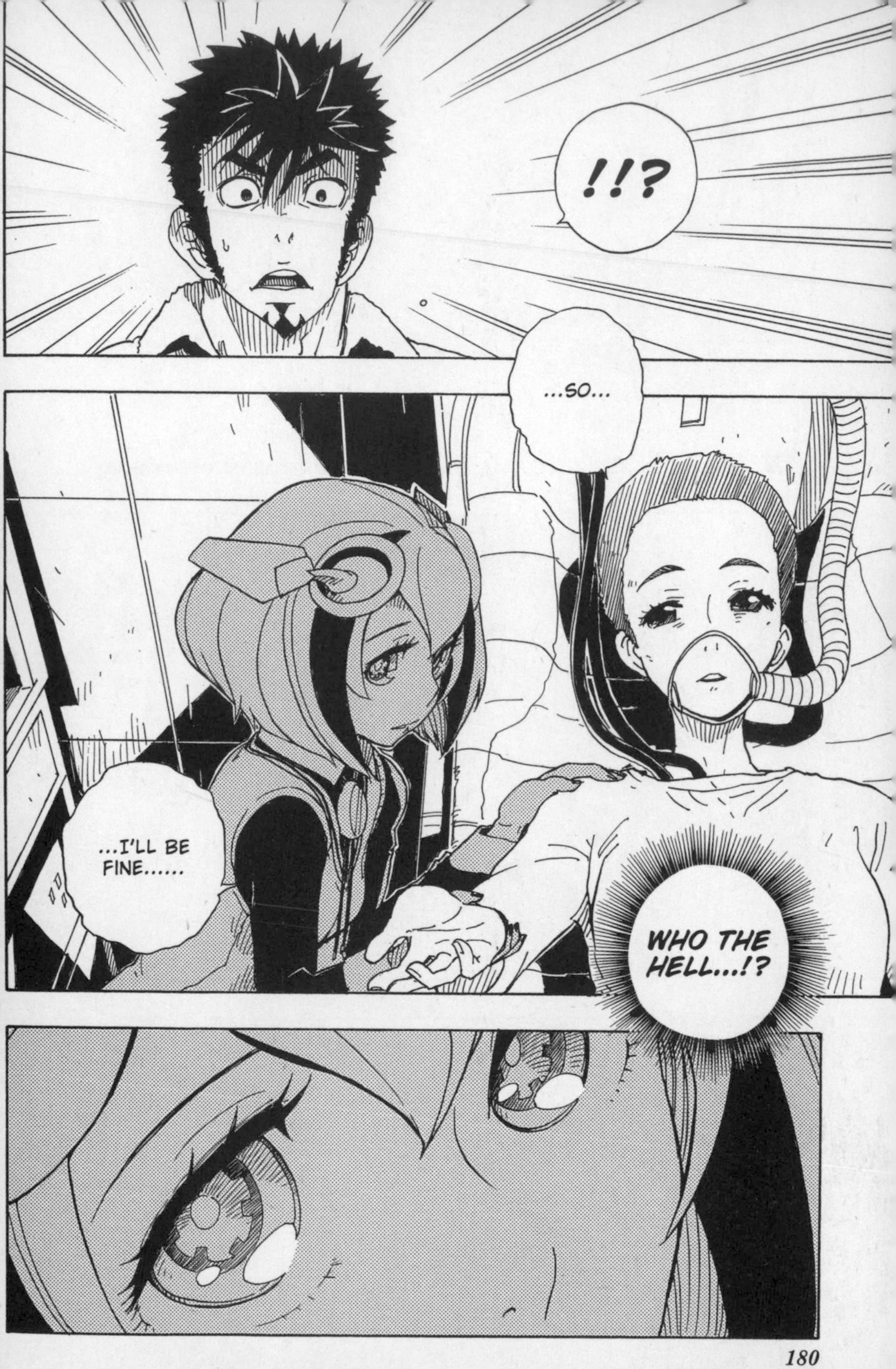
!!?
...SO...
...I'LL BE FINE......
WHO THE HELL...!?

FILE.55
LIGHT

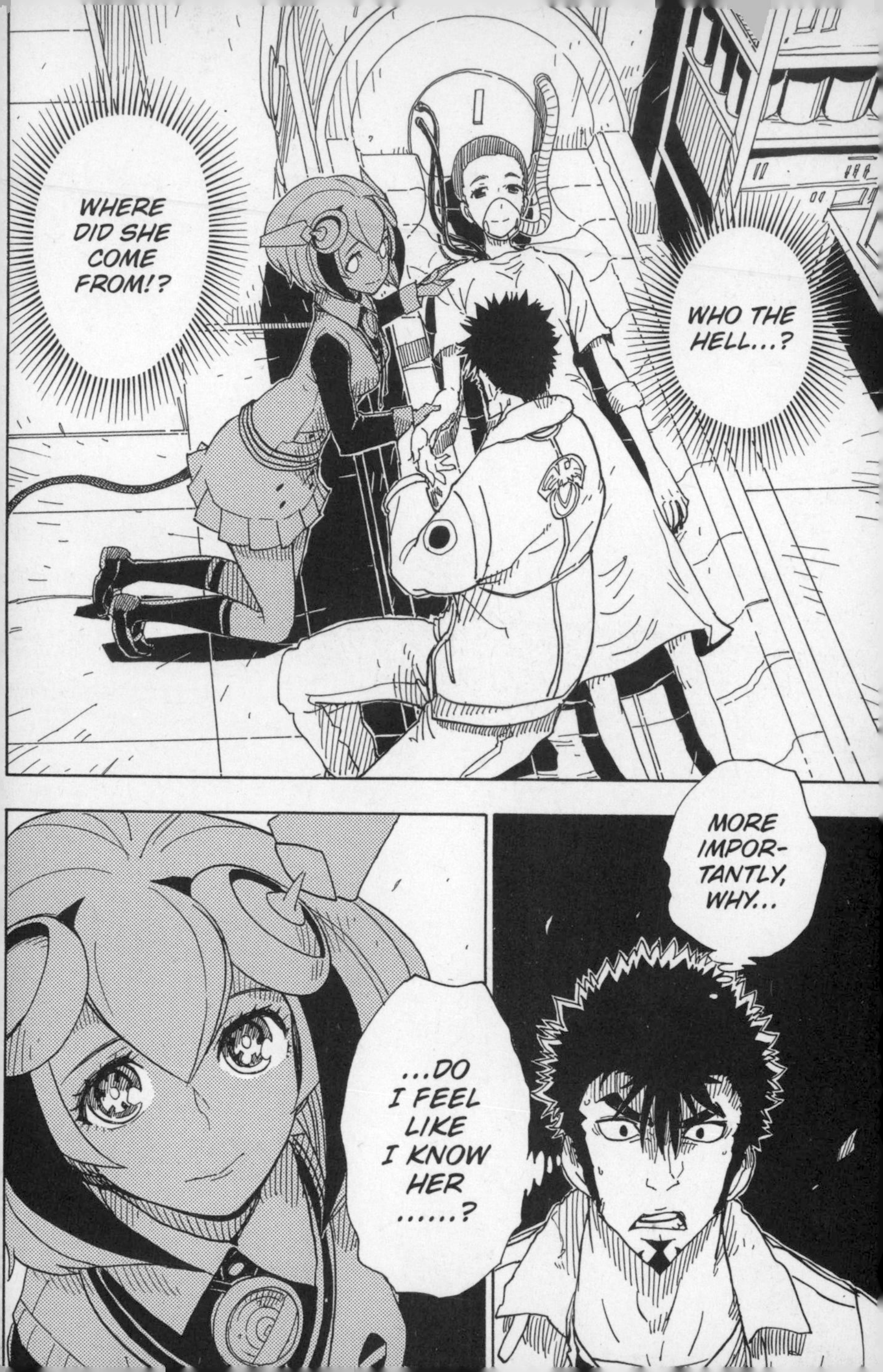
WHO THE HELL...?
WHERE DID SHE COME FROM!?
MORE IMPOR-TANTLY, WHY...
...DO I FEEL LIKE I KNOW HER ......?

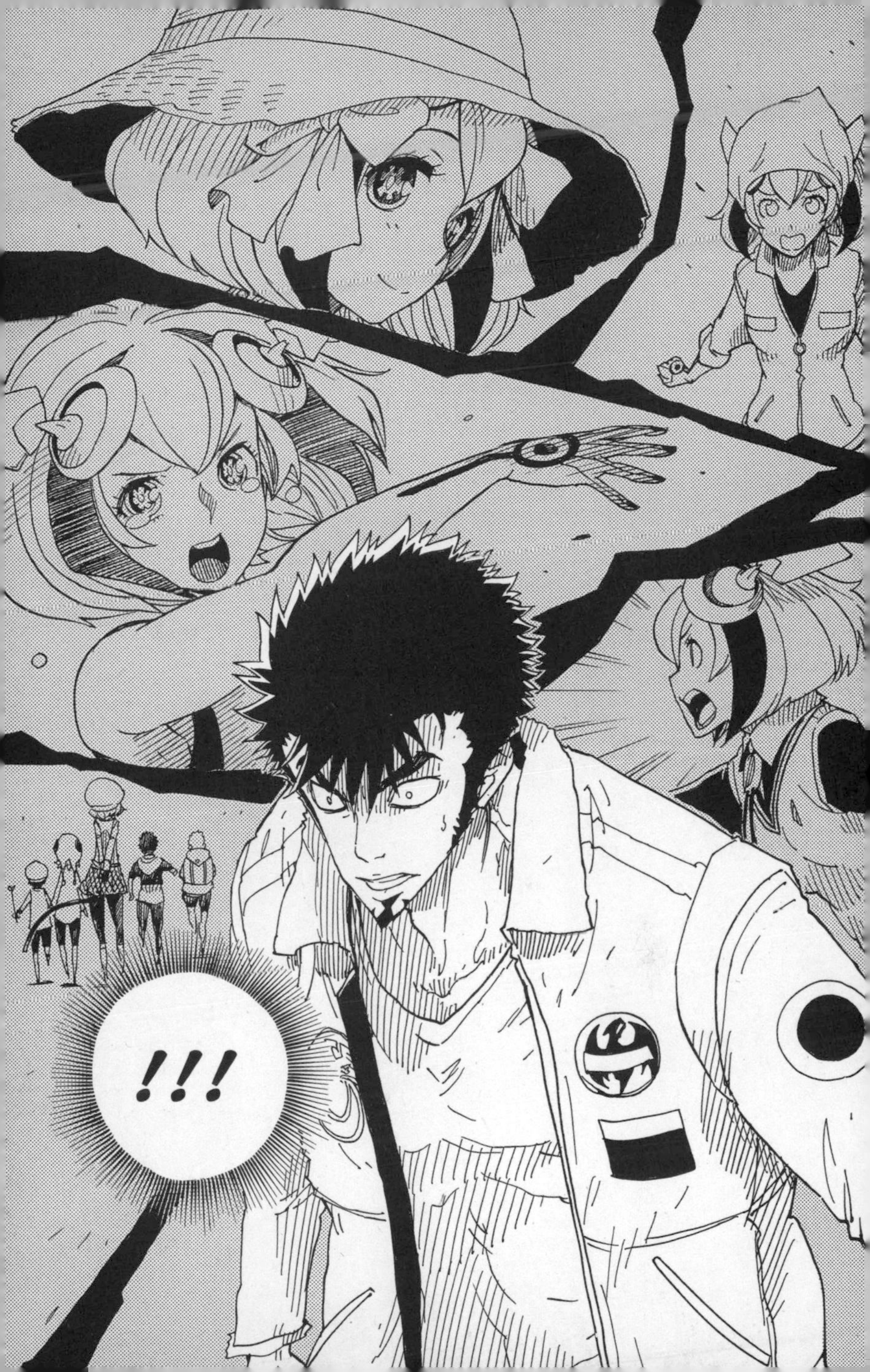
!!!

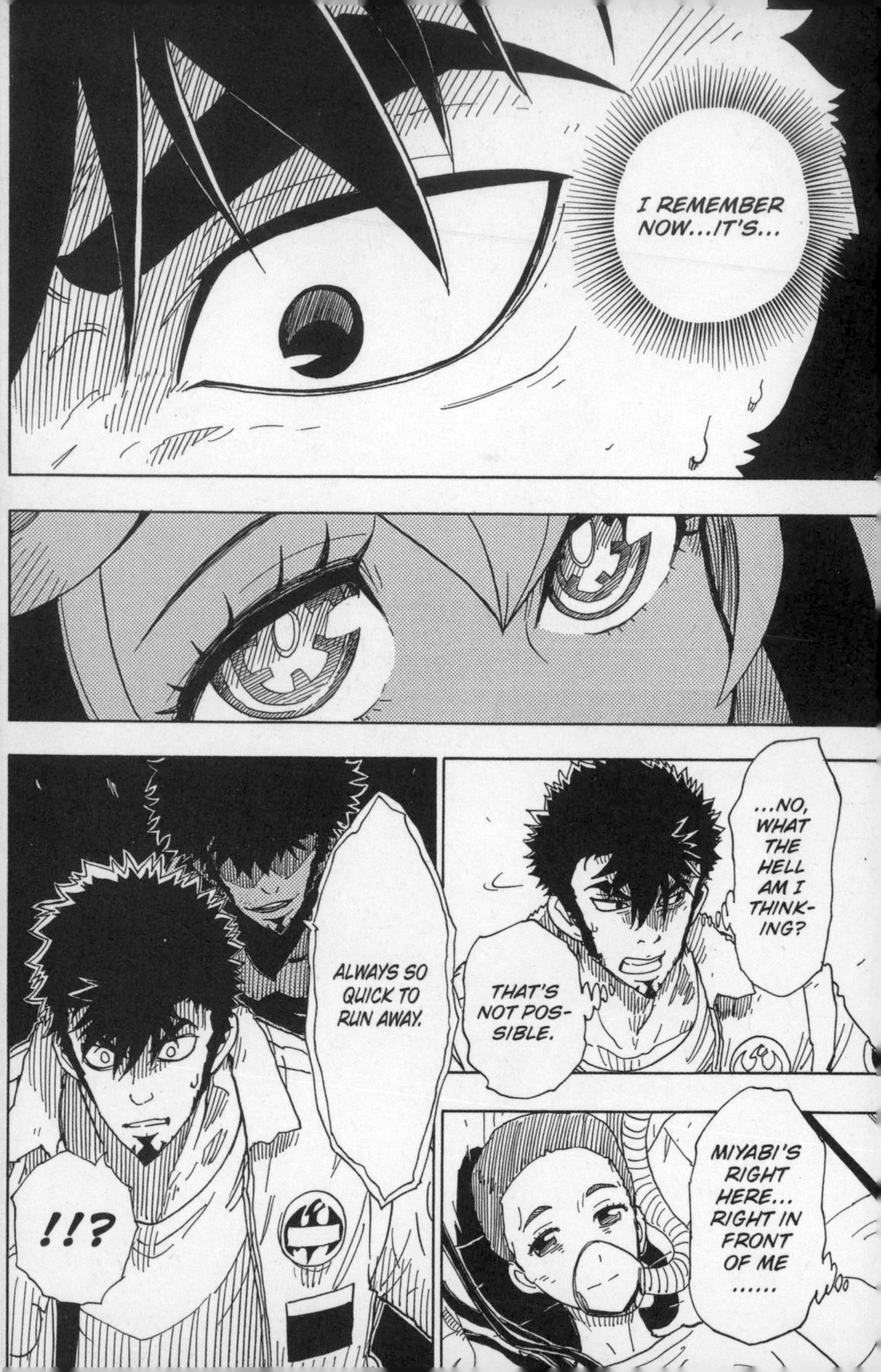
I REMEMBER NOW...IT'S...
...NO, WHAT THE HELL AM I THINKING?
THAT'S NOT POSSIBLE.
MIYABI'S RIGHT HERE... RIGHT IN FRONT OF ME ......
ALWAYS SO QUICK TO RUN AWAY.
!!?

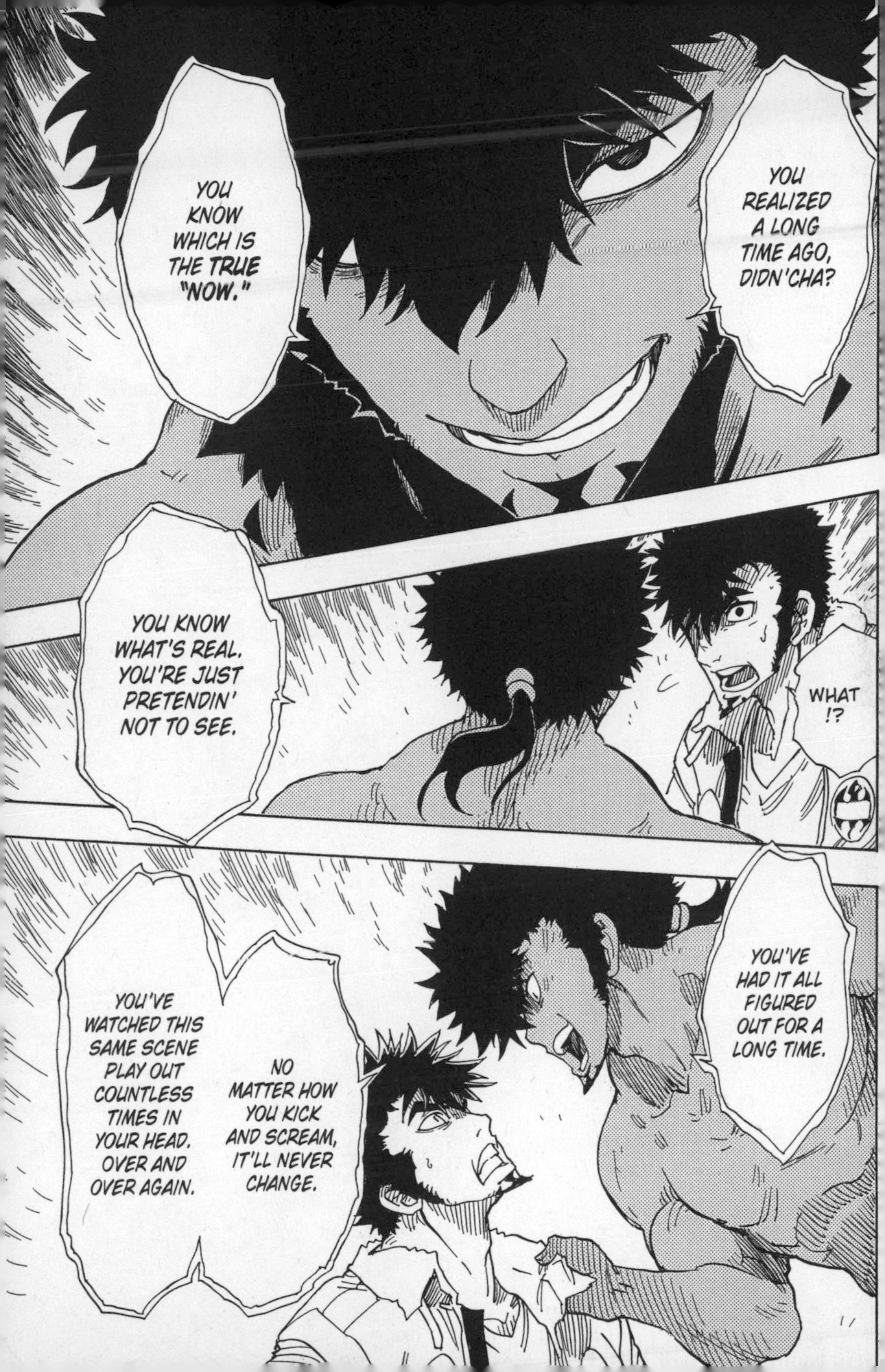
YOU REALIZED A LONG TIME AGO, DIDN'CHA?
YOU KNOW WHICH IS THE TRUE "NOW."
WHAT!?
YOU KNOW WHAT'S REAL. YOU'RE JUST PRETENDIN' NOT TO SEE.
YOU'VE HAD IT ALL FIGURED OUT FOR A LONG TIME.
NO MATTER HOW YOU KICK AND SCREAM, IT'LL NEVER CHANGE.
YOU'VE WATCHED THIS SAME SCENE PLAY OUT COUNTLESS TIMES IN YOUR HEAD. OVER AND OVER AGAIN.

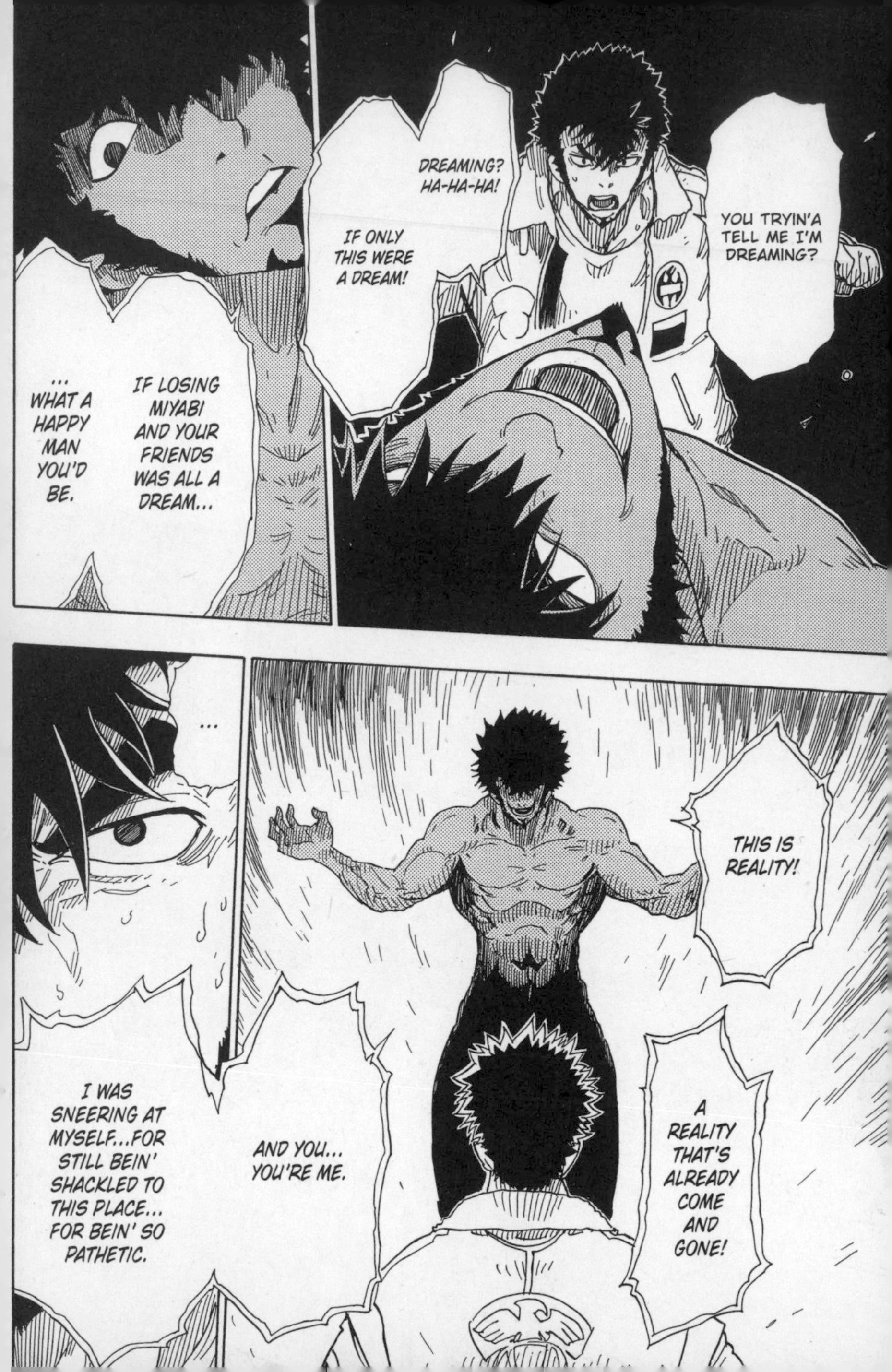
YOU TRYIN'A TELL ME I'M DREAMING?
DREAMING? HA-HA-HA!
IF ONLY THIS WERE A DREAM!
IF LOSING MIYABI AND YOUR FRIENDS WAS ALL A DREAM...
...WHAT A HAPPY MAN YOU'D BE.
THIS IS REALITY!
A REALITY THAT'S ALREADY COME AND GONE!
AND YOU... YOU'RE ME.
I WAS SNEERING AT MYSELF...FOR STILL BEIN' SHACKLED TO THIS PLACE... FOR BEIN' SO PATHETIC.
...

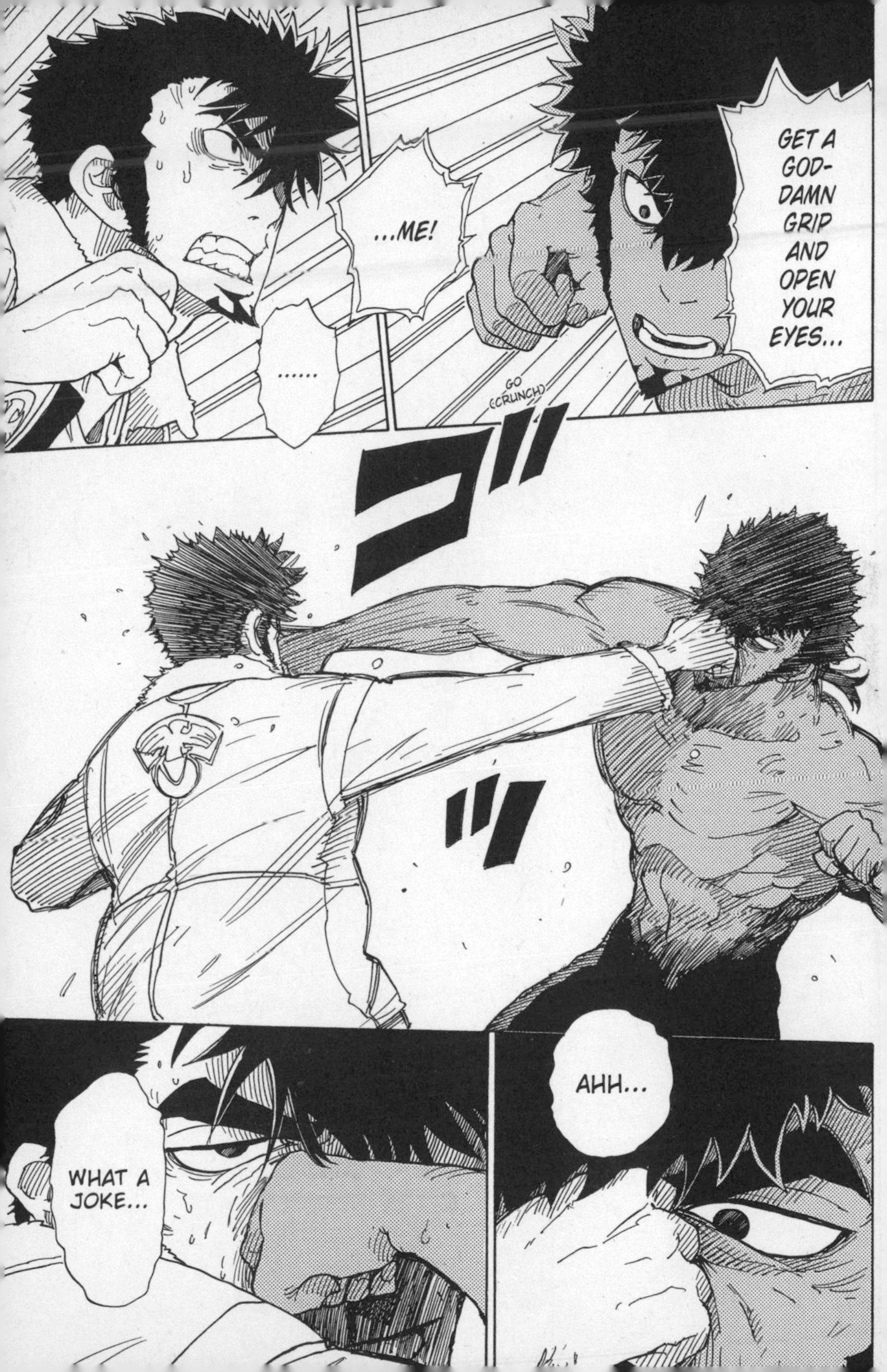

GET A GOD-DAMN GRIP AND OPEN YOUR EYES...
...ME!
......
GO (CRUNCH)
ゴッ
AHH...
WHAT A JOKE...

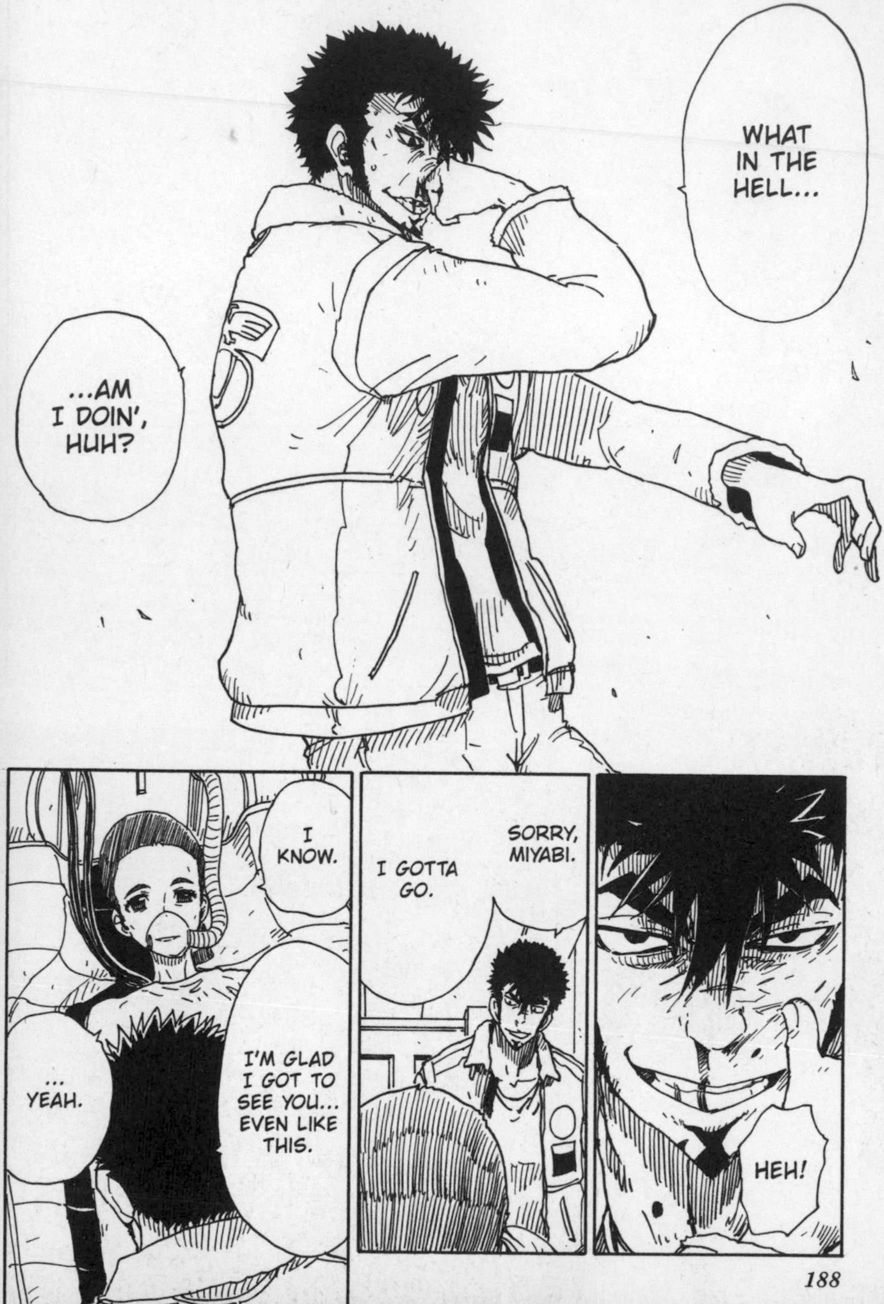
WHAT IN THE HELL...
...AM I DOIN', HUH?
HEH!
SORRY, MIYABI.
I GOTTA GO.
I KNOW.
I'M GLAD I GOT TO SEE YOU... EVEN LIKE THIS.
...YEAH.

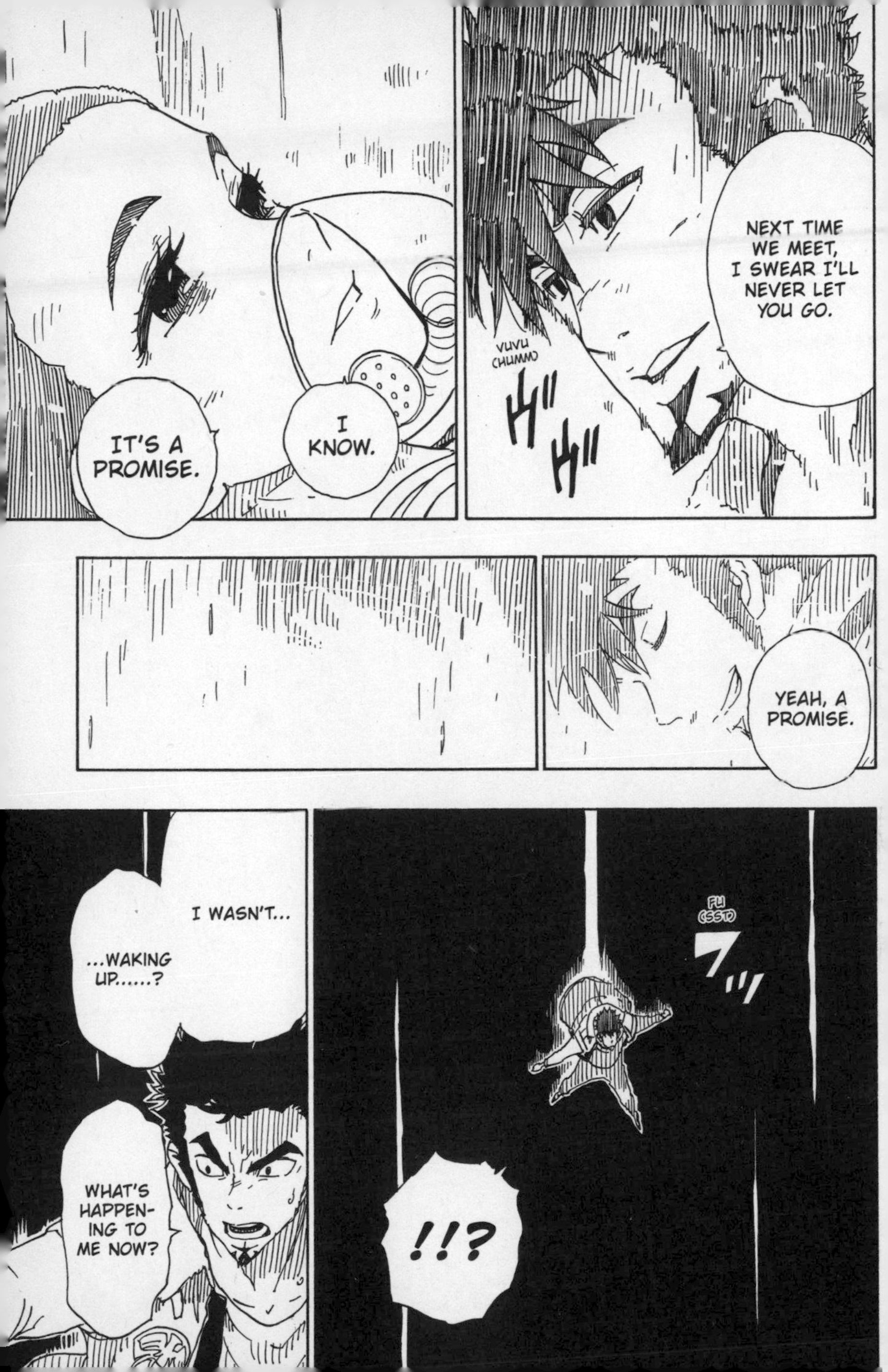
NEXT TIME WE MEET, I SWEAR I'LL NEVER LET YOU GO.
I KNOW.
IT'S A PROMISE.
YEAH, A PROMISE.
FU (SSST)
!!?
I WASN'T...
...WAKING UP......?
WHAT'S HAPPEN-ING TO ME NOW?

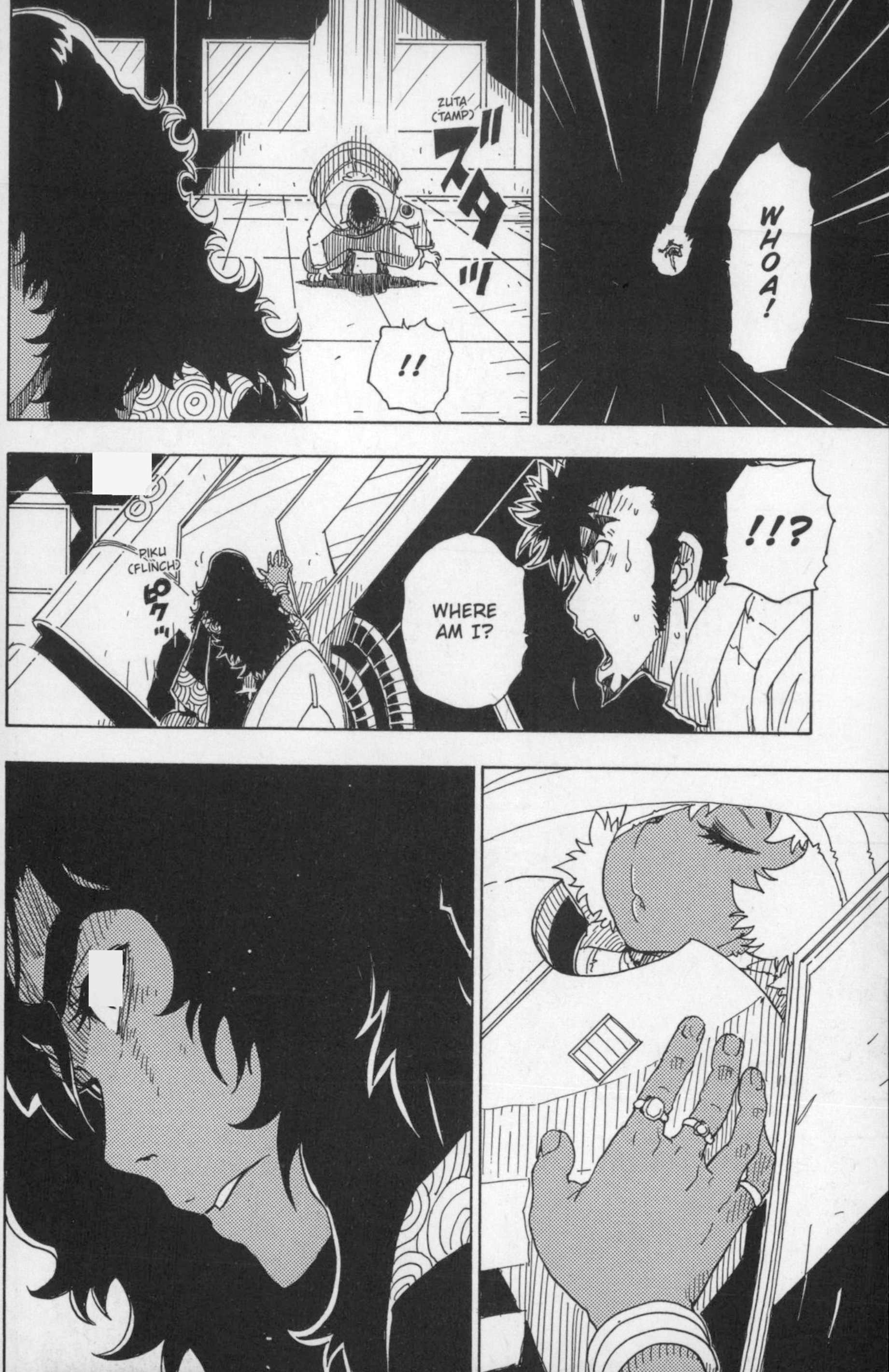
WHOA!
ZUTA (TAMP)
!!
!!?
WHERE AM I?
PIKU (FLINCH)

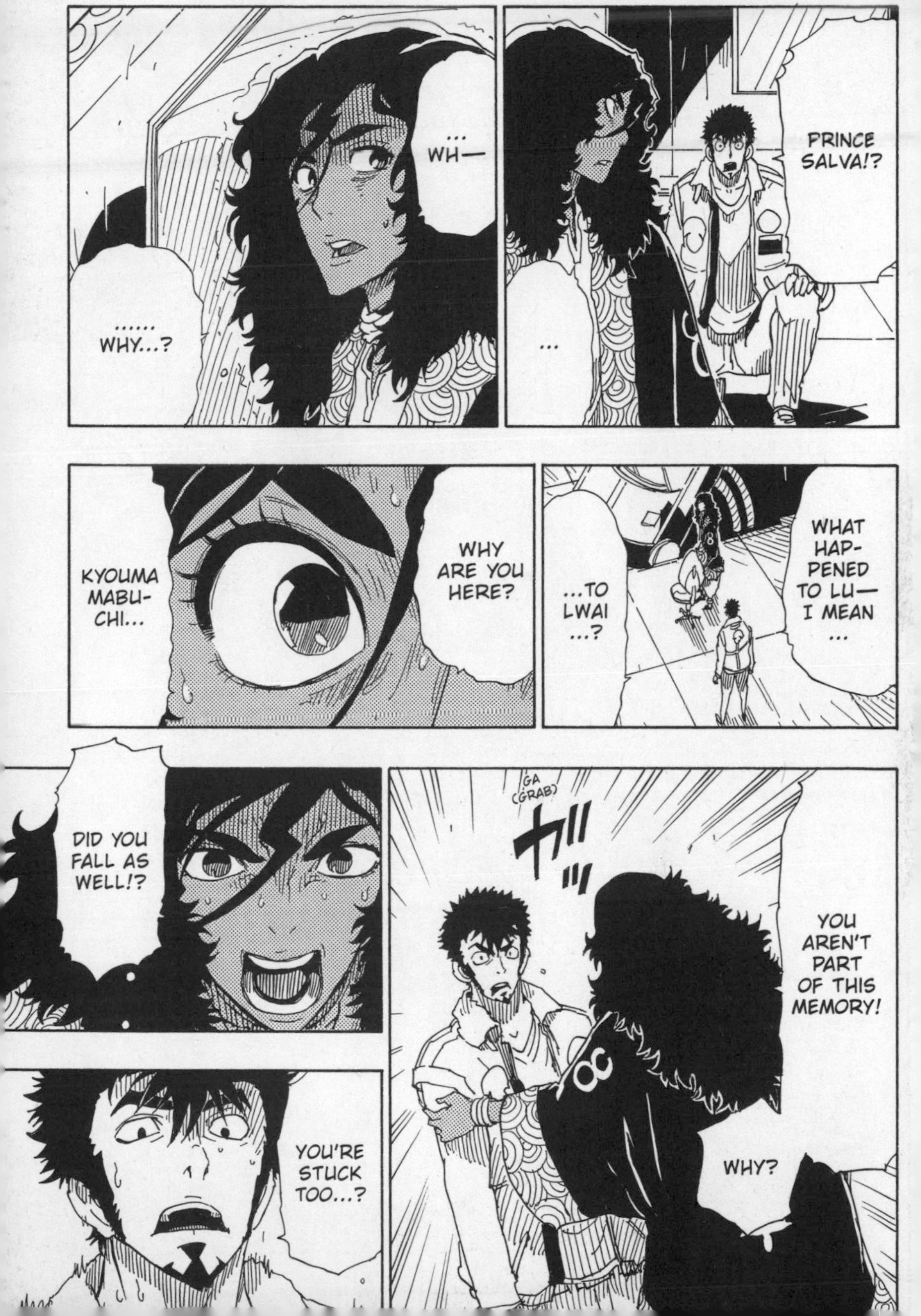
PRINCE SALVA!?
...
... WH—
...... WHY...?
WHAT HAP-PENED TO LU— I MEAN ...
...TO LWAI ...?
WHY ARE YOU HERE?
KYOUMA MABU-CHI...
GA (GRAB)
ガッ
YOU AREN'T PART OF THIS MEMORY!
WHY?
DID YOU FALL AS WELL!?
YOU'RE STUCK TOO...?

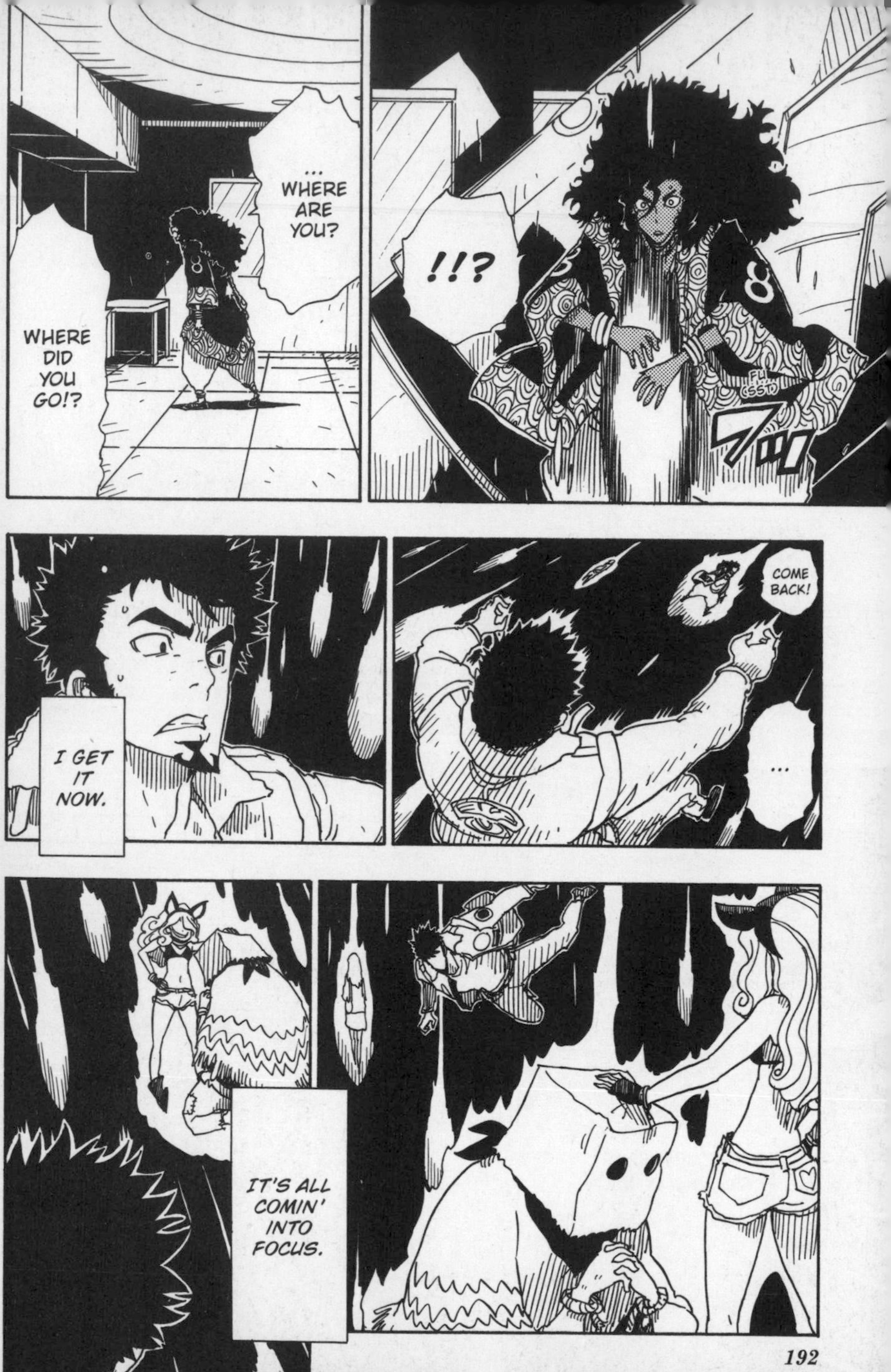
!!?
FU... (SST)
... WHERE ARE YOU?
WHERE DID YOU GO!?
COME BACK!
...
I GET IT NOW.
IT'S ALL COMIN' INTO FOCUS.

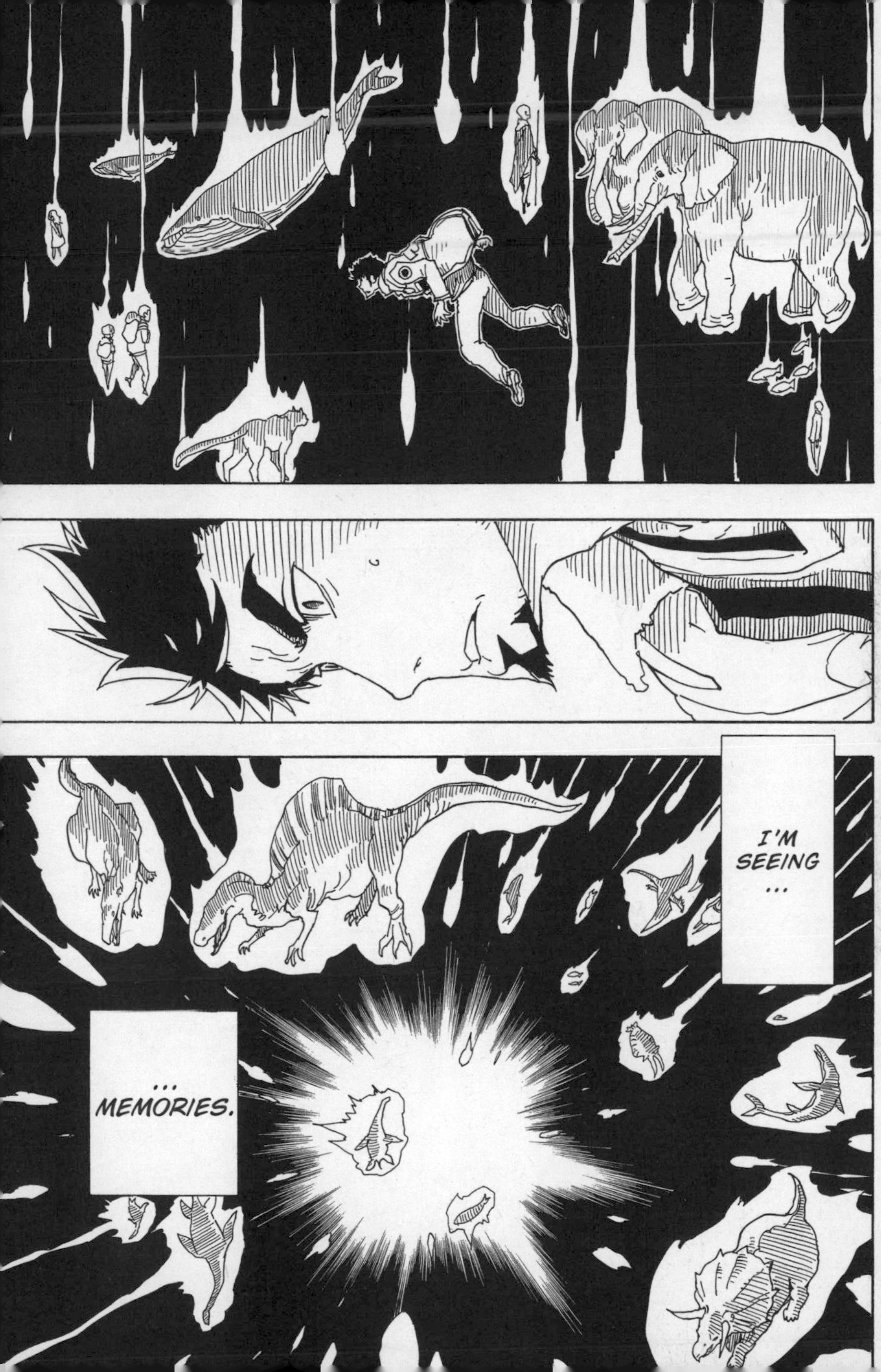
I'M SEEING ...
... MEMORIES.

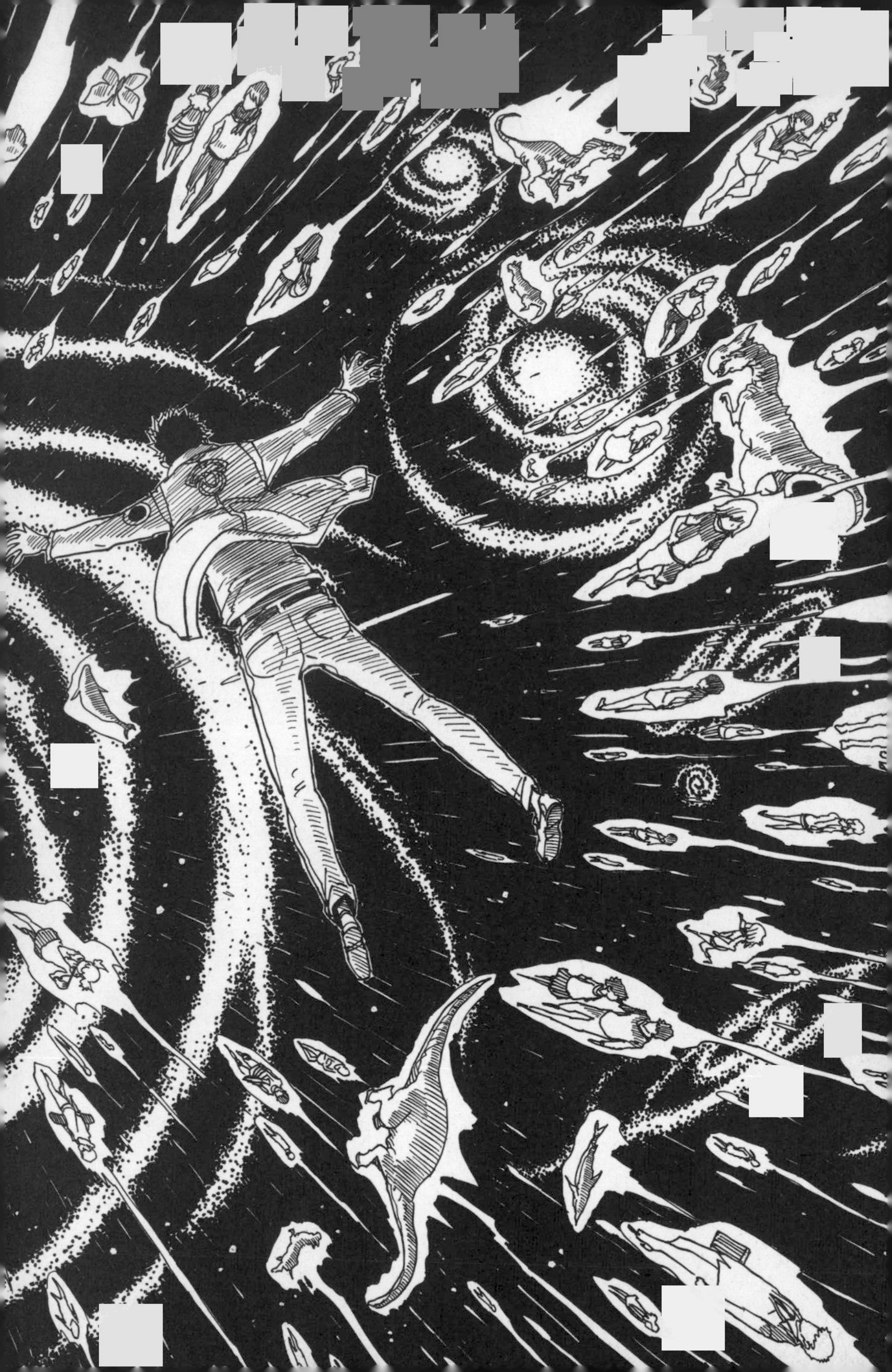

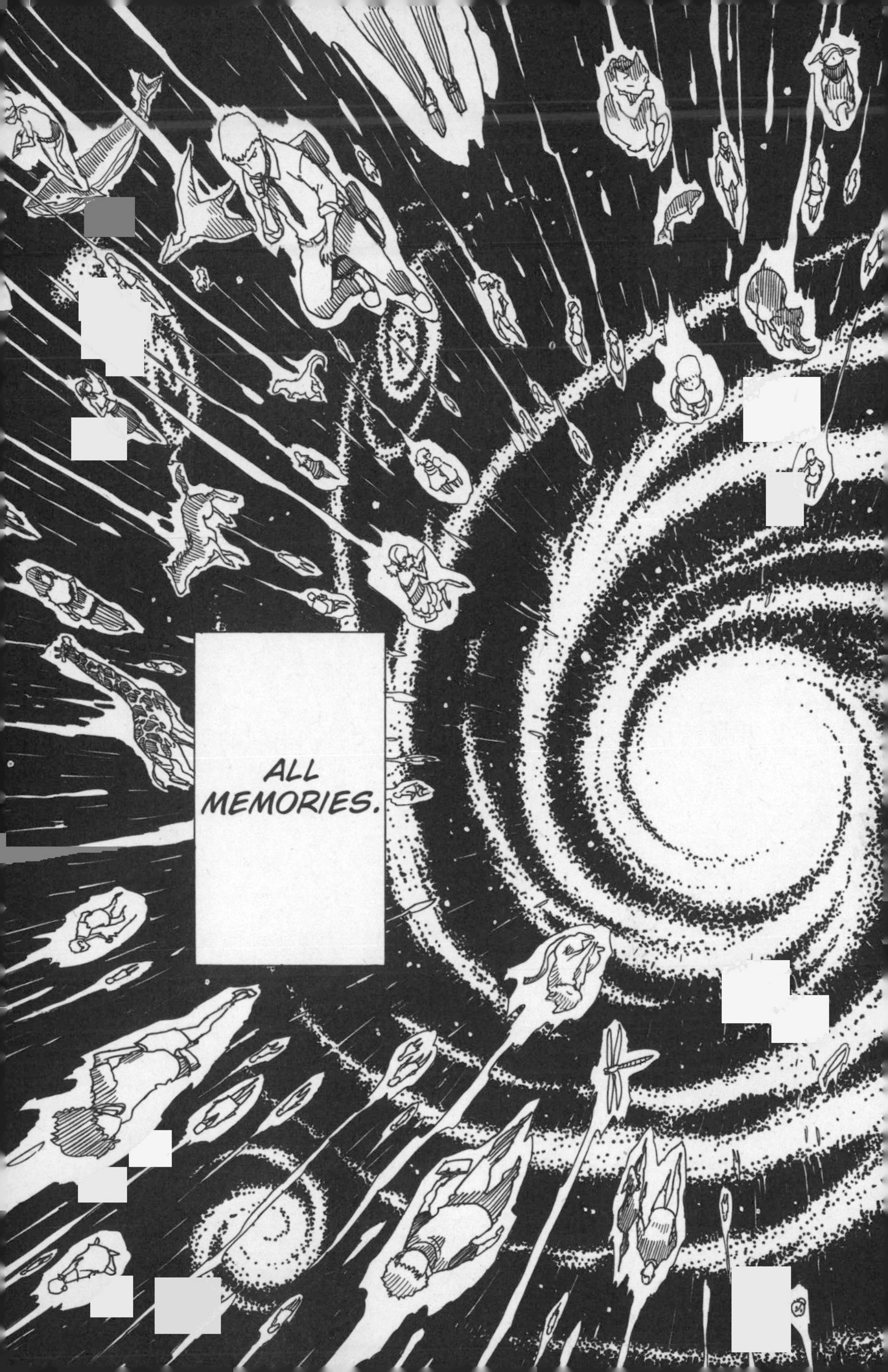
ALL MEMORIES.

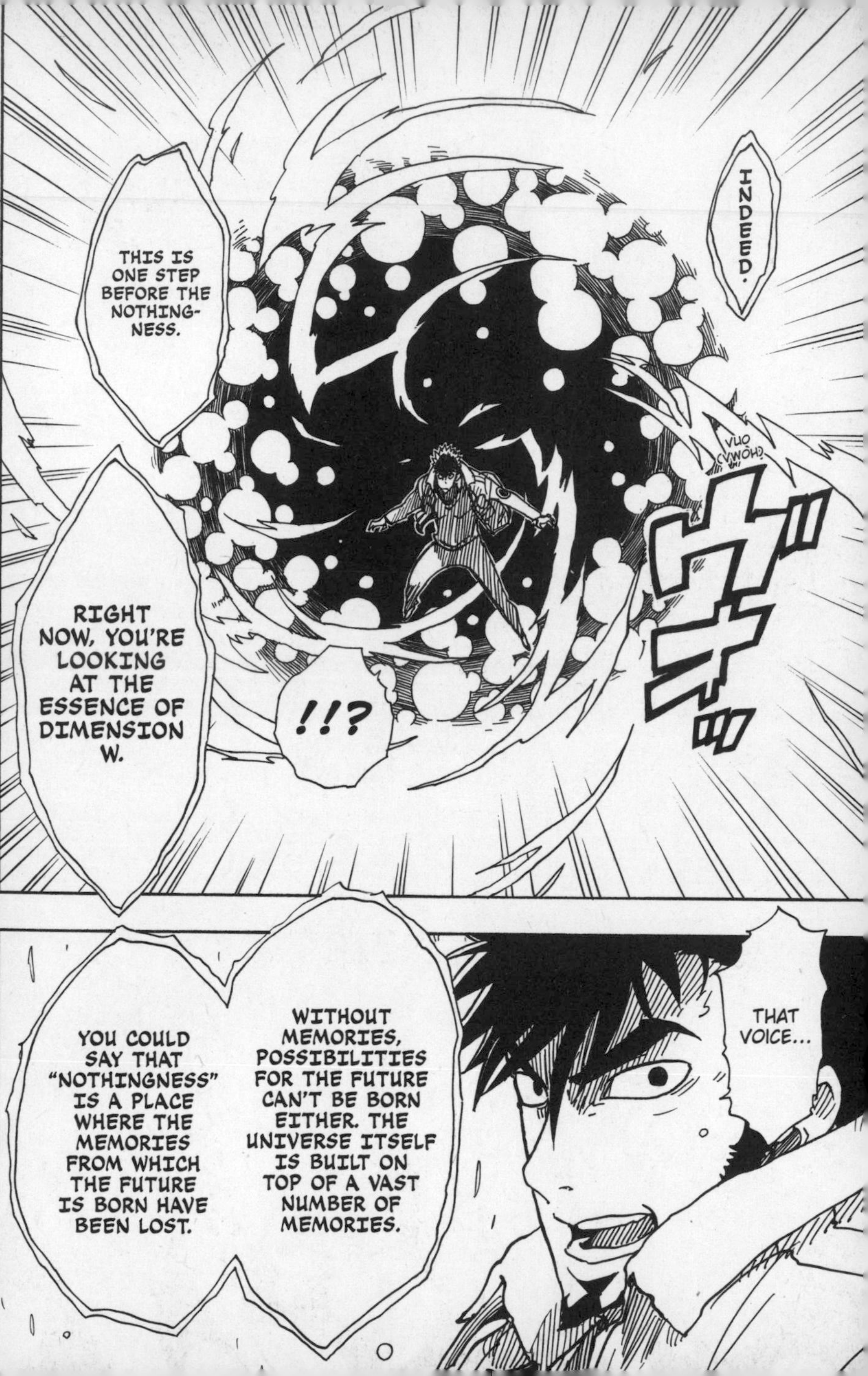
INDEED.
VUO (VWOH)
THIS IS ONE STEP BEFORE THE NOTHINGNESS.
!!?
RIGHT NOW, YOU'RE LOOKING AT THE ESSENCE OF DIMENSION W.
THAT VOICE...
YOU COULD SAY THAT "NOTHINGNESS" IS A PLACE WHERE THE MEMORIES FROM WHICH THE FUTURE IS BORN HAVE BEEN LOST.
WITHOUT MEMORIES, POSSIBILITIES FOR THE FUTURE CAN'T BE BORN EITHER. THE UNIVERSE ITSELF IS BUILT ON TOP OF A VAST NUMBER OF MEMORIES.

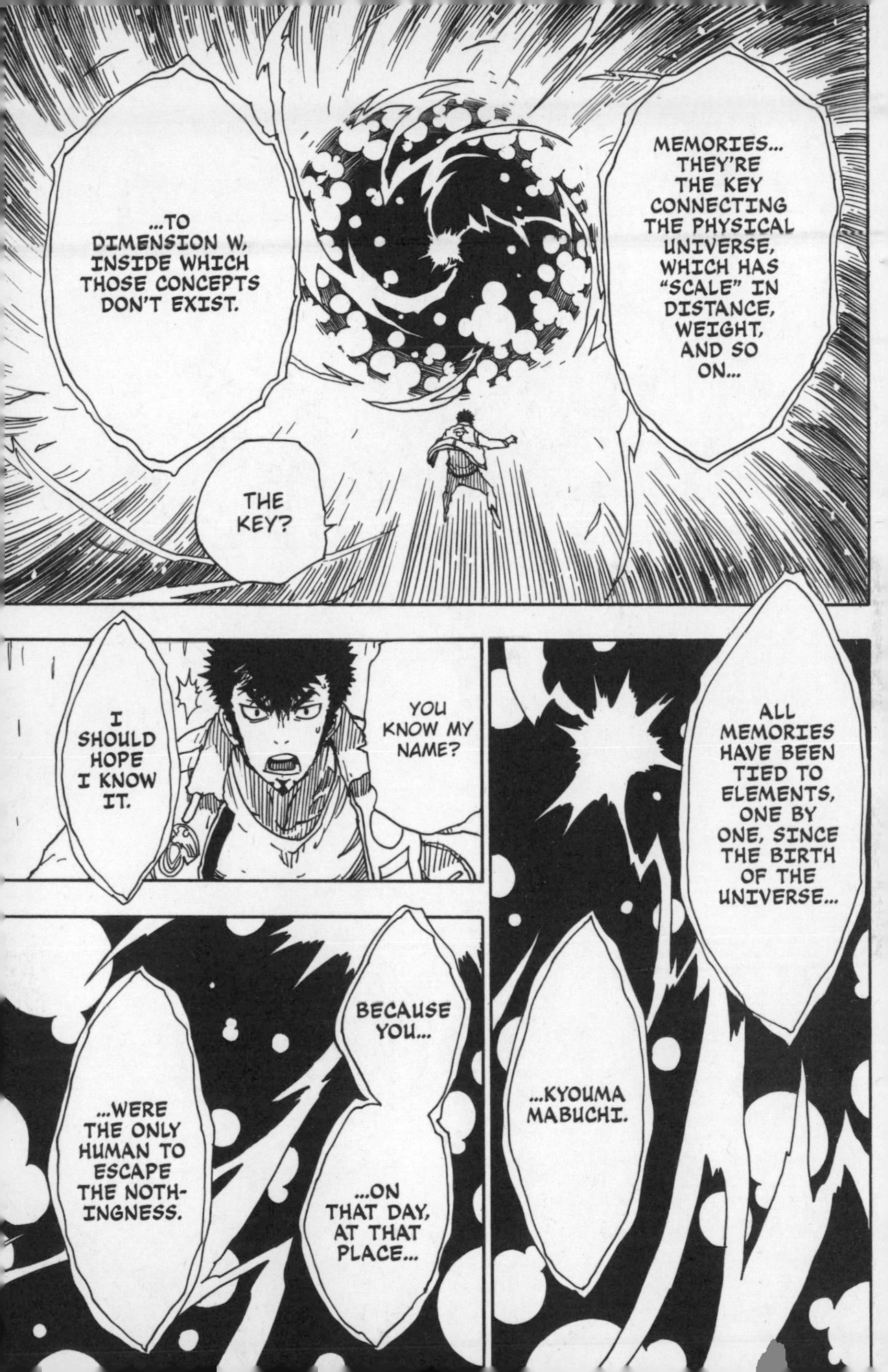
MEMORIES... THEY'RE THE KEY CONNECTING THE PHYSICAL UNIVERSE, WHICH HAS "SCALE" IN DISTANCE, WEIGHT, AND SO ON...
...TO DIMENSION W, INSIDE WHICH THOSE CONCEPTS DON'T EXIST.
THE KEY?
ALL MEMORIES HAVE BEEN TIED TO ELEMENTS, ONE BY ONE, SINCE THE BIRTH OF THE UNIVERSE...
...KYOUMA MABUCHI.
YOU KNOW MY NAME?
I SHOULD HOPE I KNOW IT.
BECAUSE YOU...
...ON THAT DAY, AT THAT PLACE...
...WERE THE ONLY HUMAN TO ESCAPE THE NOTH-INGNESS.

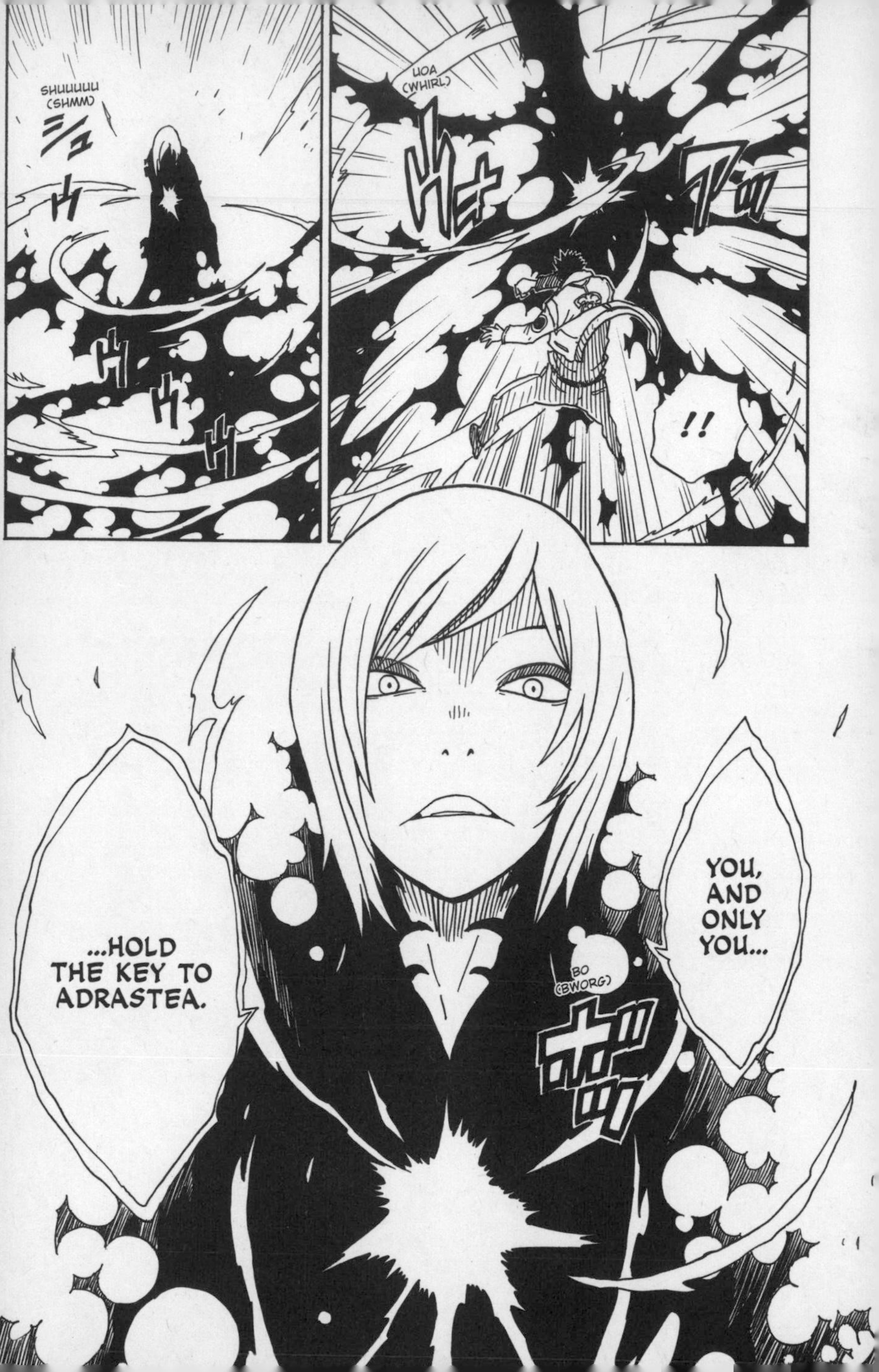
UOA (WHIRL)
!!
SHUUUUU (SHMM)
YOU, AND ONLY YOU...
BO (BWORG)
...HOLD THE KEY TO ADRASTEA.

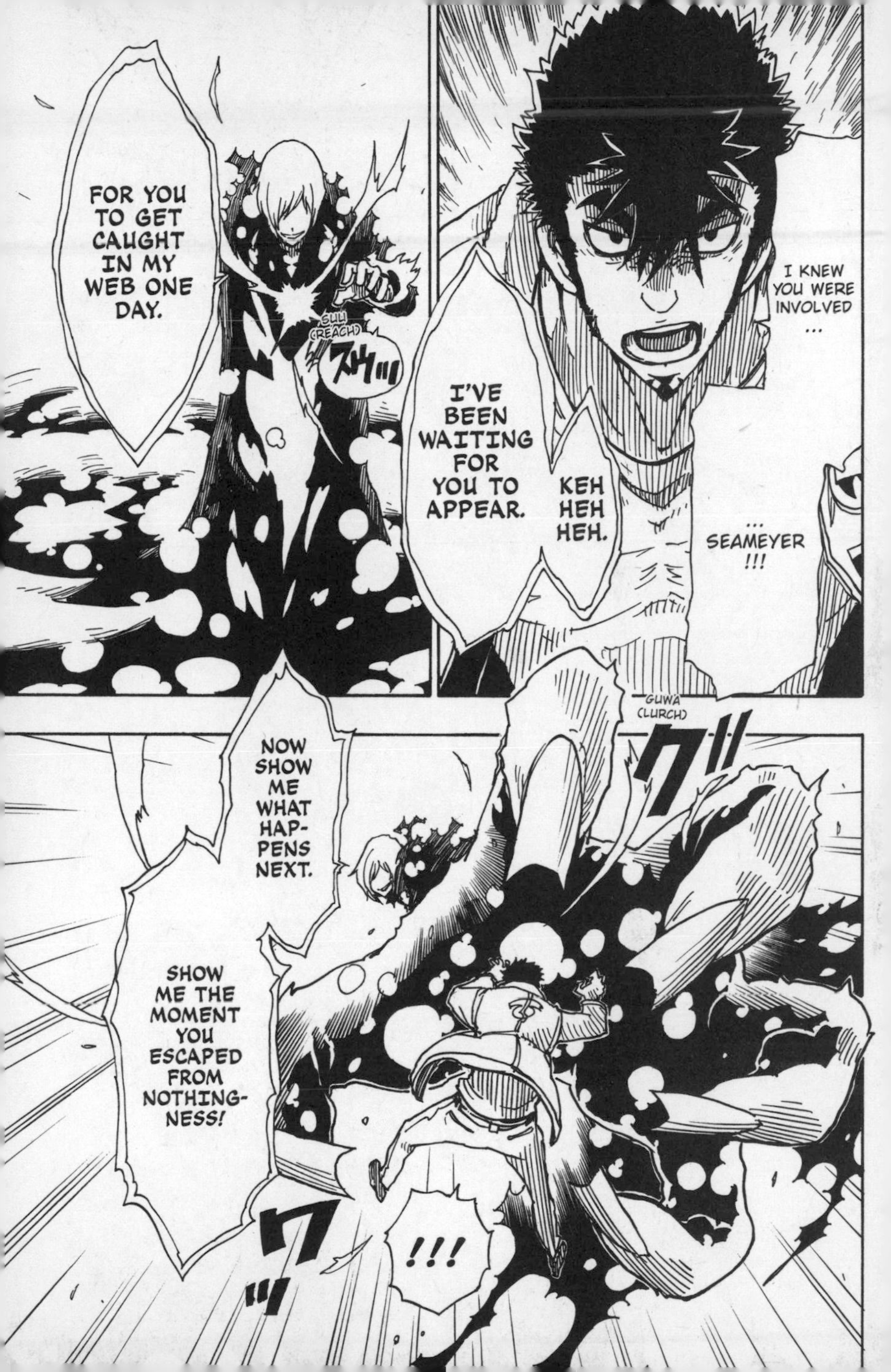
I KNEW YOU WERE INVOLVED ...
... SEAMEYER !!!
I'VE BEEN WAITING FOR YOU TO APPEAR.
KEH HEH HEH.
SULI (REACH)
FOR YOU TO GET CAUGHT IN MY WEB ONE DAY.
GUWA (LURCH)
NOW SHOW ME WHAT HAP-PENS NEXT.
SHOW ME THE MOMENT YOU ESCAPED FROM NOTHING-NESS!
!!!

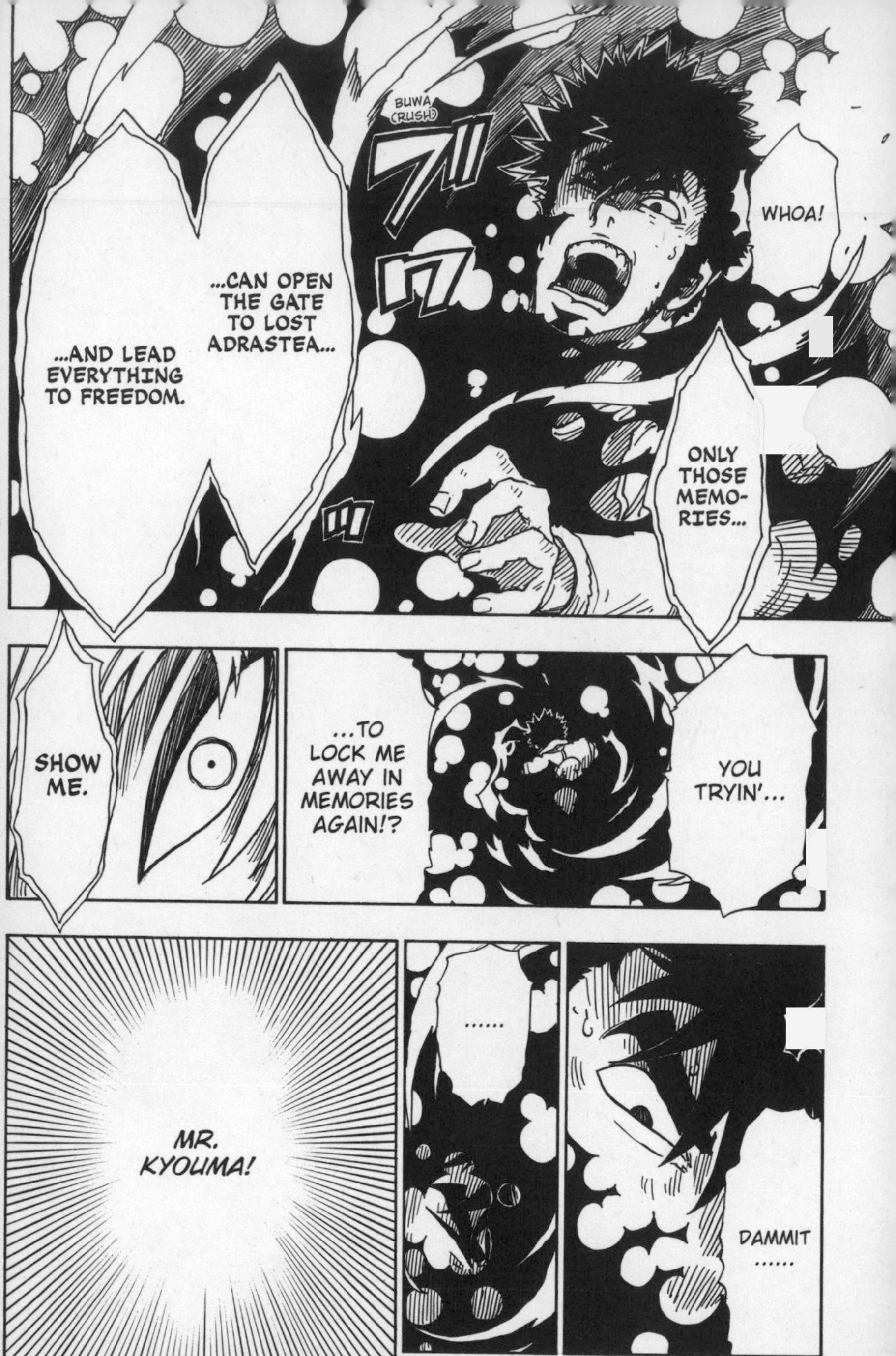
WHOA!
BUWA (CRUSH)
ONLY THOSE MEMORIES...
...CAN OPEN THE GATE TO LOST ADRASTEA...
...AND LEAD EVERYTHING TO FREEDOM.
YOU TRYIN'...
...TO LOCK ME AWAY IN MEMORIES AGAIN!?
SHOW ME.
DAMMIT ......
......
MR. KYOUMA!

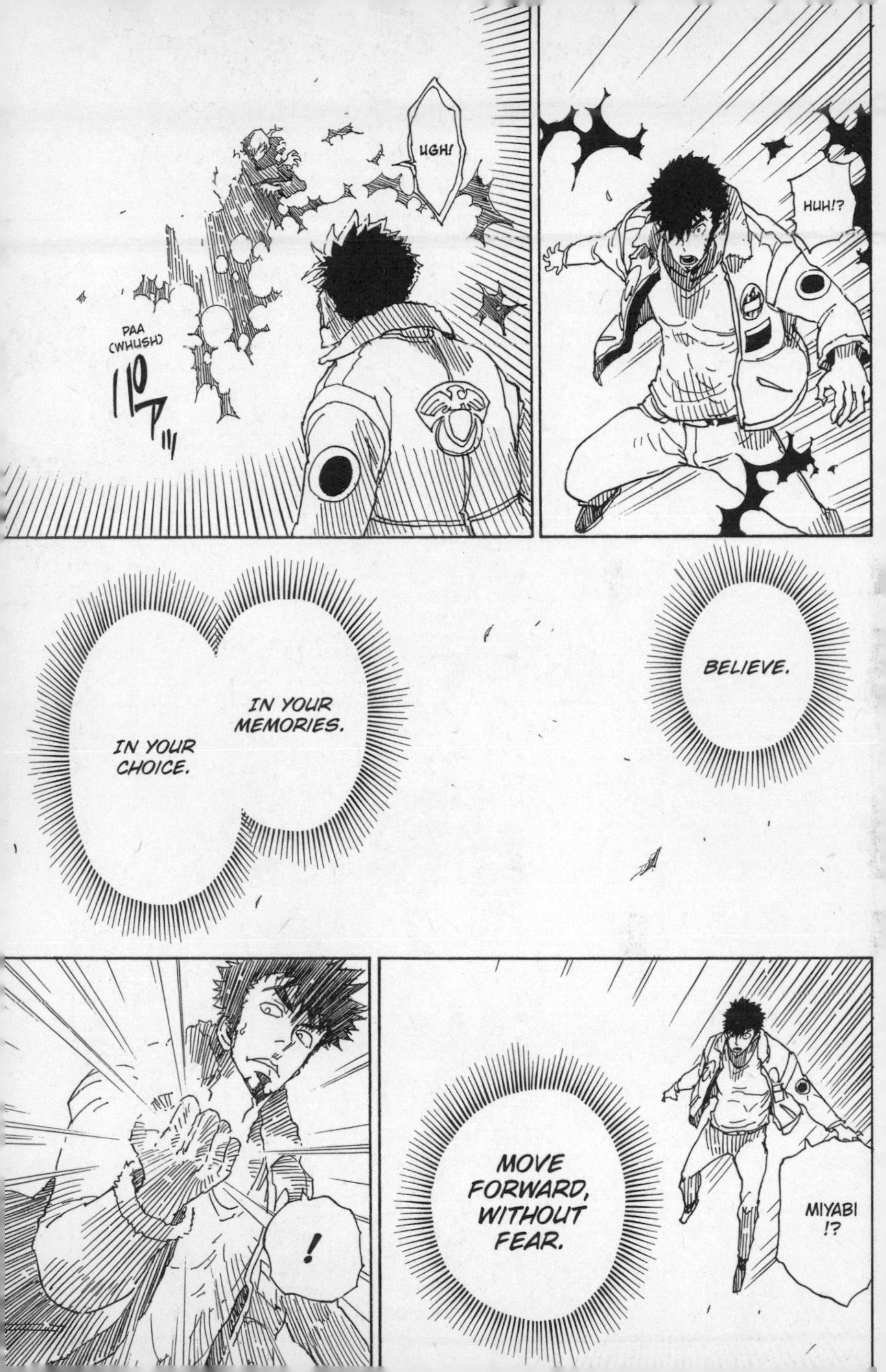
HUH!?
UGH!
PAA
(WHUSH)
パッ
BELIEVE.
IN YOUR MEMORIES.
IN YOUR CHOICE.
MIYABI
!?
MOVE FORWARD, WITHOUT FEAR.
!

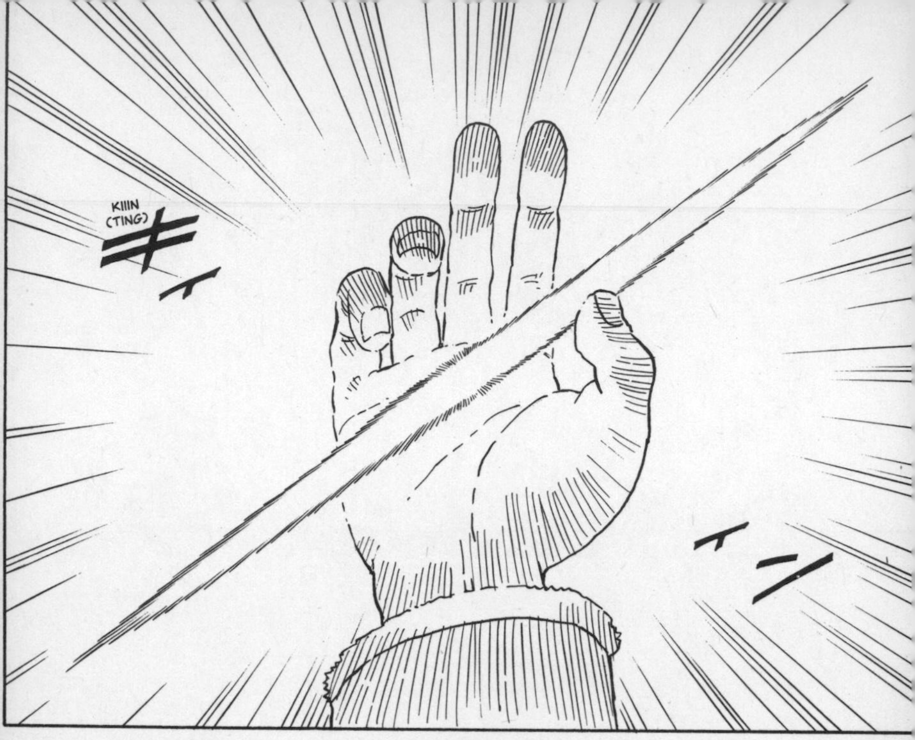
KIIIN
(TING)

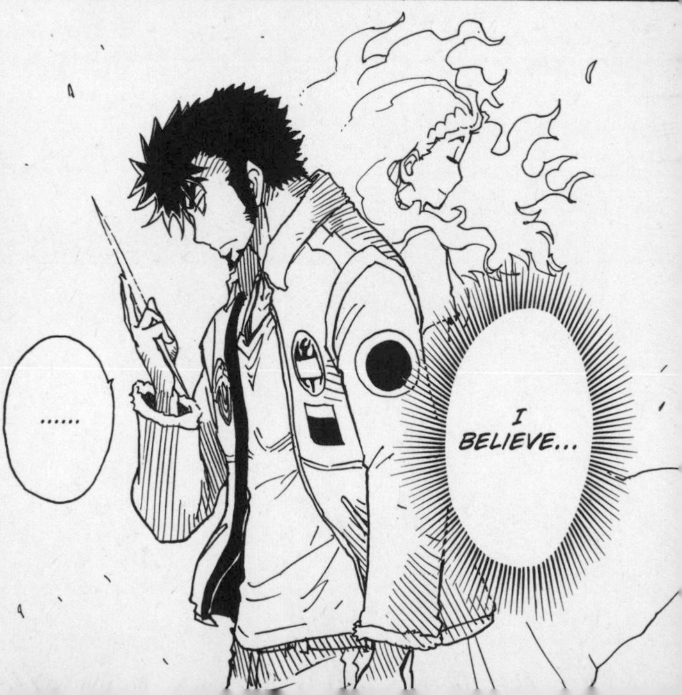
I BELIEVE...
......

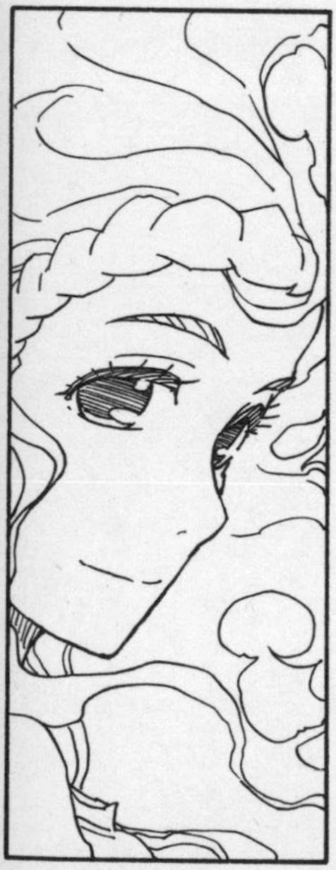

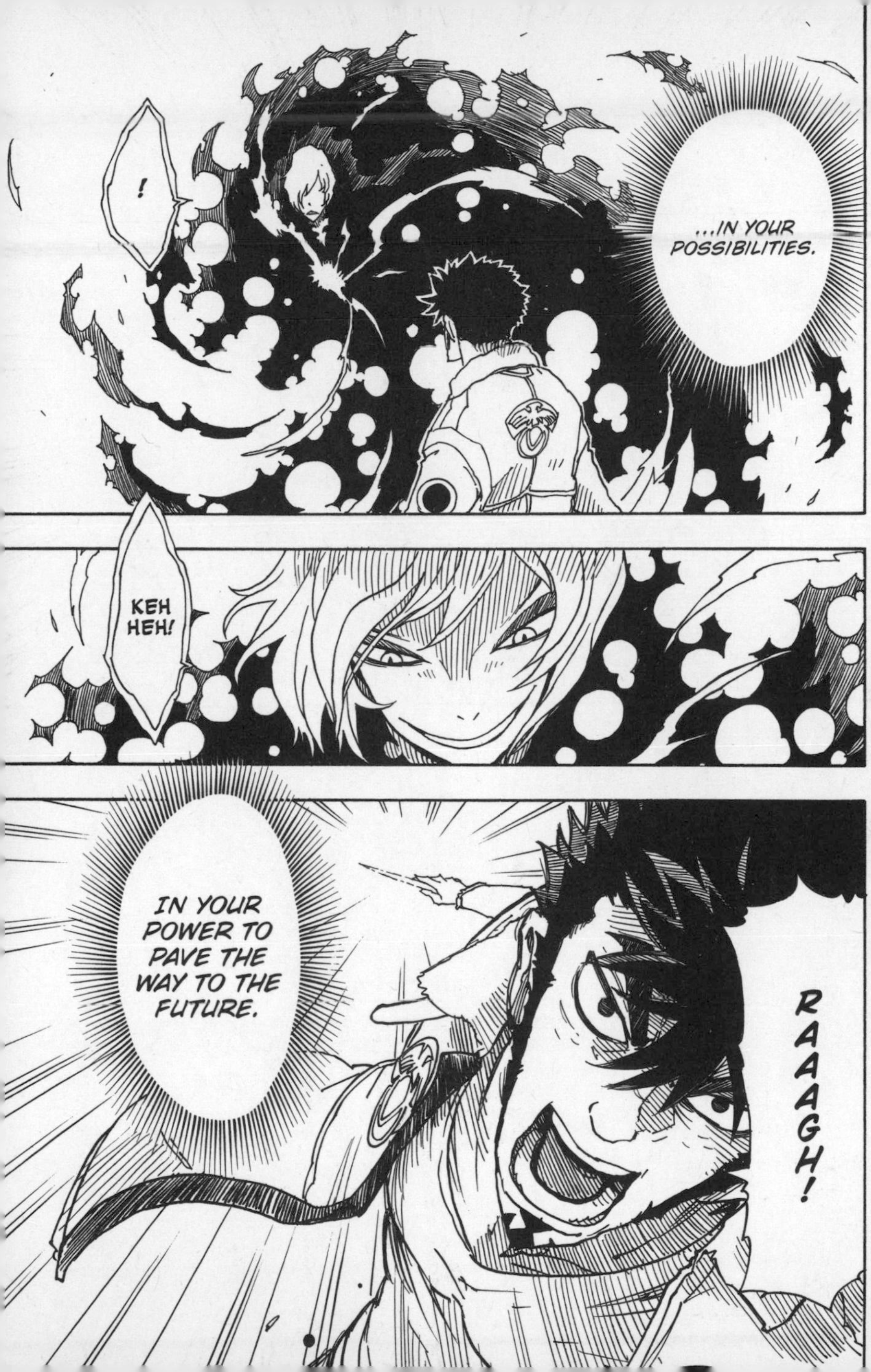
...IN YOUR POSSIBILITIES.
!
KEH HEH!
RAAAGH!
IN YOUR POWER TO PAVE THE WAY TO THE FUTURE.

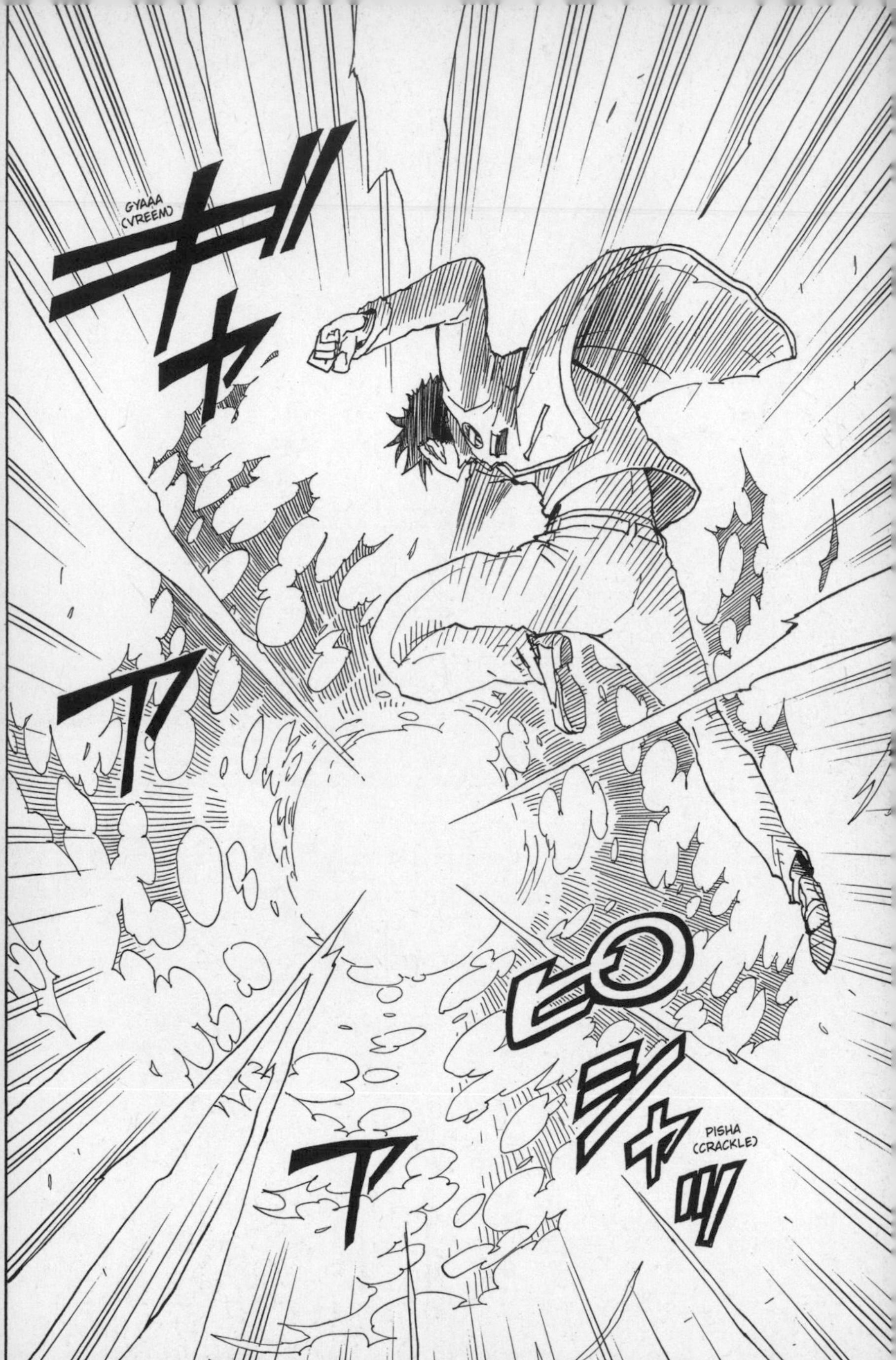
GYAAA
(VREEM)
PISHA
(CRACKLE)

DIMENSION W 7 END

Dimension W

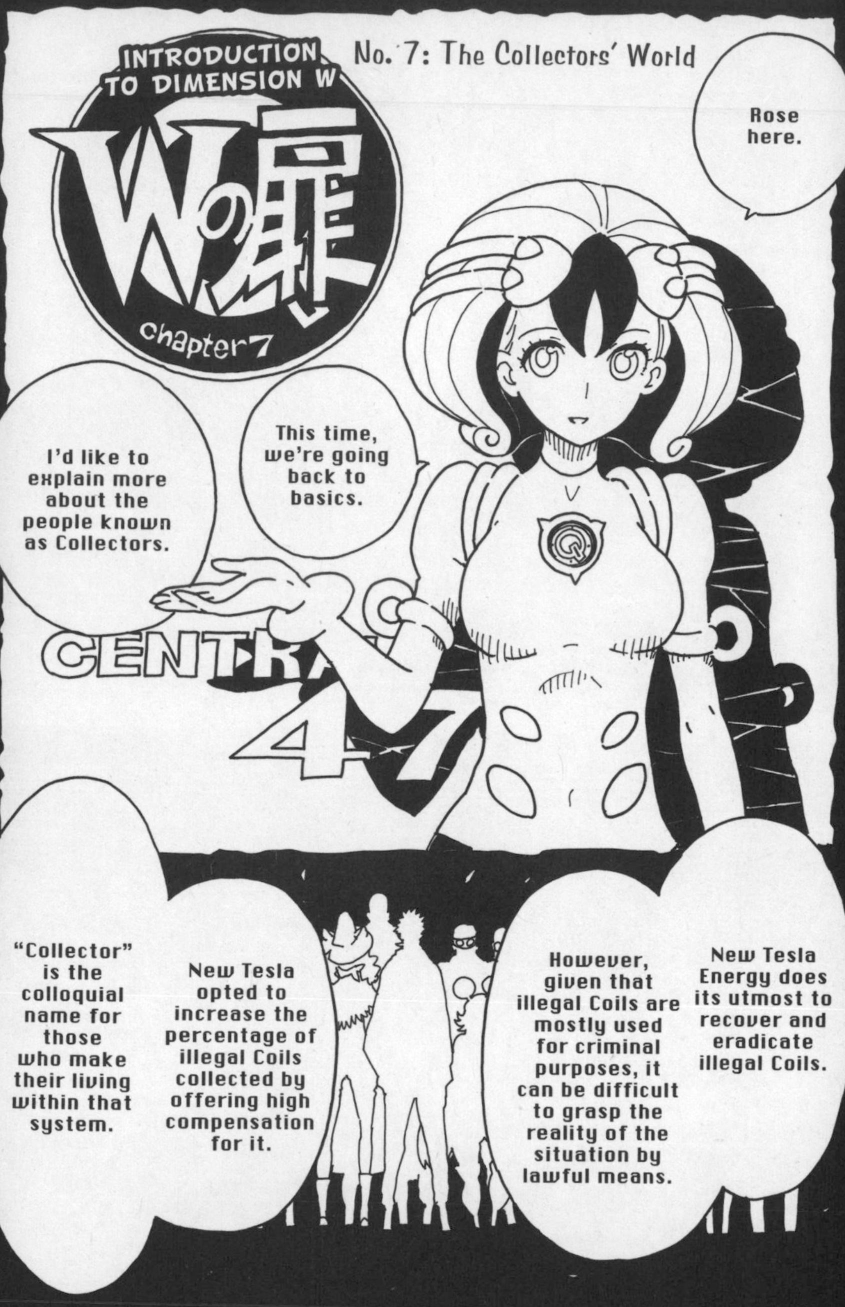

INTRODUCTION TO DIMENSION W
chapter 7
No. 7: The Collectors' World
Rose here.
This time, we're going back to basics.
I'd like to explain more about the people known as Collectors.
New Tesla Energy does its utmost to recover and eradicate illegal Coils.
However, given that illegal Coils are mostly used for criminal purposes, it can be difficult to grasp the reality of the situation by lawful means.
New Tesla opted to increase the percentage of illegal Coils collected by offering high compensation for it.
"Collector" is the colloquial name for those who make their living within that system.

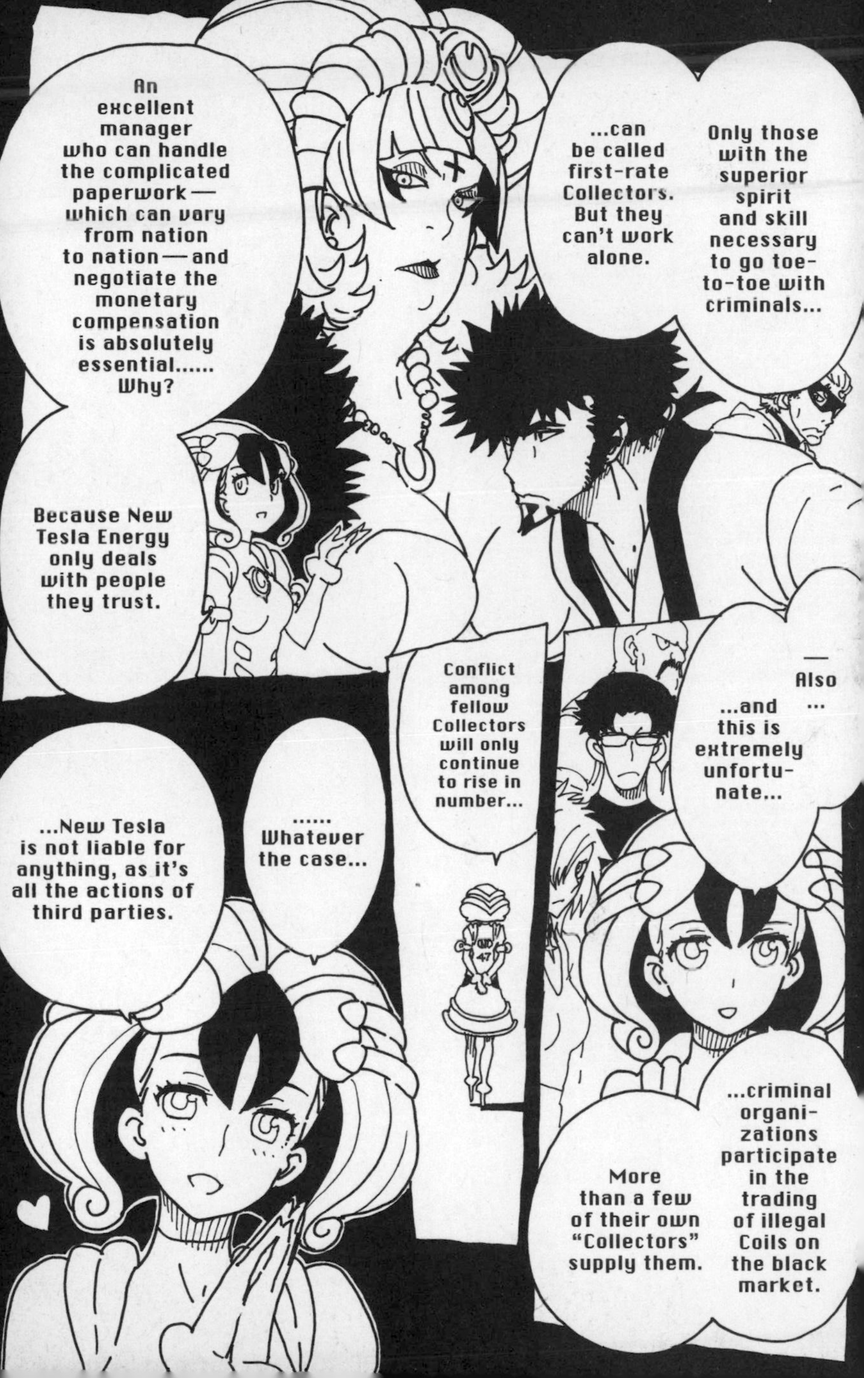
Only those with the superior spirit and skill necessary to go toe-to-toe with criminals...
...can be called first-rate Collectors. But they can't work alone.
An excellent manager who can handle the complicated paperwork — which can vary from nation to nation — and negotiate the monetary compensation is absolutely essential...... Why?
Because New Tesla Energy only deals with people they trust.
— Also ...
...and this is extremely unfortunate...
...criminal organizations participate in the trading of illegal Coils on the black market.
More than a few of their own "Collectors" supply them.
Conflict among fellow Collectors will only continue to rise in number...
...... Whatever the case...
...New Tesla is not liable for anything, as it's all the actions of third parties.

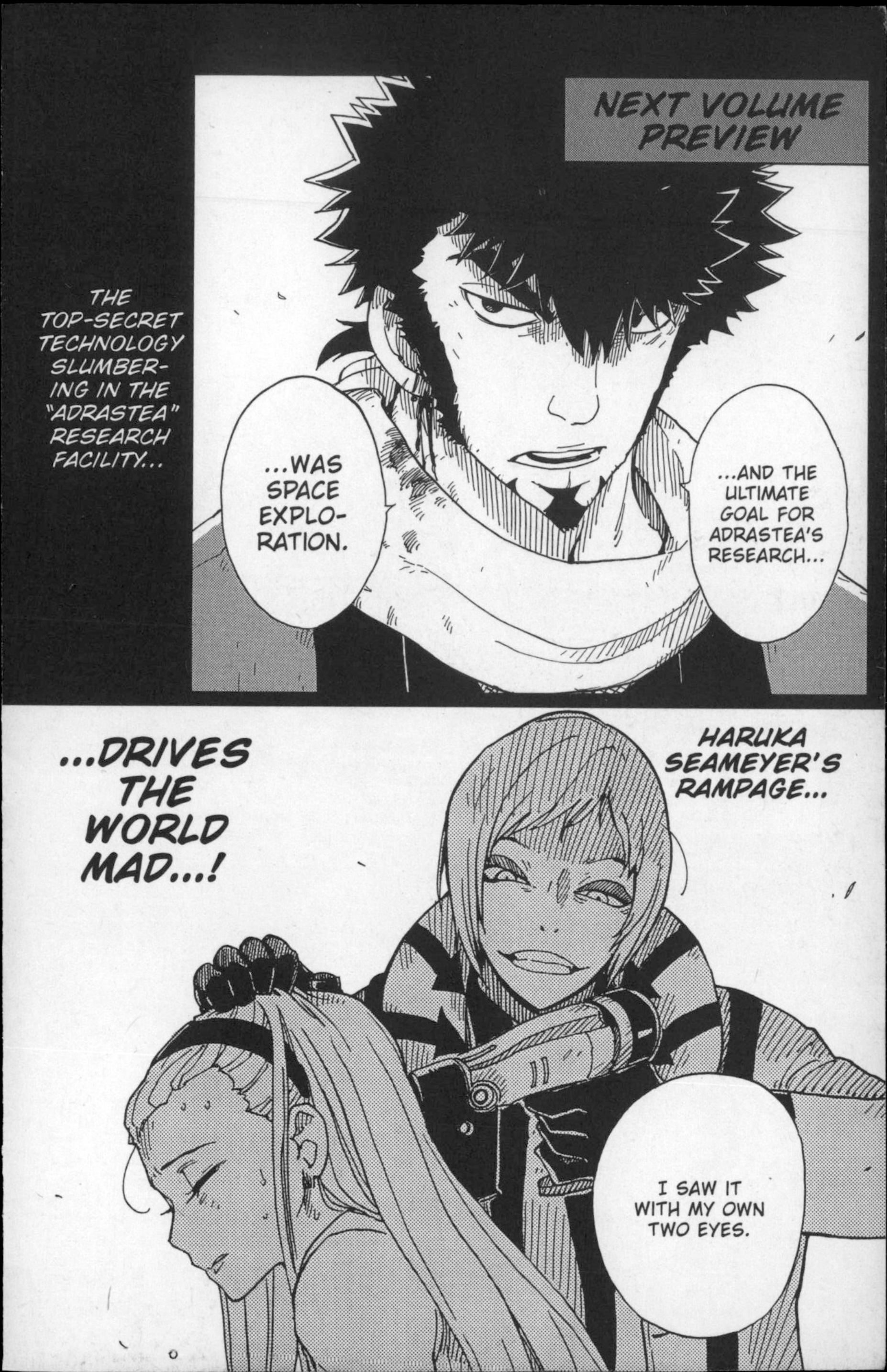
NEXT VOLUME PREVIEW
THE TOP-SECRET TECHNOLOGY SLUMBERING IN THE "ADRASTEA" RESEARCH FACILITY...
...WAS SPACE EXPLORATION.
...AND THE ULTIMATE GOAL FOR ADRASTEA'S RESEARCH...
HARUKA SEAMEYER'S RAMPAGE...
...DRIVES THE WORLD MAD...!
I SAW IT WITH MY OWN TWO EYES.

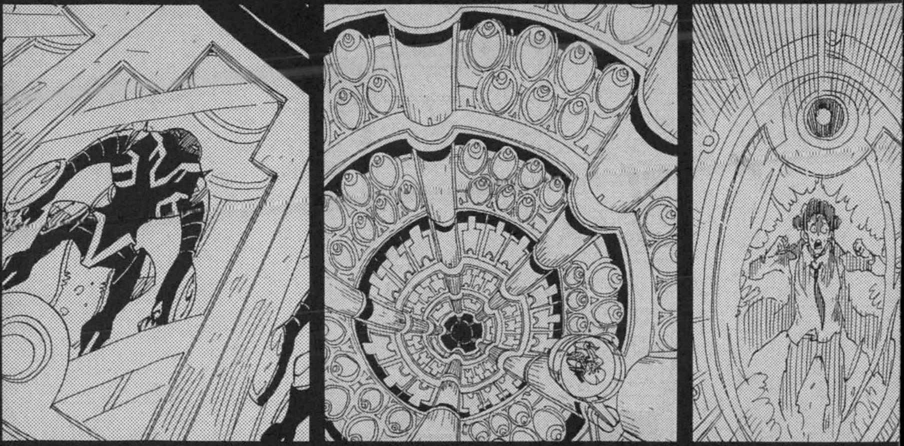

AT THE END OF A BATTLE IS A FUTURE WORTH FIGHTING FOR.

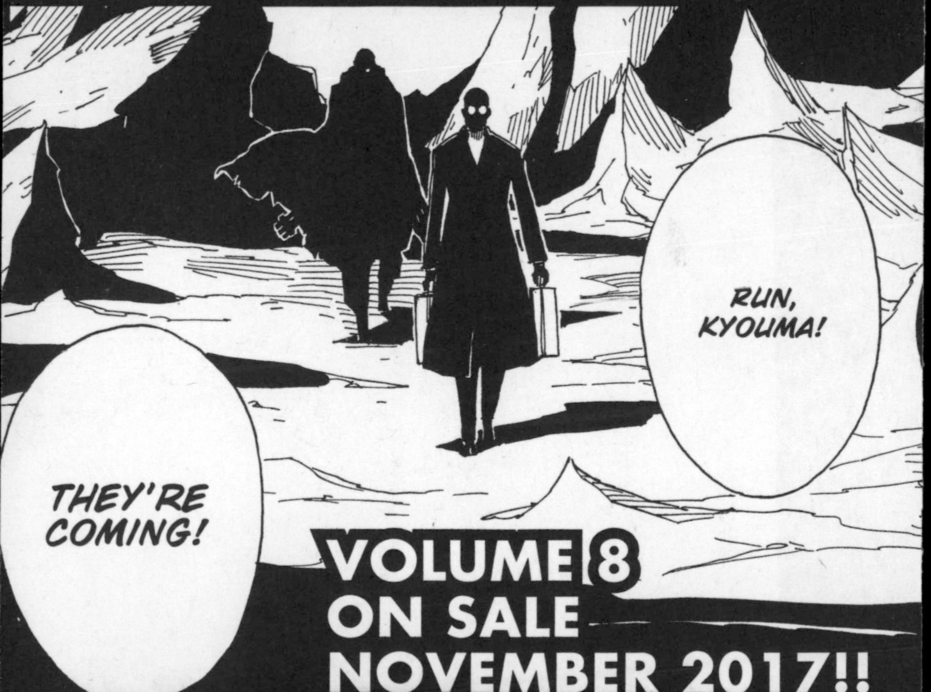
RUN, KYOUMA!
THEY'RE COMING!
VOLUME 8 ON SALE NOVEMBER 2017!!

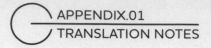

APPENDIX.01
TRANSLATION NOTES

happi coat: The short coat that Kyouma always wears. A traditional Japanese garment often worn by restaurant staff and festival performers.